SHONEN JUMP ADVANCED MANGA EDITION

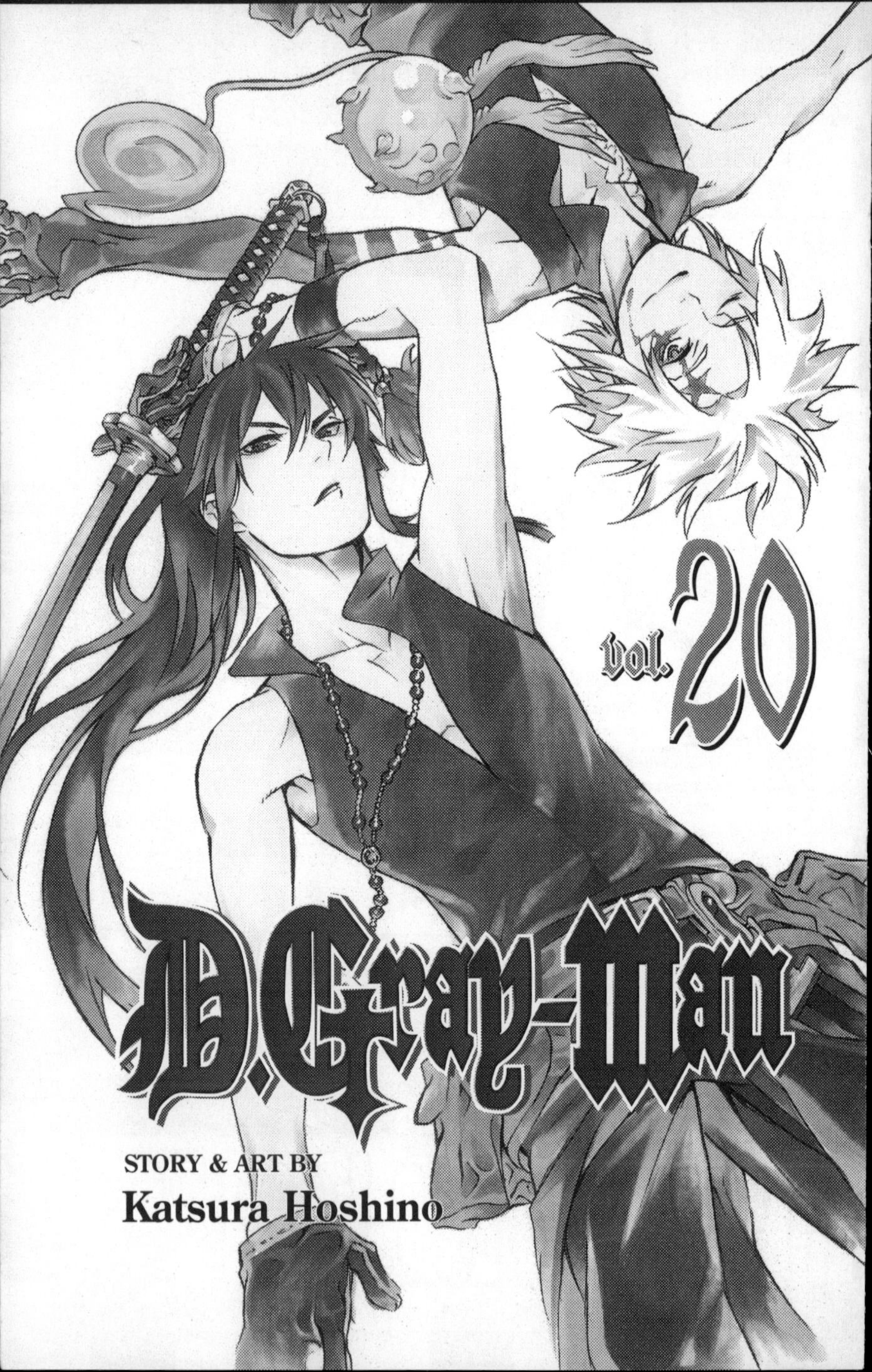
vol. 20
D.Gray-man
STORY & ART BY
Katsura Hoshino

CHARACTERS

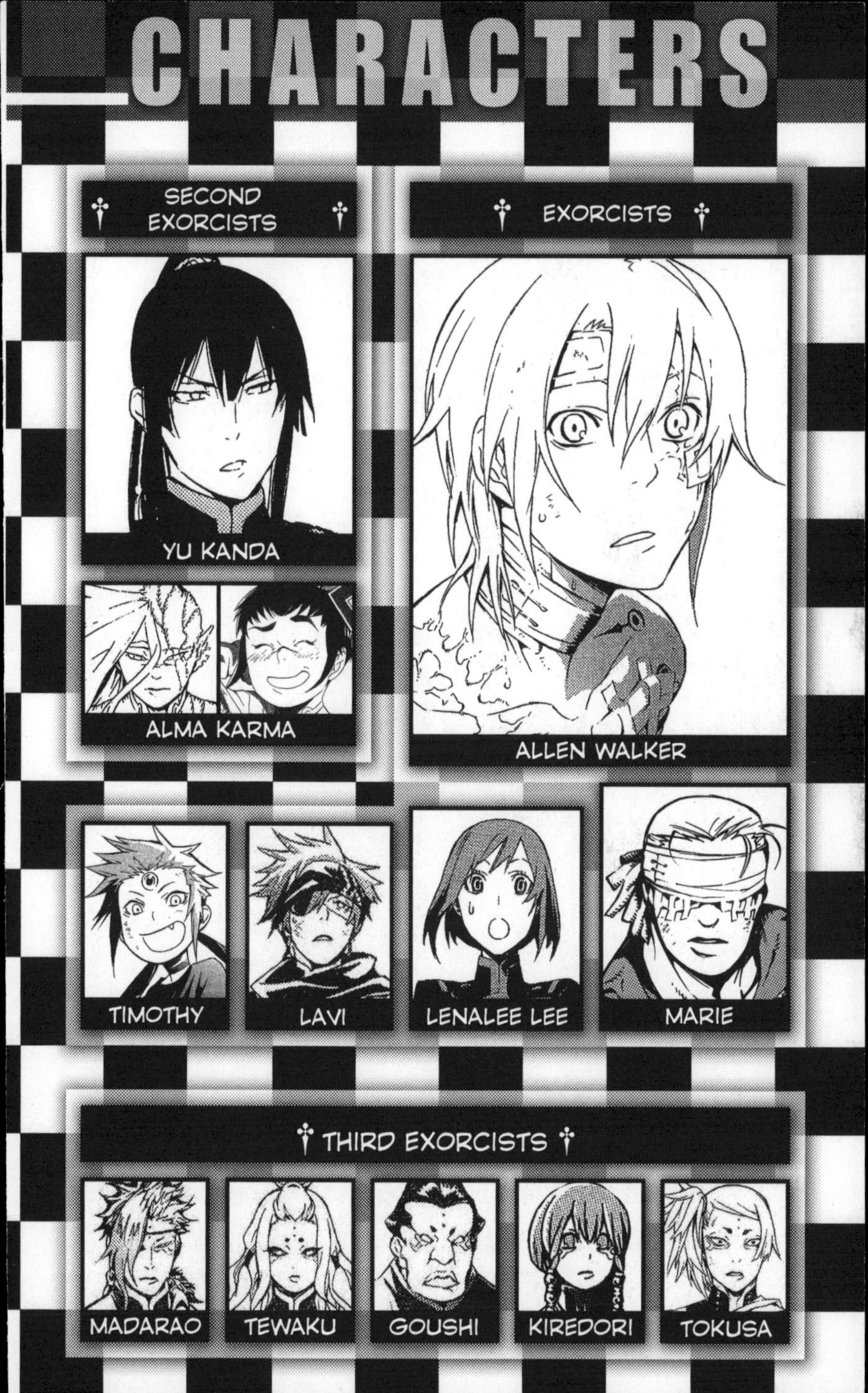
EXORCISTS
ALLEN WALKER
SECOND EXORCISTS
YU KANDA
ALMA KARMA
MARIE
LENALEE LEE
LAVI
TIMOTHY
THIRD EXORCISTS
TOKUSA
KIREDORI
GOUSHI
TEWAKU
MADARAO

D.Gray-man

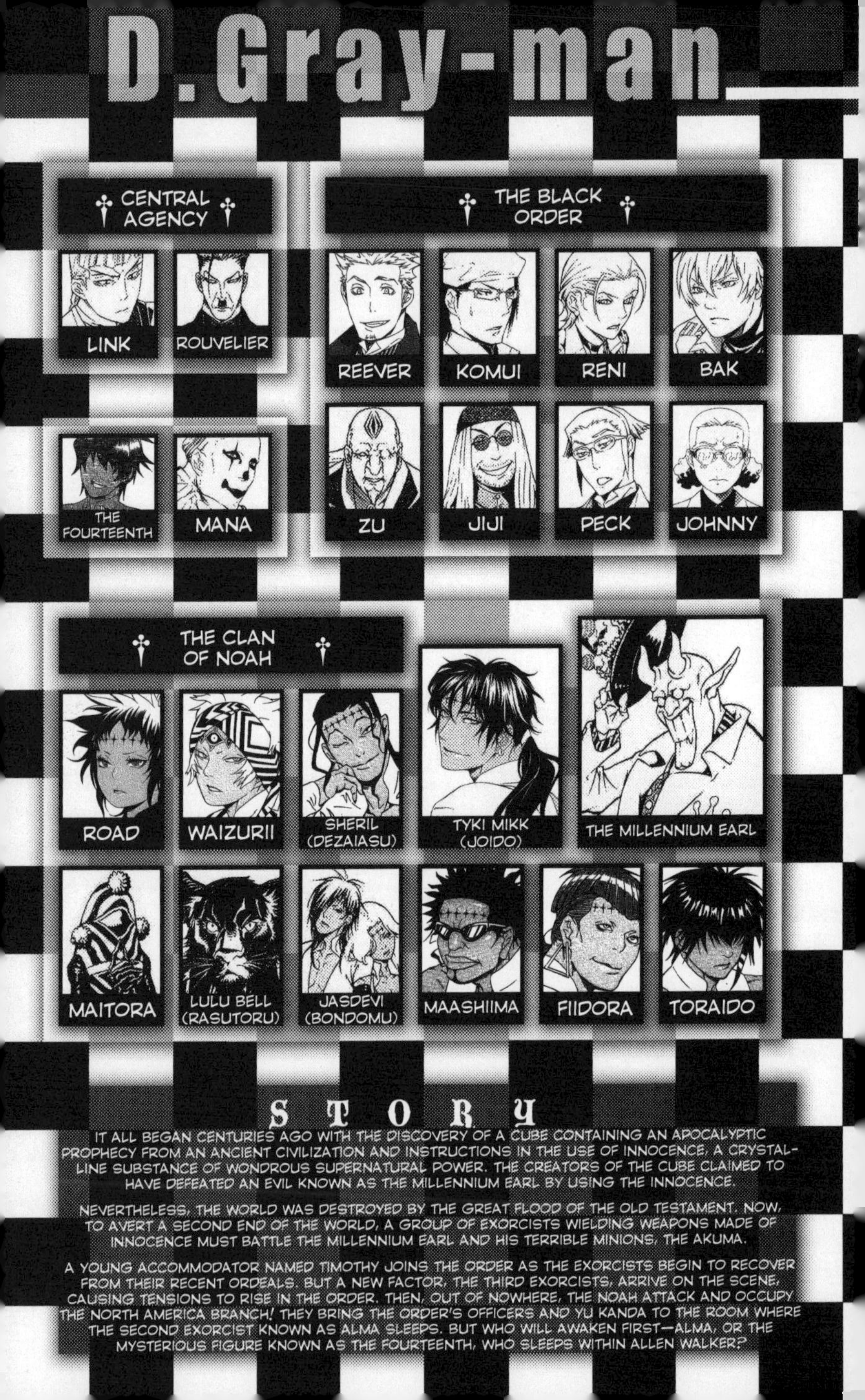

CENTRAL AGENCY
LINK
ROUVELIER
THE FOURTEENTH
MANA
THE BLACK ORDER
REEVER
KOMUI
RENI
BAK
ZU
JIJI
PECK
JOHNNY
THE CLAN OF NOAH
ROAD
WAIZURII
SHERIL (DEZAIASU)
TYKI MIKK (JOIDO)
THE MILLENNIUM EARL
MAITORA
LULU BELL (RASUTORU)
JASDEVI (BONDOMU)
MAASHIIMA
FIIDORA
TORAIDO

STORY

IT ALL BEGAN CENTURIES AGO WITH THE DISCOVERY OF A CUBE CONTAINING AN APOCALYPTIC PROPHECY FROM AN ANCIENT CIVILIZATION AND INSTRUCTIONS IN THE USE OF INNOCENCE, A CRYSTALLINE SUBSTANCE OF WONDROUS SUPERNATURAL POWER. THE CREATORS OF THE CUBE CLAIMED TO HAVE DEFEATED AN EVIL KNOWN AS THE MILLENNIUM EARL BY USING THE INNOCENCE.

NEVERTHELESS, THE WORLD WAS DESTROYED BY THE GREAT FLOOD OF THE OLD TESTAMENT. NOW, TO AVERT A SECOND END OF THE WORLD, A GROUP OF EXORCISTS WIELDING WEAPONS MADE OF INNOCENCE MUST BATTLE THE MILLENNIUM EARL AND HIS TERRIBLE MINIONS, THE AKUMA.

A YOUNG ACCOMMODATOR NAMED TIMOTHY JOINS THE ORDER AS THE EXORCISTS BEGIN TO RECOVER FROM THEIR RECENT ORDEALS. BUT A NEW FACTOR, THE THIRD EXORCISTS, ARRIVE ON THE SCENE, CAUSING TENSIONS TO RISE IN THE ORDER. THEN, OUT OF NOWHERE, THE NOAH ATTACK AND OCCUPY THE NORTH AMERICA BRANCH! THEY BRING THE ORDER'S OFFICERS AND YU KANDA TO THE ROOM WHERE THE SECOND EXORCIST KNOWN AS ALMA SLEEPS. BUT WHO WILL AWAKEN FIRST—ALMA, OR THE MYSTERIOUS FIGURE KNOWN AS THE FOURTEENTH, WHO SLEEPS WITHIN ALLEN WALKER?

D.GRAY-MAN
Vol. 20

CONTENTS

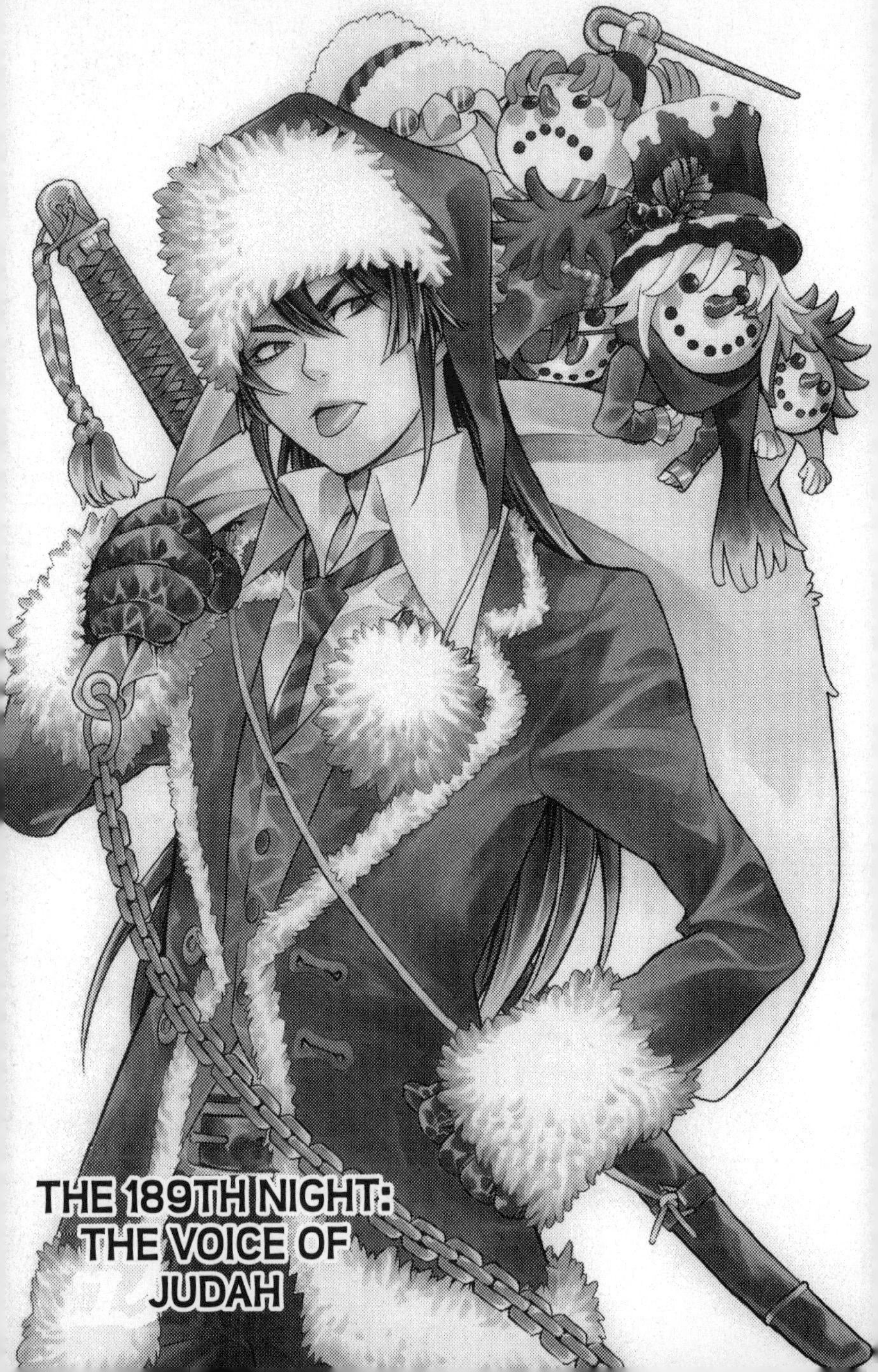
THE 189TH NIGHT: THE VOICE OF JUDAH

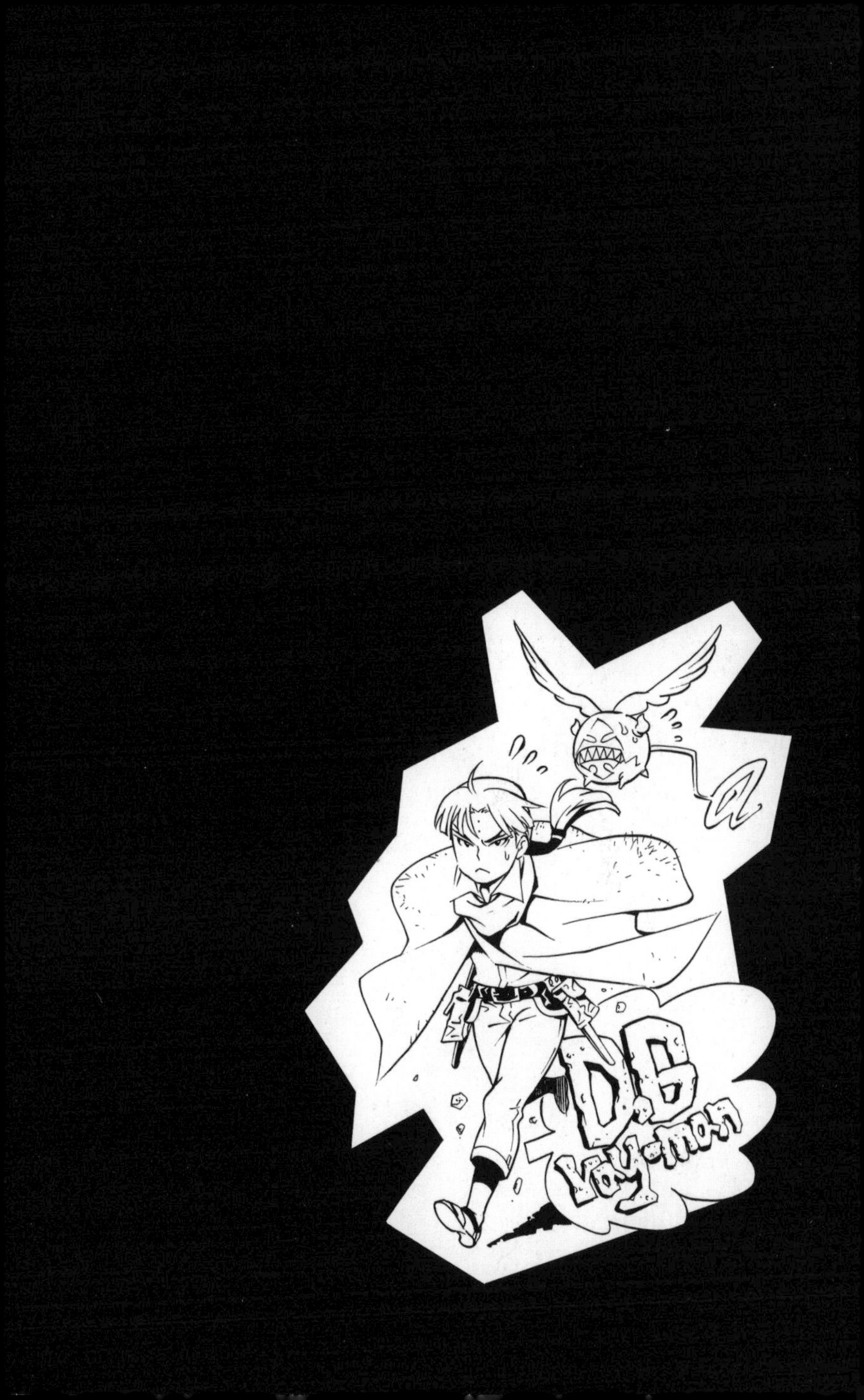
D.Gray-man

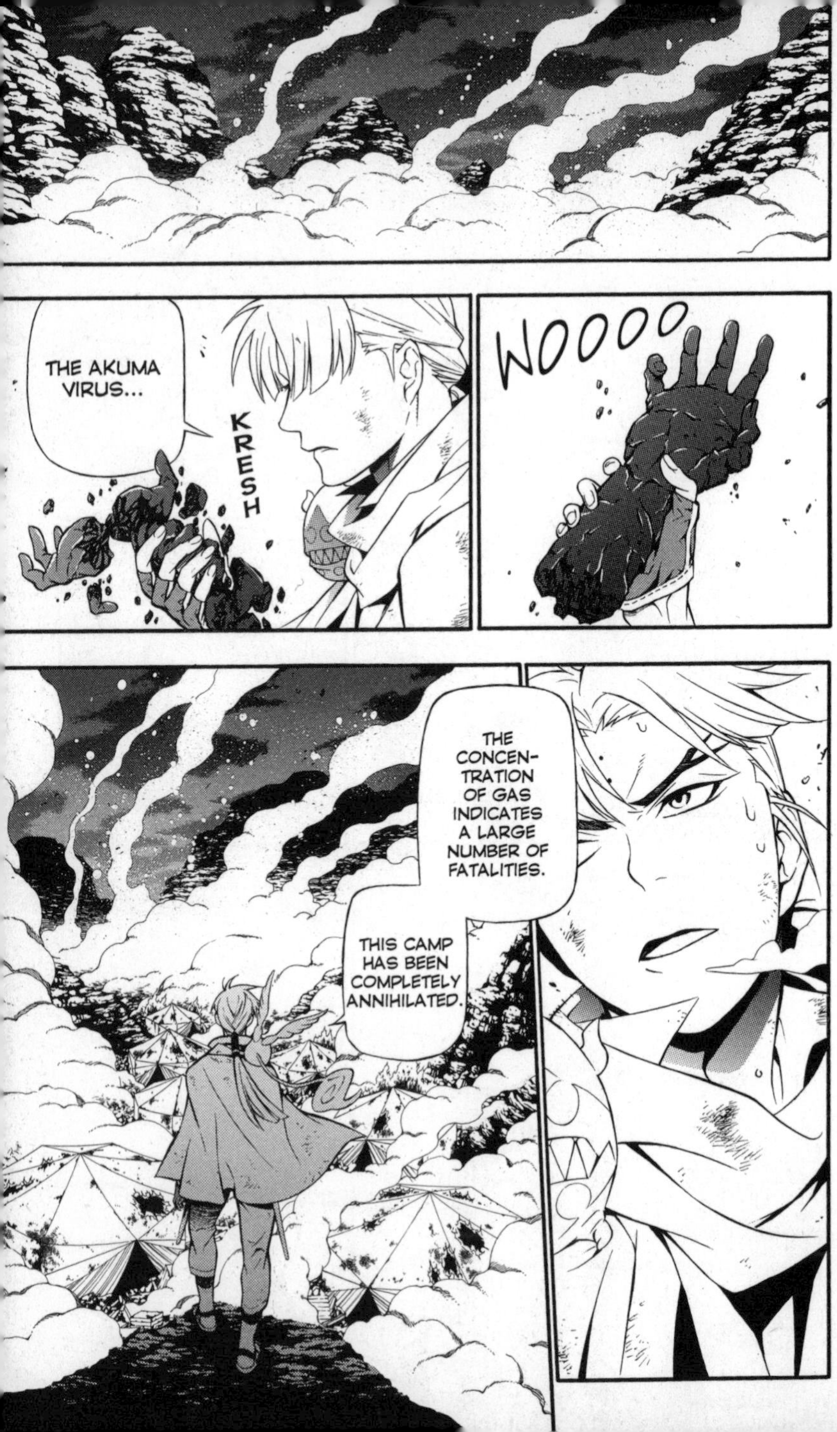
WOOOO
THE AKUMA VIRUS...
KRESH
THE CONCEN-TRATION OF GAS INDICATES A LARGE NUMBER OF FATALITIES.
THIS CAMP HAS BEEN COMPLETELY ANNIHILATED.

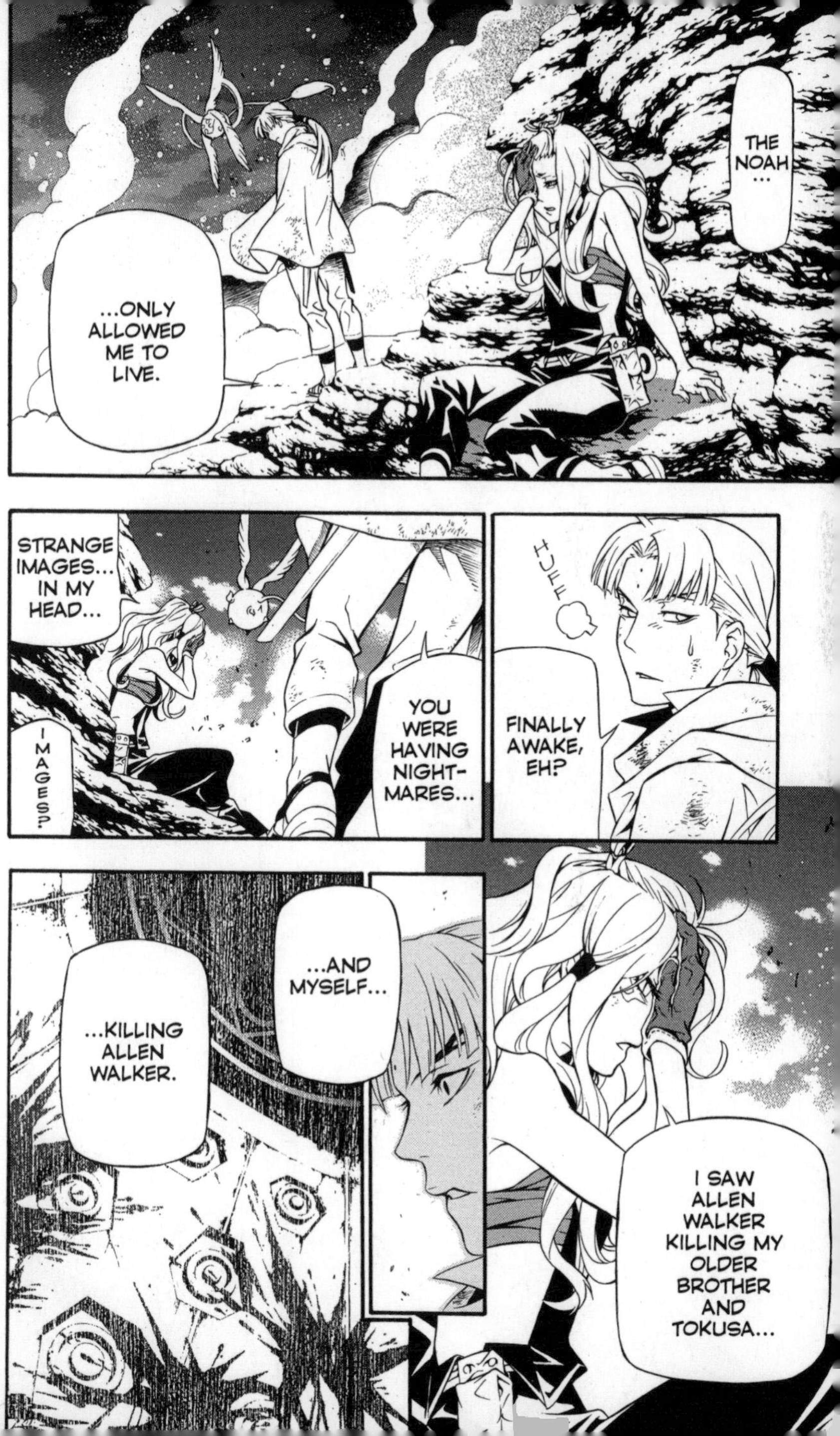
THE NOAH...
...ONLY ALLOWED ME TO LIVE.
HUFF
FINALLY AWAKE, EH?
YOU WERE HAVING NIGHT-MARES...
STRANGE IMAGES... IN MY HEAD...
IMAGES?
I SAW ALLEN WALKER KILLING MY OLDER BROTHER AND TOKUSA...
...AND MYSELF...
...KILLING ALLEN WALKER.

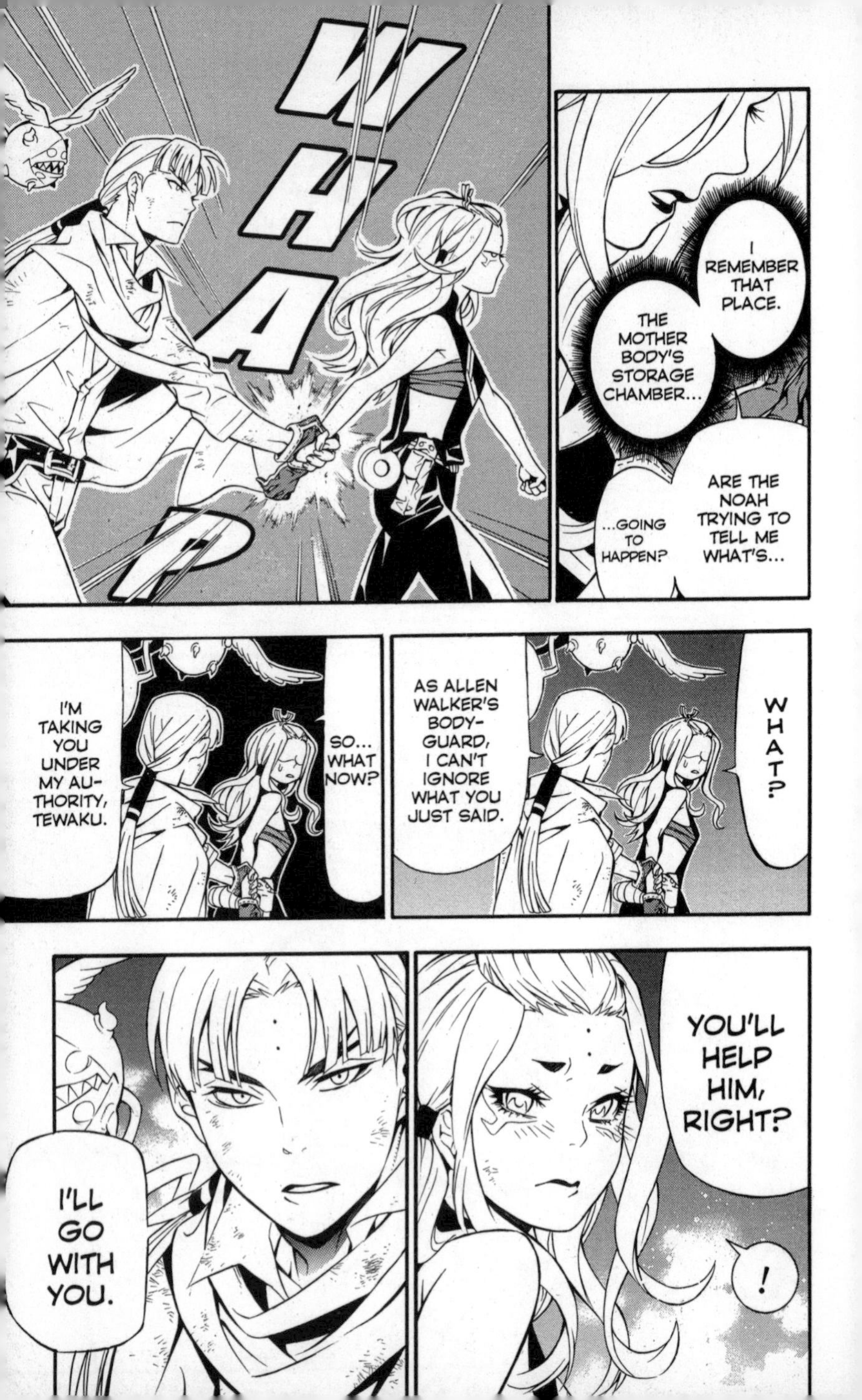
I REMEMBER THAT PLACE.
THE MOTHER BODY'S STORAGE CHAMBER...
ARE THE NOAH TRYING TO TELL ME WHAT'S...
...GOING TO HAPPEN?
WHAP
WHAT?
AS ALLEN WALKER'S BODY-GUARD, I CAN'T IGNORE WHAT YOU JUST SAID.
SO... WHAT NOW?
I'M TAKING YOU UNDER MY AU-THORITY, TEWAKU.
YOU'LL HELP HIM, RIGHT?
!
I'LL GO WITH YOU.

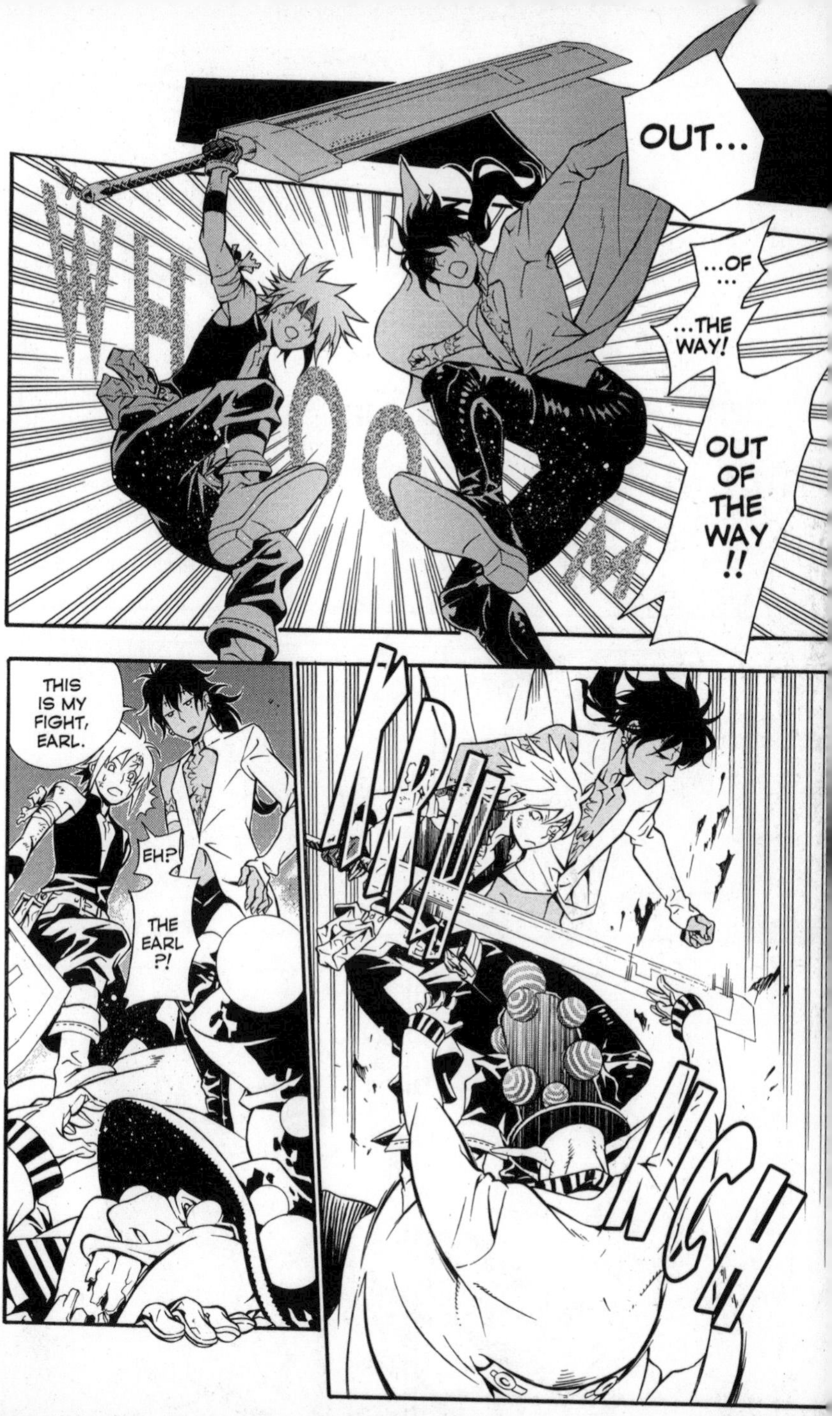
OUT...
...OF ...
...THE WAY!
OUT OF THE WAY !!
WHOOM
THIS IS MY FIGHT, EARL.
EH?
THE EARL ?!

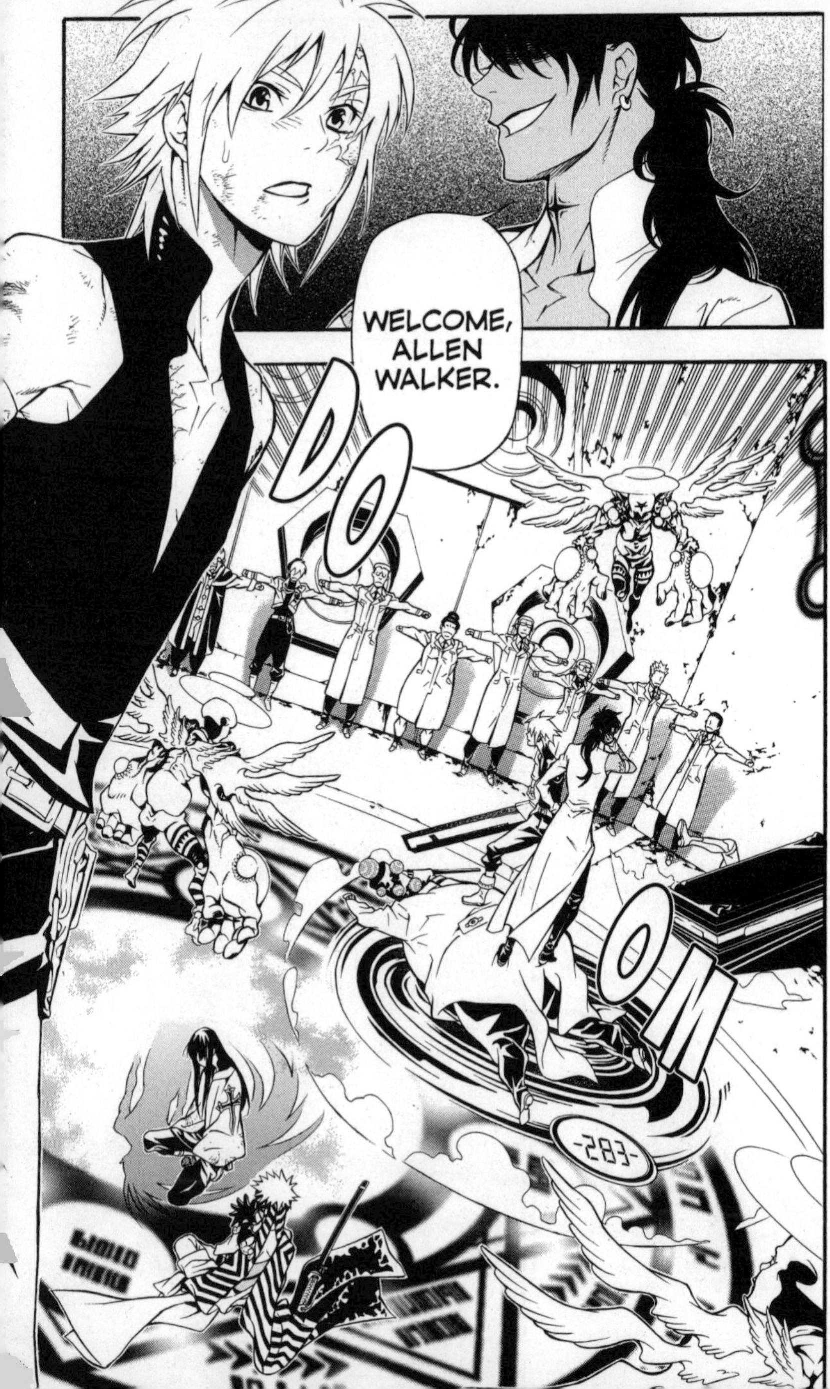
WELCOME, ALLEN WALKER.
DOOM

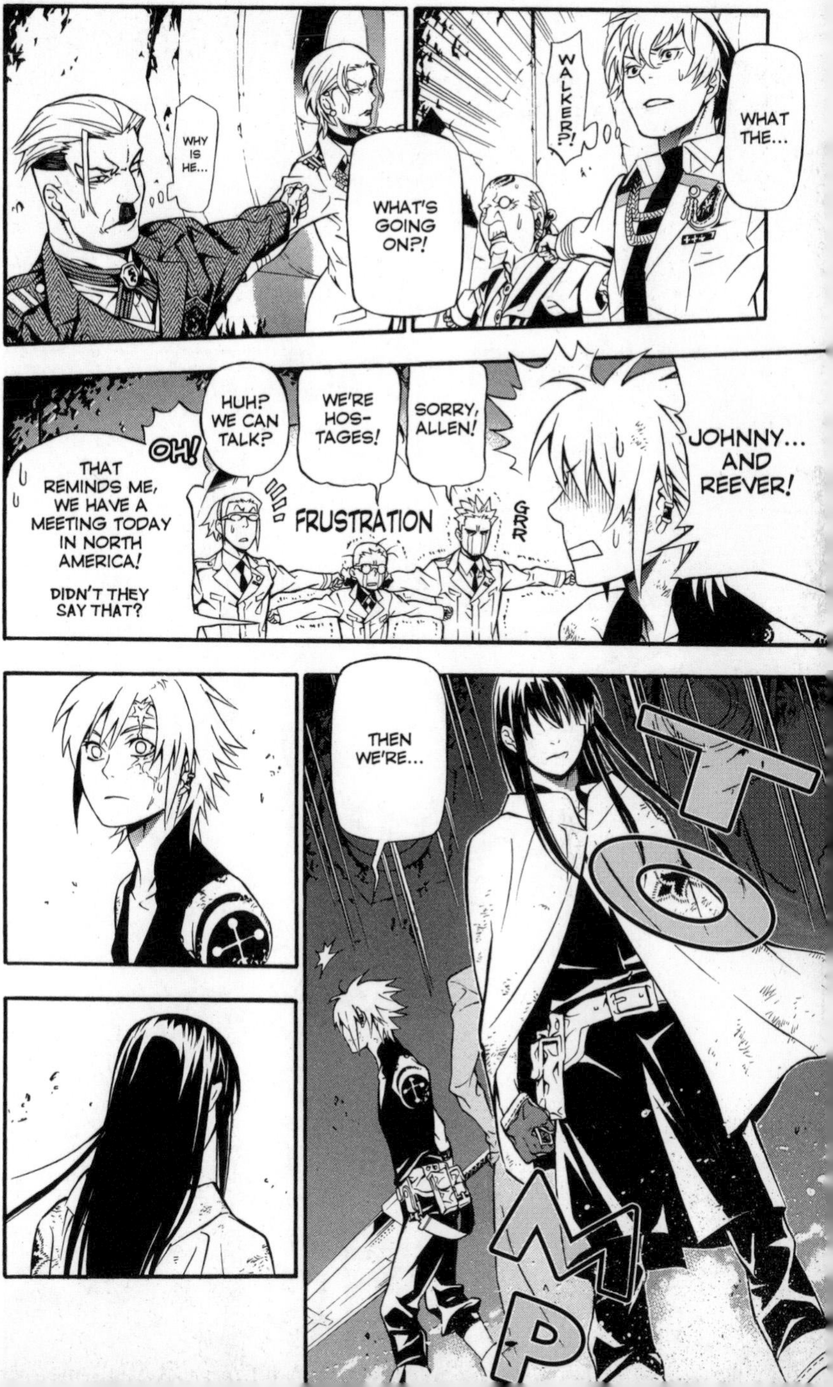
WHAT THE...
WALKER?!
WHAT'S GOING ON?!
WHY IS HE...
JOHNNY... AND REEVER!
SORRY, ALLEN!
GRR
WE'RE HOS-TAGES!
FRUSTRATION
HUH? WE CAN TALK?
OH!
THAT REMINDS ME, WE HAVE A MEETING TODAY IN NORTH AMERICA!
DIDN'T THEY SAY THAT?
THEN WE'RE...
TOMP

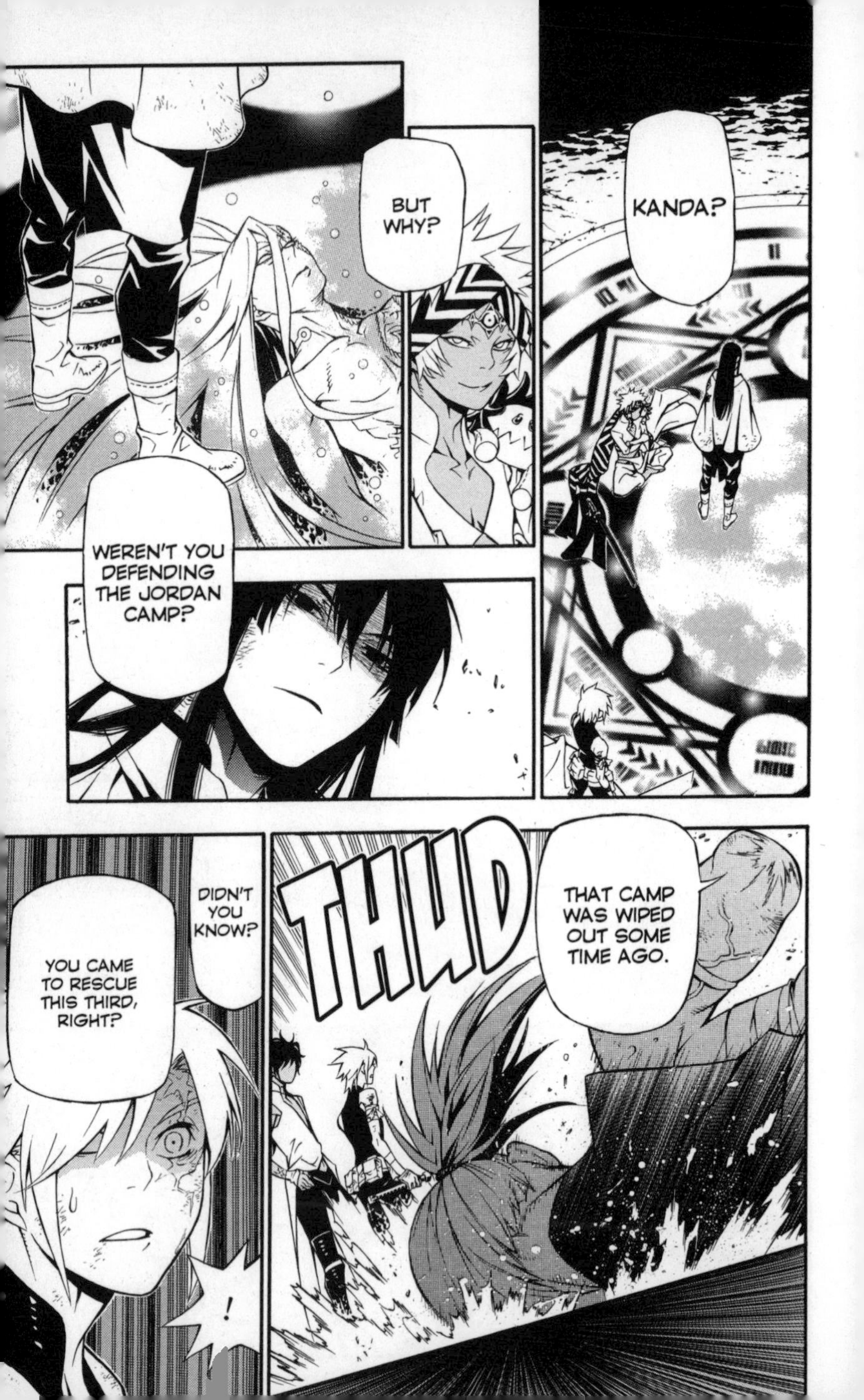
KANDA?
BUT WHY?
WEREN'T YOU DEFENDING THE JORDAN CAMP?
THAT CAMP WAS WIPED OUT SOME TIME AGO.
THUD
DIDN'T YOU KNOW?
YOU CAME TO RESCUE THIS THIRD, RIGHT?
!

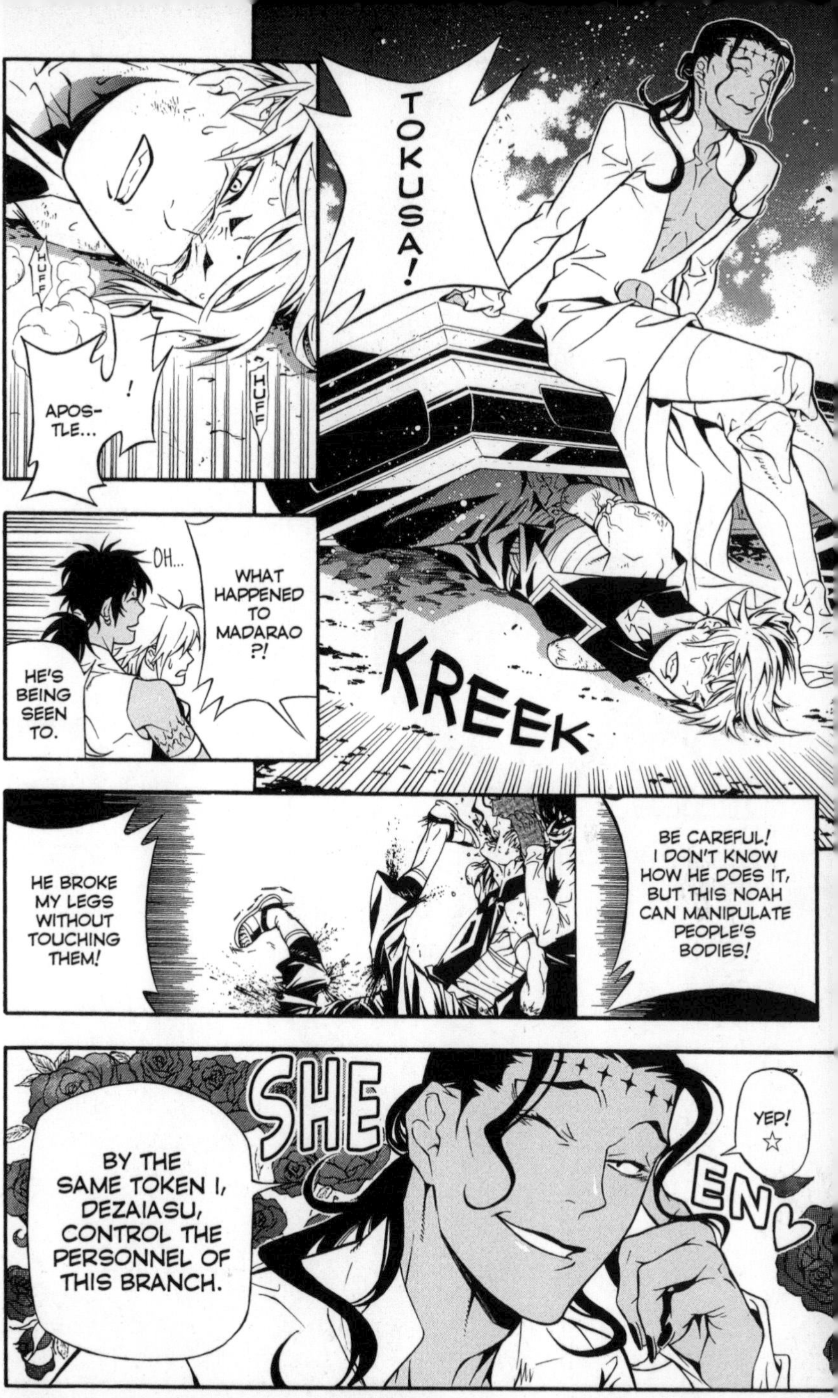
TOKUSA!
KREEK
HUFF
HUFF
!
APOS-
TLE...
WHAT HAPPENED TO MADARAO ?!
OH...
HE'S BEING SEEN TO.
BE CAREFUL! I DON'T KNOW HOW HE DOES IT, BUT THIS NOAH CAN MANIPULATE PEOPLE'S BODIES!
HE BROKE MY LEGS WITHOUT TOUCHING THEM!
YEP! ☆
SHEEN
BY THE SAME TOKEN I, DEZAIASU, CONTROL THE PERSONNEL OF THIS BRANCH.

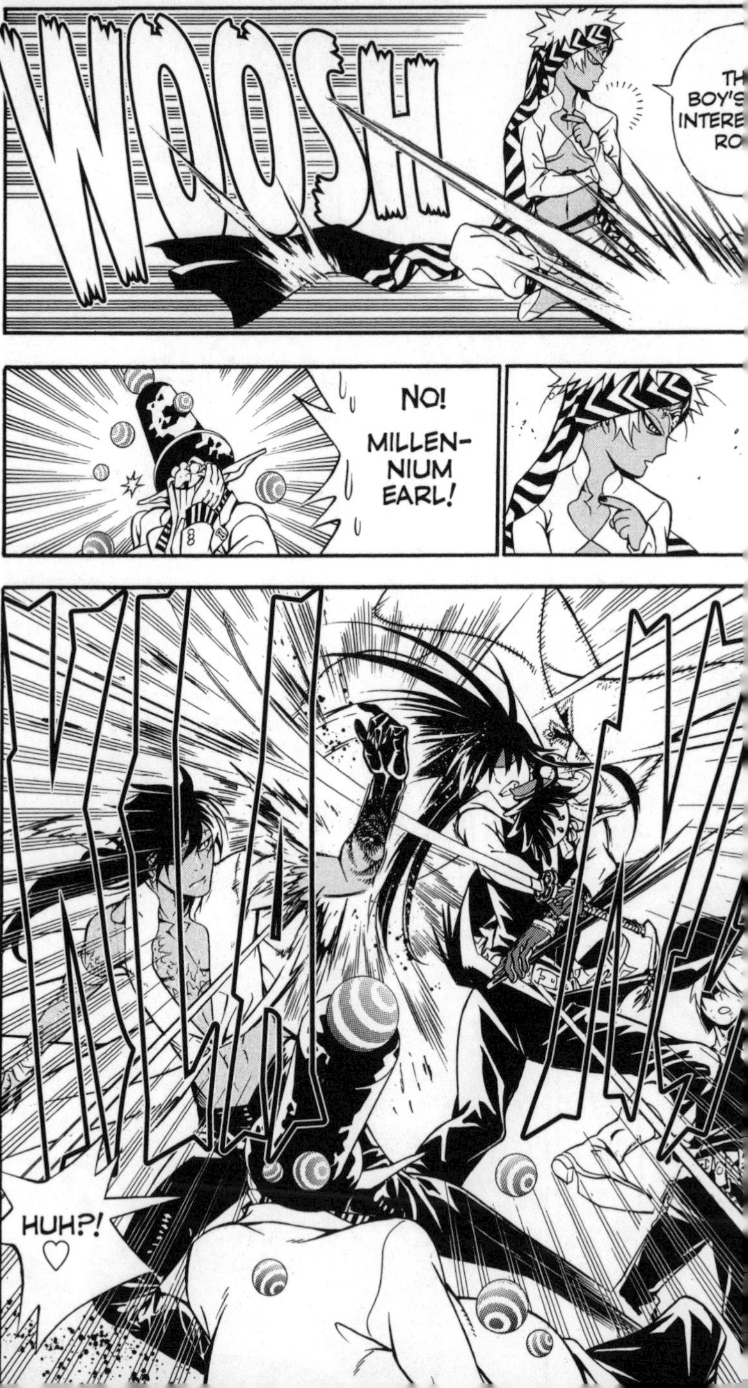
TH
BOY'S
INTERE
RO
WOOSH
NO!
MILLEN-NIUM EARL!
HUH?! ♡

READ THIS WAY

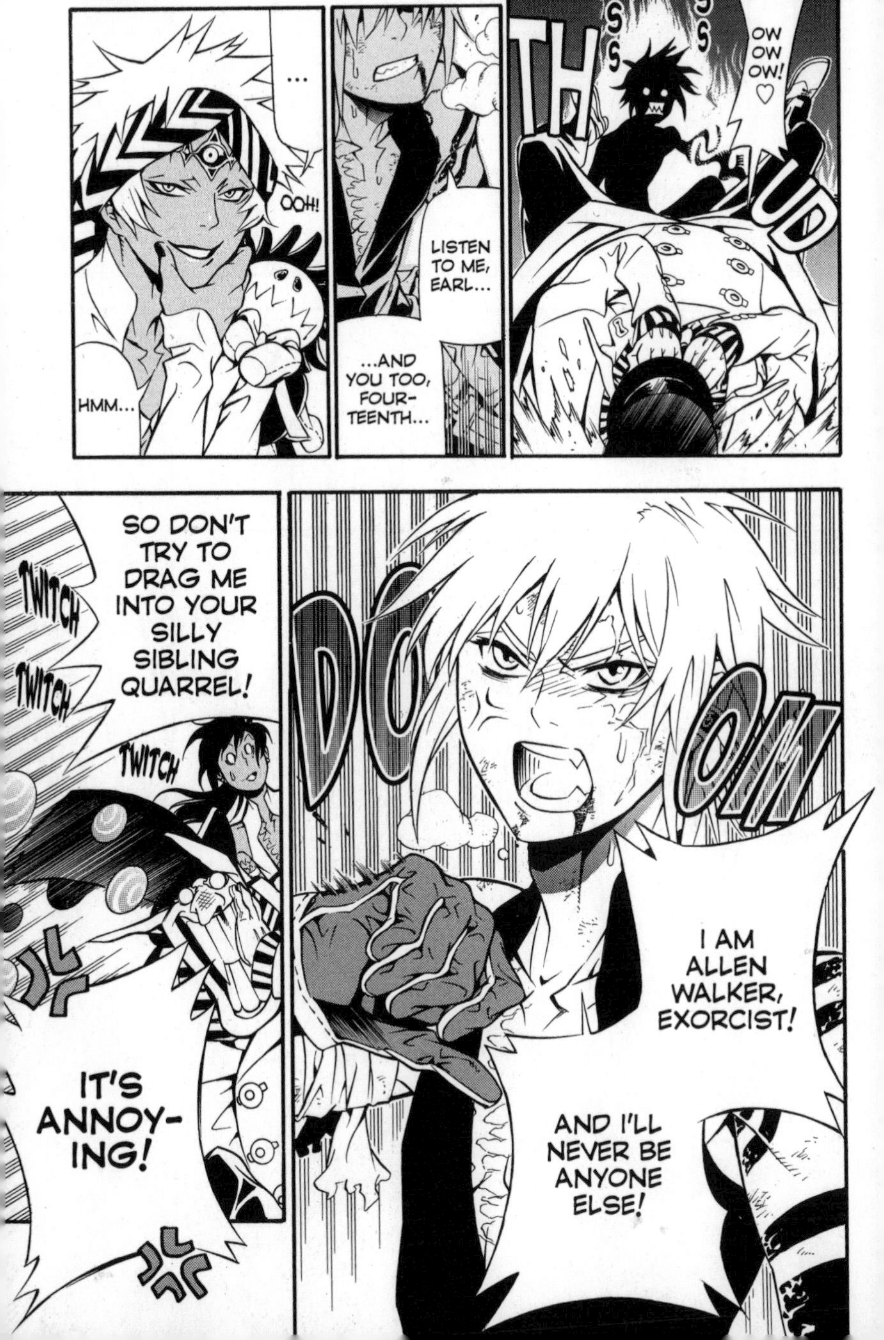
FSS
FSS
OW OW OW! ♥
THUD
LISTEN TO ME, EARL...
...AND YOU TOO, FOURTEENTH...
...
OOH!
HMM...
DOOM
I AM ALLEN WALKER, EXORCIST!
AND I'LL NEVER BE ANYONE ELSE!
SO DON'T TRY TO DRAG ME INTO YOUR SILLY SIBLING QUARREL!
TWITCH
TWITCH
TWITCH
IT'S ANNOYING!

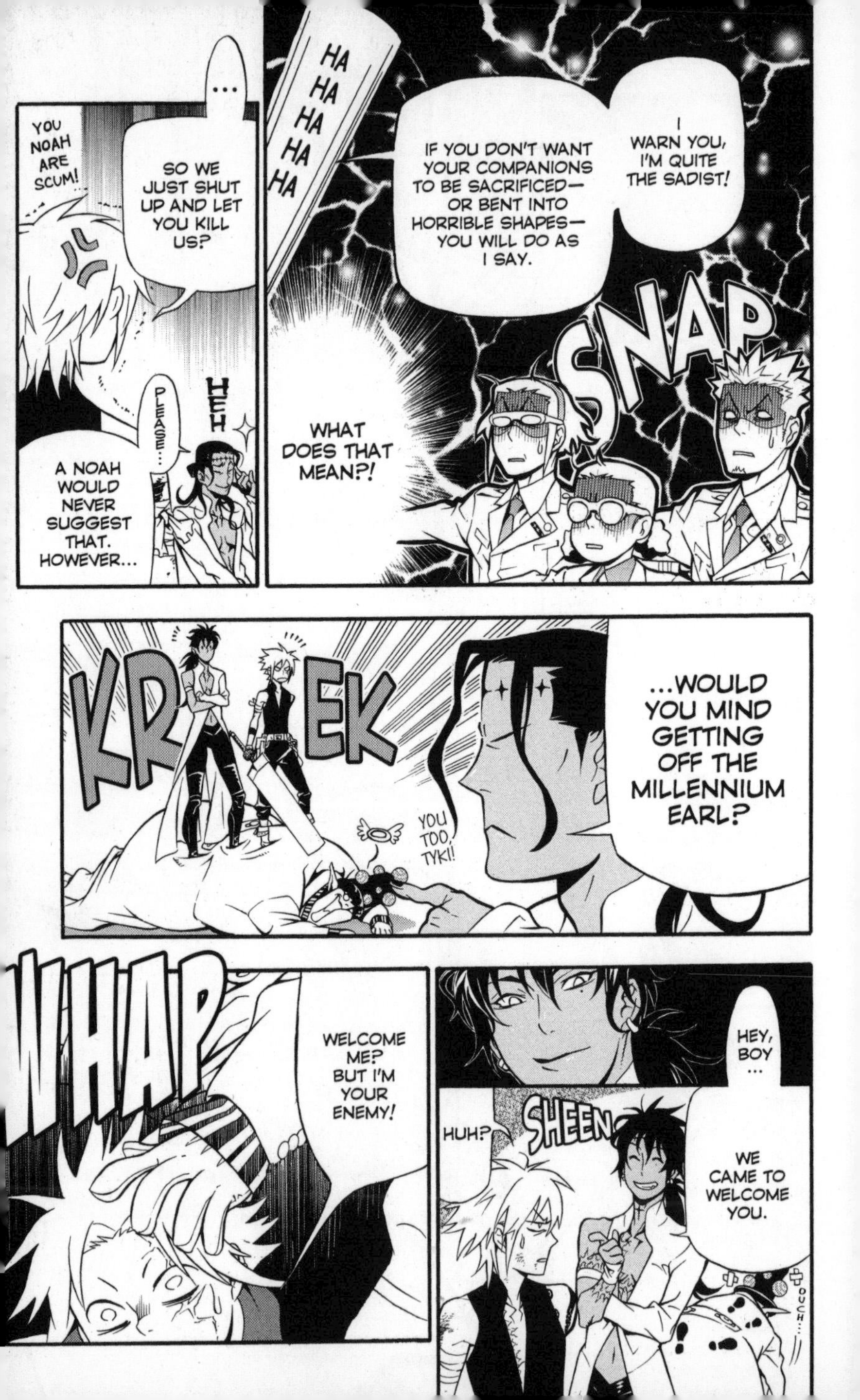
HA HA HA HA HA HA
I WARN YOU, I'M QUITE THE SADIST!
IF YOU DON'T WANT YOUR COMPANIONS TO BE SACRIFICED—OR BENT INTO HORRIBLE SHAPES—YOU WILL DO AS I SAY.
SNAP
WHAT DOES THAT MEAN?!
...
YOU NOAH ARE SCUM!
SO WE JUST SHUT UP AND LET YOU KILL US?
HEH
PLEASE...
A NOAH WOULD NEVER SUGGEST THAT. HOWEVER...
...WOULD YOU MIND GETTING OFF THE MILLENNIUM EARL?
KR EK
YOU TOO, TYKI!
HEY, BOY...
WE CAME TO WELCOME YOU.
SHEEN
HUH?
OUCH...
WHAP
WELCOME ME? BUT I'M YOUR ENEMY!

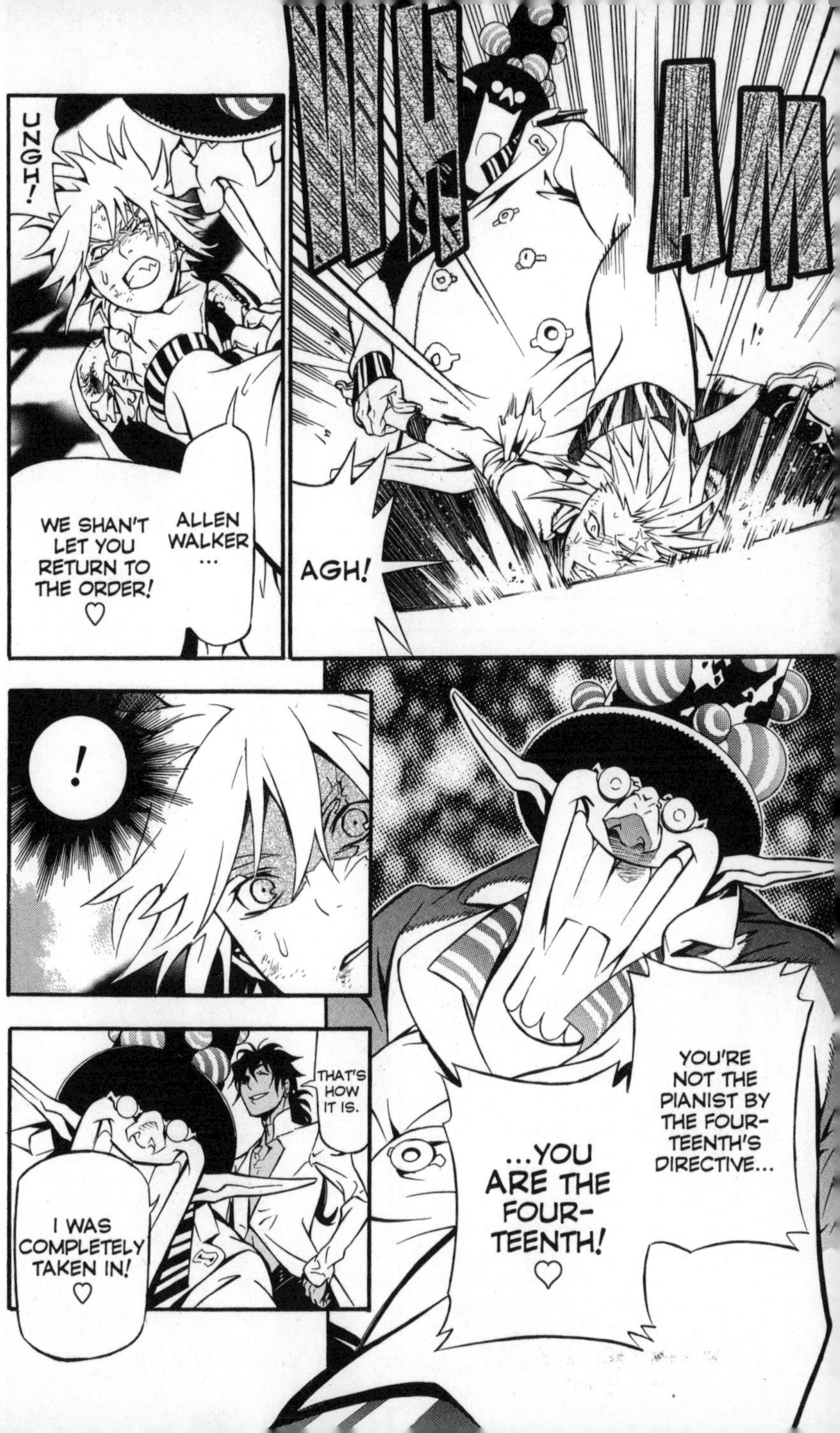
WHAM
AGH!
UNGH!
ALLEN WALKER ...
WE SHAN'T LET YOU RETURN TO THE ORDER! ♡
YOU'RE NOT THE PIANIST BY THE FOURTEENTH'S DIRECTIVE...
...YOU ARE THE FOURTEENTH! ♡
!
THAT'S HOW IT IS.
I WAS COMPLETELY TAKEN IN! ♡

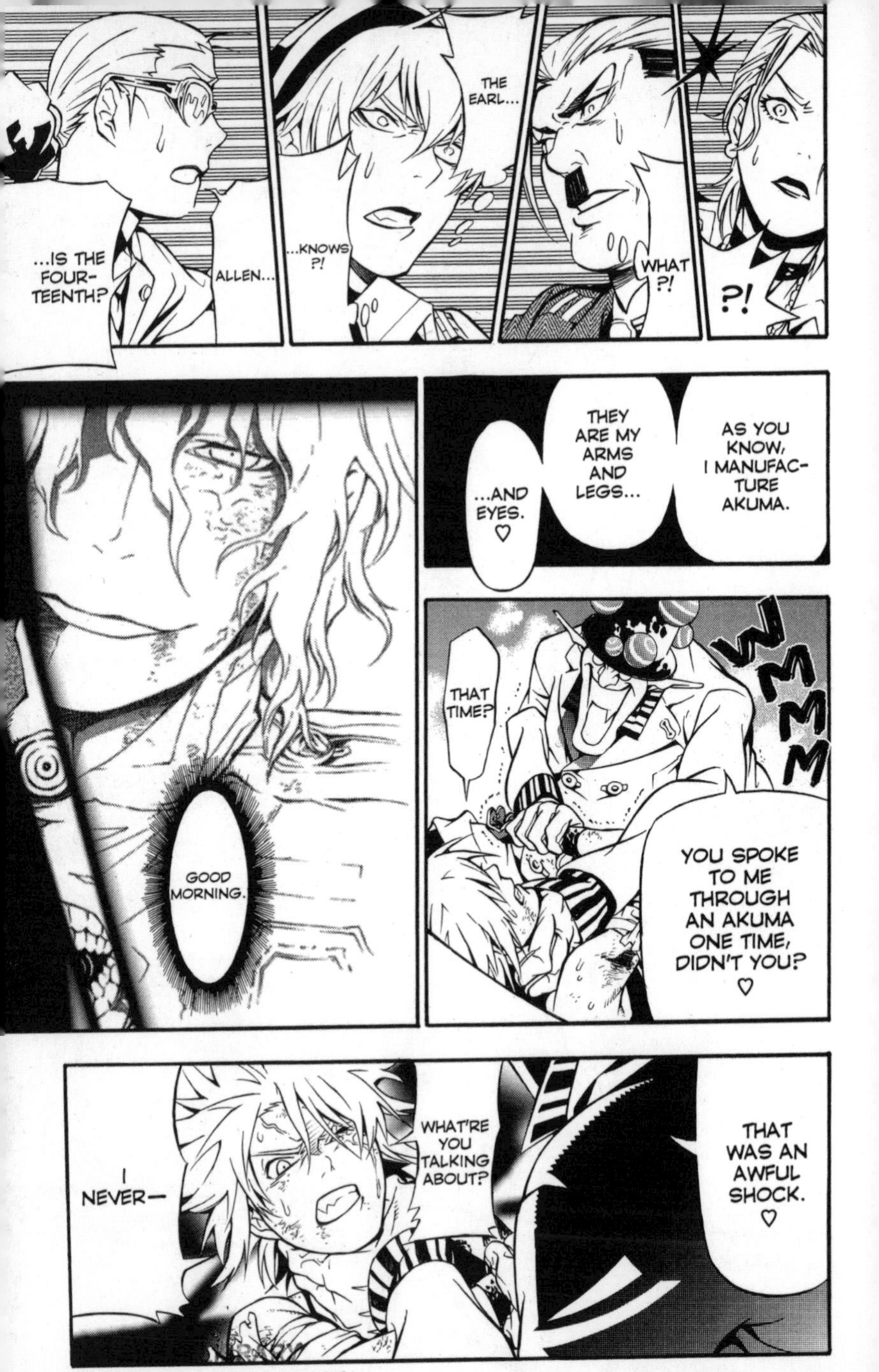
?!
WHAT ?!
THE EARL...
...KNOWS ?!
ALLEN...
...IS THE FOURTEENTH?
AS YOU KNOW, I MANUFACTURE AKUMA.
THEY ARE MY ARMS AND LEGS...
...AND EYES. ♡
WMMM
YOU SPOKE TO ME THROUGH AN AKUMA ONE TIME, DIDN'T YOU? ♡
THAT TIME?
GOOD MORNING.
THAT WAS AN AWFUL SHOCK. ♡
WHAT'RE YOU TALKING ABOUT?
I NEVER—

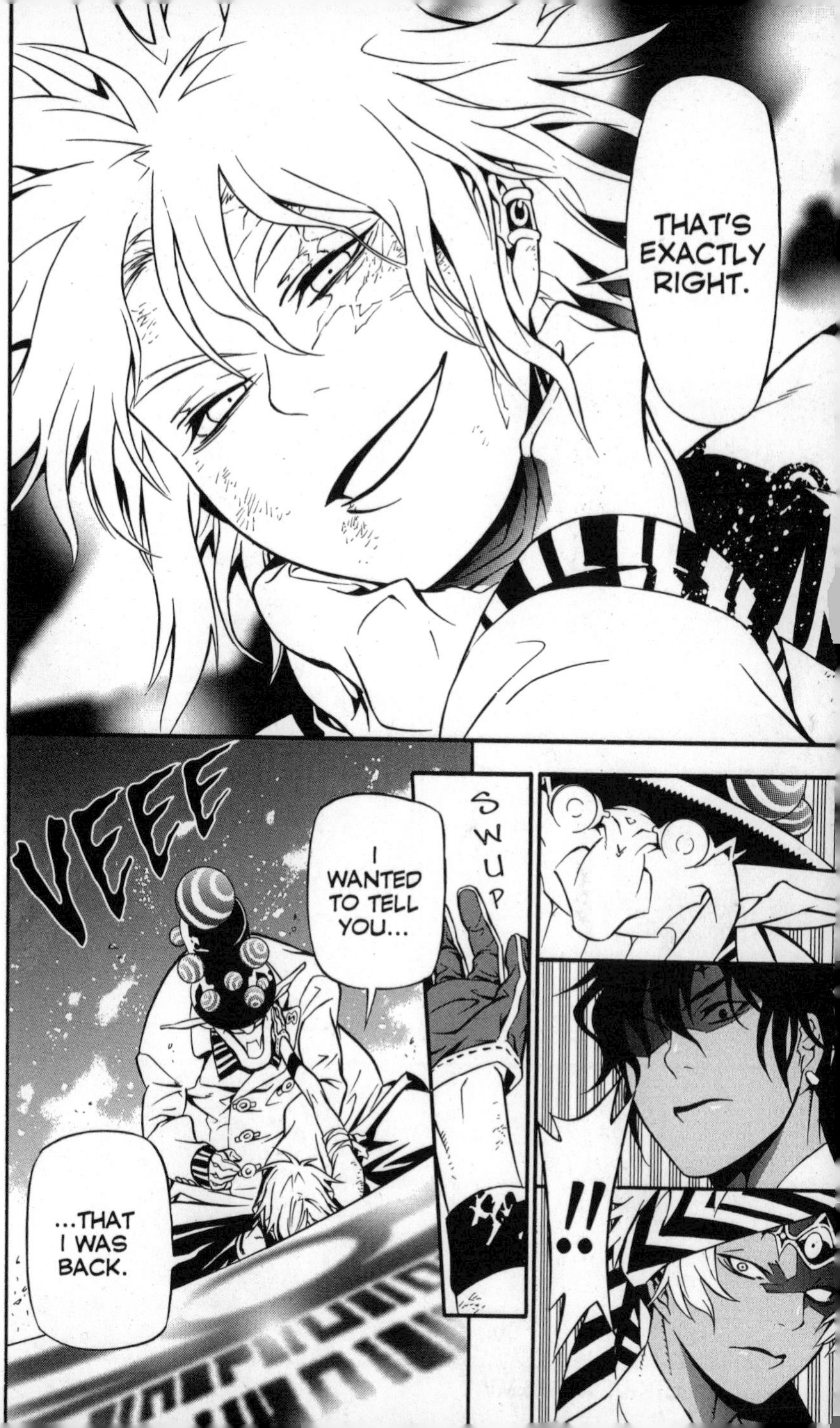
THAT'S EXACTLY RIGHT.
!!
SWUP
I WANTED TO TELL YOU...
VEEE
...THAT I WAS BACK.

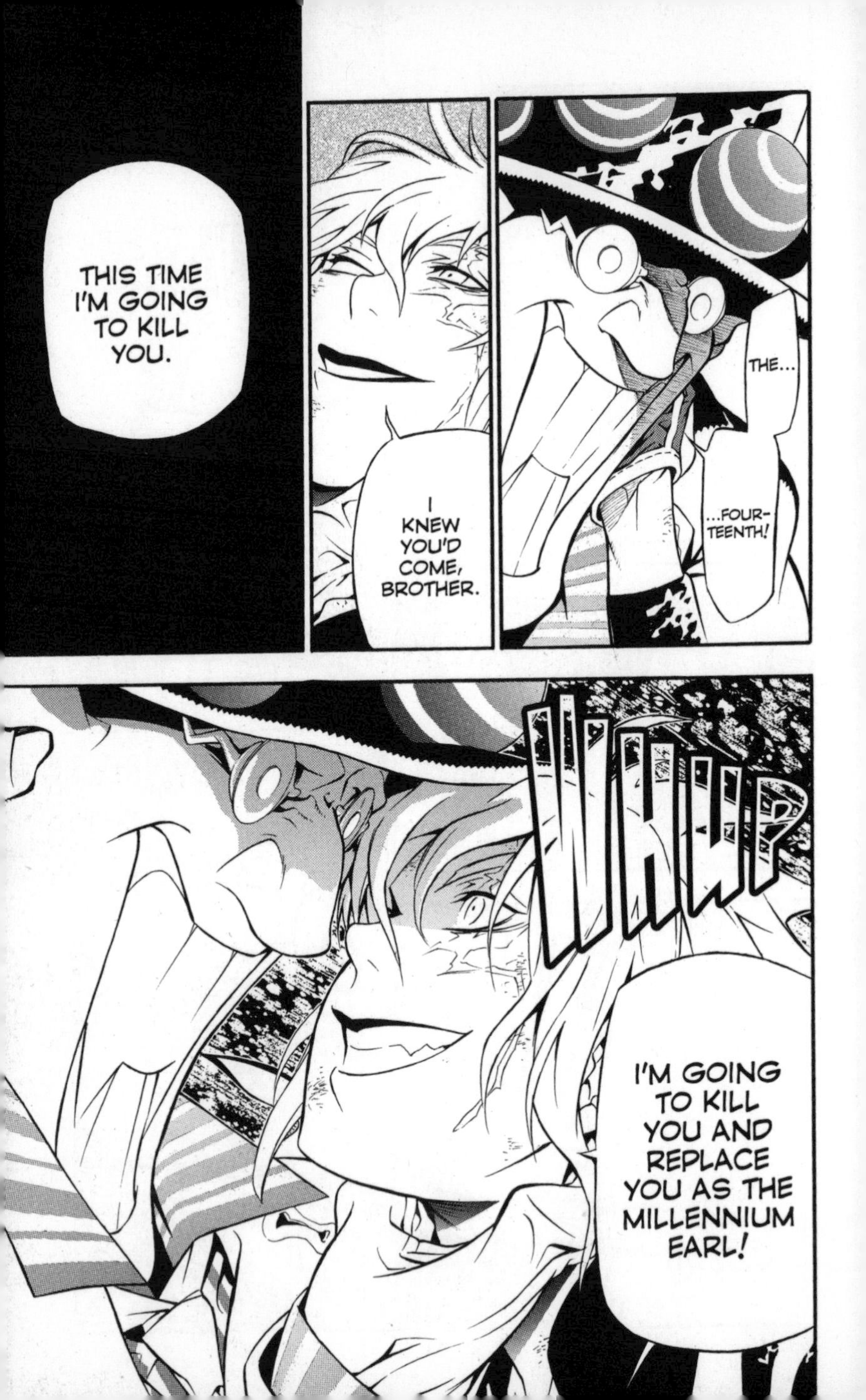
THE...
...FOURTEENTH!
I KNEW YOU'D COME, BROTHER.
THIS TIME I'M GOING TO KILL YOU.
WHUP
I'M GOING TO KILL YOU AND REPLACE YOU AS THE MILLENNIUM EARL!

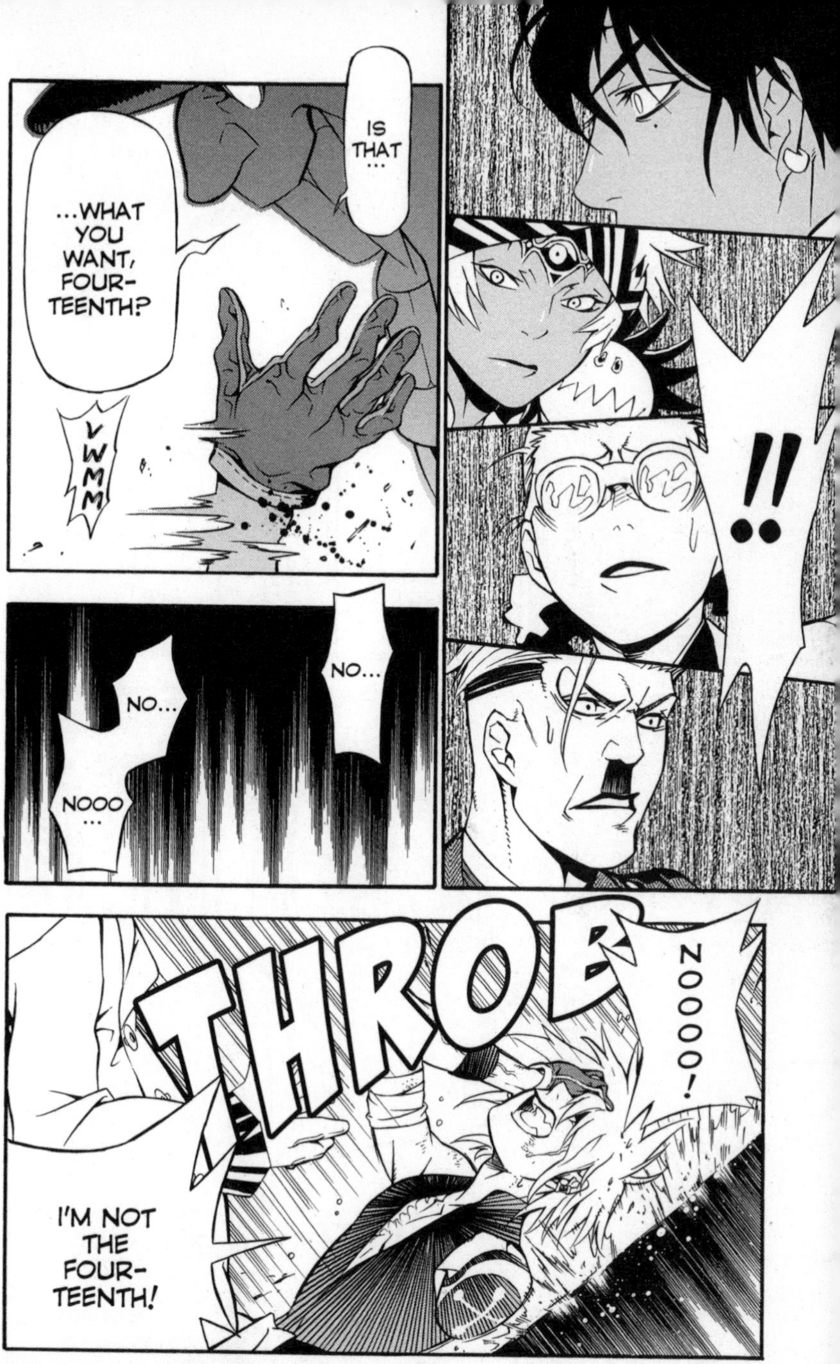
!!
IS THAT ...
...WHAT YOU WANT, FOURTEENTH?
VWMM
NO...
NO...
NOOO ...
NOOOOO!
THROB
I'M NOT THE FOURTEENTH!

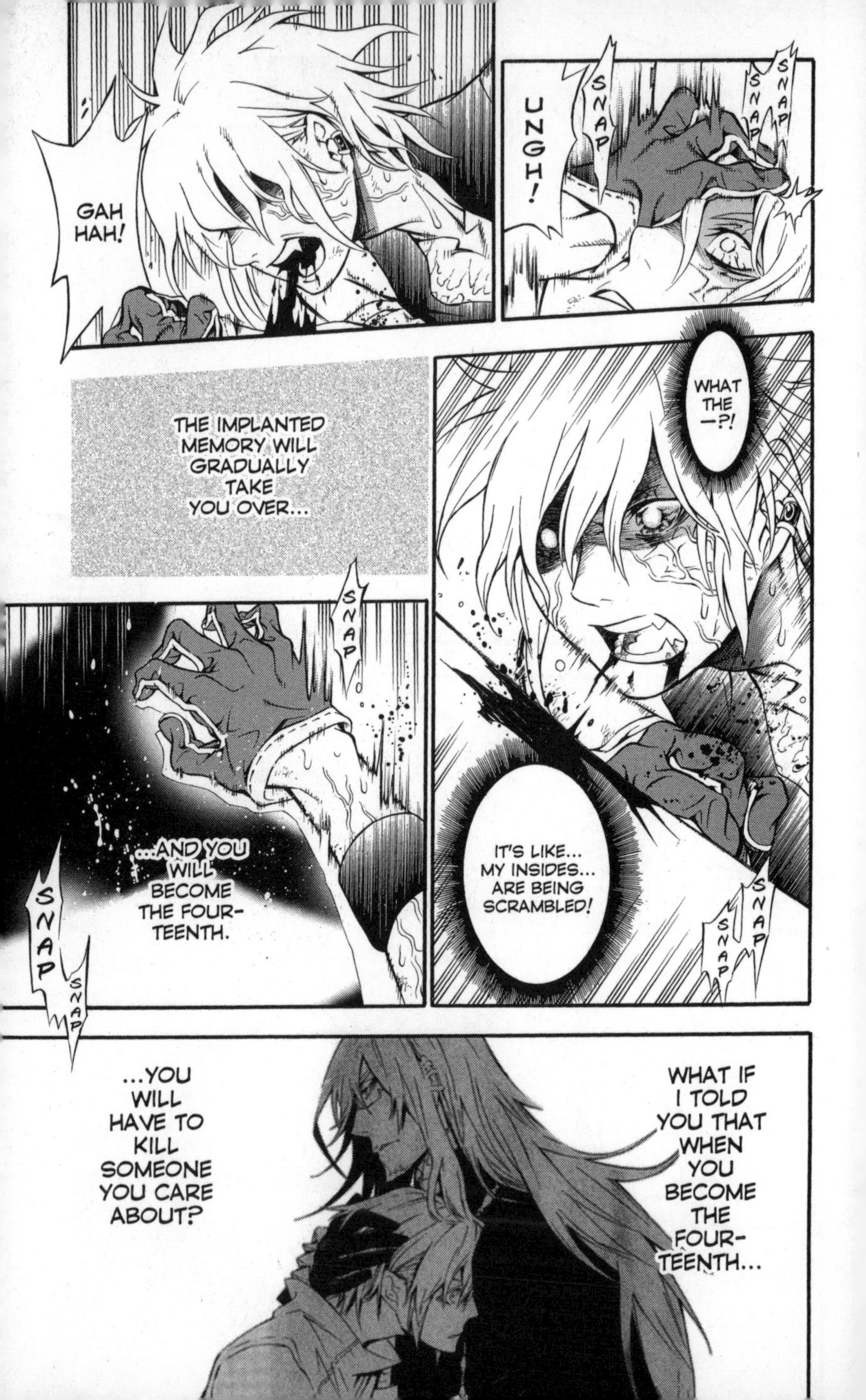
SNAP
SNAP
SNAP
UNGH!
GAH HAH!
WHAT THE—?!
IT'S LIKE... MY INSIDES... ARE BEING SCRAMBLED!
SNAP
SNAP
THE IMPLANTED MEMORY WILL GRADUALLY TAKE YOU OVER...
SNAP
...AND YOU WILL BECOME THE FOUR-TEENTH.
SNAP
SNAP
WHAT IF I TOLD YOU THAT WHEN YOU BECOME THE FOUR-TEENTH...
...YOU WILL HAVE TO KILL SOMEONE YOU CARE ABOUT?

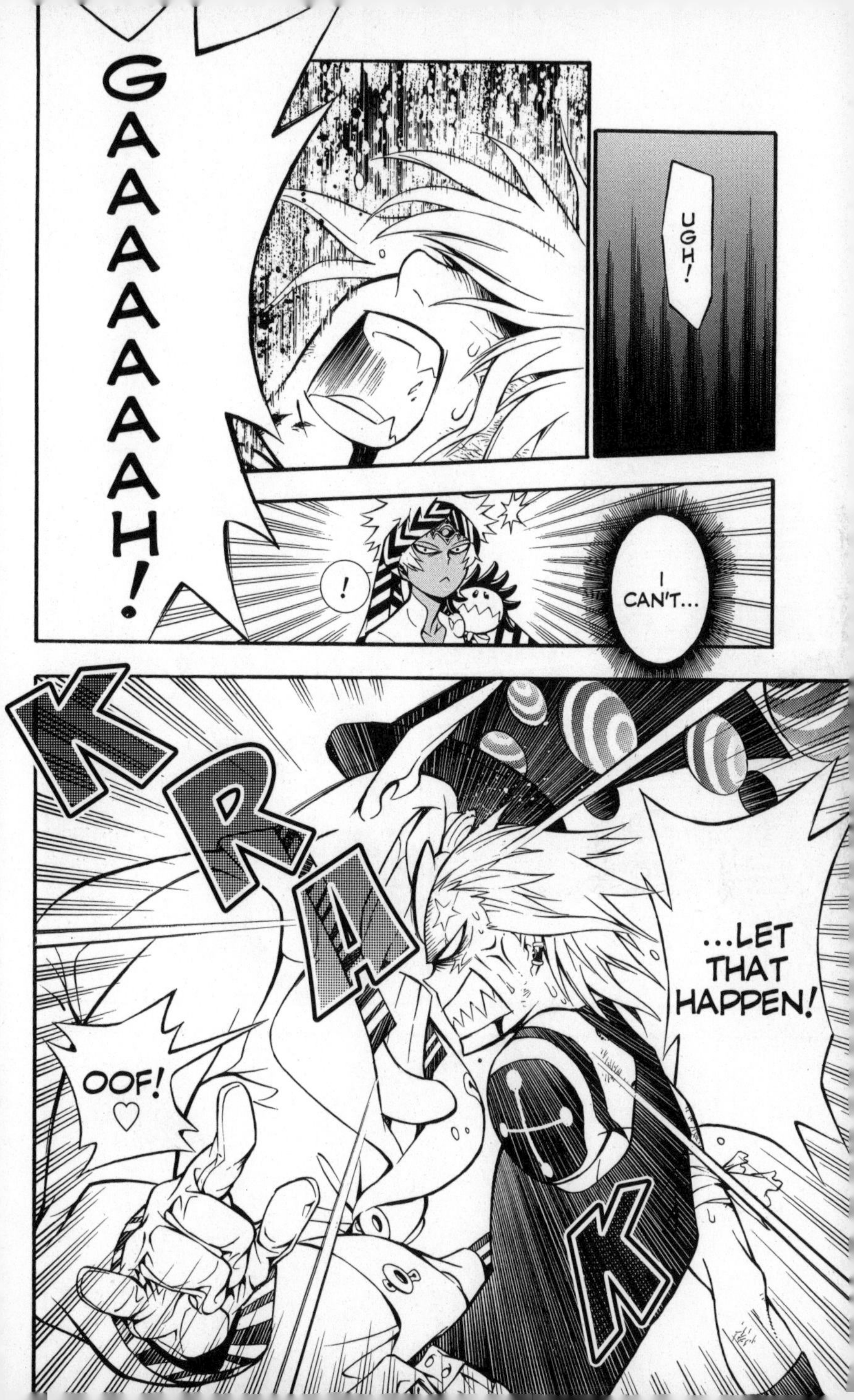

UGH!
GAAAAAAAH!
I CAN'T...
!
...LET THAT HAPPEN!
KRAAK
OOF! ♡

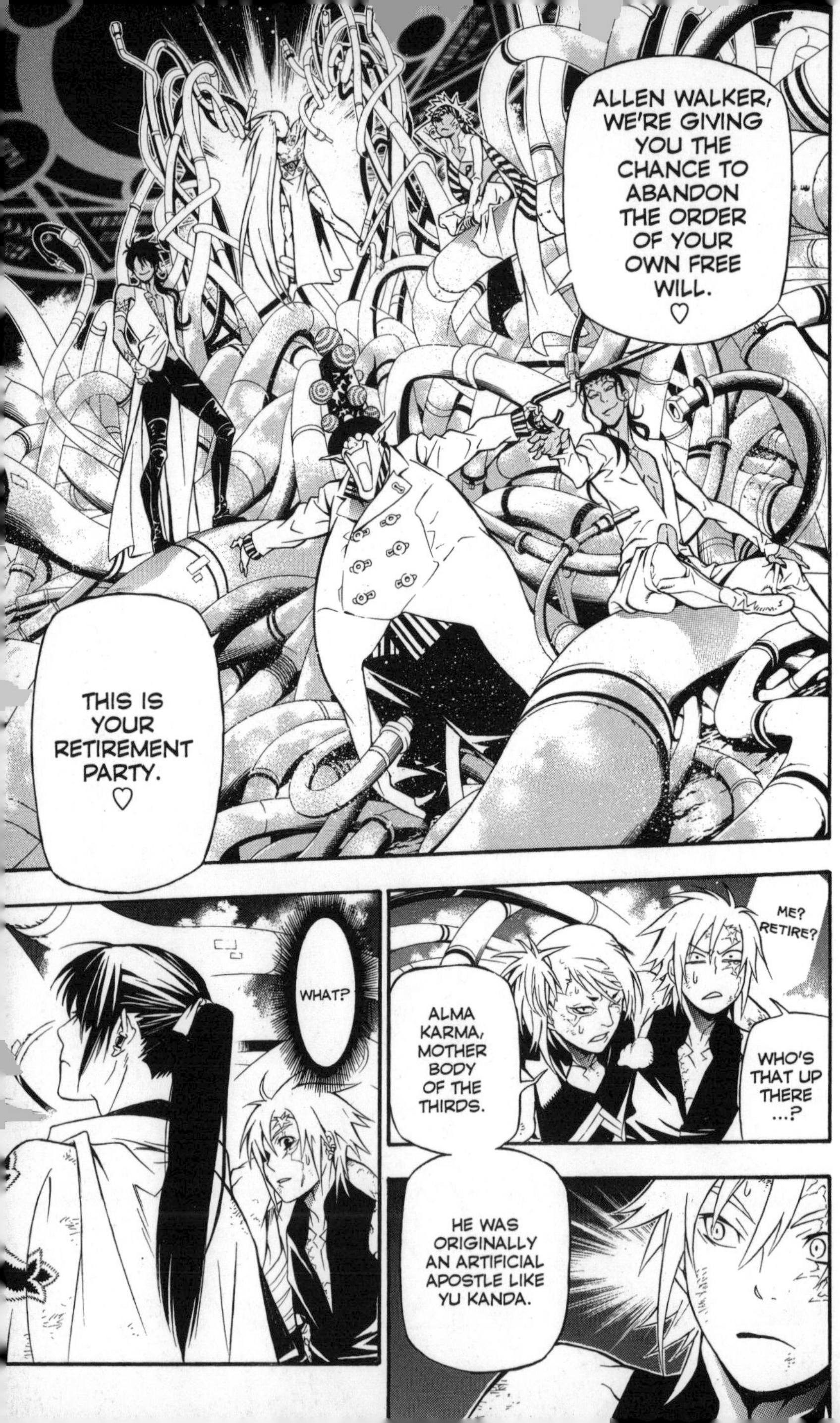
ALLEN WALKER, WE'RE GIVING YOU THE CHANCE TO ABANDON THE ORDER OF YOUR OWN FREE WILL. ♡
THIS IS YOUR RETIREMENT PARTY. ♡
ME? RETIRE?
WHO'S THAT UP THERE ...?
ALMA KARMA, MOTHER BODY OF THE THIRDS.
HE WAS ORIGINALLY AN ARTIFICIAL APOSTLE LIKE YU KANDA.
WHAT?

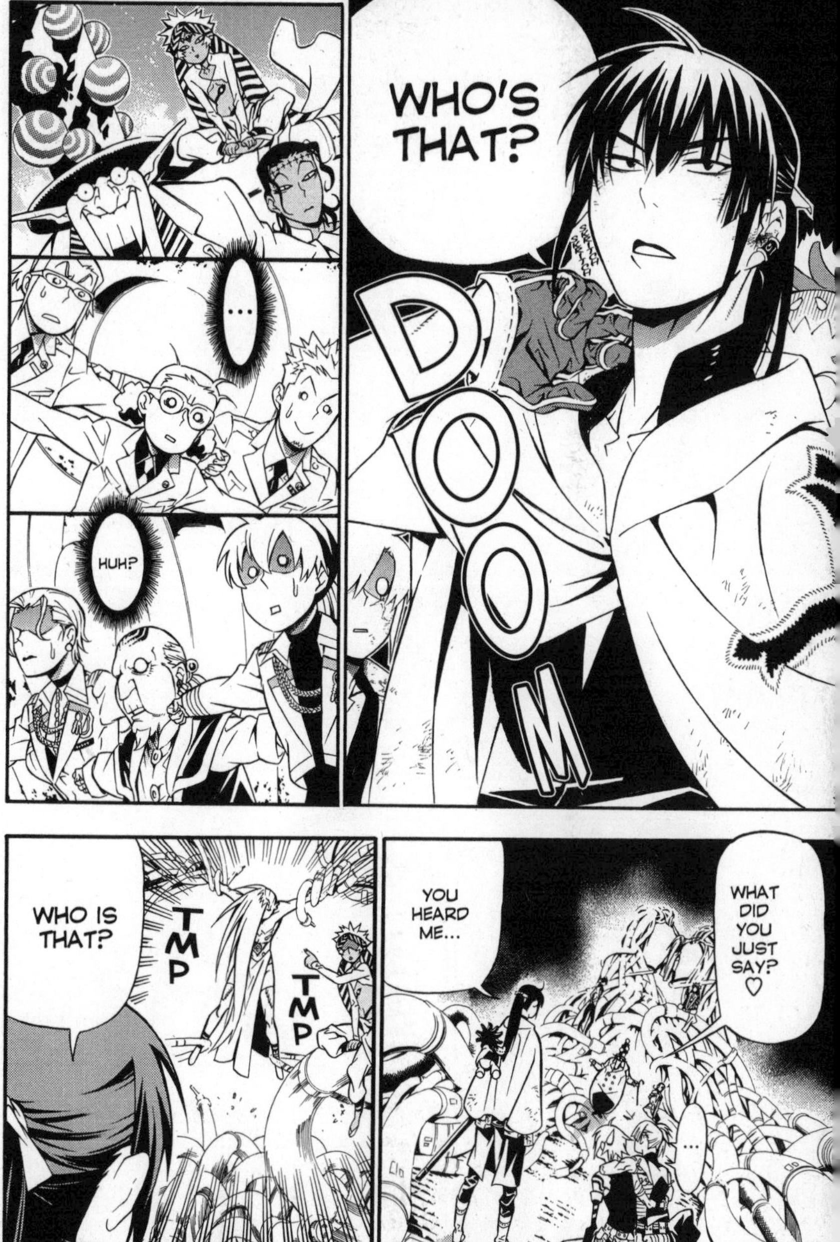
WHO'S THAT?
SKRITCH SKRITCH
DOOOM
...
HUH?
WHAT DID YOU JUST SAY? ♡
YOU HEARD ME...
...
WHO IS THAT?
TMP
TMP

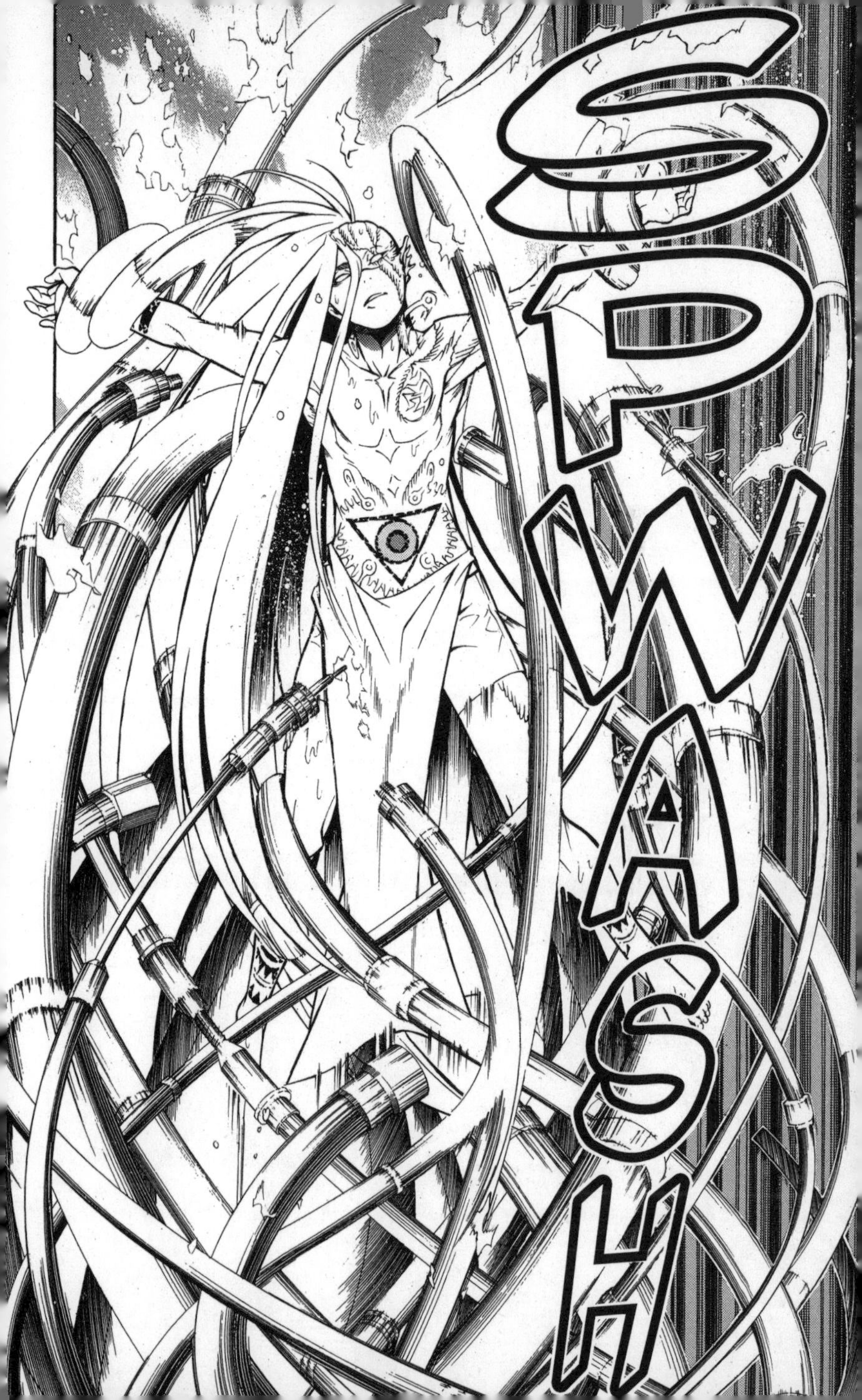
SPWASH

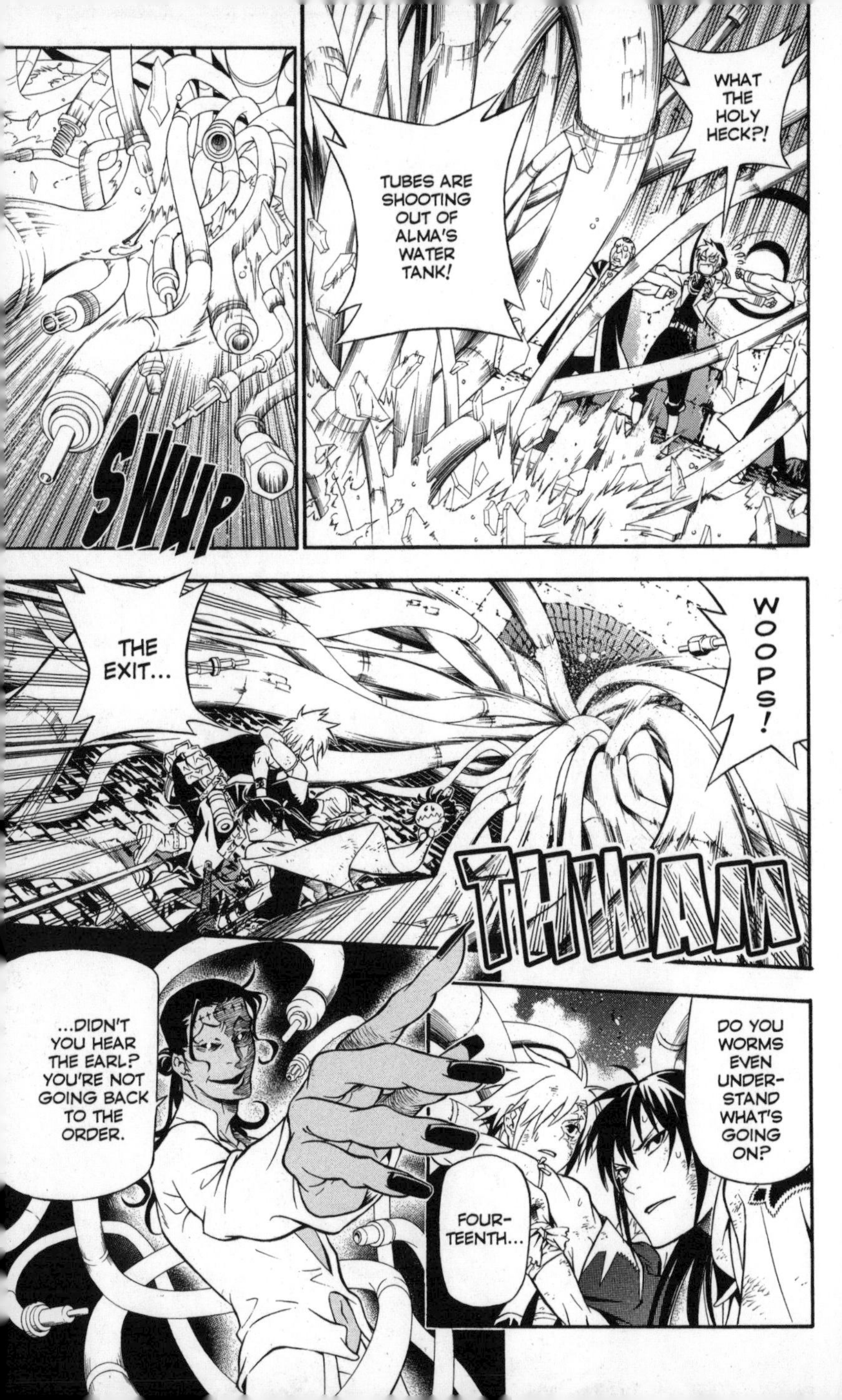
WHAT THE HOLY HECK?!
TUBES ARE SHOOTING OUT OF ALMA'S WATER TANK!
SWUP
WOOPS!
THE EXIT...
THWAM
DO YOU WORMS EVEN UNDER-STAND WHAT'S GOING ON?
FOUR-TEENTH...
...DIDN'T YOU HEAR THE EARL? YOU'RE NOT GOING BACK TO THE ORDER.

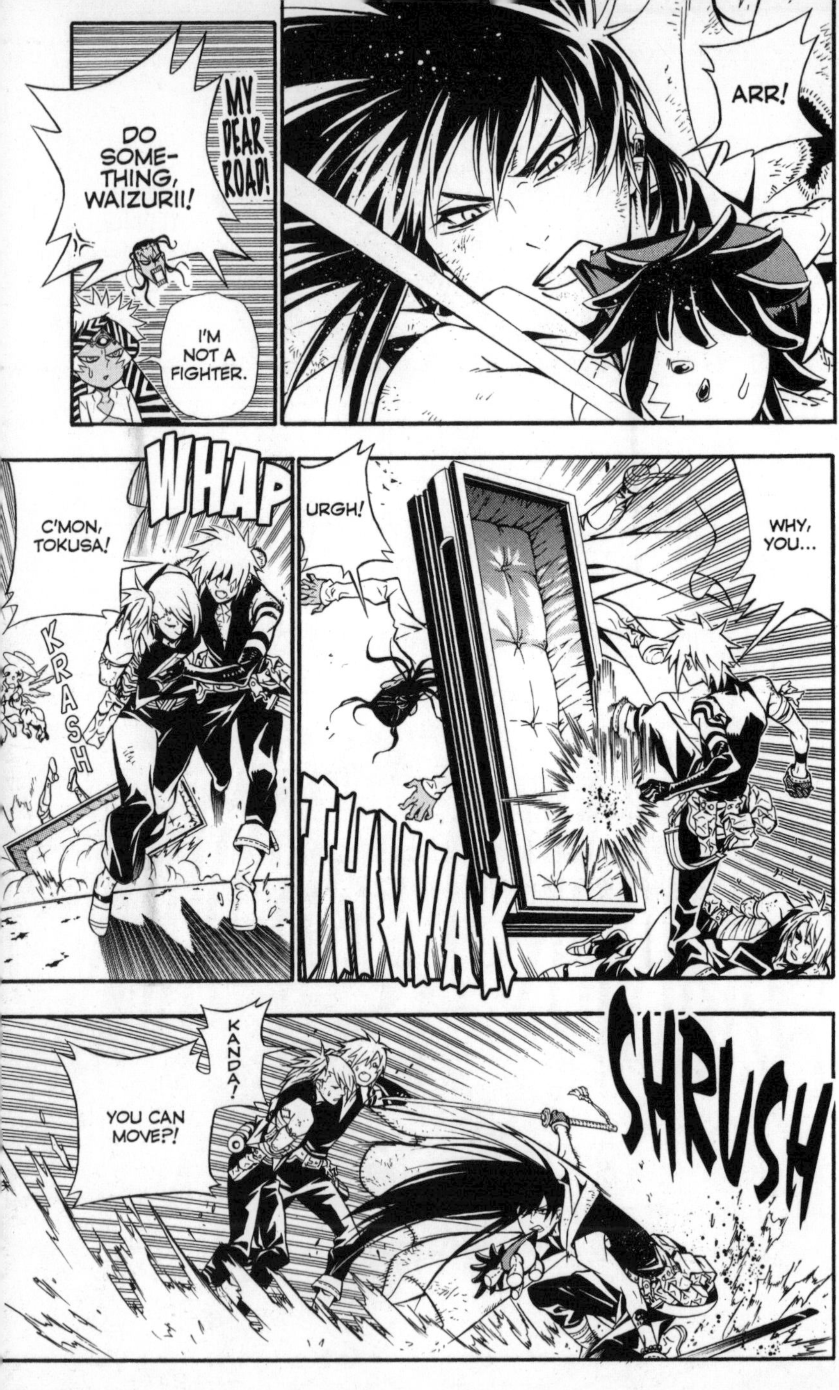
ARR!
MY DEAR ROAD!
DO SOME-THING, WAIZURII!
I'M NOT A FIGHTER.
WHY, YOU...
URGH!
THWAK
WHAP
C'MON, TOKUSA!
KRASH
SHRUSH
KANDA!
YOU CAN MOVE?!

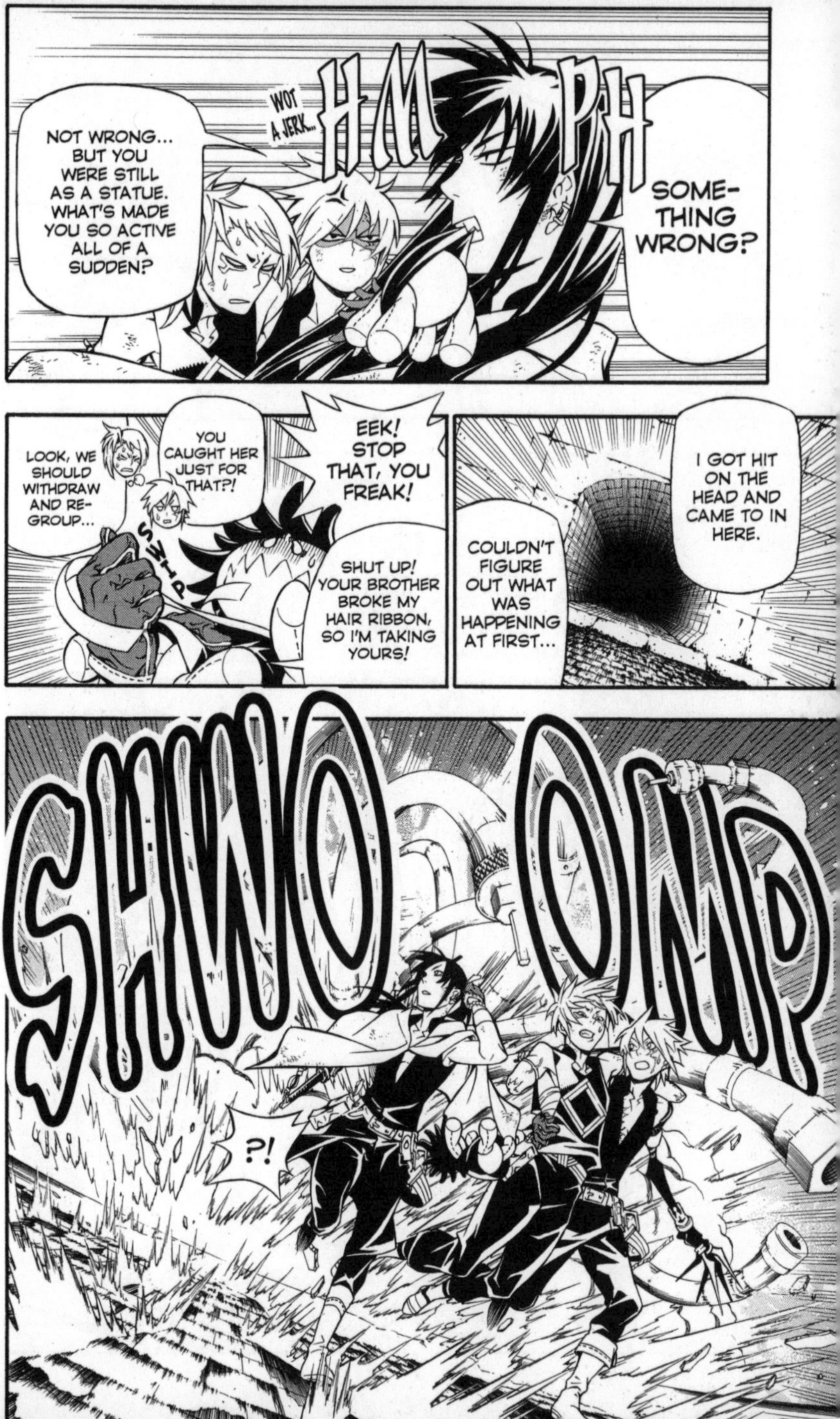
SOMETHING WRONG?
HMPH
WOT A JERK...
NOT WRONG... BUT YOU WERE STILL AS A STATUE. WHAT'S MADE YOU SO ACTIVE ALL OF A SUDDEN?
I GOT HIT ON THE HEAD AND CAME TO IN HERE.
COULDN'T FIGURE OUT WHAT WAS HAPPENING AT FIRST...
EEK! STOP THAT, YOU FREAK!
YOU CAUGHT HER JUST FOR THAT?!
LOOK, WE SHOULD WITHDRAW AND REGROUP...
SHUT UP! YOUR BROTHER BROKE MY HAIR RIBBON, SO I'M TAKING YOURS!
SWIP
SHWOOMP
?!

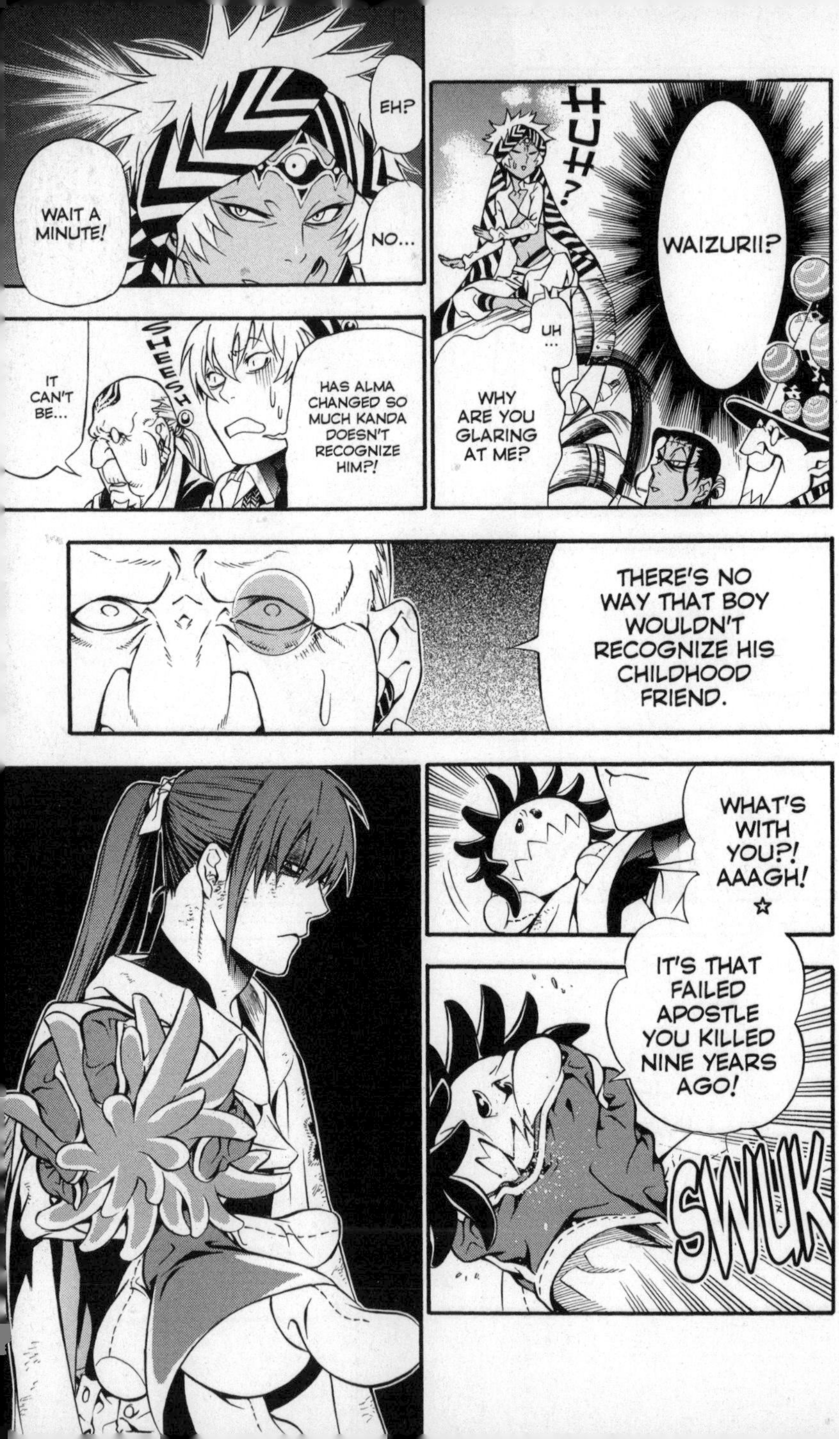
HUH?!
WAIZURII?
UH...
WHY ARE YOU GLARING AT ME?
EH?
NO...
WAIT A MINUTE!
HAS ALMA CHANGED SO MUCH KANDA DOESN'T RECOGNIZE HIM?!
SHEESH
IT CAN'T BE...
THERE'S NO WAY THAT BOY WOULDN'T RECOGNIZE HIS CHILDHOOD FRIEND.
WHAT'S WITH YOU?! AAAGH! ☆
IT'S THAT FAILED APOSTLE YOU KILLED NINE YEARS AGO!
SWUK

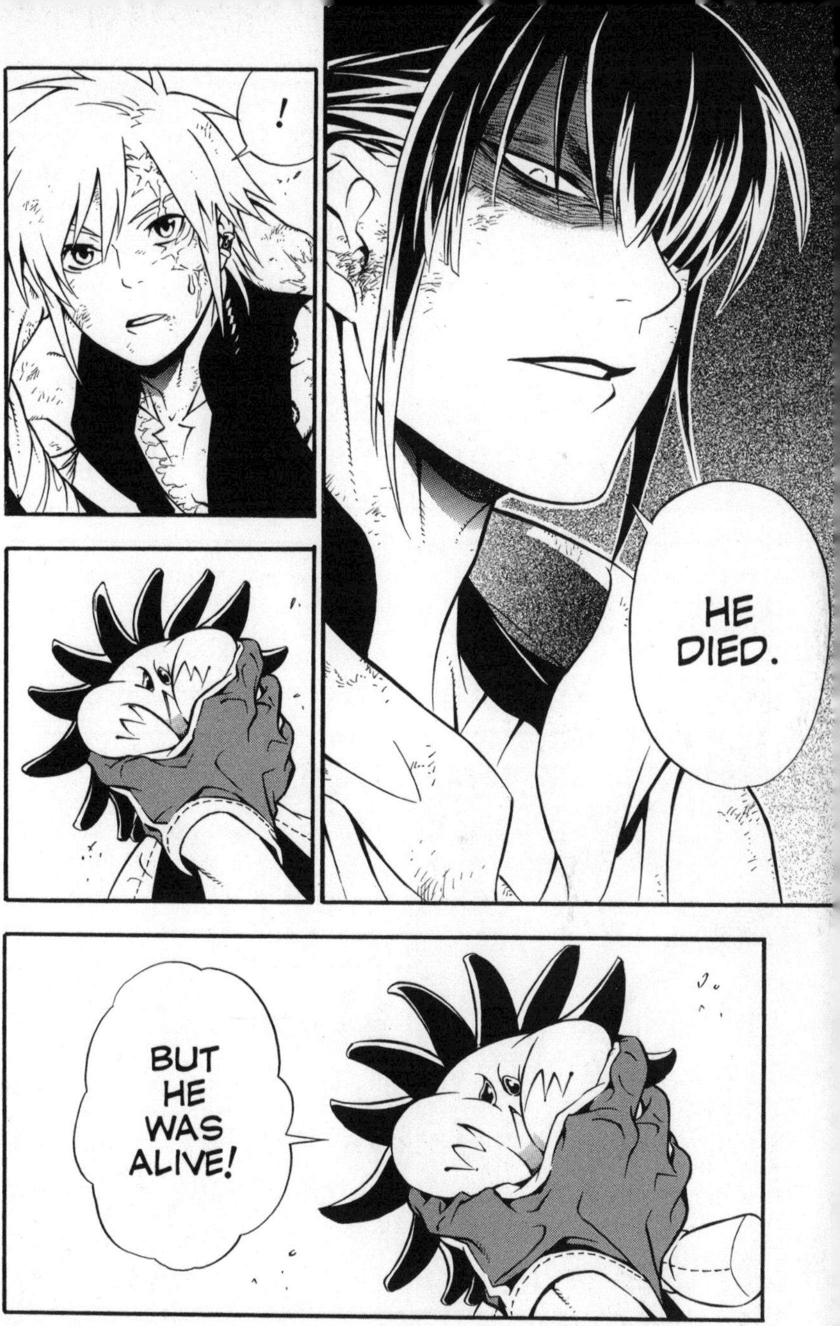
HE DIED.
!
BUT HE WAS ALIVE!

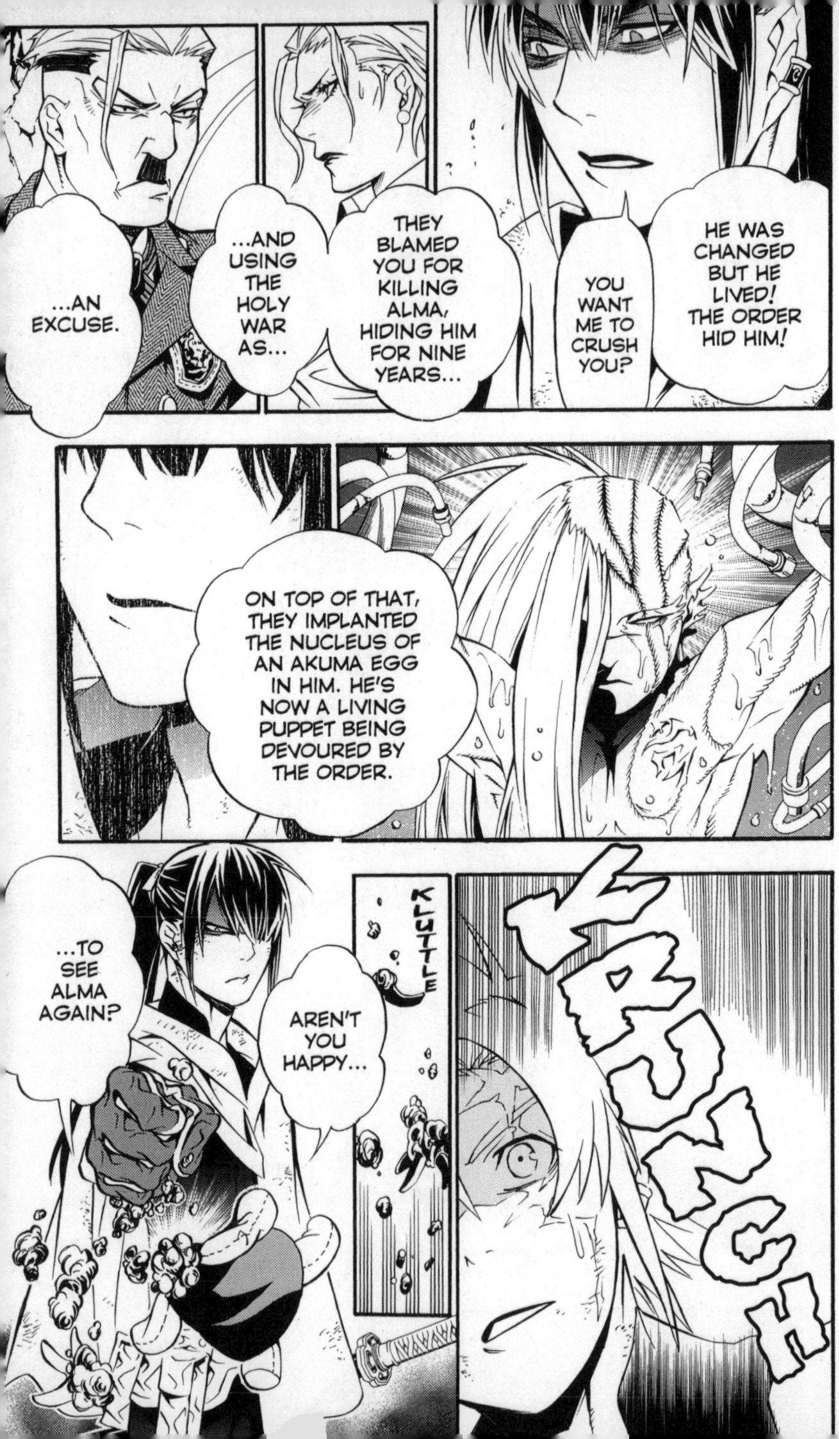
HE WAS CHANGED BUT HE LIVED! THE ORDER HID HIM!
YOU WANT ME TO CRUSH YOU?
THEY BLAMED YOU FOR KILLING ALMA, HIDING HIM FOR NINE YEARS...
...AND USING THE HOLY WAR AS...
...AN EXCUSE.
ON TOP OF THAT, THEY IMPLANTED THE NUCLEUS OF AN AKUMA EGG IN HIM. HE'S NOW A LIVING PUPPET BEING DEVOURED BY THE ORDER.
KRUNCH
KLUTTLE
AREN'T YOU HAPPY...
...TO SEE ALMA AGAIN?

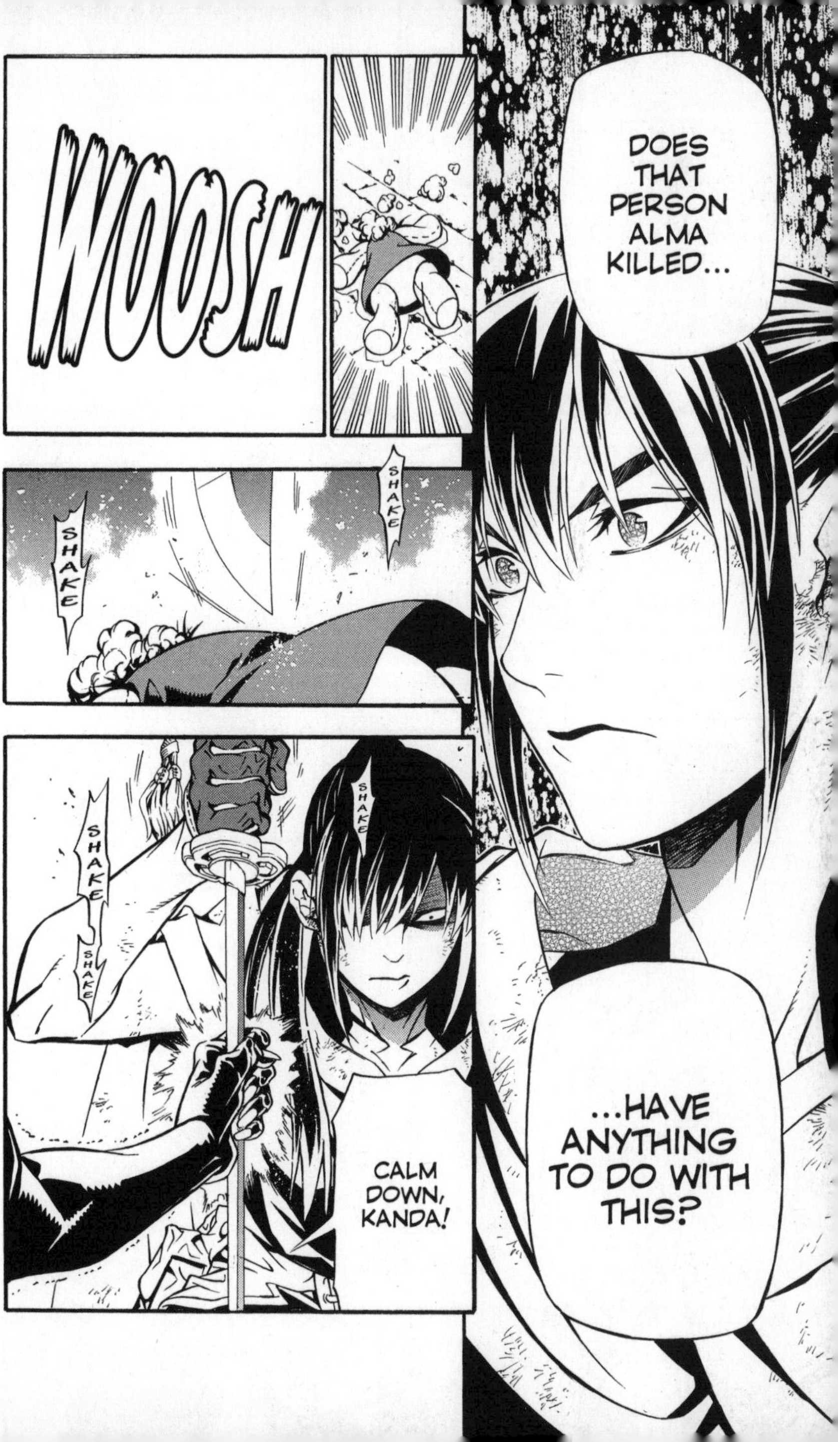
DOES THAT PERSON ALMA KILLED...
...HAVE ANYTHING TO DO WITH THIS?
WOOSH
SHAKE
SHAKE
SHAKE
SHAKE
SHAKE
CALM DOWN, KANDA!

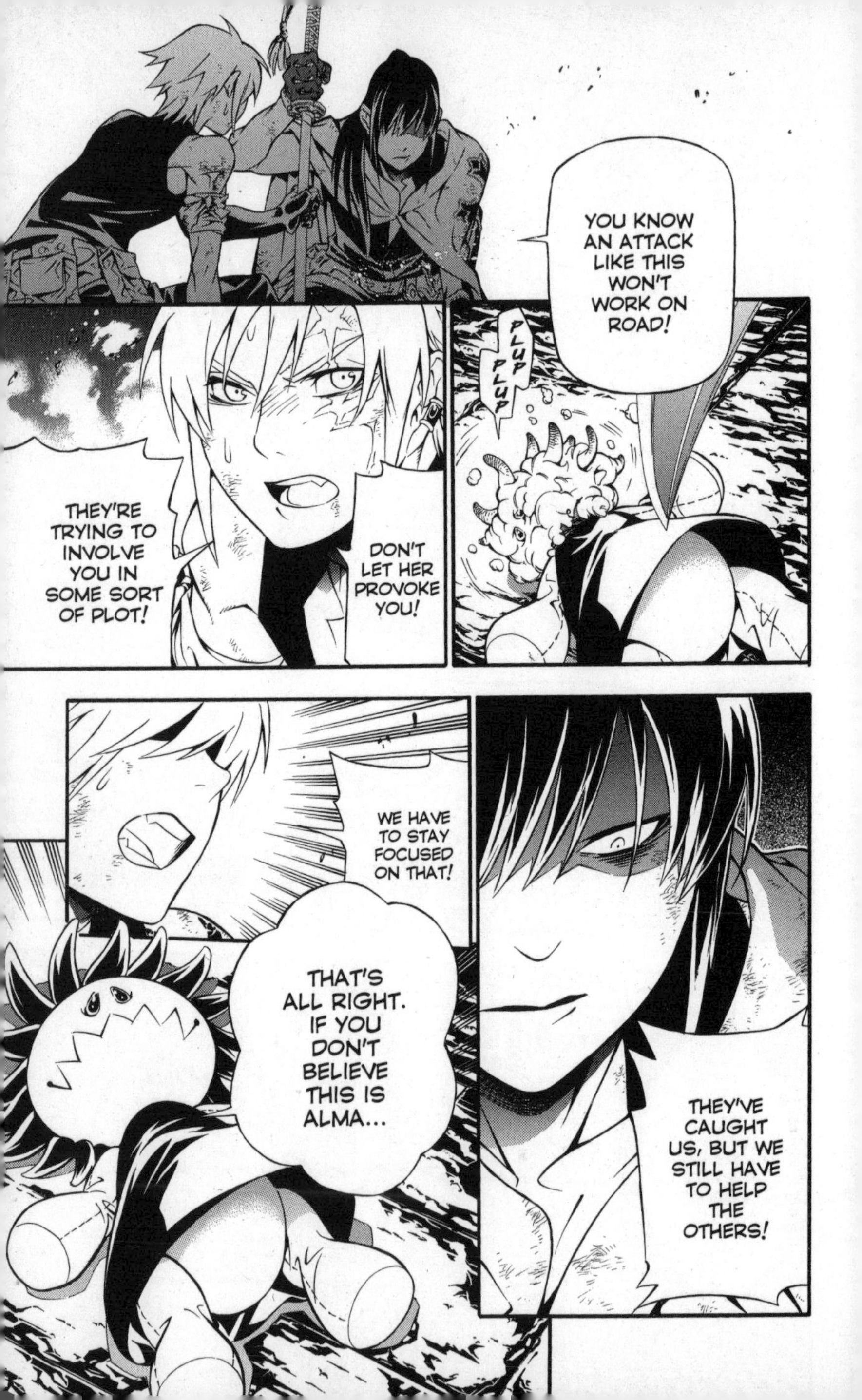
YOU KNOW AN ATTACK LIKE THIS WON'T WORK ON ROAD!
PLUP PLUP
DON'T LET HER PROVOKE YOU!
THEY'RE TRYING TO INVOLVE YOU IN SOME SORT OF PLOT!
THEY'VE CAUGHT US, BUT WE STILL HAVE TO HELP THE OTHERS!
WE HAVE TO STAY FOCUSED ON THAT!
THAT'S ALL RIGHT. IF YOU DON'T BELIEVE THIS IS ALMA...

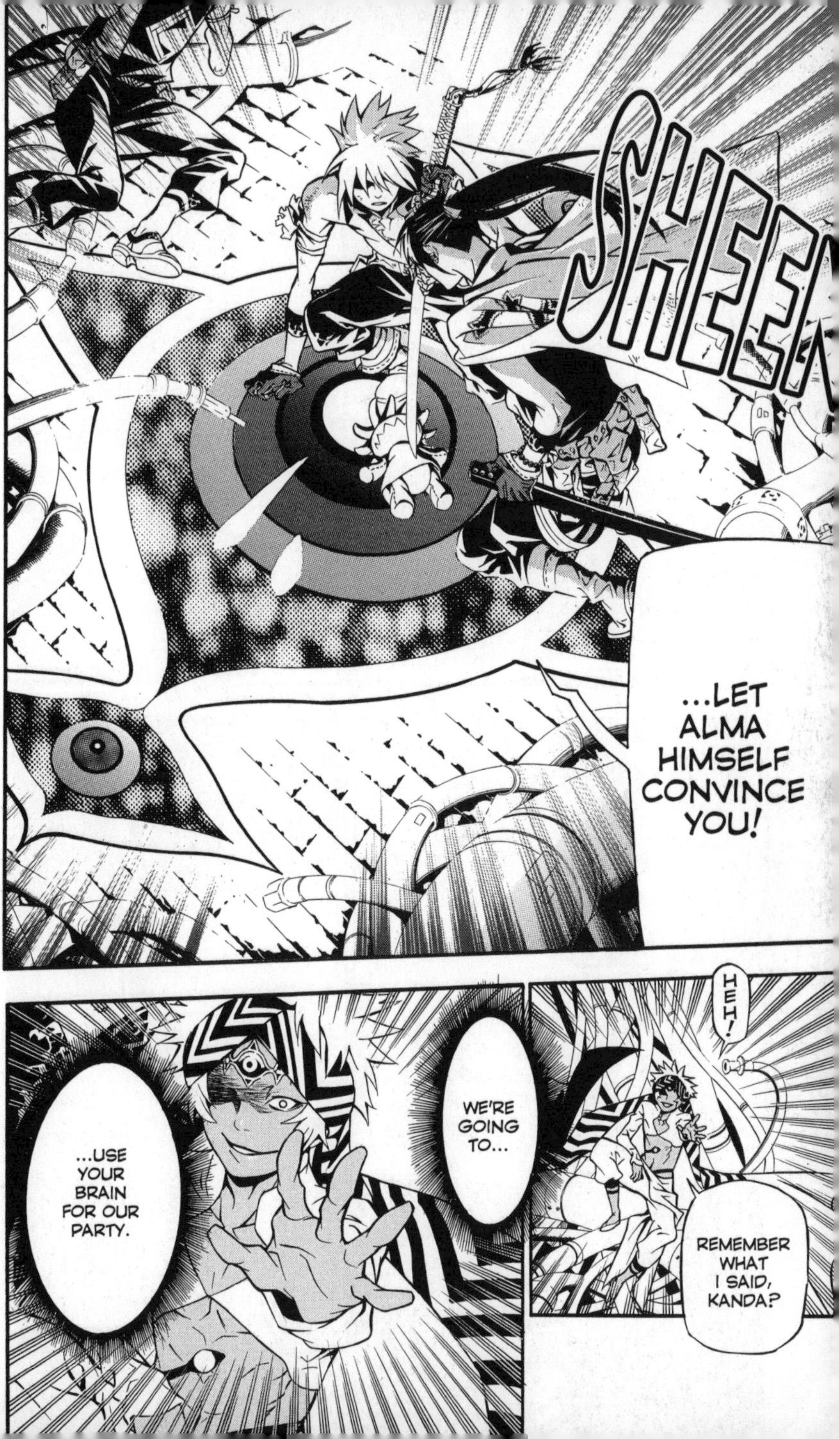
SHEE
...LET ALMA HIMSELF CONVINCE YOU!
HEH!
REMEMBER WHAT I SAID, KANDA?
WE'RE GOING TO...
...USE YOUR BRAIN FOR OUR PARTY.

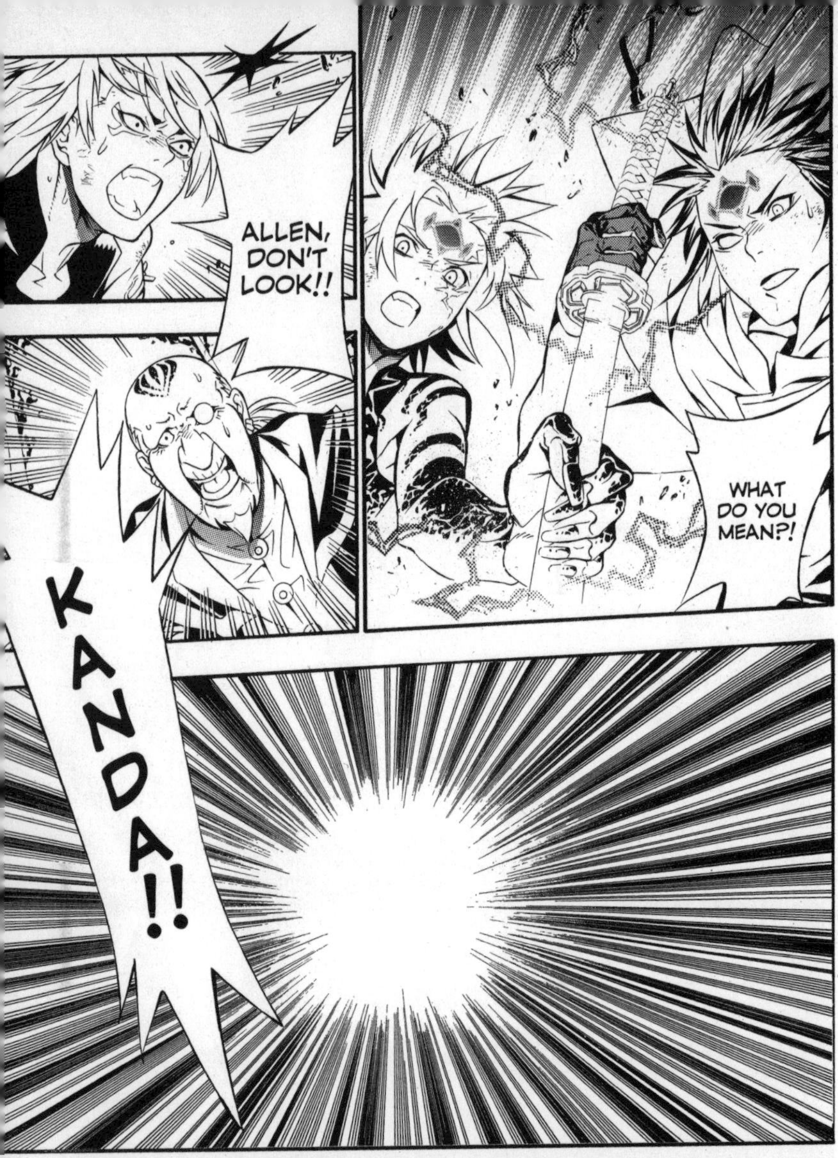
WHAT DO YOU MEAN?!
ALLEN, DON'T LOOK!!
KANDA!!

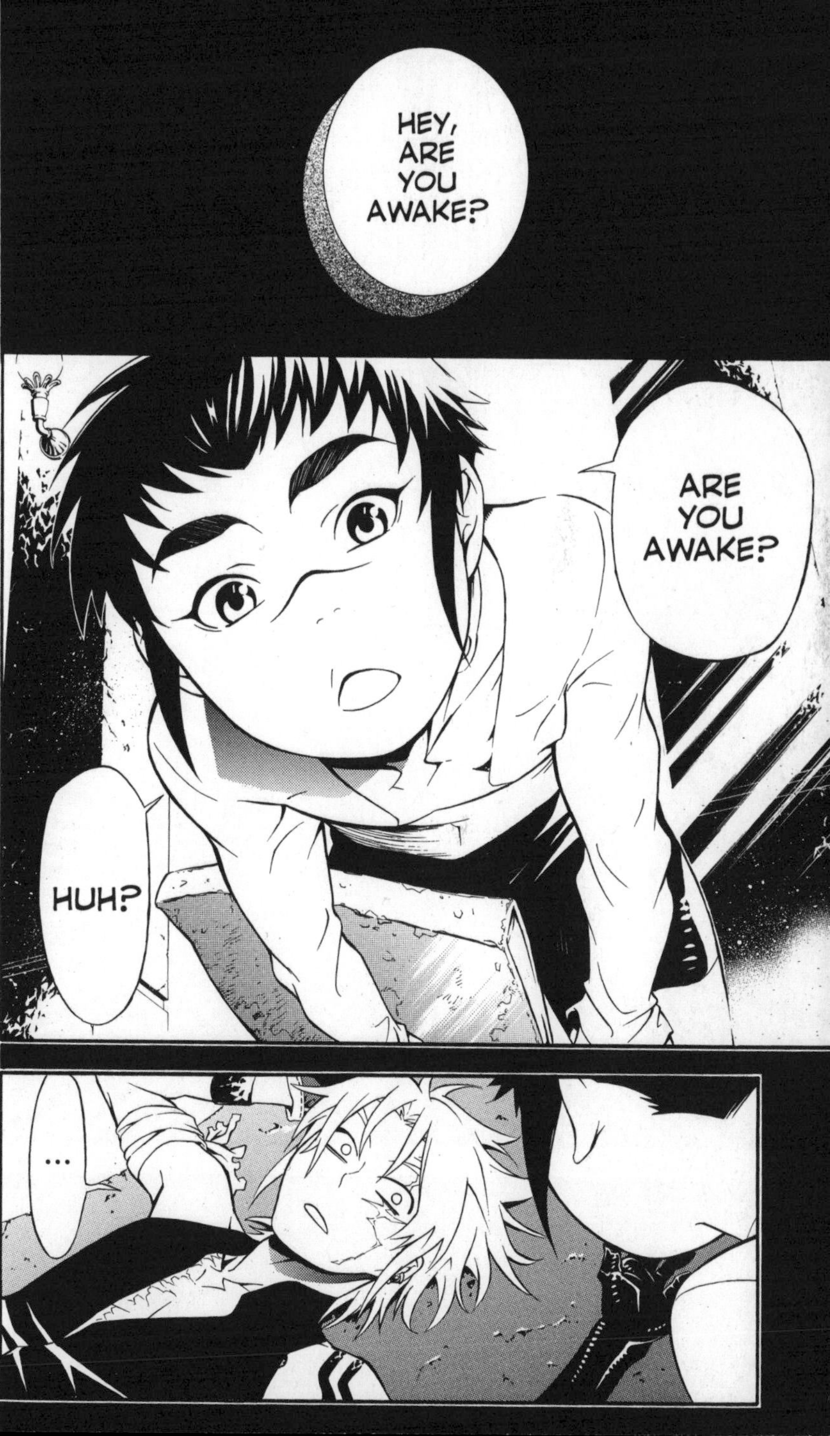
HEY, ARE YOU AWAKE?
ARE YOU AWAKE?
HUH?
...

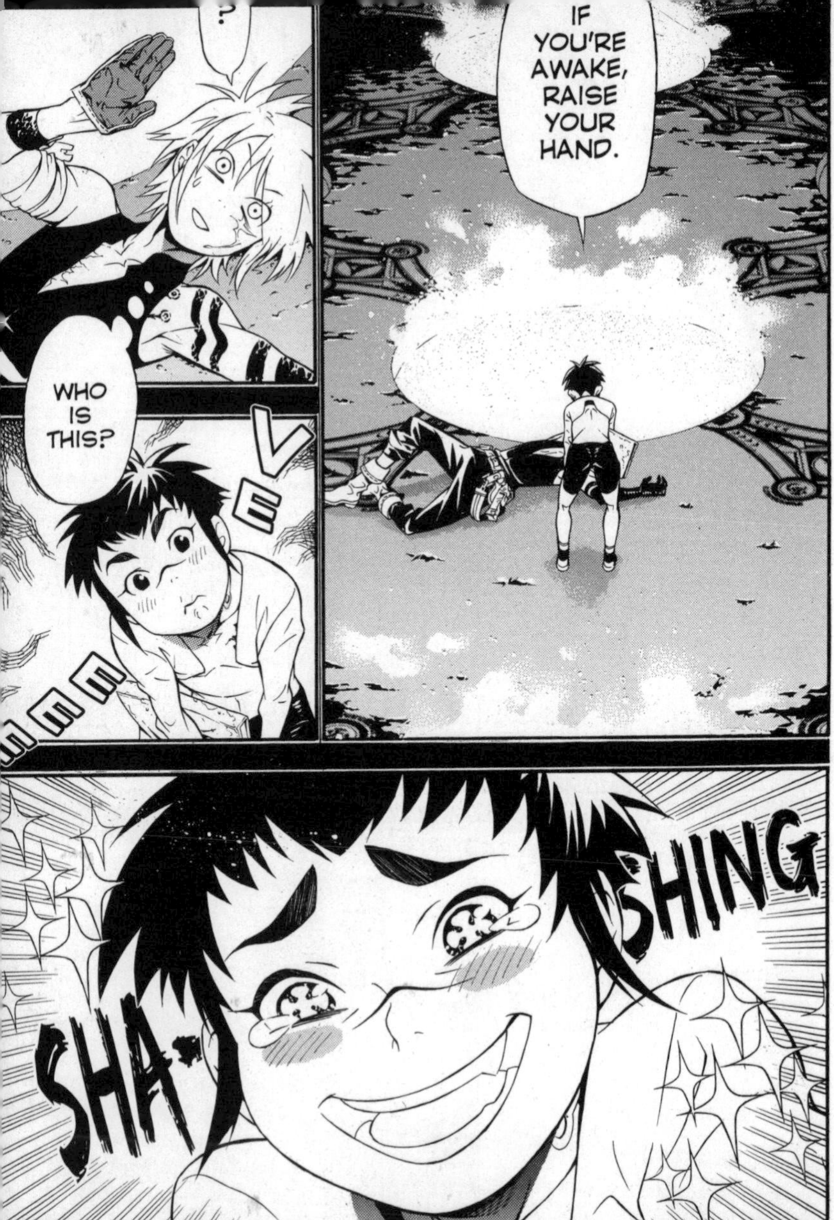

IF YOU'RE AWAKE, RAISE YOUR HAND.
?
WHO IS THIS?
VEEEE
SHING
SHA-

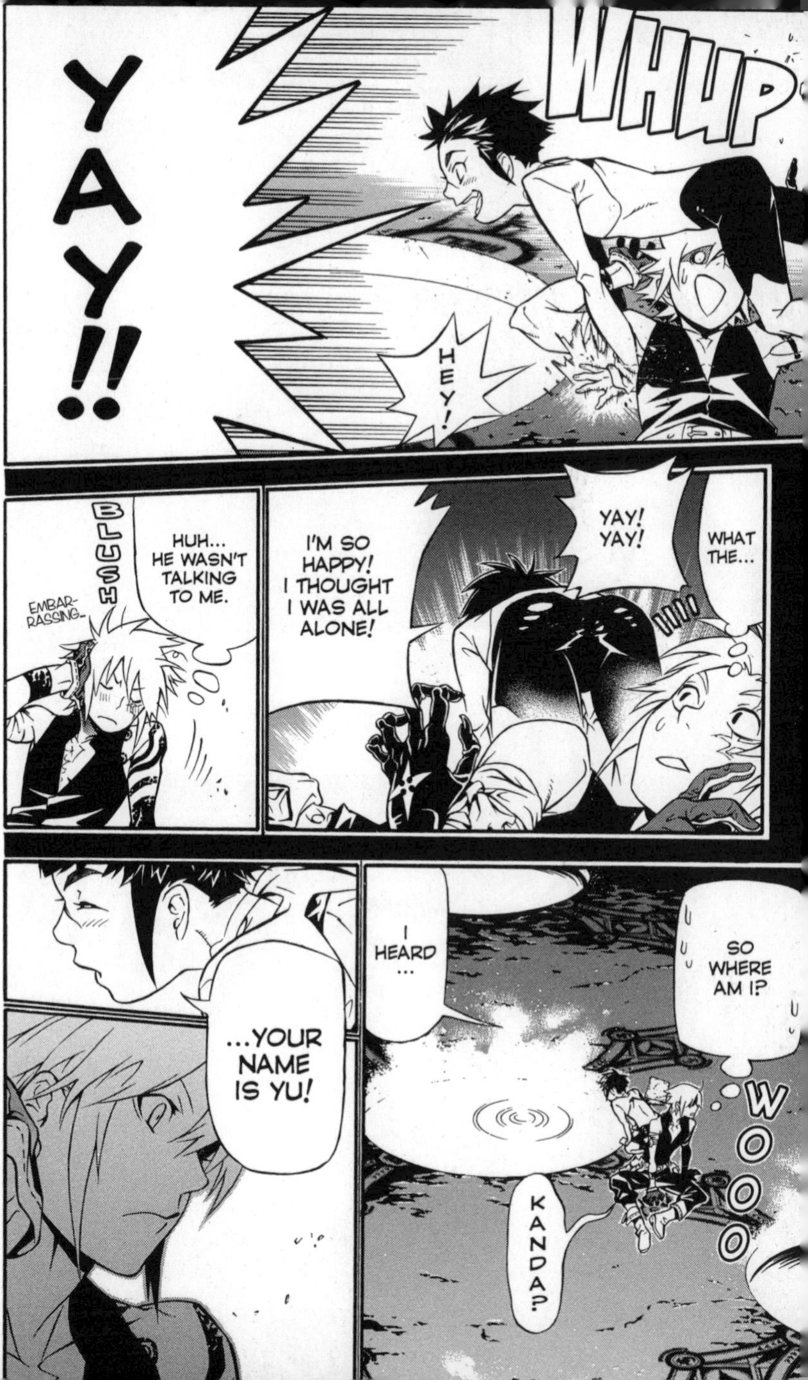
WHUP
HEY!
YAY!!
WHAT THE...
YAY! YAY!
I'M SO HAPPY! I THOUGHT I WAS ALL ALONE!
BLUSH
HUH... HE WASN'T TALKING TO ME.
EMBARRASSING...
WOOO
SO WHERE AM I?
KANDA?
I HEARD...
...YOUR NAME IS YU!

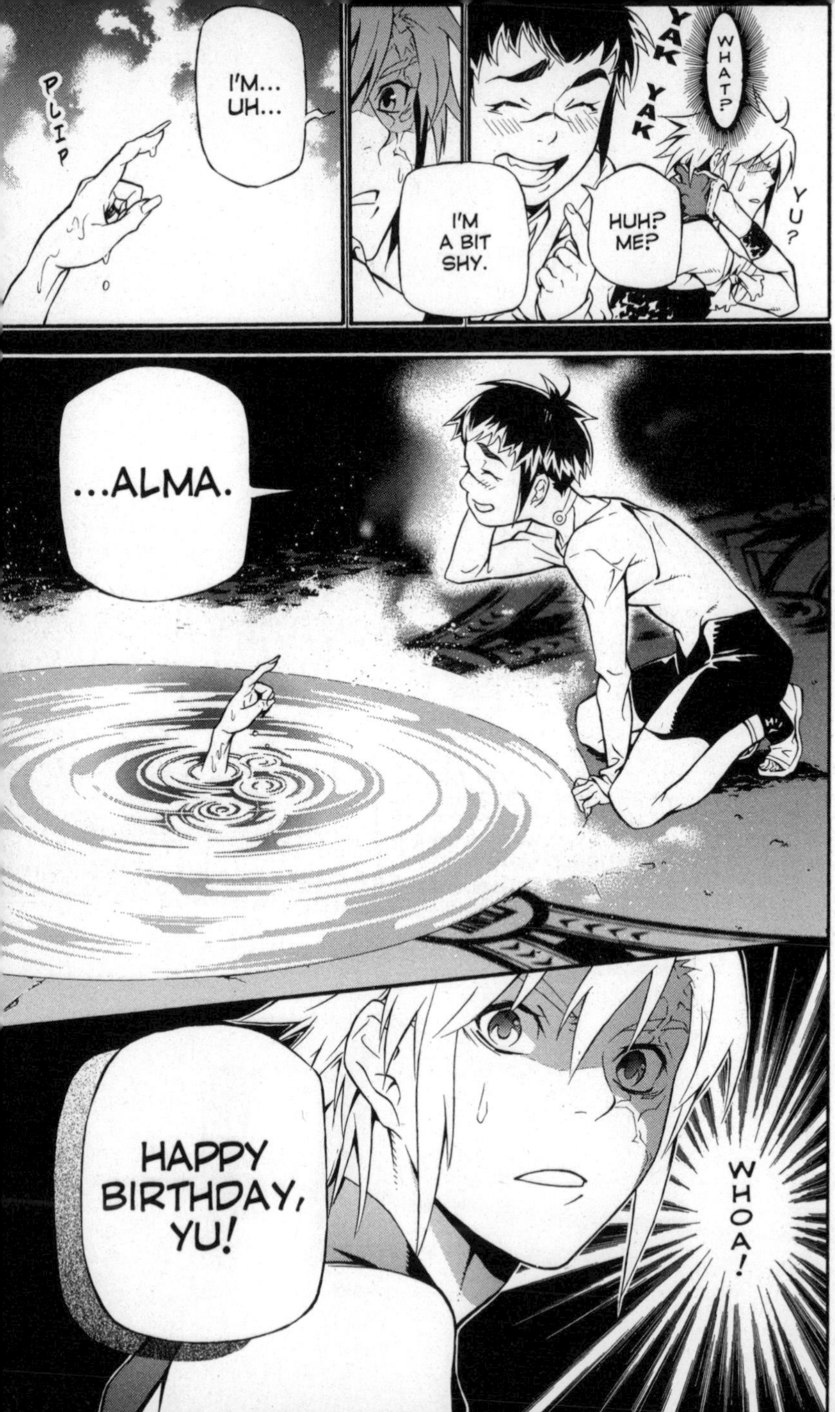
WHAT?
YU?
YAK YAK
HUH? ME?
I'M A BIT SHY.
PLIP
I'M... UH...
...ALMA.
WHOA!
HAPPY BIRTHDAY, YU!

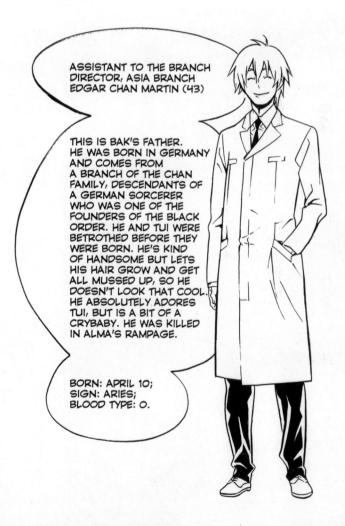

ASSISTANT TO THE BRANCH
DIRECTOR, ASIA BRANCH
EDGAR CHAN MARTIN (43)

THIS IS BAK'S FATHER.
HE WAS BORN IN GERMANY
AND COMES FROM
A BRANCH OF THE CHAN
FAMILY, DESCENDANTS OF
A GERMAN SORCERER
WHO WAS ONE OF THE
FOUNDERS OF THE BLACK
ORDER. HE AND TUI WERE
BETROTHED BEFORE THEY
WERE BORN. HE'S KIND
OF HANDSOME BUT LETS
HIS HAIR GROW AND GET
ALL MUSSED UP, SO HE
DOESN'T LOOK THAT COOL.
HE ABSOLUTELY ADORES
TUI, BUT IS A BIT OF A
CRYBABY. HE WAS KILLED
IN ALMA'S RAMPAGE.

BORN: APRIL 10;
SIGN: ARIES;
BLOOD TYPE: O.

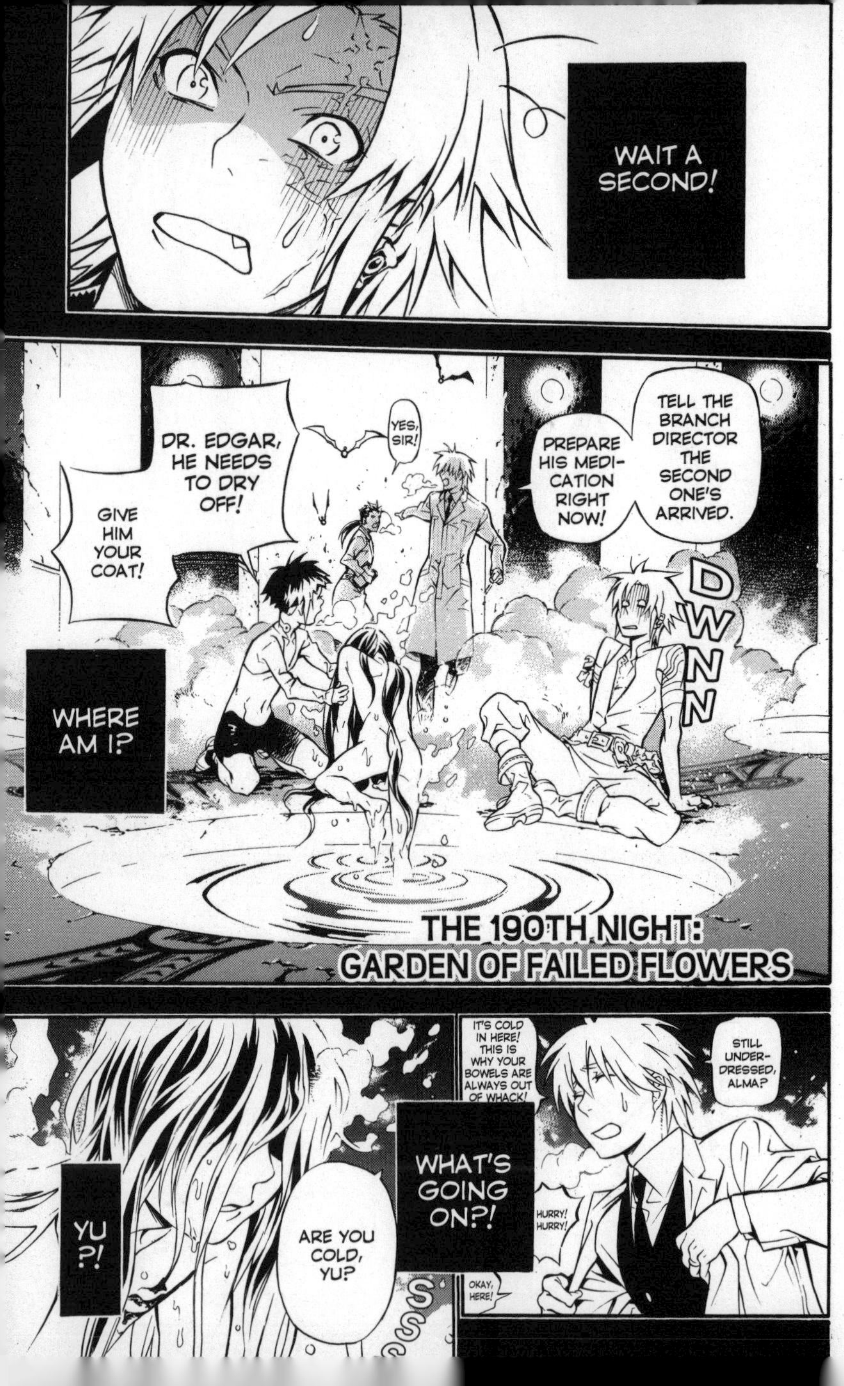
WAIT A SECOND!
TELL THE BRANCH DIRECTOR THE SECOND ONE'S ARRIVED.
PREPARE HIS MEDICATION RIGHT NOW!
YES, SIR!
DR. EDGAR, HE NEEDS TO DRY OFF!
GIVE HIM YOUR COAT!
DWNN
WHERE AM I?
THE 190TH NIGHT: GARDEN OF FAILED FLOWERS
STILL UNDER-DRESSED, ALMA?
IT'S COLD IN HERE! THIS IS WHY YOUR BOWELS ARE ALWAYS OUT OF WHACK!
HURRY! HURRY!
OKAY, HERE!
WHAT'S GOING ON?!
ARE YOU COLD, YU?
YU?!

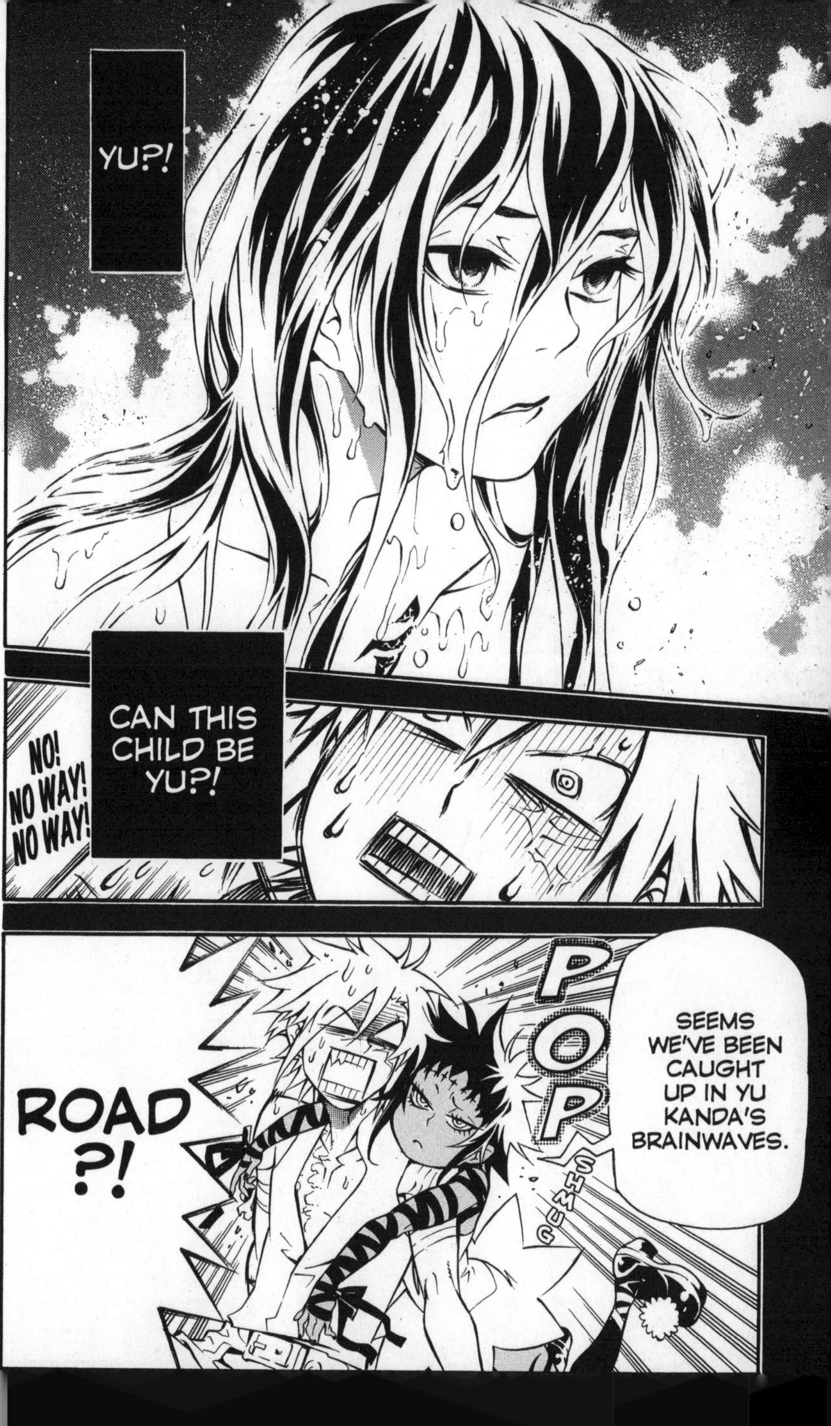
YU?!
CAN THIS CHILD BE YU?!
NO! NO WAY! NO WAY!
SEEMS WE'VE BEEN CAUGHT UP IN YU KANDA'S BRAINWAVES.
POP
SHMUG
ROAD?!

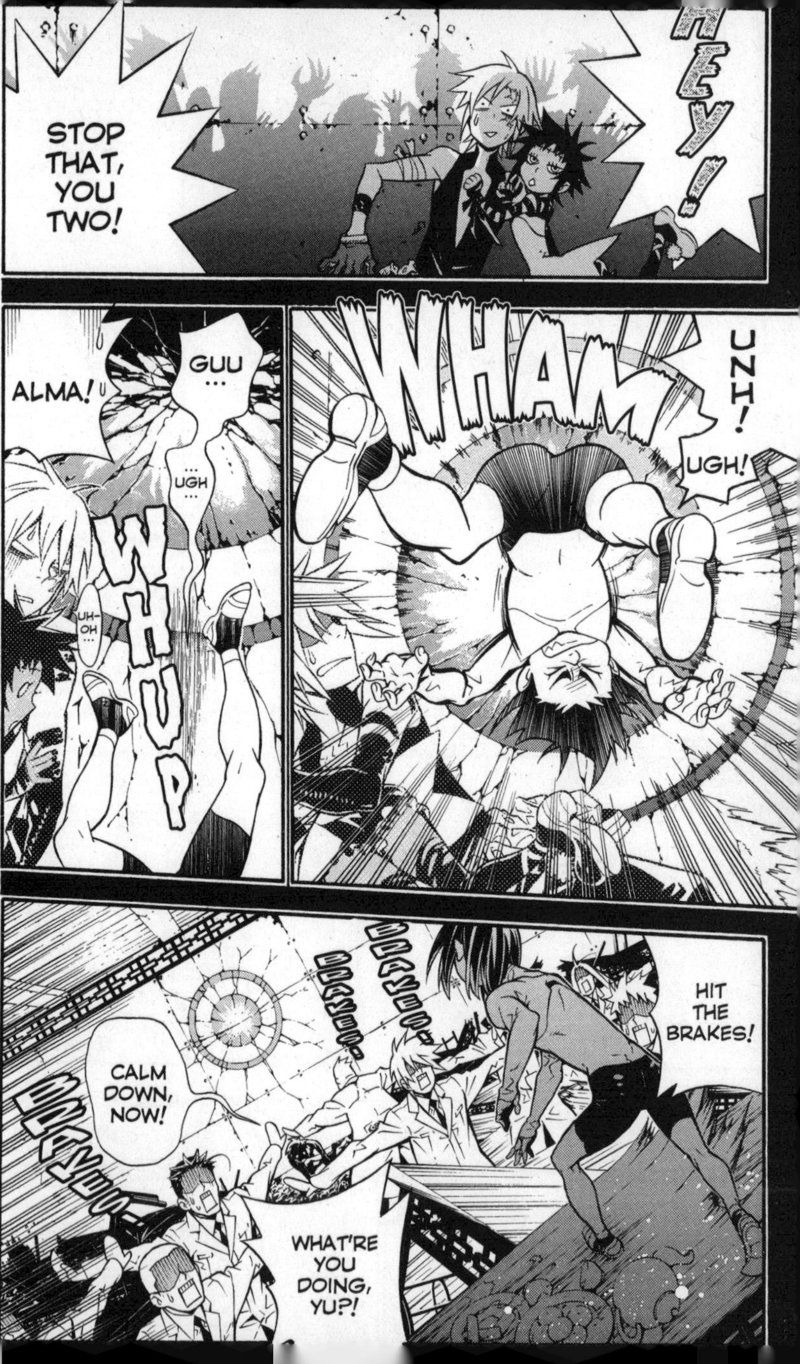
HEY!
STOP THAT, YOU TWO!
UNH!
WHAM
UGH!
GUU ...
ALMA!
... UGH ...
WHUP
UH-OH ...
HIT THE BRAKES!
BRAKES!
BRAKES!
CALM DOWN, NOW!
BRAKES
WHAT'RE YOU DOING, YU?!

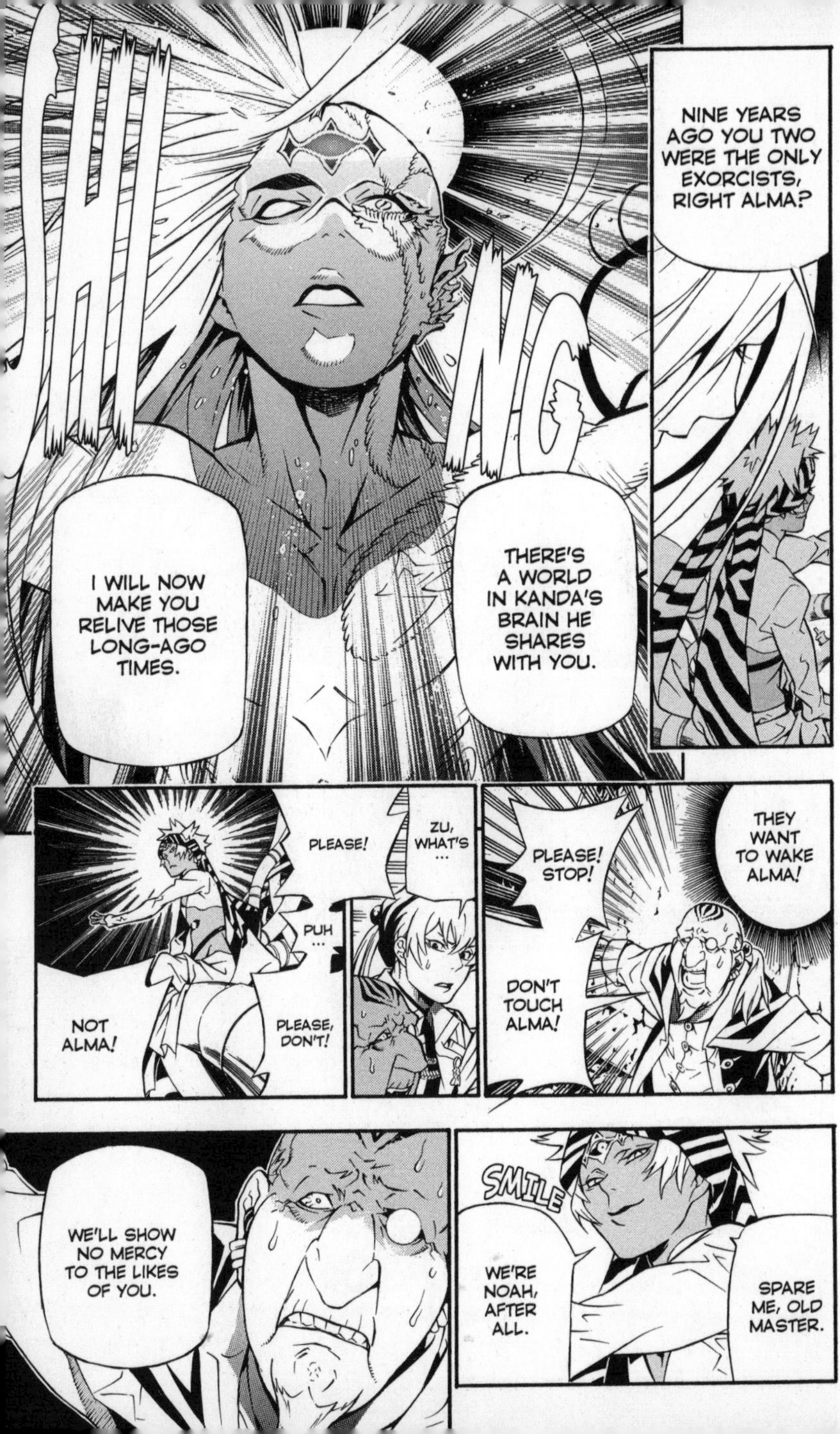
NINE YEARS AGO YOU TWO WERE THE ONLY EXORCISTS, RIGHT ALMA?
THERE'S A WORLD IN KANDA'S BRAIN HE SHARES WITH YOU.
I WILL NOW MAKE YOU RELIVE THOSE LONG-AGO TIMES.
THEY WANT TO WAKE ALMA!
PLEASE! STOP!
DON'T TOUCH ALMA!
ZU, WHAT'S ...
PUH ...
PLEASE, DON'T!
PLEASE!
NOT ALMA!
SMILE
SPARE ME, OLD MASTER.
WE'RE NOAH, AFTER ALL.
WE'LL SHOW NO MERCY TO THE LIKES OF YOU.

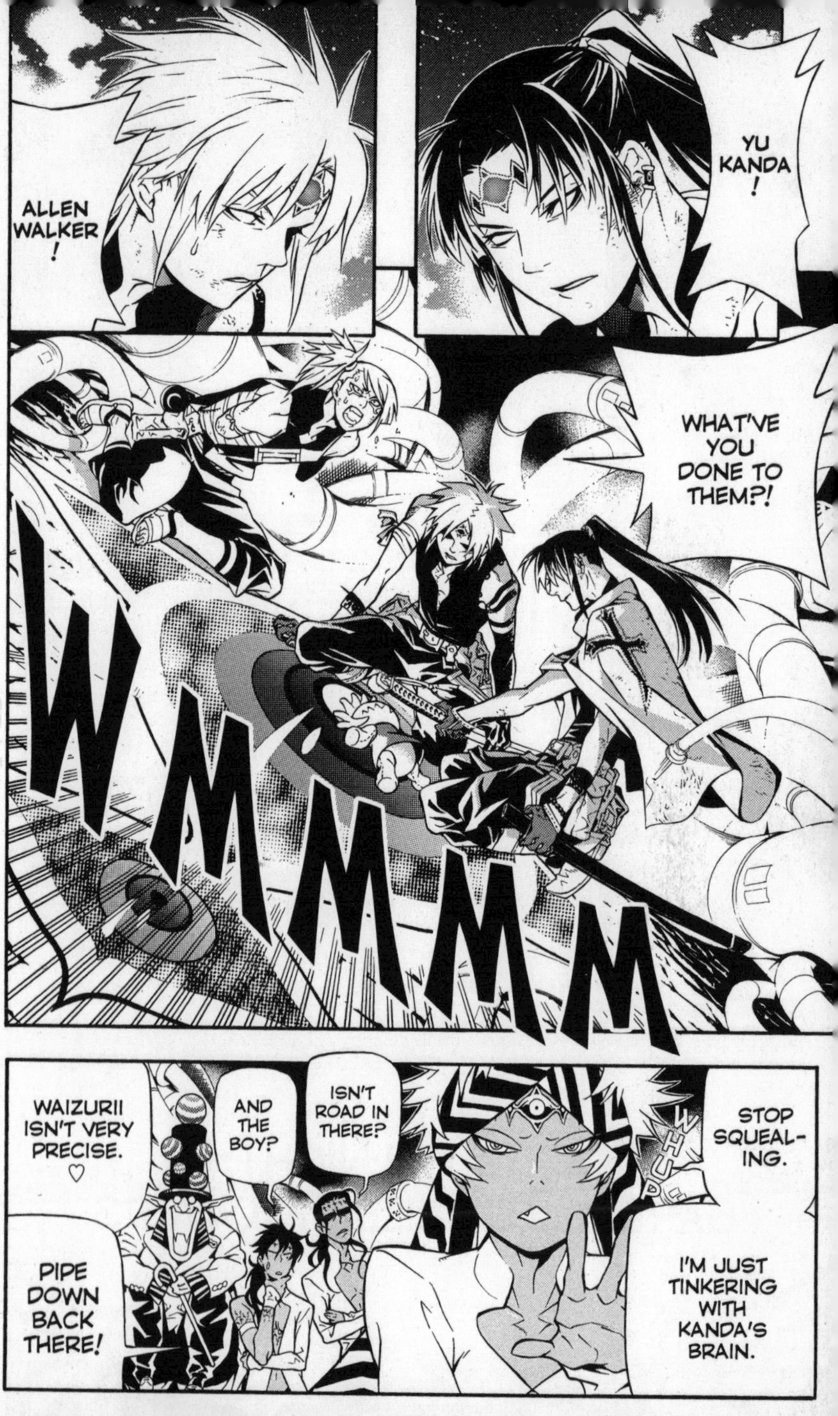
YU KANDA!
ALLEN WALKER!
WHAT'VE YOU DONE TO THEM?!
WMMMMM
STOP SQUEAL-ING.
I'M JUST TINKERING WITH KANDA'S BRAIN.
ISN'T ROAD IN THERE?
AND THE BOY?
WAIZURII ISN'T VERY PRECISE. ♡
PIPE DOWN BACK THERE!

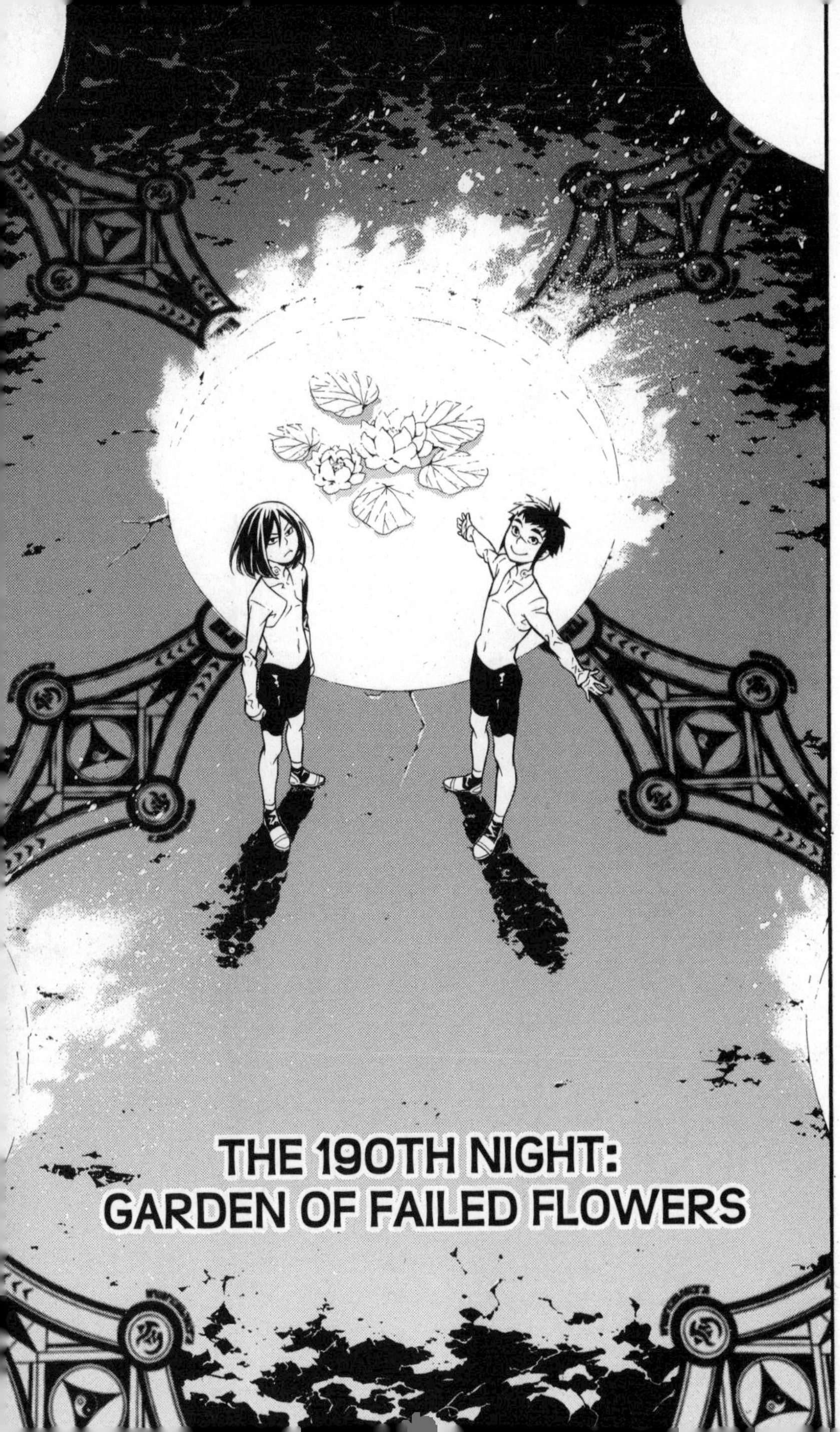
THE 190TH NIGHT:
GARDEN OF FAILED FLOWERS

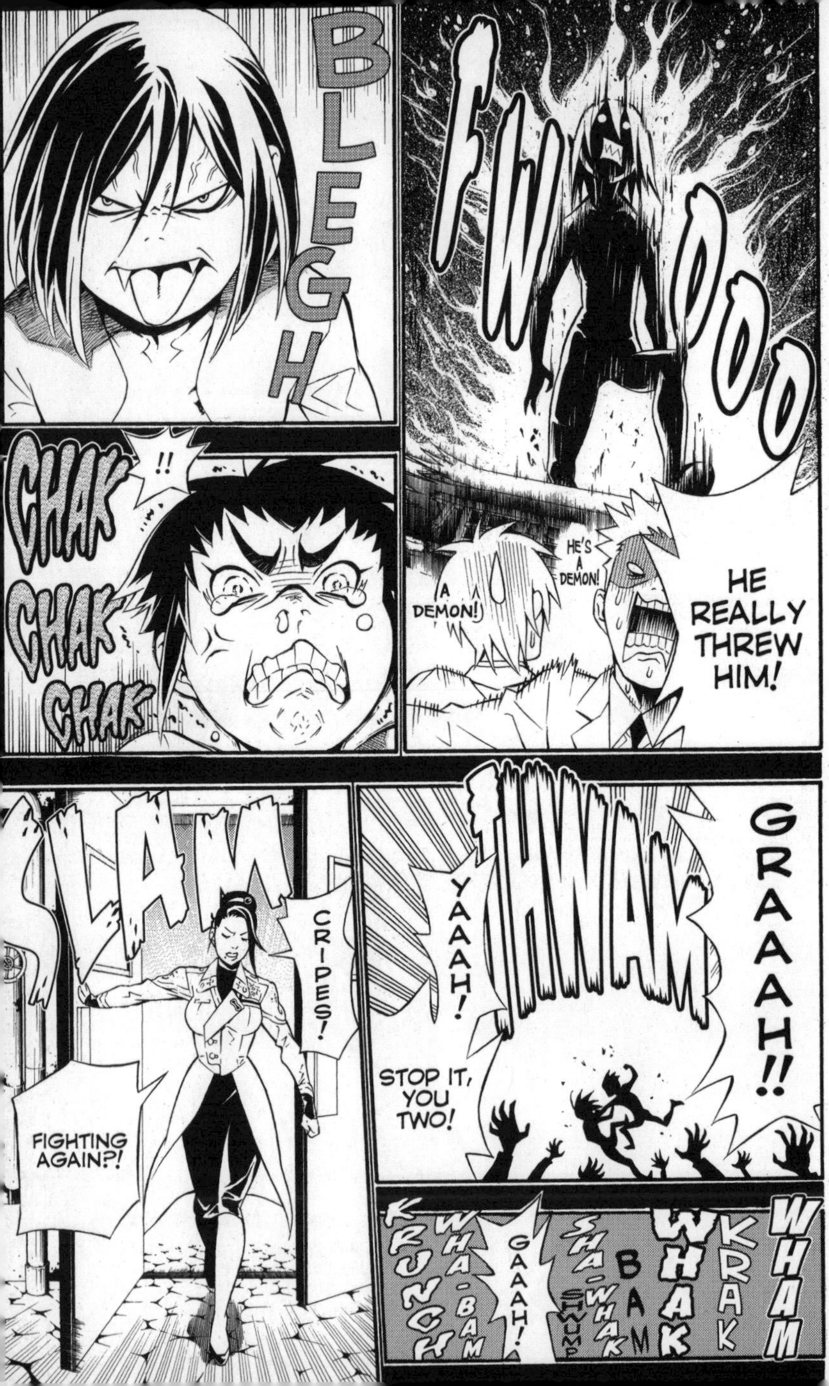
FWOOOO
HE REALLY THREW HIM!
HE'S A DEMON!
A DEMON!
BLEGH
!!
CHAK
CHAK
CHAK
GRAAAAH!!
THWAK
YAAAAH!
STOP IT, YOU TWO!
WHAM
KRAK
WHAK
BAM
SHWUMP
SHA-WHAK
GAAAH!
WHA-BAM
KRUNCH
SLAM
CRIPES!
FIGHTING AGAIN?!

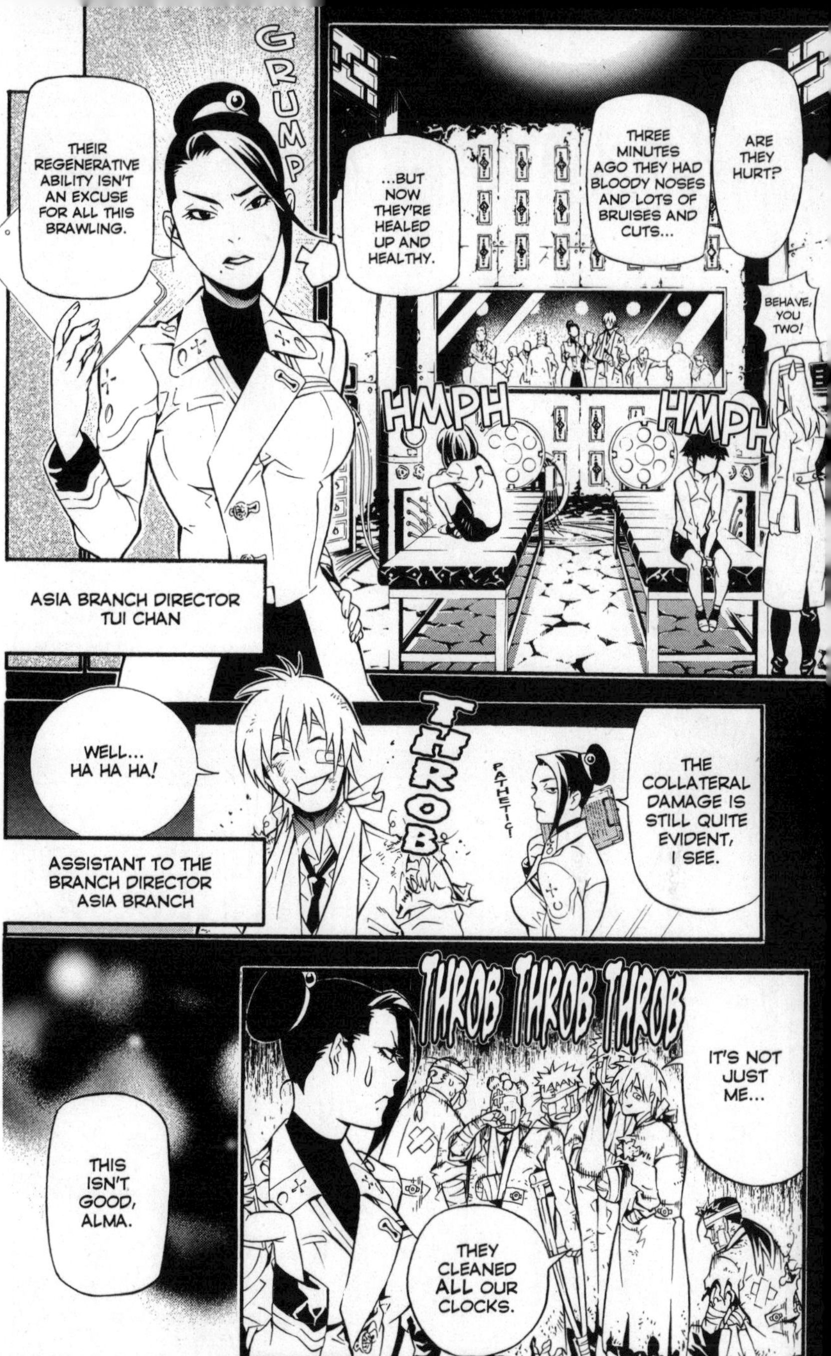
ARE THEY HURT?
THREE MINUTES AGO THEY HAD BLOODY NOSES AND LOTS OF BRUISES AND CUTS...
...BUT NOW THEY'RE HEALED UP AND HEALTHY.
BEHAVE, YOU TWO!
HMPH
HMPH
GRUMP
THEIR REGENERATIVE ABILITY ISN'T AN EXCUSE FOR ALL THIS BRAWLING.
ASIA BRANCH DIRECTOR TUI CHAN
THE COLLATERAL DAMAGE IS STILL QUITE EVIDENT, I SEE.
PATHETIC!
THROB
WELL... HA HA HA!
ASSISTANT TO THE BRANCH DIRECTOR ASIA BRANCH
THROB THROB THROB
IT'S NOT JUST ME...
THEY CLEANED ALL OUR CLOCKS.
THIS ISN'T GOOD, ALMA.

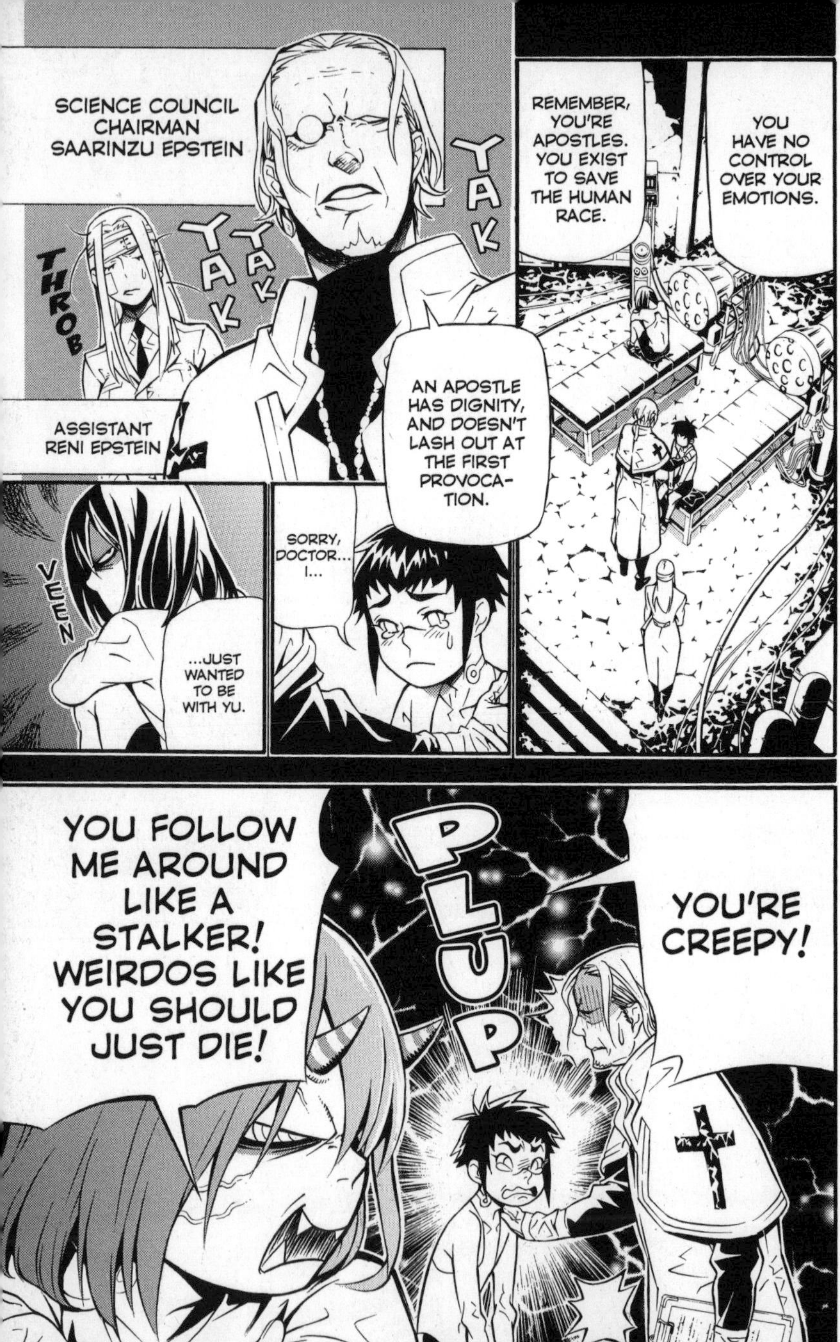
YOU HAVE NO CONTROL OVER YOUR EMOTIONS.
REMEMBER, YOU'RE APOSTLES. YOU EXIST TO SAVE THE HUMAN RACE.
YAK
SCIENCE COUNCIL CHAIRMAN SAARINZU EPSTEIN
YAK YAK
AN APOSTLE HAS DIGNITY, AND DOESN'T LASH OUT AT THE FIRST PROVOCA-TION.
THROB
ASSISTANT RENI EPSTEIN
SORRY, DOCTOR... I...
VEEN
...JUST WANTED TO BE WITH YU.
YOU'RE CREEPY!
PLUP
YOU FOLLOW ME AROUND LIKE A STALKER! WEIRDOS LIKE YOU SHOULD JUST DIE!

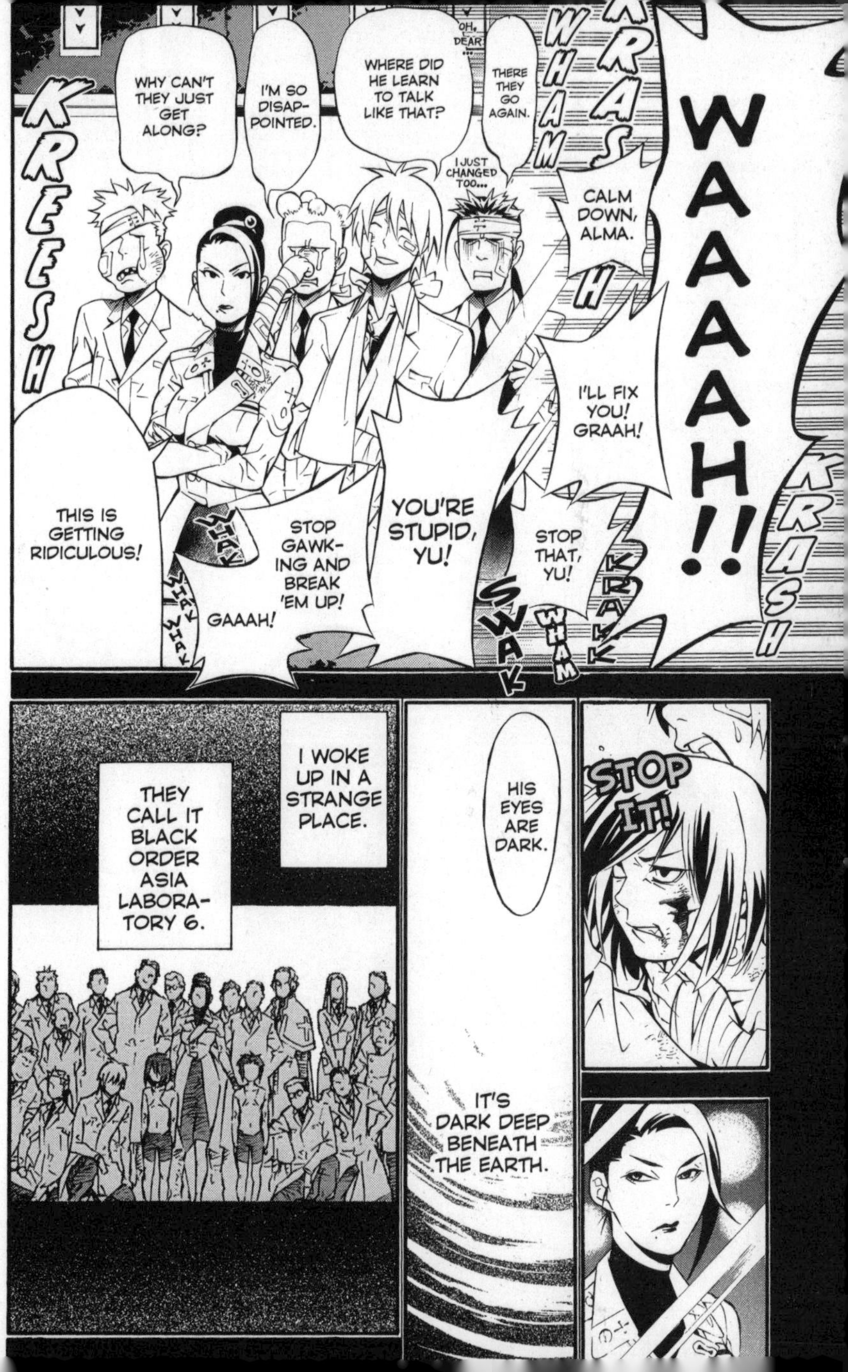
WAAAH!!
KRASH
WHAM
THERE THEY GO AGAIN.
OH, DEAR...
I JUST CHANGED TOO...
WHERE DID HE LEARN TO TALK LIKE THAT?
I'M SO DISAPPOINTED.
WHY CAN'T THEY JUST GET ALONG?
KREESH
CALM DOWN, ALMA.
WHAM
I'LL FIX YOU! GRAAH!
KRASH
KRAK
STOP THAT, YU!
YOU'RE STUPID, YU!
SWAK
WHAM
STOP GAWKING AND BREAK 'EM UP!
WHAK
THIS IS GETTING RIDICULOUS!
WHAK WHAK
GAAAH!
STOP IT!
HIS EYES ARE DARK.
IT'S DARK DEEP BENEATH THE EARTH.
I WOKE UP IN A STRANGE PLACE.
THEY CALL IT BLACK ORDER ASIA LABORATORY 6.

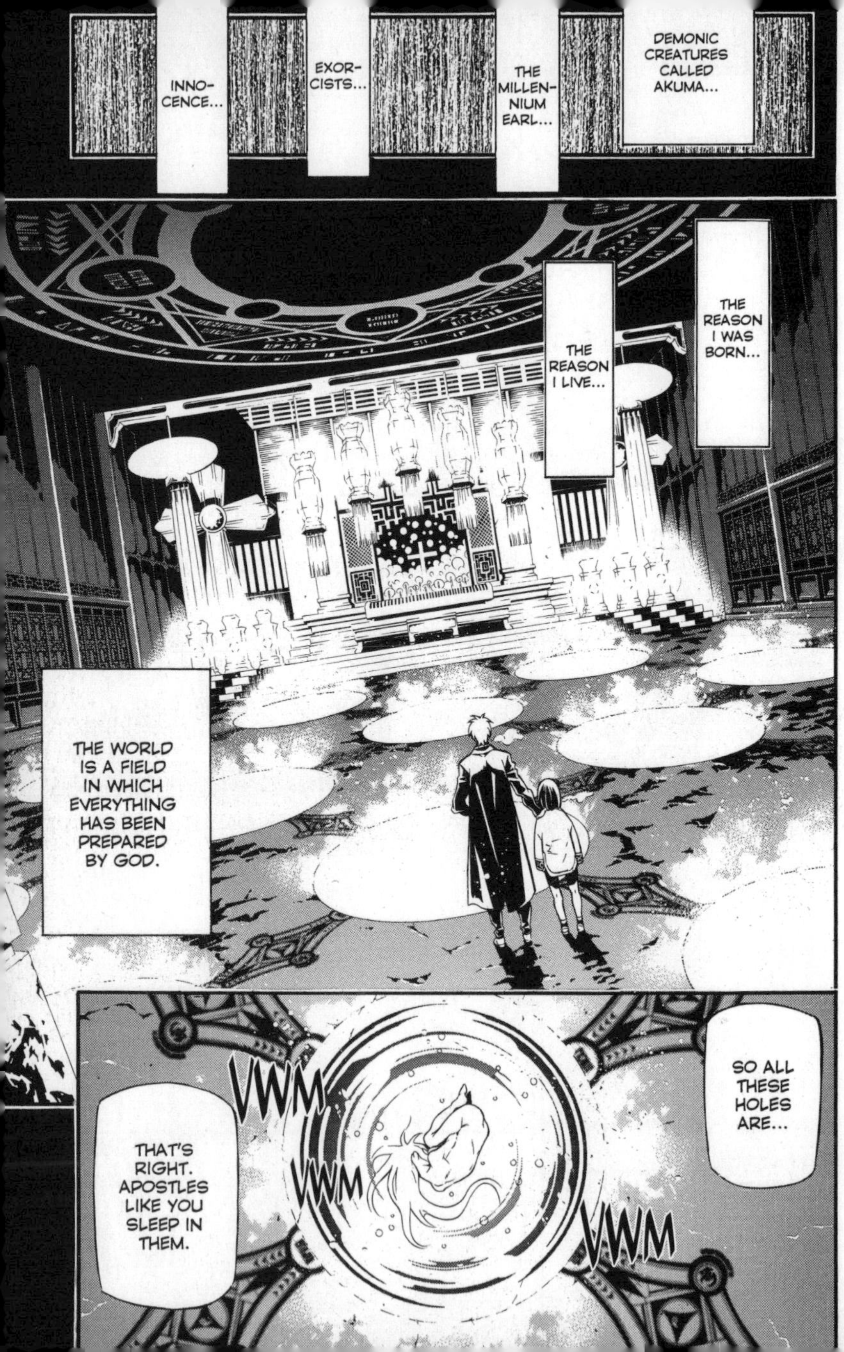
DEMONIC CREATURES CALLED AKUMA...
THE MILLENNIUM EARL...
EXORCISTS...
INNOCENCE...
THE REASON I WAS BORN...
THE REASON I LIVE...
THE WORLD IS A FIELD IN WHICH EVERYTHING HAS BEEN PREPARED BY GOD.
SO ALL THESE HOLES ARE...
VWM
VWM
VWM
THAT'S RIGHT. APOSTLES LIKE YOU SLEEP IN THEM.

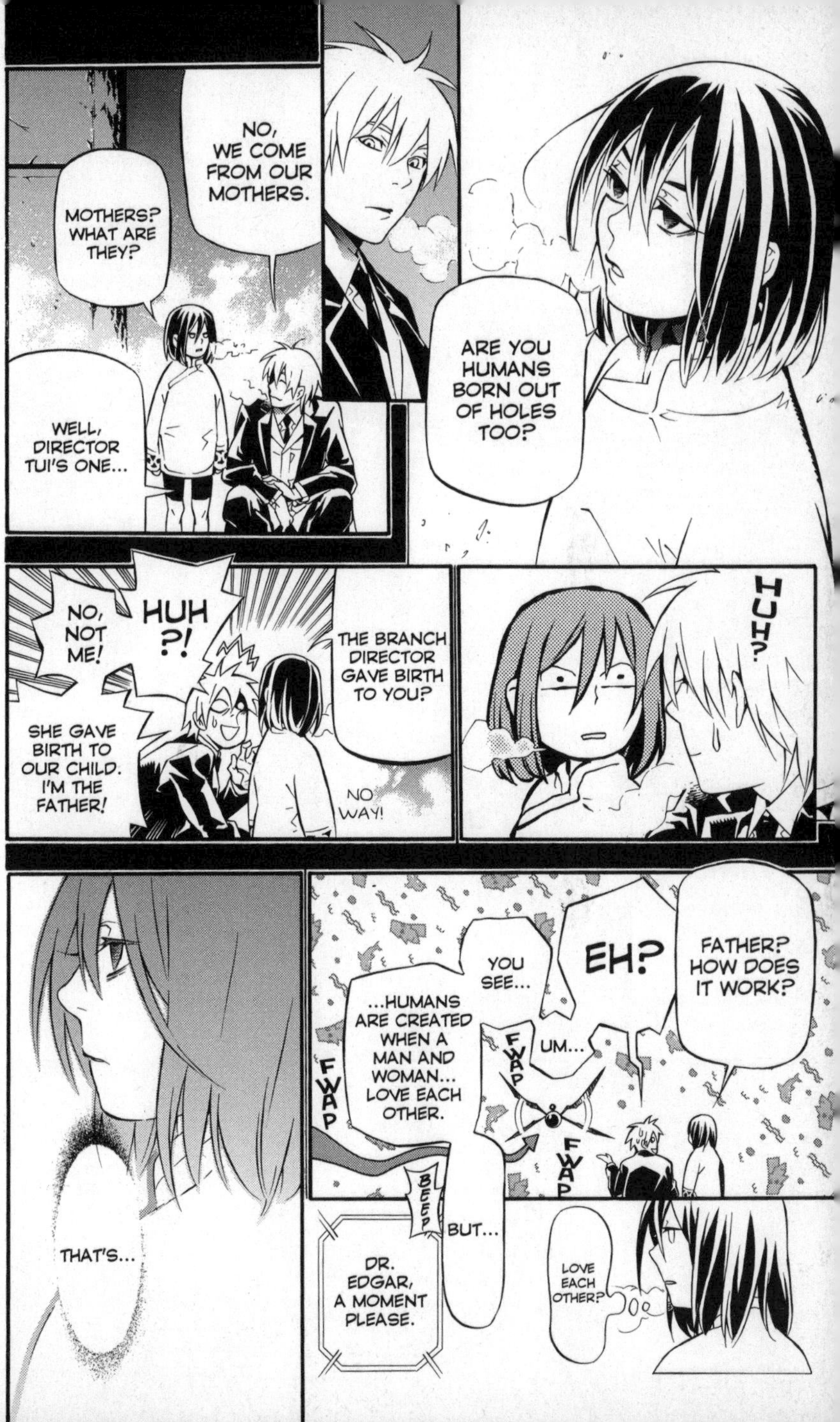
ARE YOU HUMANS BORN OUT OF HOLES TOO?
NO, WE COME FROM OUR MOTHERS.
MOTHERS? WHAT ARE THEY?
WELL, DIRECTOR TUI'S ONE...
HUH?
THE BRANCH DIRECTOR GAVE BIRTH TO YOU?
HUH?!
NO, NOT ME!
SHE GAVE BIRTH TO OUR CHILD. I'M THE FATHER!
NO WAY!
FATHER? HOW DOES IT WORK?
EH?
YOU SEE...
UM...
FWAP
...HUMANS ARE CREATED WHEN A MAN AND WOMAN... LOVE EACH OTHER.
FWAP
FWAP
LOVE EACH OTHER?
BUT...
BEEEP
DR. EDGAR, A MOMENT PLEASE.
THAT'S...

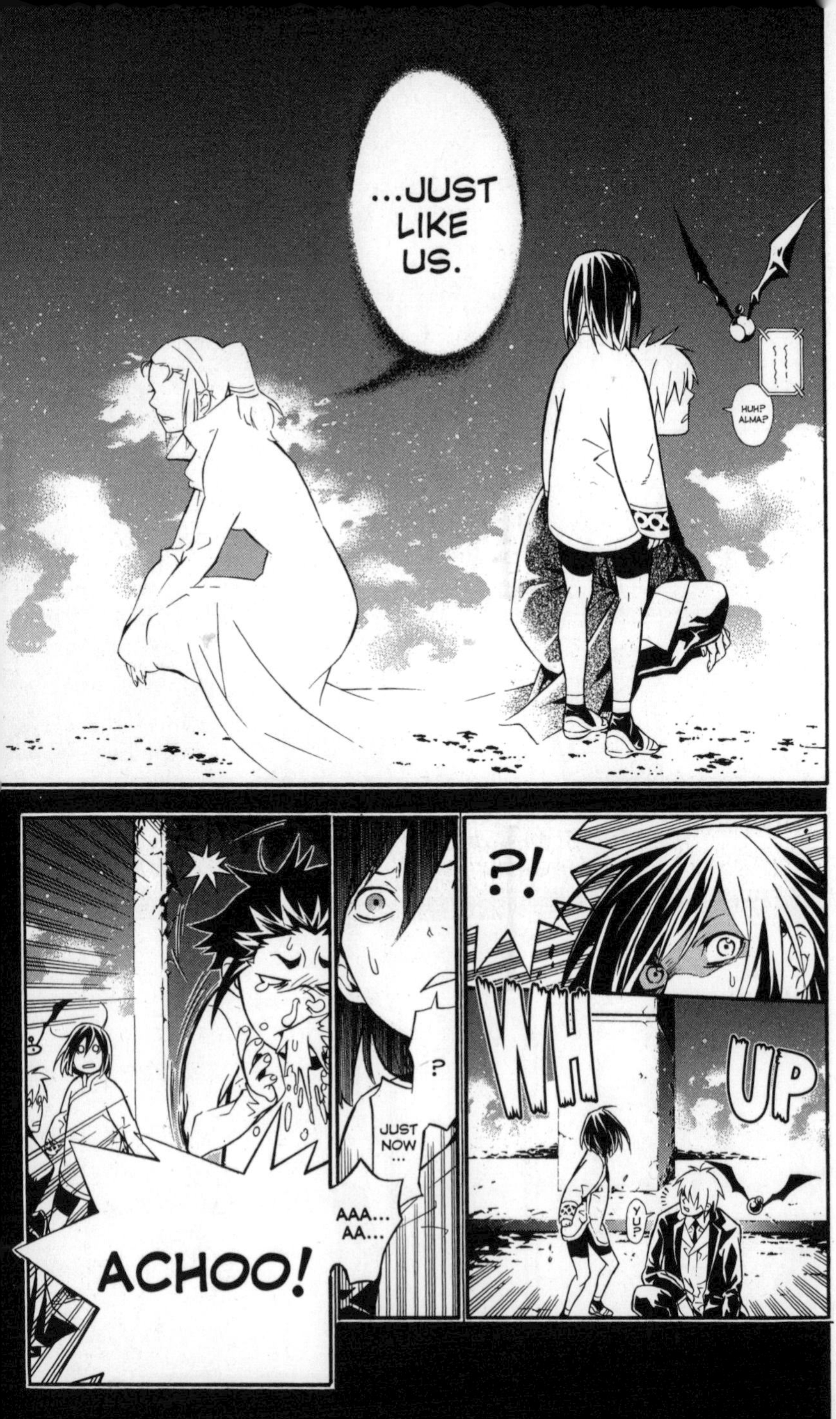
...JUST LIKE US.
HUH? ALMA?
?!
WH
UP
YUP.
?
JUST NOW ...
AAA... AA...
ACHOO!

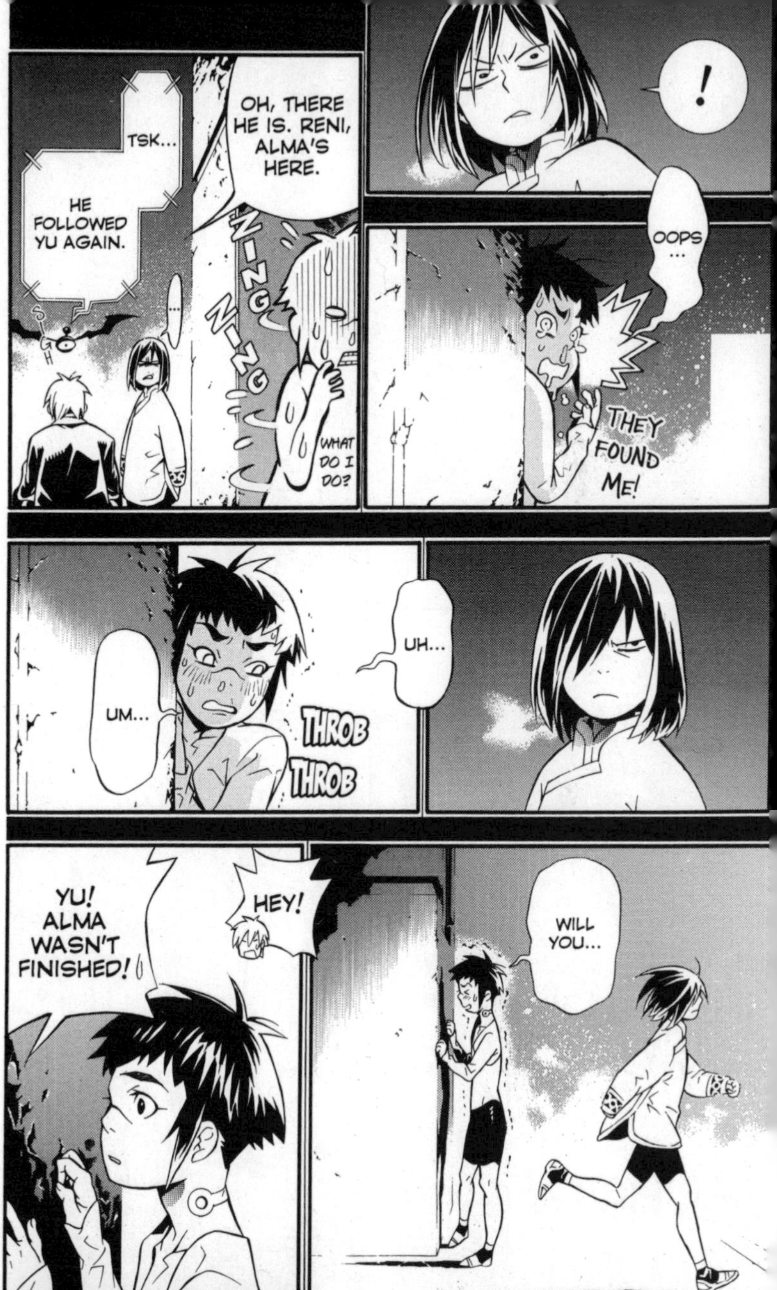
!
OOPS...
THEY FOUND ME!
OH, THERE HE IS. RENI, ALMA'S HERE.
ZING ZING
WHAT DO I DO?
TSK...
HE FOLLOWED YU AGAIN.
SIGH
...
UH...
THROB THROB
UM...
WILL YOU...
HEY!
YU! ALMA WASN'T FINISHED!

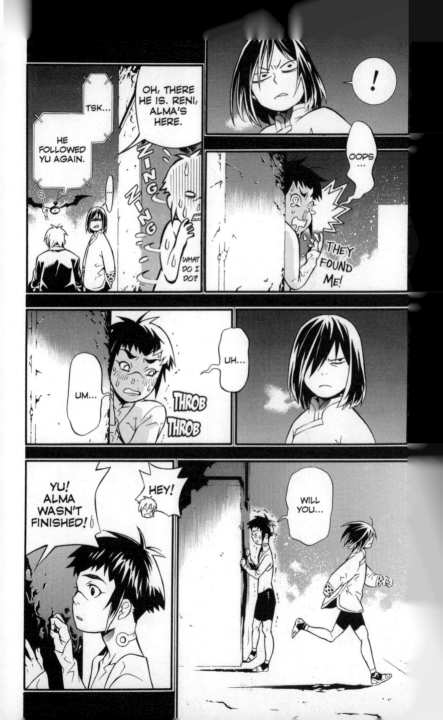

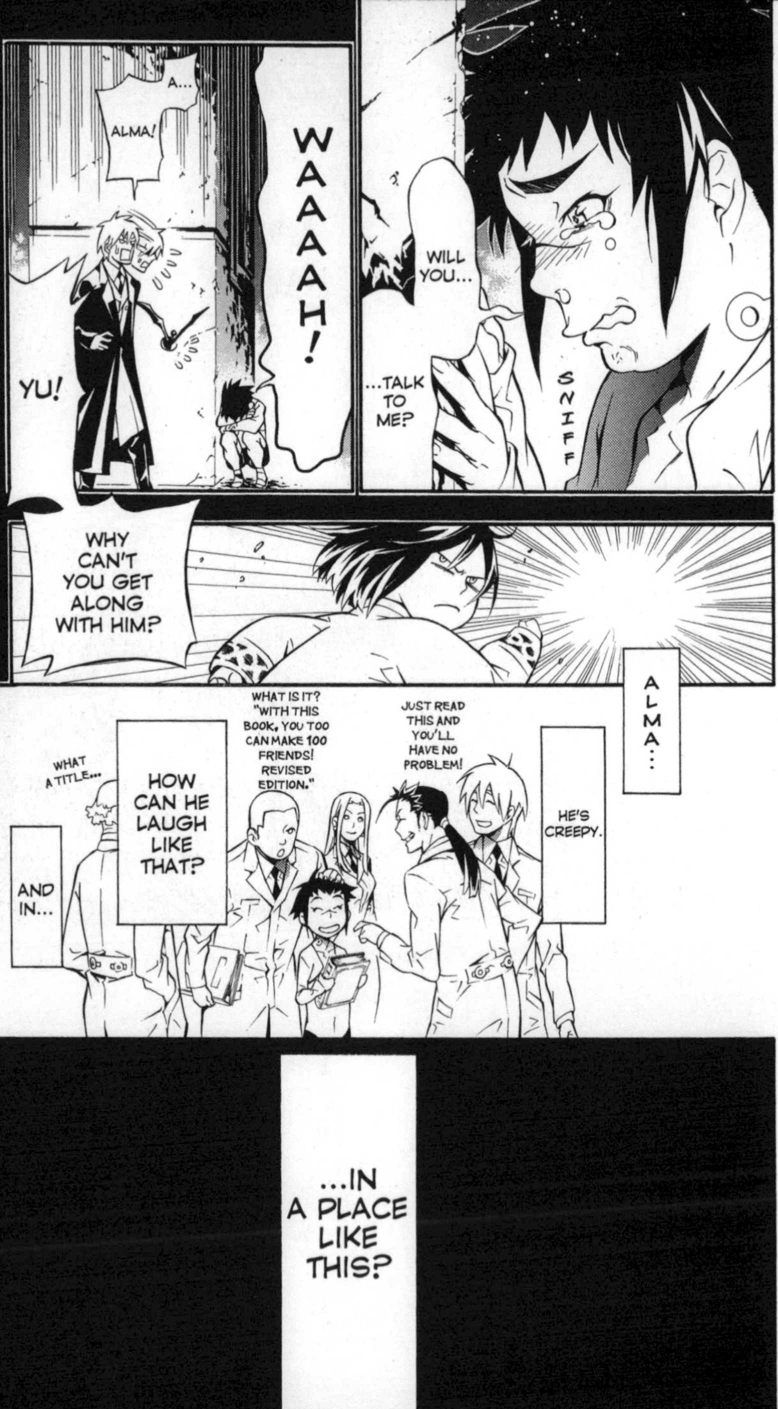
WILL YOU...
...TALK TO ME?
SNIFF
A...
ALMA!
WAAAAH!
YU!
WHY CAN'T YOU GET ALONG WITH HIM?
ALMA...
HE'S CREEPY.
JUST READ THIS AND YOU'LL HAVE NO PROBLEM!
WHAT IS IT? "WITH THIS BOOK, YOU TOO CAN MAKE 100 FRIENDS! REVISED EDITION."
HOW CAN HE LAUGH LIKE THAT?
WHAT A TITLE...
AND IN...
...IN A PLACE LIKE THIS?

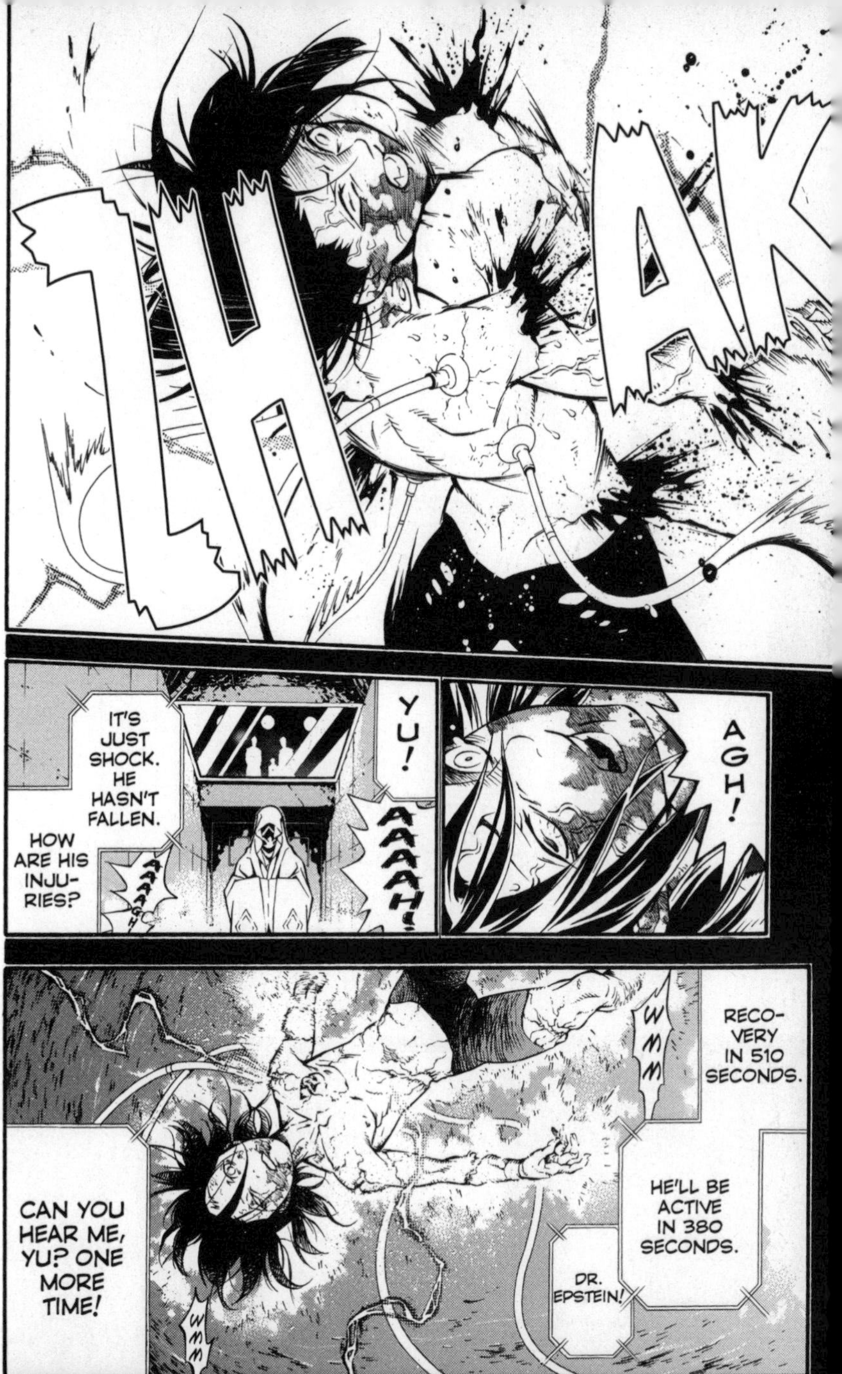
AGH!
YU!
AAAAAH!
IT'S JUST SHOCK. HE HASN'T FALLEN.
HOW ARE HIS INJU-RIES?
AAAAGH
RECO-VERY IN 510 SECONDS.
WMM
HE'LL BE ACTIVE IN 380 SECONDS.
DR. EPSTEIN!
CAN YOU HEAR ME, YU? ONE MORE TIME!
WMM

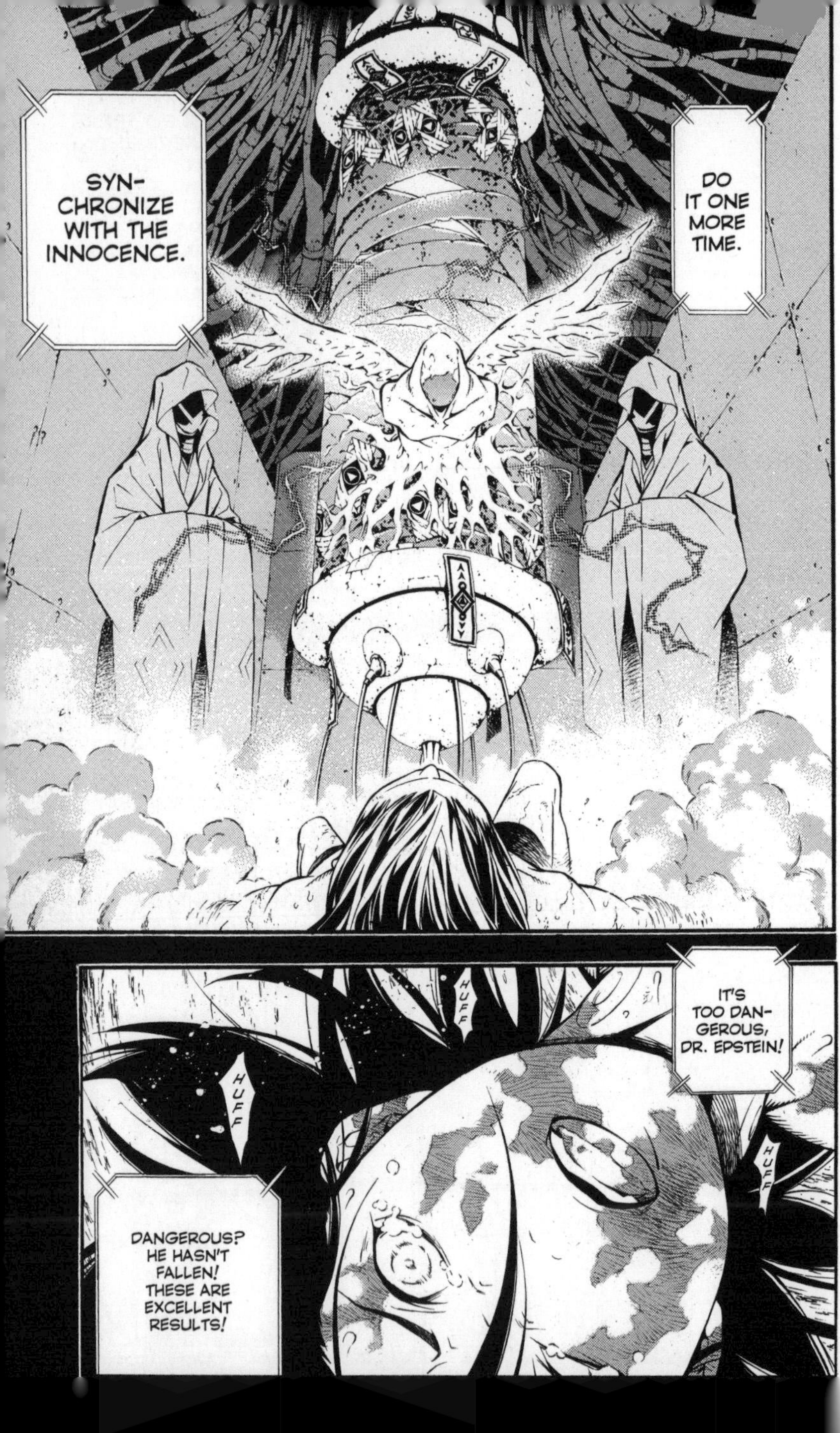
DO IT ONE MORE TIME.
SYN-CHRONIZE WITH THE INNOCENCE.
IT'S TOO DAN-GEROUS, DR. EPSTEIN!
HUFF
HUFF
HUFF
DANGEROUS? HE HASN'T FALLEN! THESE ARE EXCELLENT RESULTS!

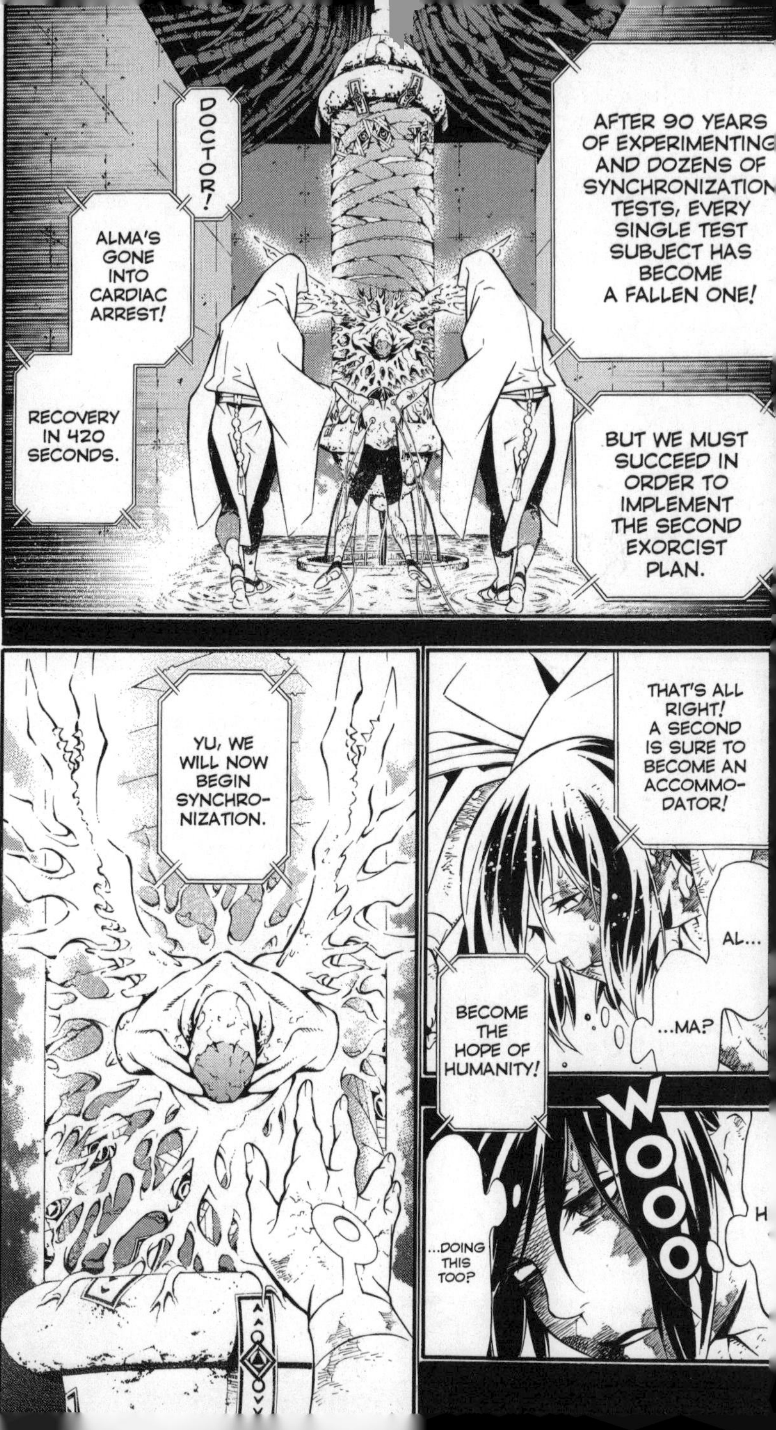
AFTER 90 YEARS OF EXPERIMENTING AND DOZENS OF SYNCHRONIZATION TESTS, EVERY SINGLE TEST SUBJECT HAS BECOME A FALLEN ONE!
BUT WE MUST SUCCEED IN ORDER TO IMPLEMENT THE SECOND EXORCIST PLAN.
DOCTOR!
ALMA'S GONE INTO CARDIAC ARREST!
RECOVERY IN 420 SECONDS.
THAT'S ALL RIGHT! A SECOND IS SURE TO BECOME AN ACCOMMO-DATOR!
AL...
...MA?
BECOME THE HOPE OF HUMANITY!
WOOOO
H
...DOING THIS TOO?
YU, WE WILL NOW BEGIN SYNCHRO-NIZATION.

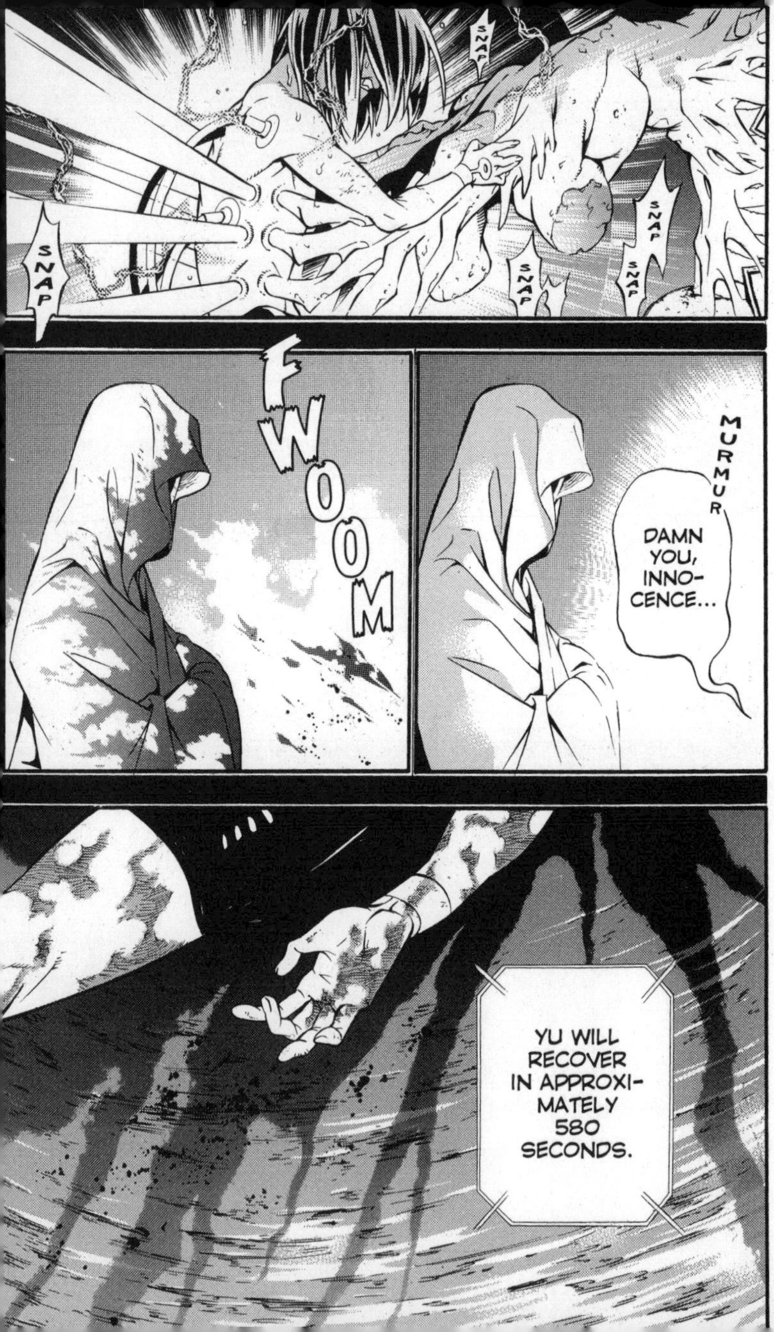
SNAP
SNAP
SNAP
SNAP
SNAP
MURMUR
DAMN YOU, INNO- CENCE...
FWOOM
YU WILL RECOVER IN APPROXI- MATELY 580 SECONDS.

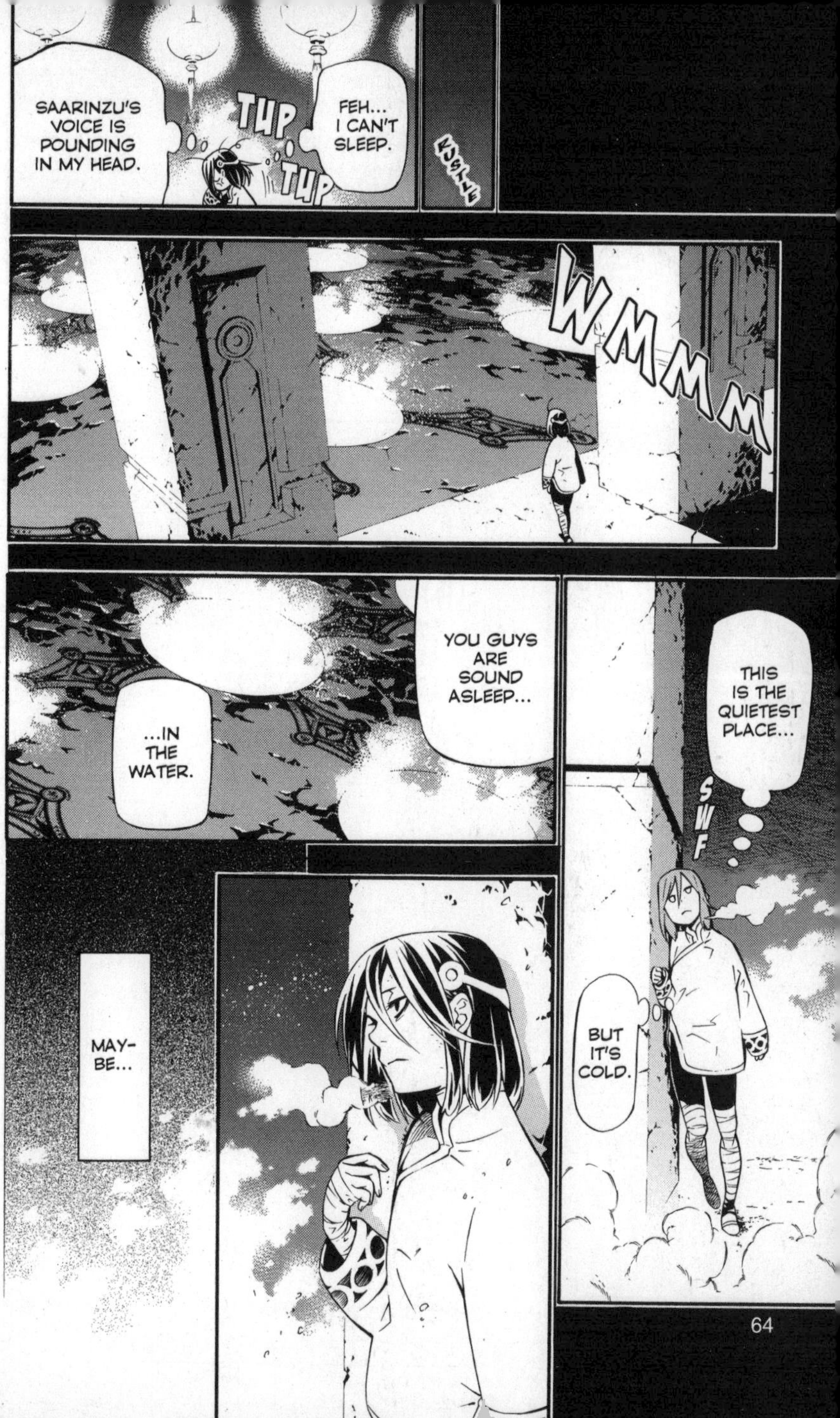
RUSTLE
FEH... I CAN'T SLEEP.
TUP
TUP
SAARINZU'S VOICE IS POUNDING IN MY HEAD.
WMMMM
THIS IS THE QUIETEST PLACE...
SWF
BUT IT'S COLD.
YOU GUYS ARE SOUND ASLEEP...
...IN THE WATER.
MAY-BE...

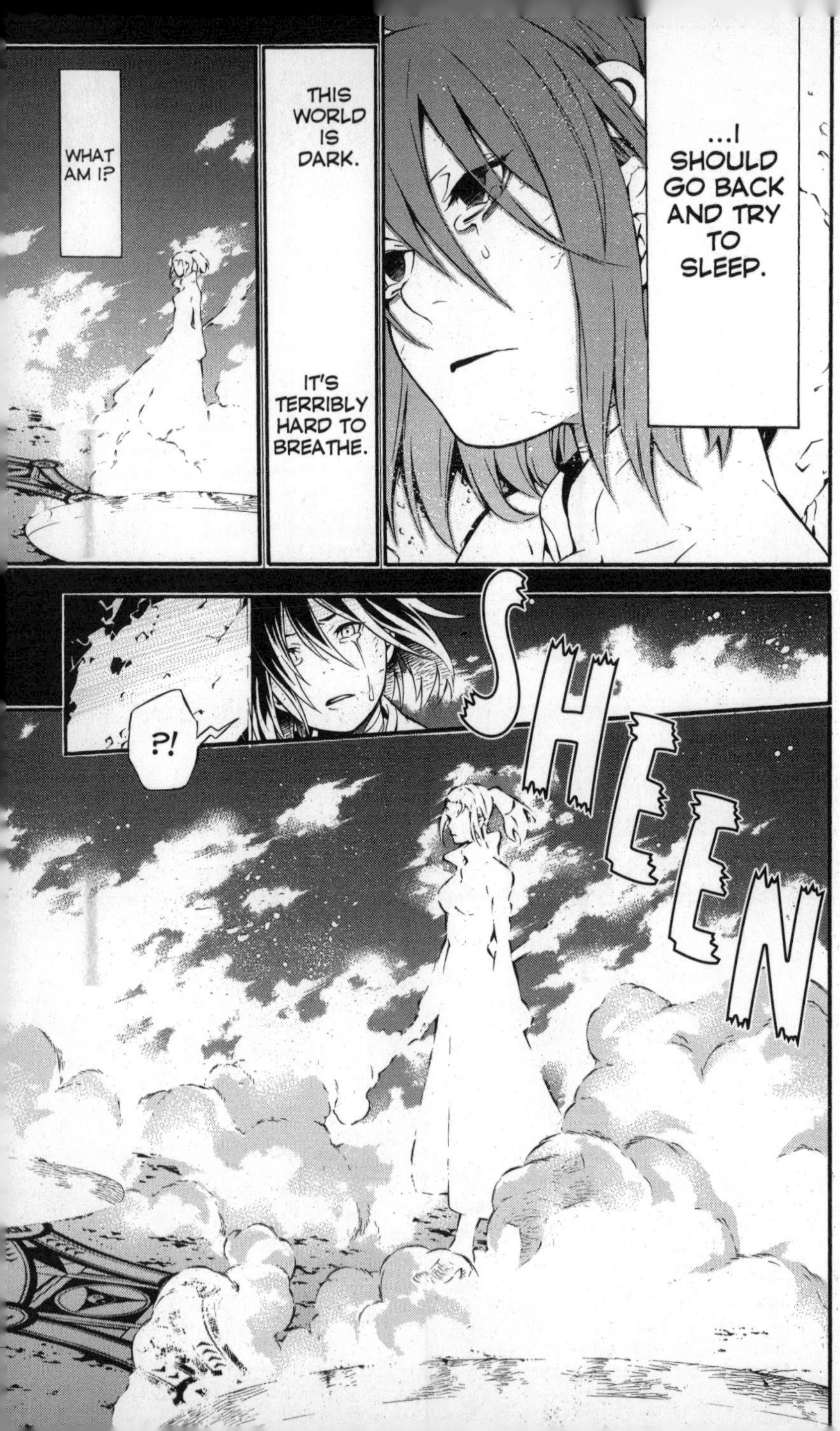
...I SHOULD GO BACK AND TRY TO SLEEP.
THIS WORLD IS DARK.
IT'S TERRIBLY HARD TO BREATHE.
WHAT AM I?
SHEEN
?!

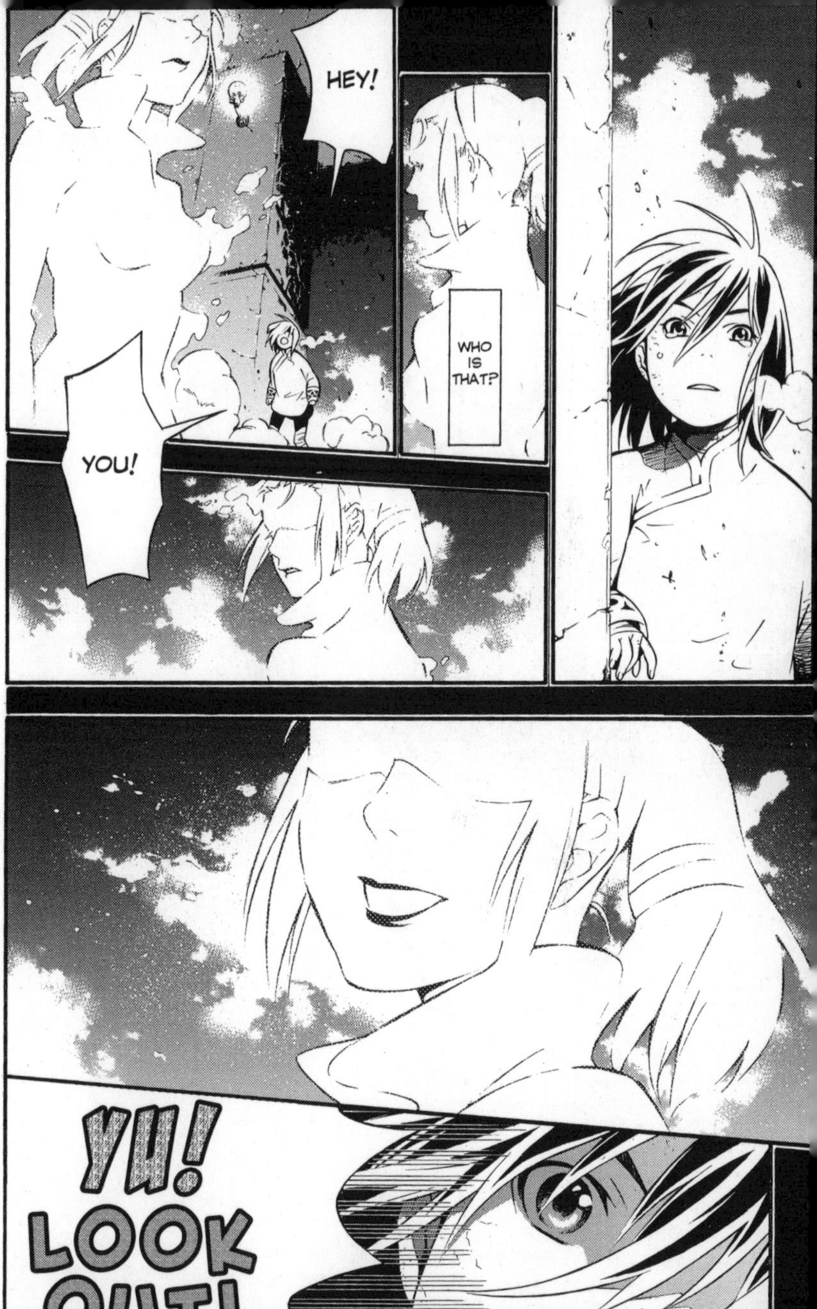
WHO IS THAT?
HEY!
YOU!
YU! LOOK OUT!

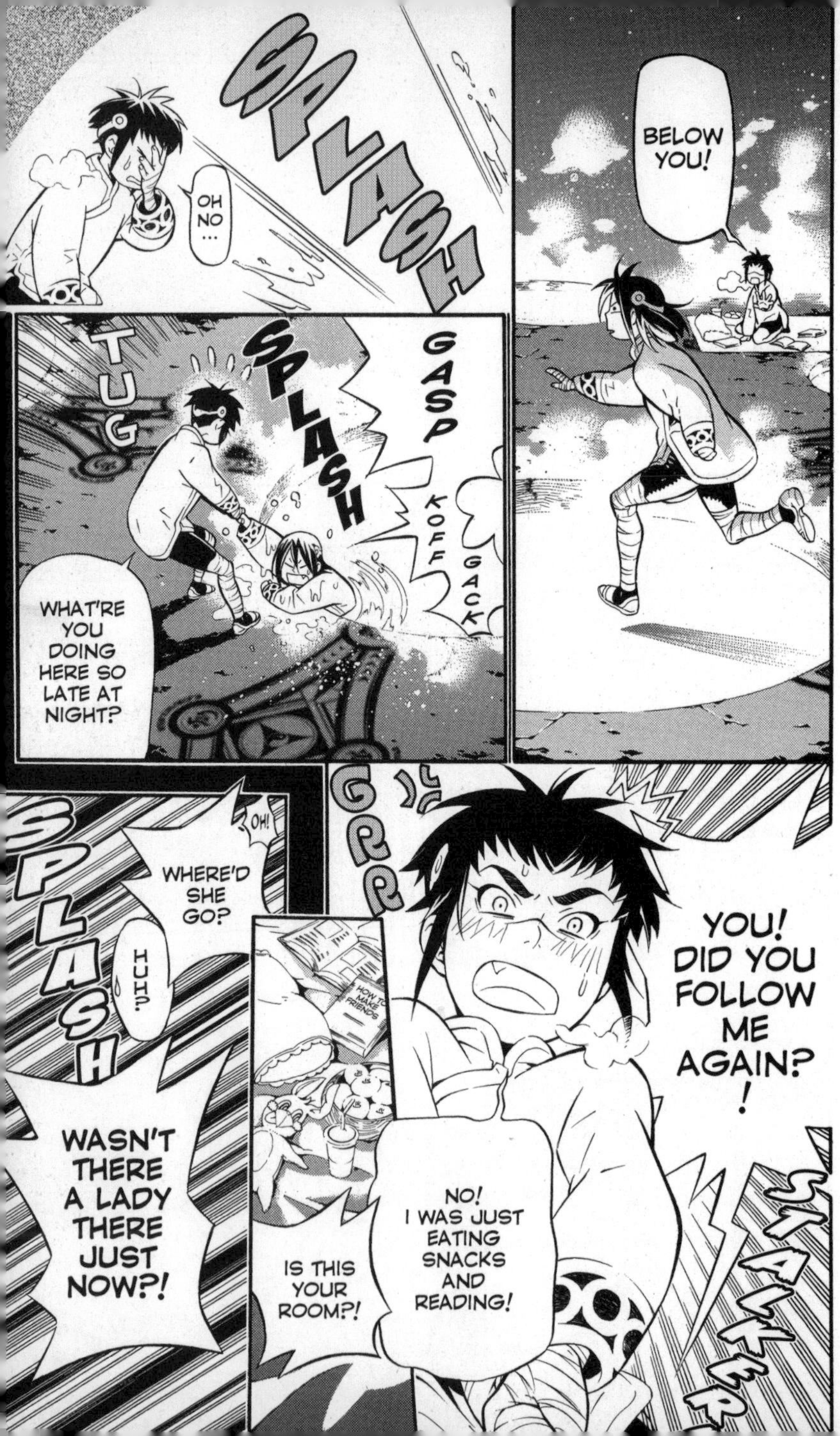

BELOW YOU!
SPLASH
OH NO ...
GASP
SPLASH
TUG
KOFF
GACK
WHAT'RE YOU DOING HERE SO LATE AT NIGHT?
GRR
YOU! DID YOU FOLLOW ME AGAIN?!
STALKER
NO! I WAS JUST EATING SNACKS AND READING!
HOW TO MAKE FRIENDS
IS THIS YOUR ROOM?!
OH!
WHERE'D SHE GO?
HUH?
SPLASH
WASN'T THERE A LADY THERE JUST NOW?!

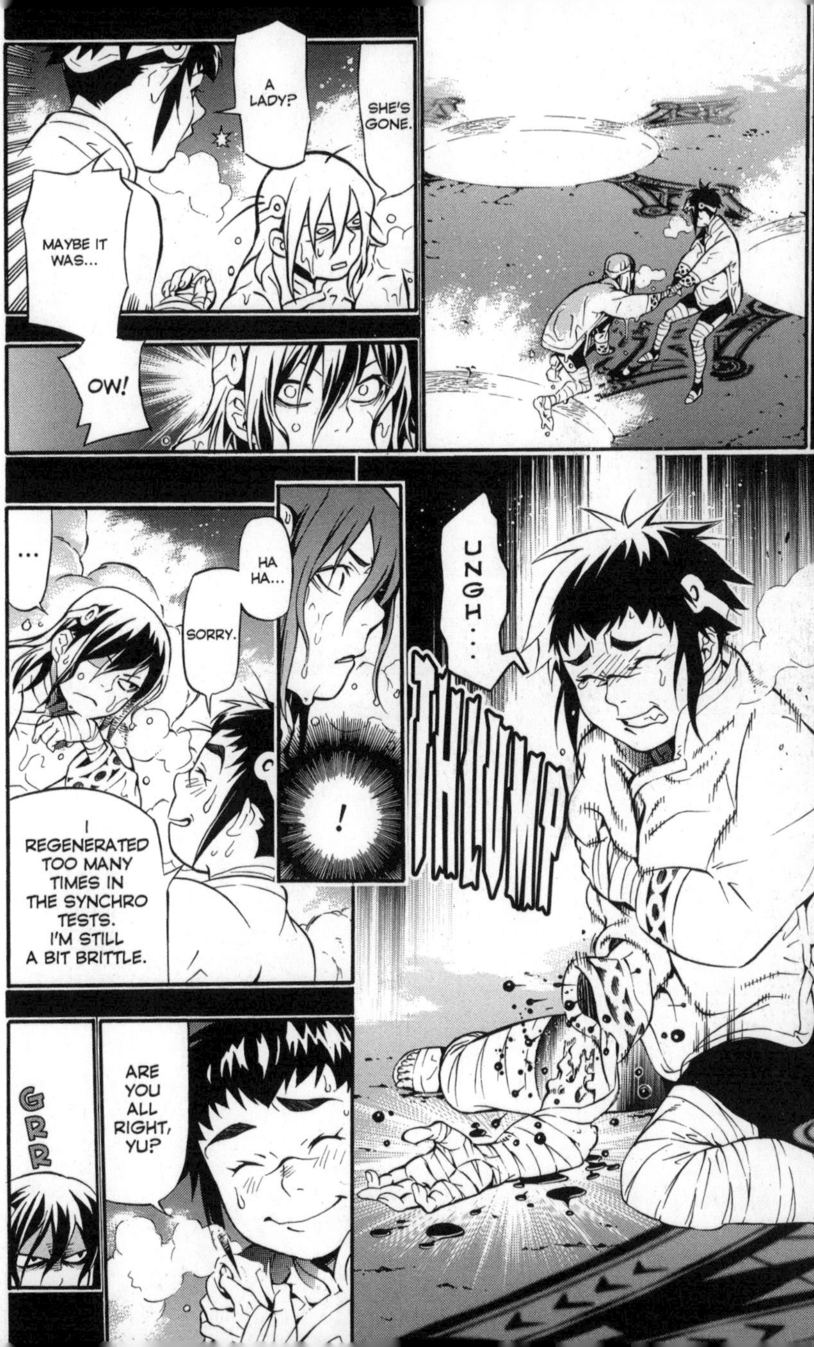
SHE'S GONE.
A LADY?
MAYBE IT WAS...
OW!
UNGH...
THLUMP
!
HA HA...
SORRY.
...
I REGENERATED TOO MANY TIMES IN THE SYNCHRO TESTS. I'M STILL A BIT BRITTLE.
ARE YOU ALL RIGHT, YU?
GRR

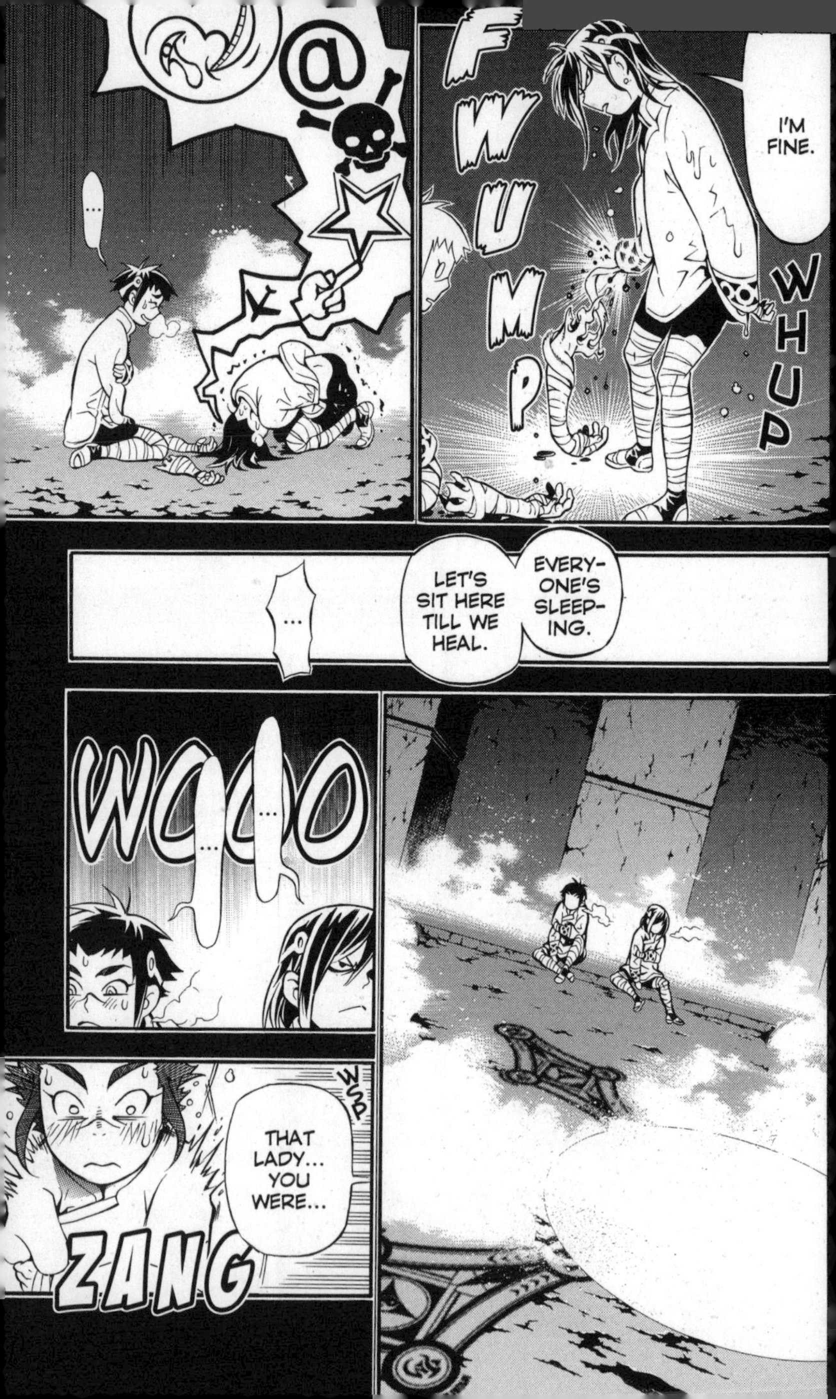
I'M FINE.
FWUMP
WHUP
...
@
EVERY-ONE'S SLEEP-ING.
LET'S SIT HERE TILL WE HEAL.
...
WOOO
...
...
WSP
THAT LADY... YOU WERE...
ZANG

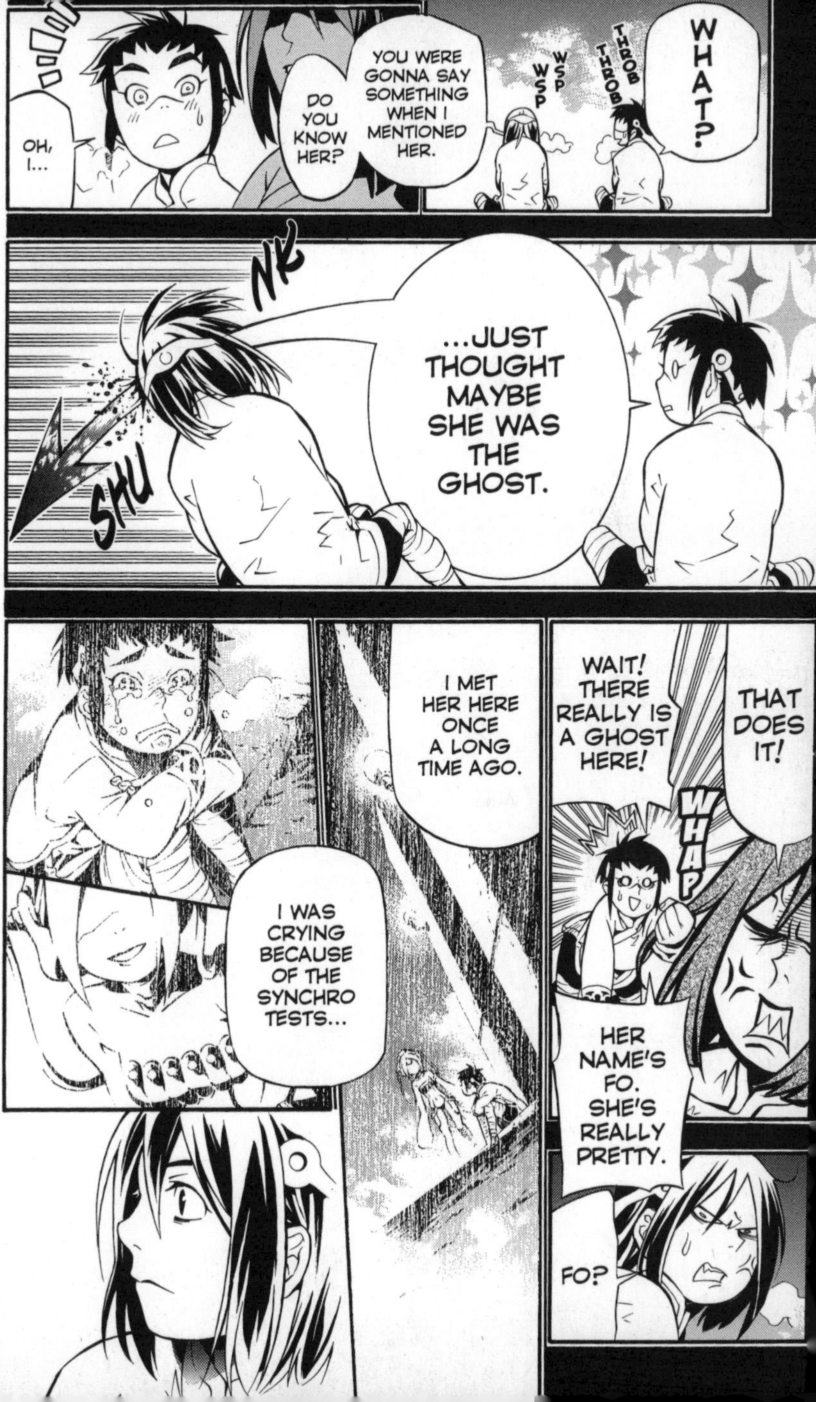
WHAT?
THROB THROB
WSP WSP
YOU WERE GONNA SAY SOMETHING WHEN I MENTIONED HER.
DO YOU KNOW HER?
OH, I...
...JUST THOUGHT MAYBE SHE WAS THE GHOST.
NK
SHU
THAT DOES IT!
WAIT! THERE REALLY IS A GHOST HERE!
WHAP
HER NAME'S FO. SHE'S REALLY PRETTY.
FO?
I MET HER HERE ONCE A LONG TIME AGO.
I WAS CRYING BECAUSE OF THE SYNCHRO TESTS...

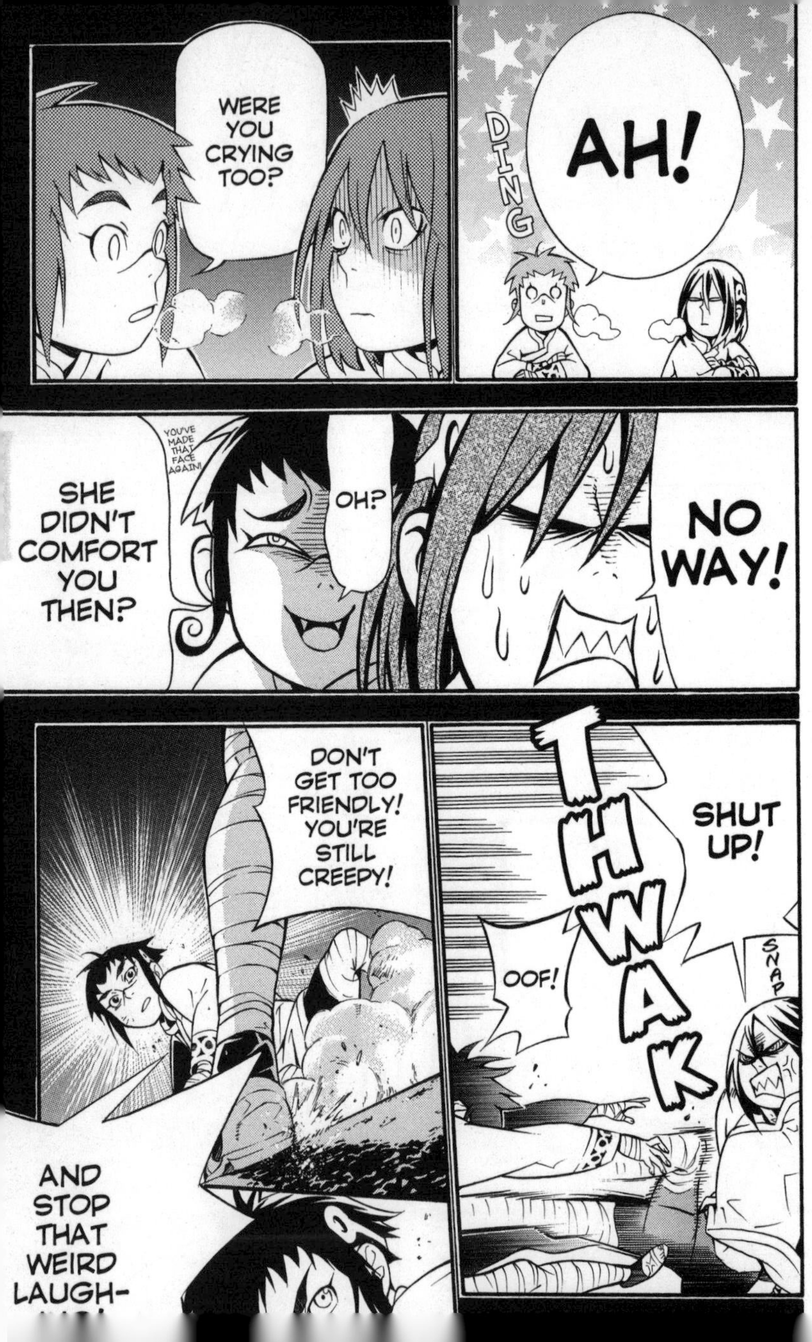
DING
AH!
WERE YOU CRYING TOO?
NO WAY!
OH?
SHE DIDN'T COMFORT YOU THEN?
YOU'VE MADE THAT FACE AGAIN!
SHUT UP!
THWAK
SNAP
OOF!
DON'T GET TOO FRIENDLY! YOU'RE STILL CREEPY!
AND STOP THAT WEIRD LAUGH-

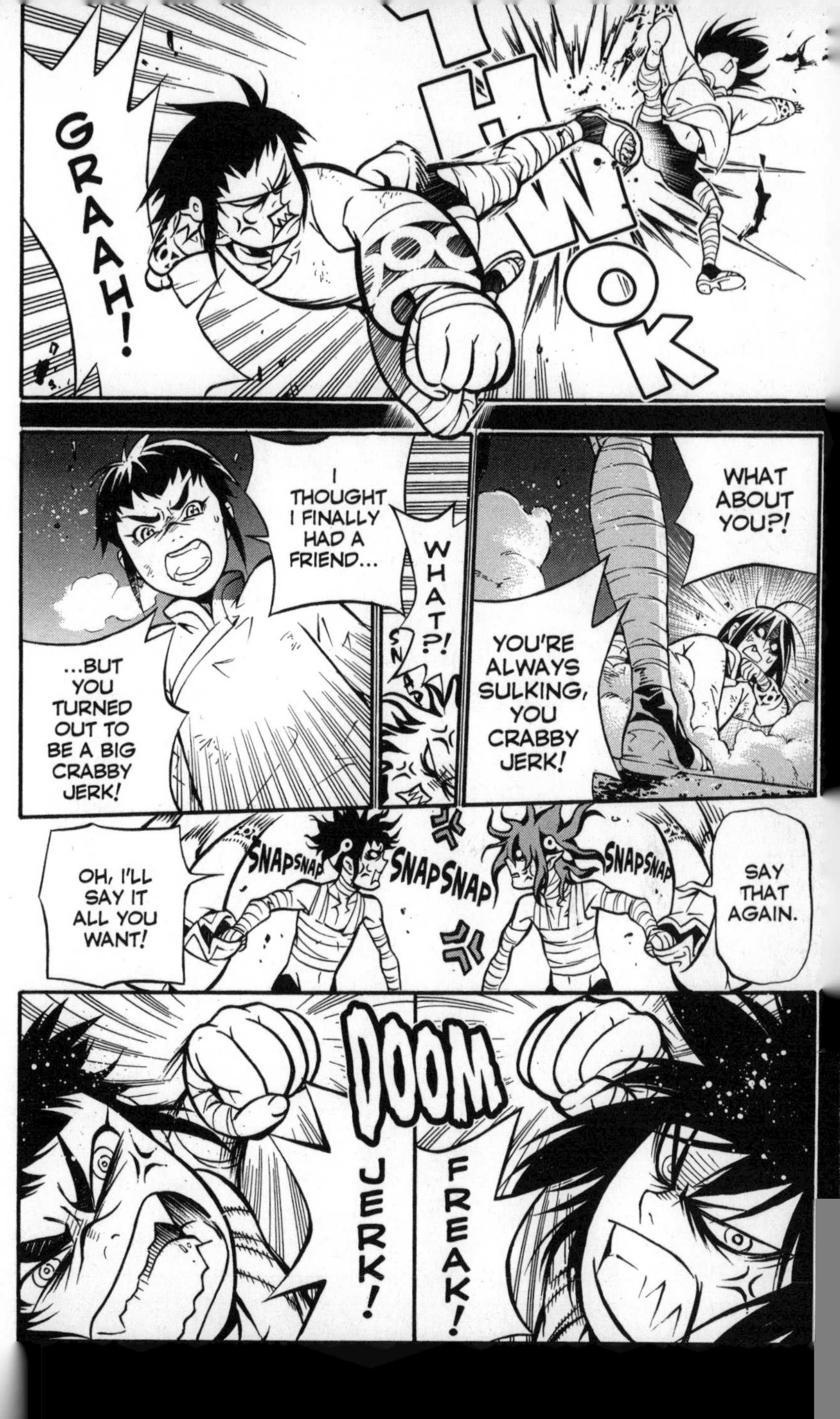
WHOK
GRAAH!
WHAT ABOUT YOU?!
YOU'RE ALWAYS SULKING, YOU CRABBY JERK!
WHAT?!
SNAP
I THOUGHT I FINALLY HAD A FRIEND...
...BUT YOU TURNED OUT TO BE A BIG CRABBY JERK!
SAY THAT AGAIN.
SNAPSNAP
SNAPSNAP
SNAPSNAP
OH, I'LL SAY IT ALL YOU WANT!
DOOM
FREAK!
JERK!

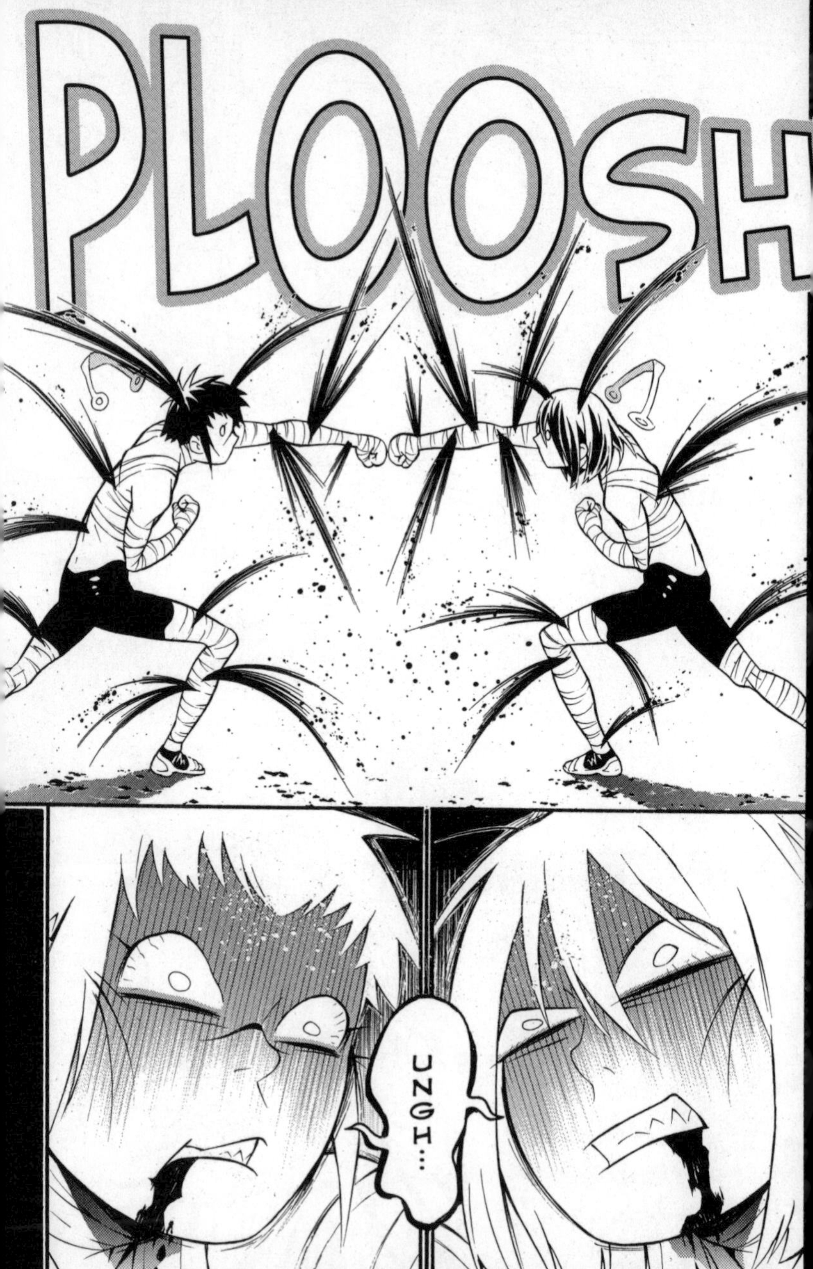
PLOOSH
UNGH...

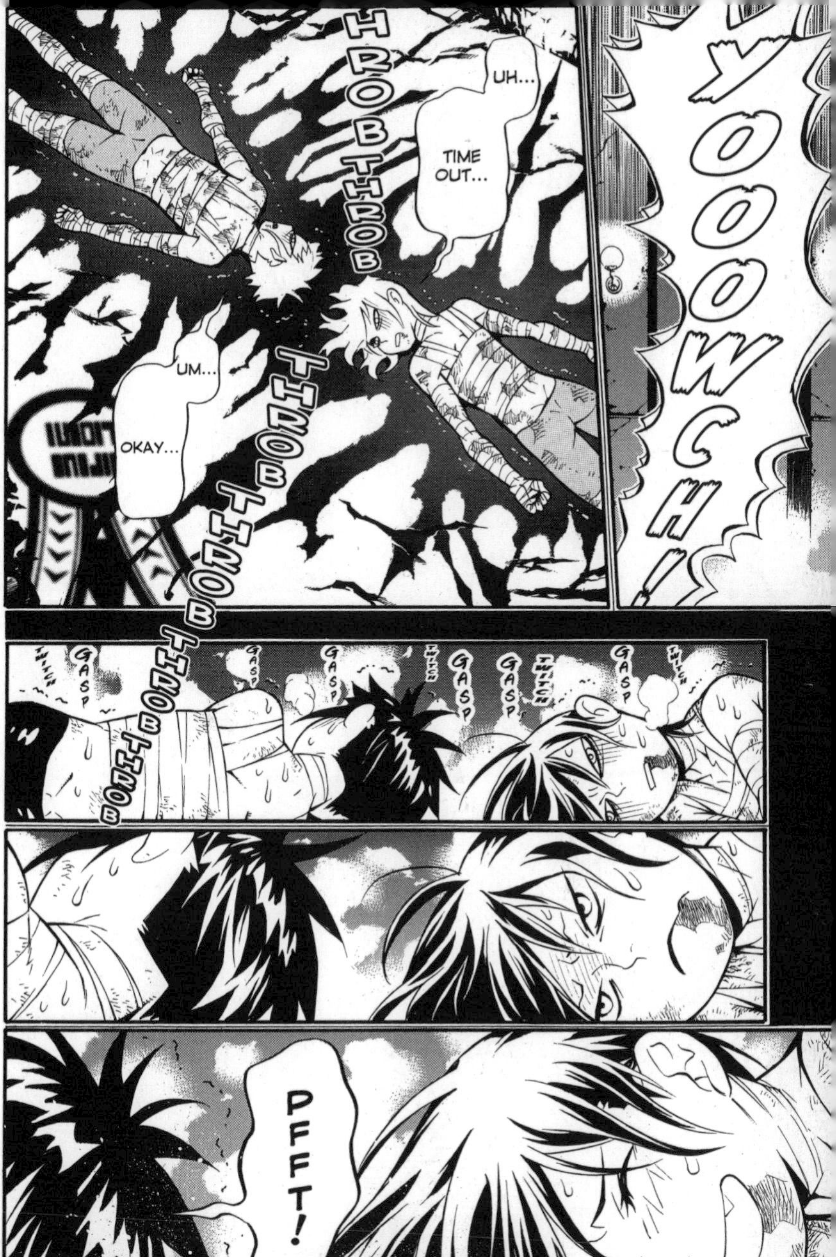

YOOOWCH!!
UH...
TIME OUT...
HROB THROB
UM...
OKAY...
THROB THROB THROB THROB
TWITCH
GASP
TWITCH
GASP
GASP
TWITCH
GASP
GASP
TWITCH
PFFT!

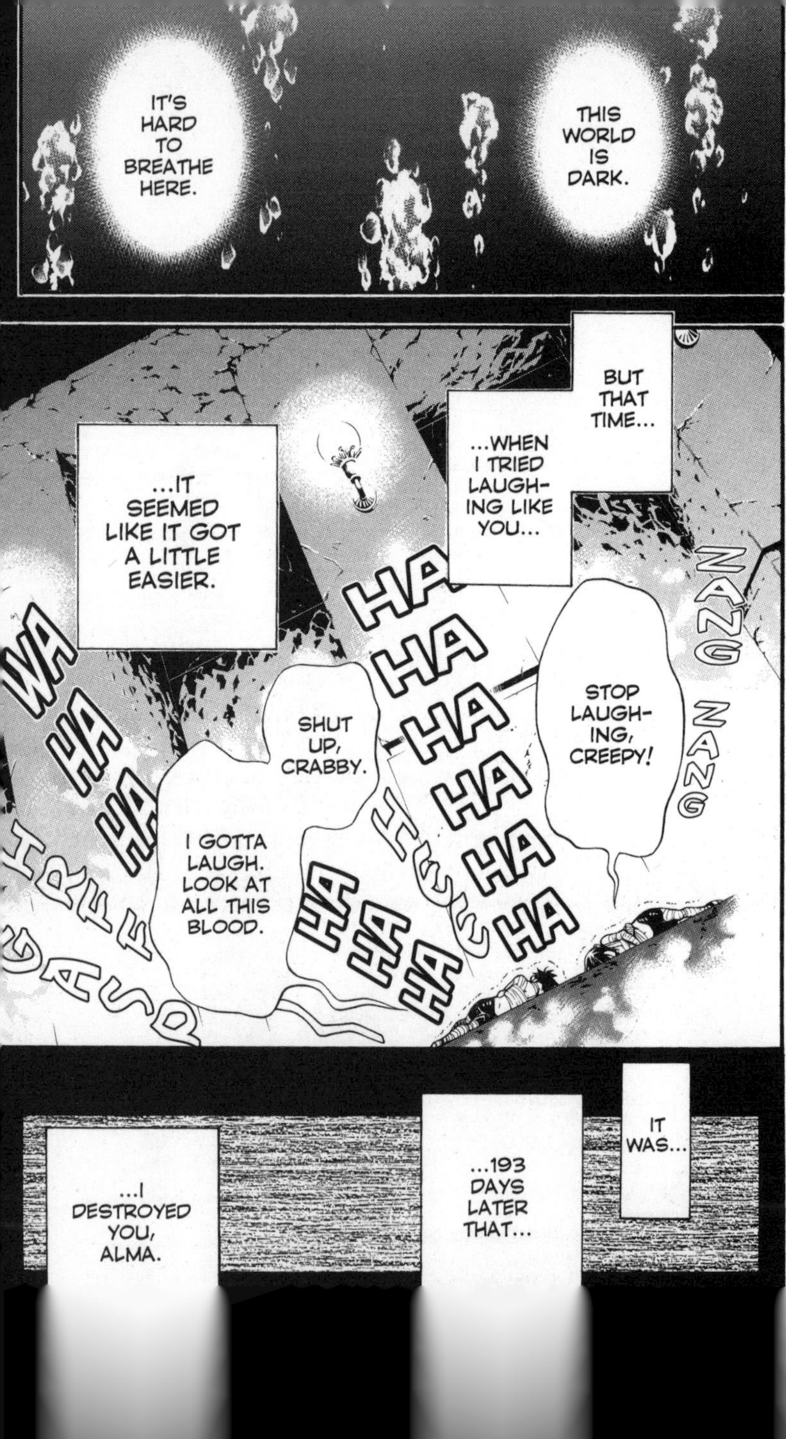
THIS WORLD IS DARK.
IT'S HARD TO BREATHE HERE.
BUT THAT TIME...
...WHEN I TRIED LAUGHING LIKE YOU...
...IT SEEMED LIKE IT GOT A LITTLE EASIER.
ZANG ZANG ZANG
STOP LAUGHING, CREEPY!
HA HA HA HA HA HA HA
SHUT UP, CRABBY.
HA HA HA
I GOTTA LAUGH. LOOK AT ALL THIS BLOOD.
WA HA HA
IT WAS...
...193 DAYS LATER THAT...
...I DESTROYED YOU, ALMA.

DIRECTOR,
ASIA BRANCH
TUI CHAN (39)

SHE IS BAK'S MOTHER.
AS HEAD OF THE CHAN
FAMILY WITH ITS LONG
TRADITION OF MAGIC,
SHE'S IN CHARGE OF
THE TECHNOLOGICAL
ASPECTS OF THE
SECOND EXORCIST
PLAN. YU'S AND ALMA'S
REGENERATIVE ABILITIES
ARE THE RESULT OF
THE CHAN FAMILY'S
SECRET ARTS.

SHE SUCCEEDED HER FATHER
AS HEAD OF THE FAMILY. ZU IS
HER FATHER'S BROTHER. SHE
RAISED HER HEIR, BAK, WITH
STRICT DISCIPLINE BECAUSE
SHE HOPED HE WOULD SOMEDAY
BECOME A LEADER AND CHANGE
THE ORDER'S INHUMANE
CULTURE. WHEN ALMA WENT
ON HIS RAMPAGE, SHE
SACRIFICED HERSELF SO THAT
RENI COULD ESCAPE.

BORN: SEPTEMBER 29;
SIGN: LIBRA;
BLOOD TYPE: A.

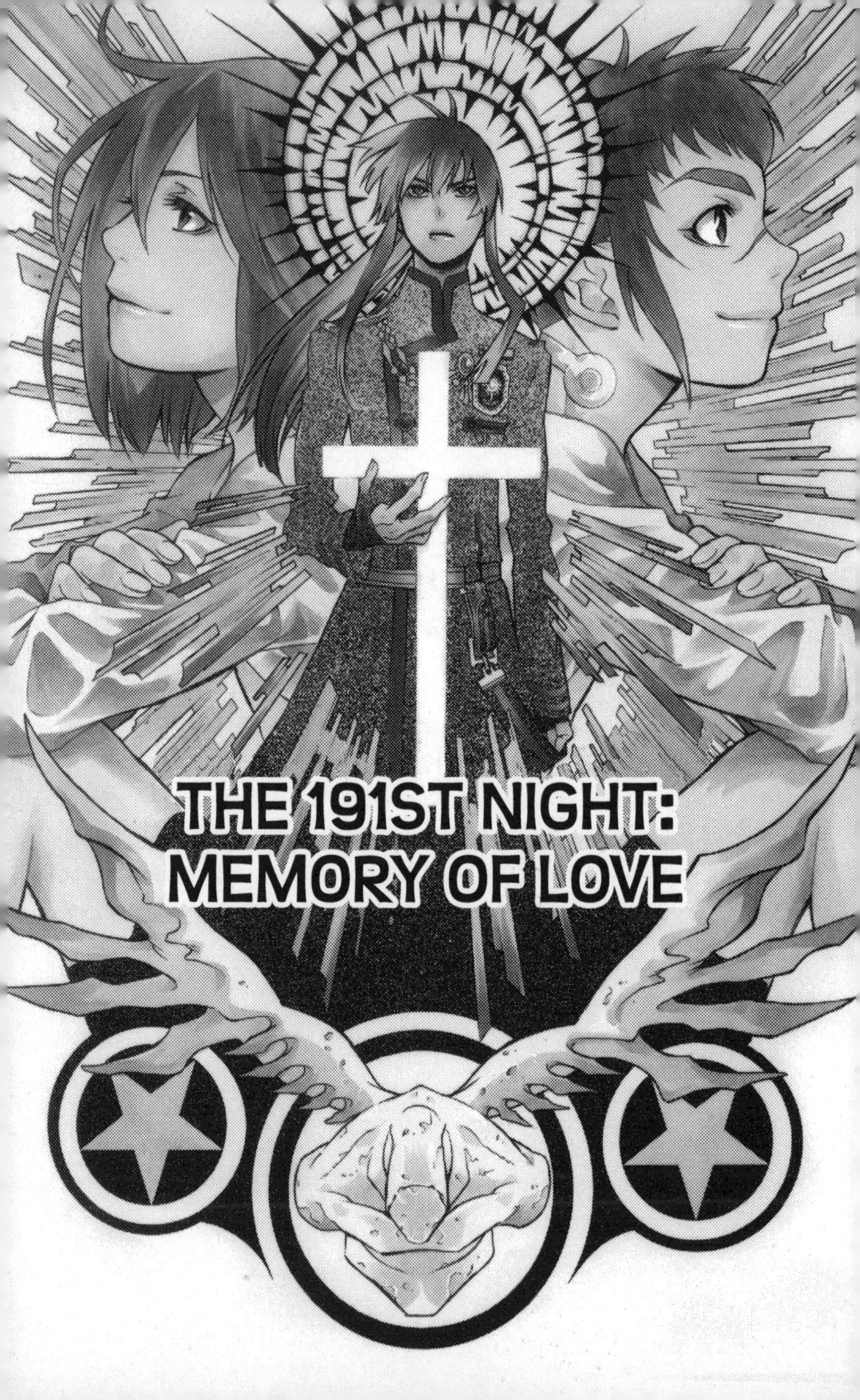
THE 191ST NIGHT:
MEMORY OF LOVE

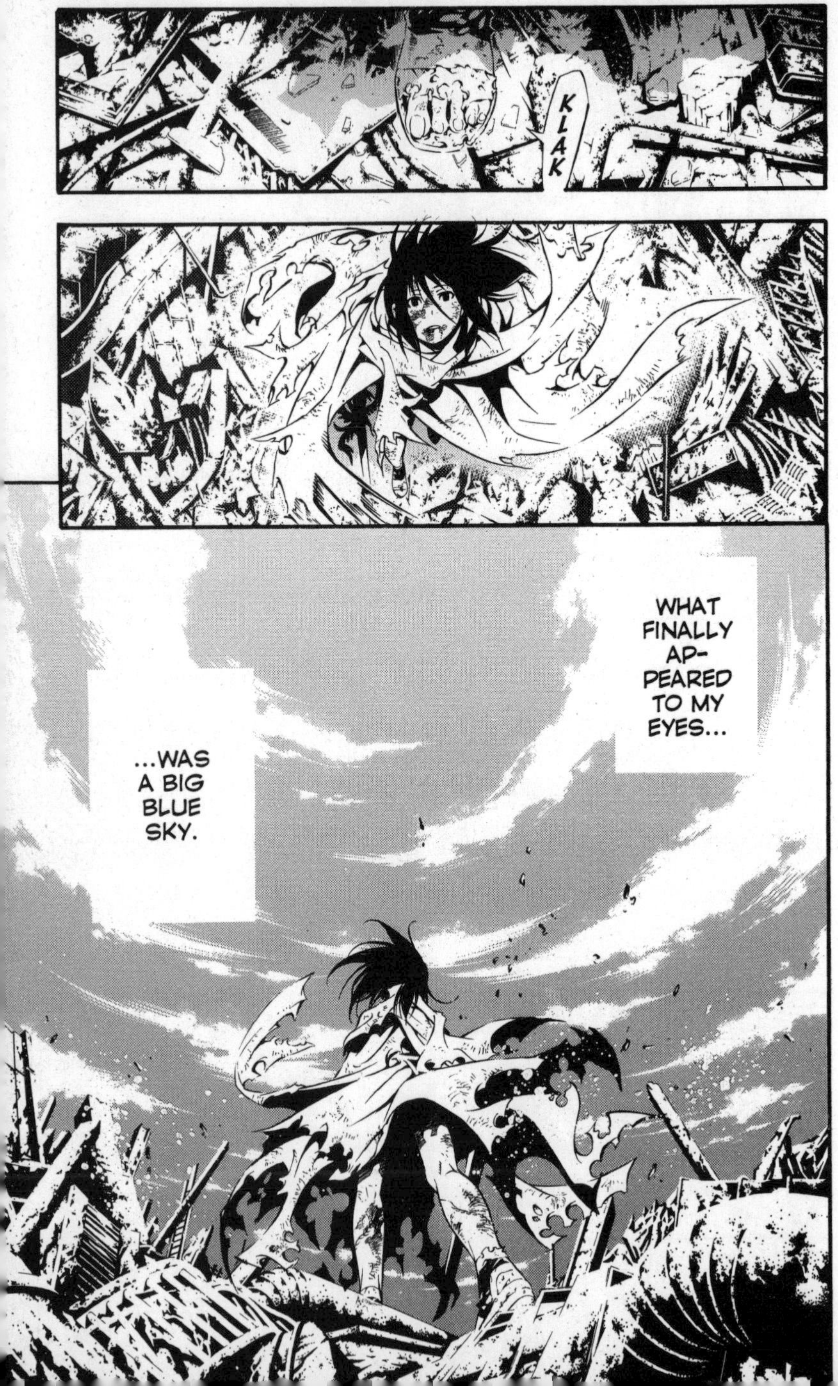
KLAK
WHAT FINALLY AP-PEARED TO MY EYES...
...WAS A BIG BLUE SKY.

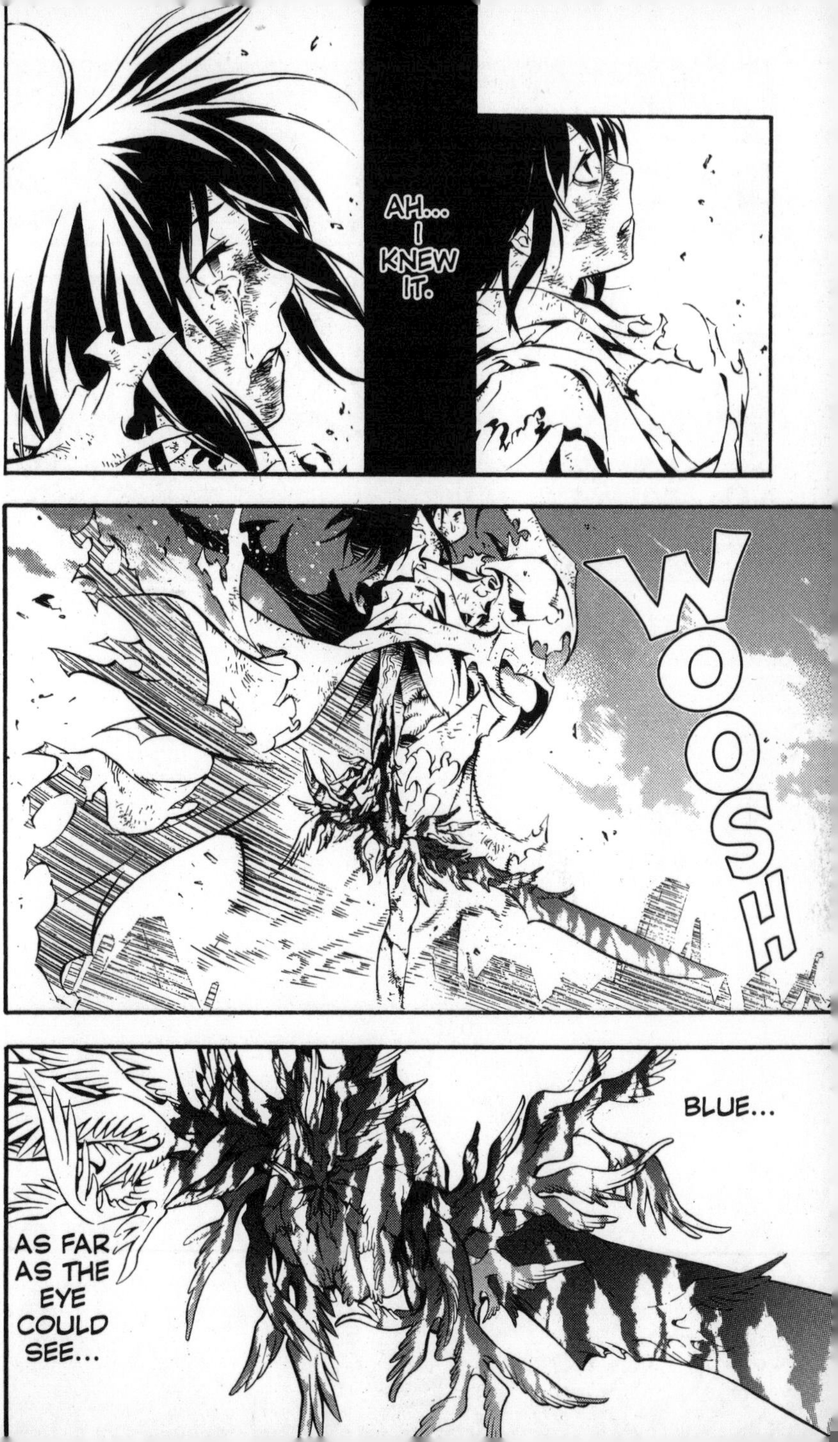
AH... I KNEW IT.
WOOSH
BLUE...
AS FAR AS THE EYE COULD SEE...

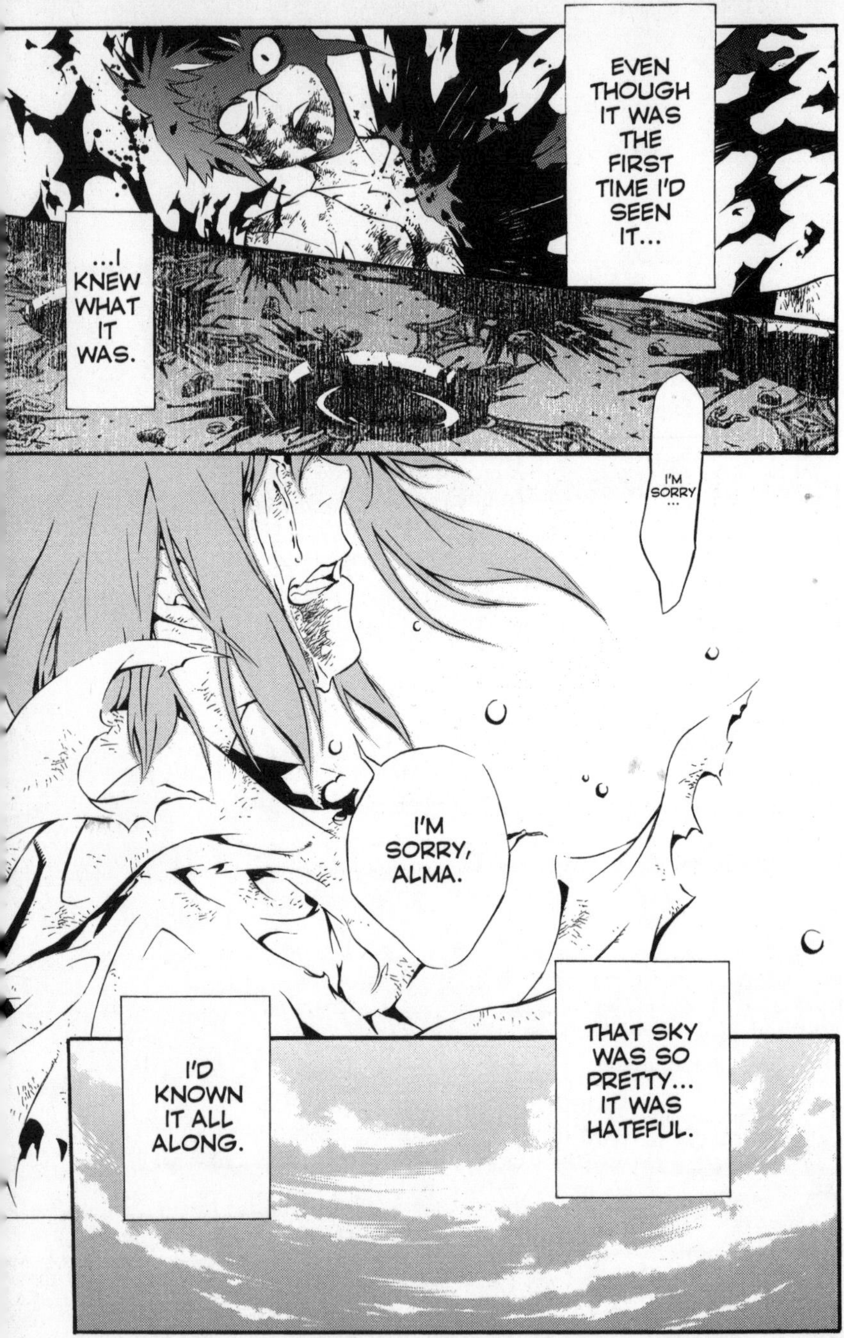
EVEN THOUGH IT WAS THE FIRST TIME I'D SEEN IT...
...I KNEW WHAT IT WAS.
I'M SORRY...
I'M SORRY, ALMA.
THAT SKY WAS SO PRETTY... IT WAS HATEFUL.
I'D KNOWN IT ALL ALONG.

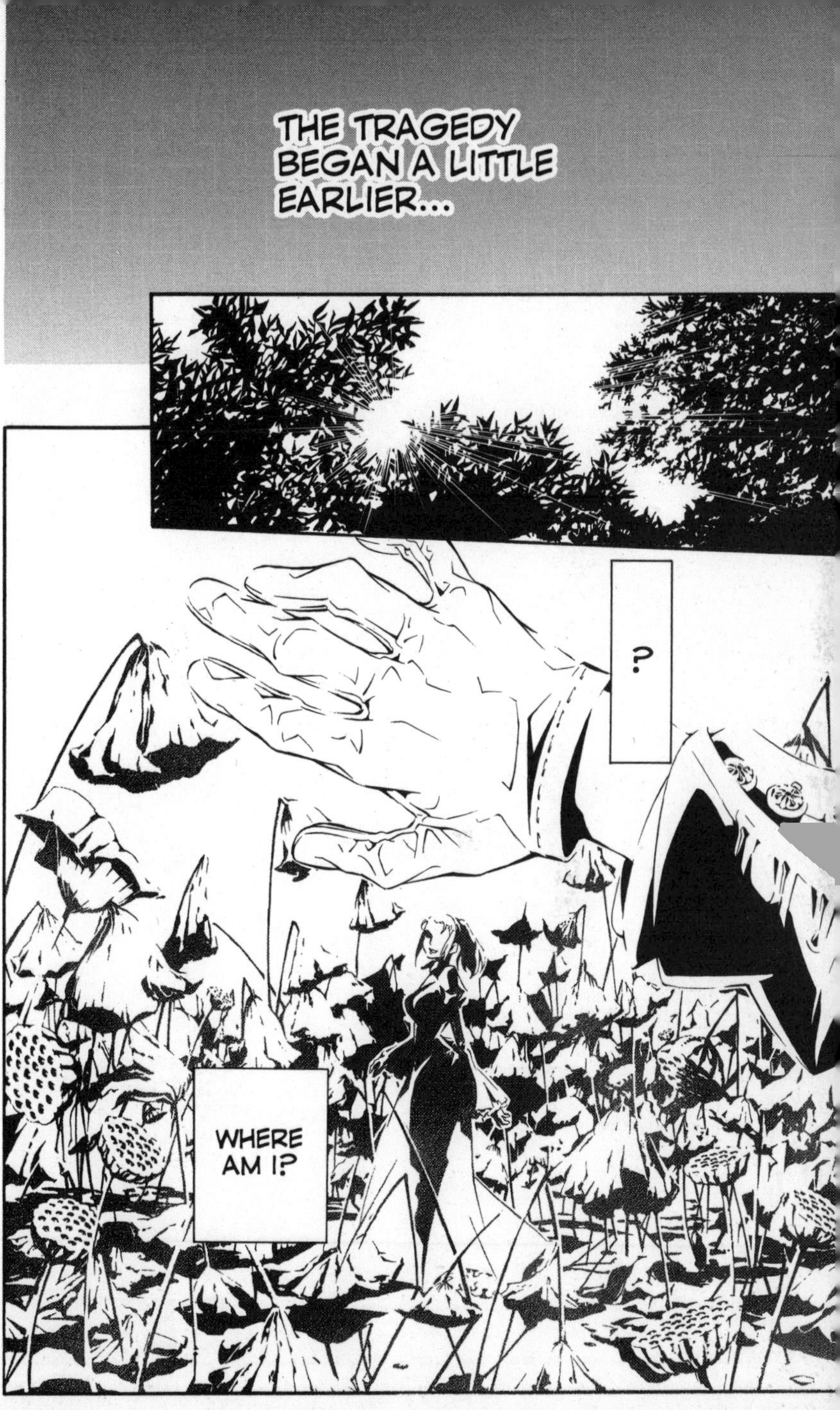
THE TRAGEDY BEGAN A LITTLE EARLIER...
?
WHERE AM I?

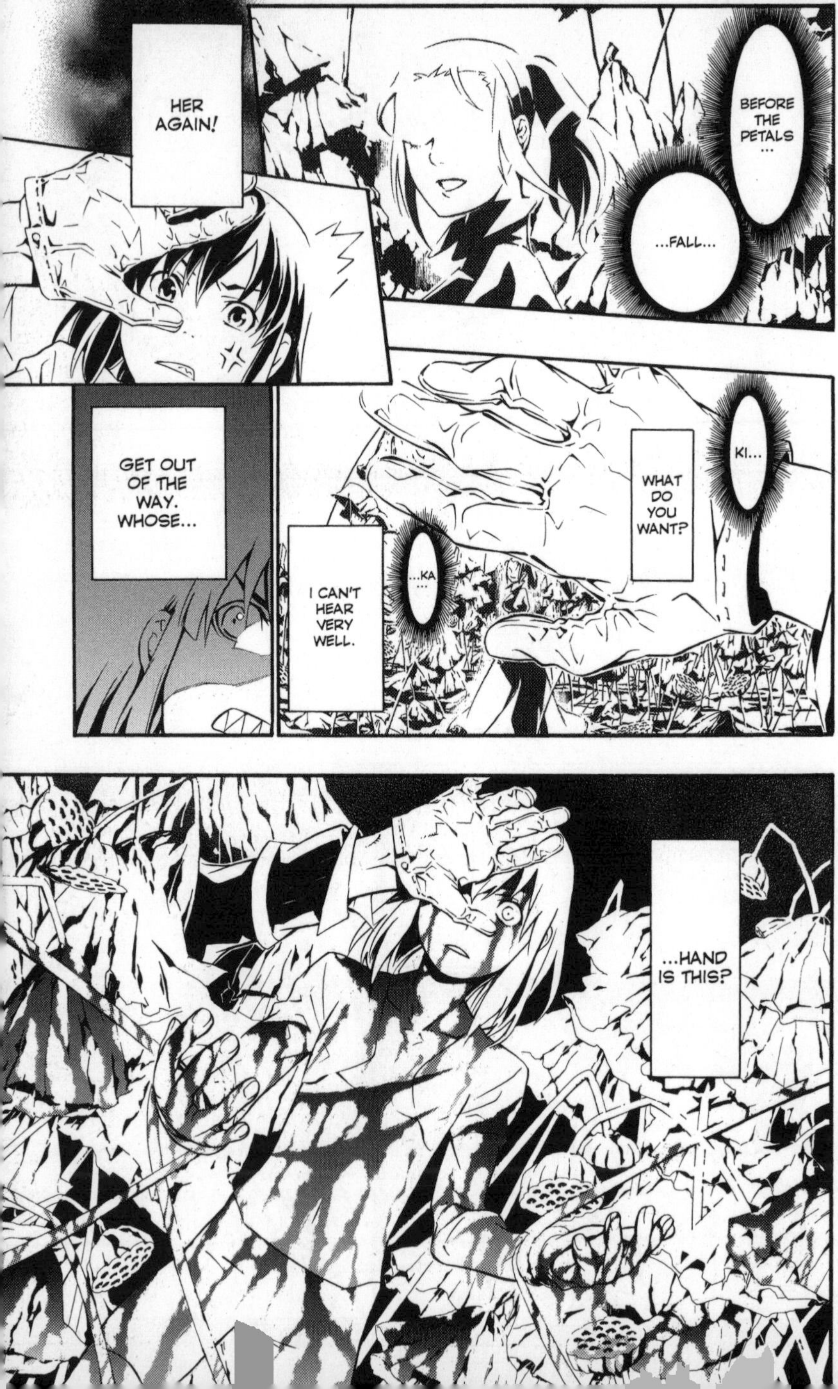
BEFORE THE PETALS...
...FALL...
HER AGAIN!
KI...
WHAT DO YOU WANT?
...KA...
I CAN'T HEAR VERY WELL.
GET OUT OF THE WAY. WHOSE...
...HAND IS THIS?

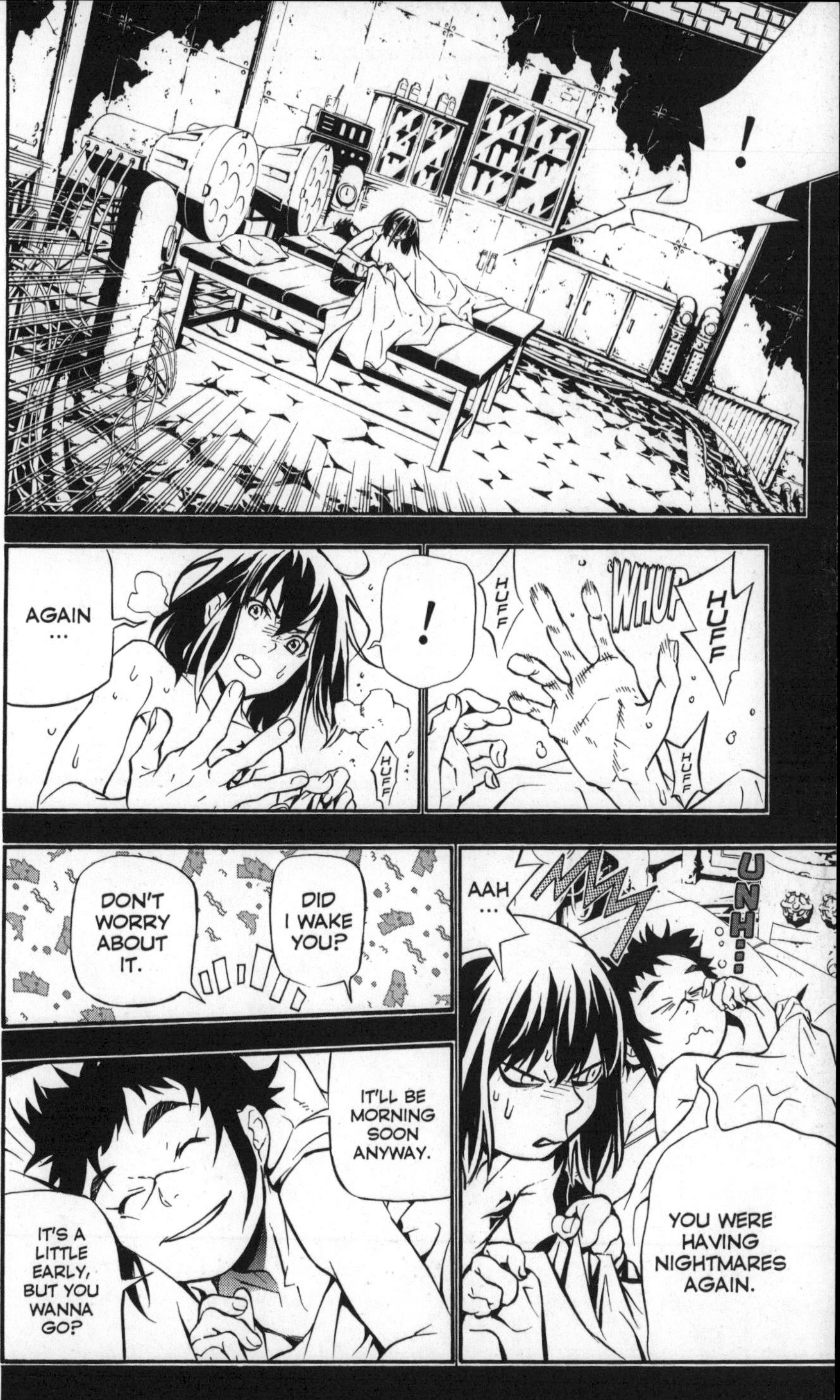
!
HUFF
WHUP
HUFF
HUFF
!
AGAIN ...
HUFF
UNH...
AAH ...
YOU WERE HAVING NIGHTMARES AGAIN.
DID I WAKE YOU?
DON'T WORRY ABOUT IT.
IT'LL BE MORNING SOON ANYWAY.
IT'S A LITTLE EARLY, BUT YOU WANNA GO?

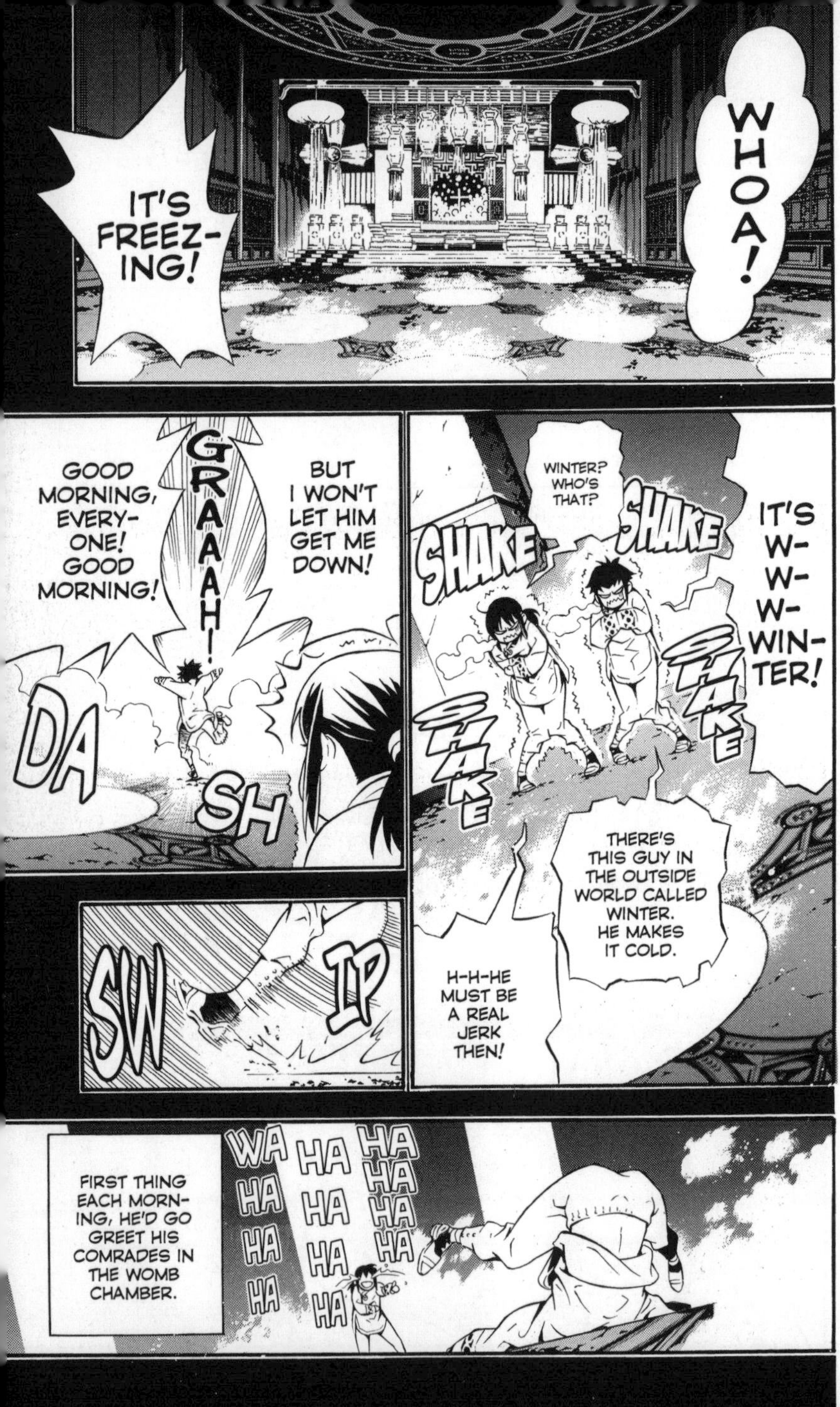
WHOA!
IT'S FREEZ-ING!
IT'S W-W-W-WIN-TER!
SHAKE
WINTER? WHO'S THAT?
SHAKE
SHAKE
SHAKE
THERE'S THIS GUY IN THE OUTSIDE WORLD CALLED WINTER. HE MAKES IT COLD.
H-H-HE MUST BE A REAL JERK THEN!
BUT I WON'T LET HIM GET ME DOWN!
GRAAAAH!
GOOD MORNING, EVERY-ONE! GOOD MORNING!
DASH
SWIP
WA HA HA HA HA HA HA HA HA HA HA HA HA HA
FIRST THING EACH MORN-ING, HE'D GO GREET HIS COMRADES IN THE WOMB CHAMBER.

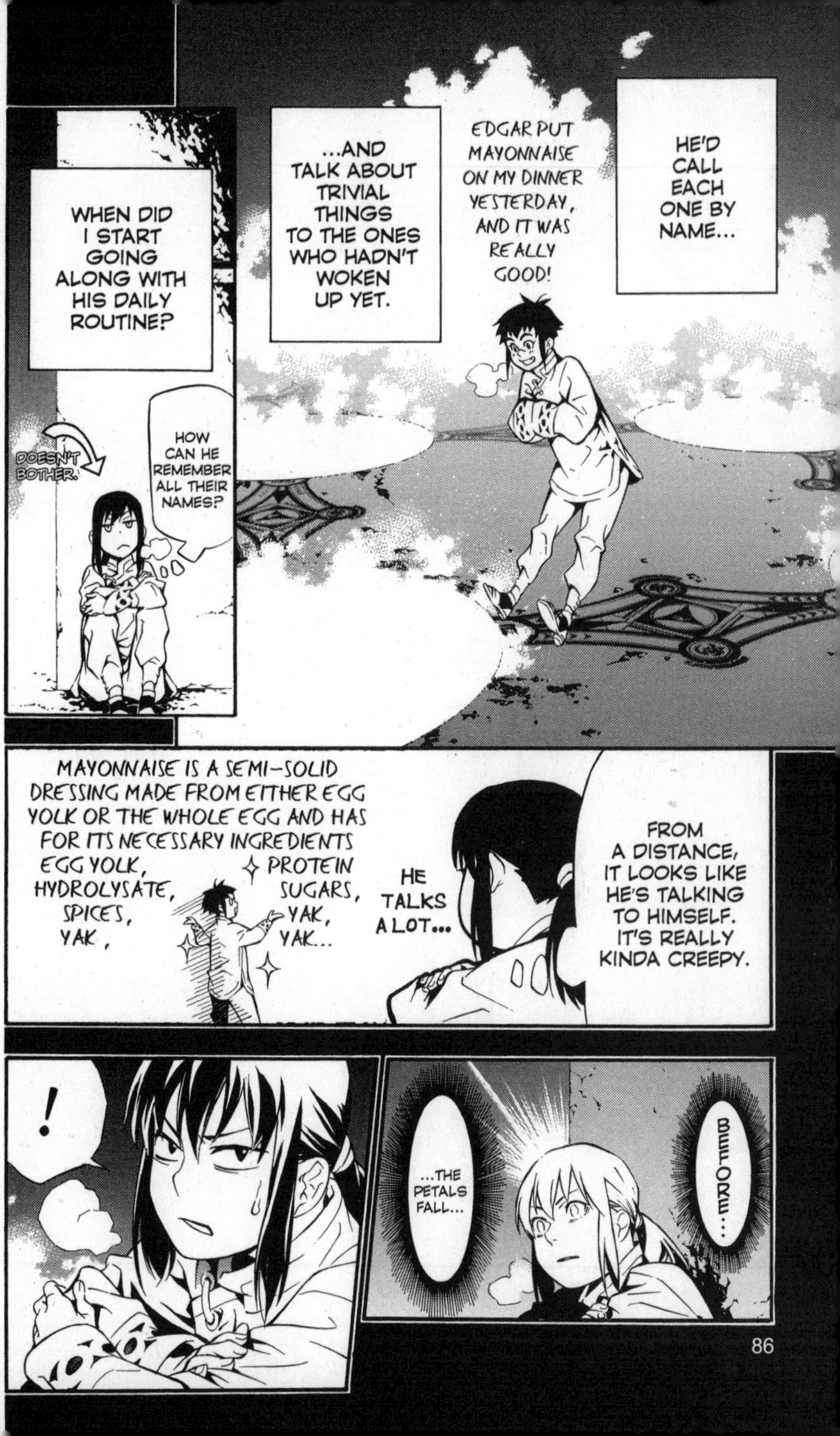
HE'D CALL EACH ONE BY NAME...
EDGAR PUT MAYONNAISE ON MY DINNER YESTERDAY, AND IT WAS REALLY GOOD!
...AND TALK ABOUT TRIVIAL THINGS TO THE ONES WHO HADN'T WOKEN UP YET.
WHEN DID I START GOING ALONG WITH HIS DAILY ROUTINE?
HOW CAN HE REMEMBER ALL THEIR NAMES?
DOESN'T BOTHER.
FROM A DISTANCE, IT LOOKS LIKE HE'S TALKING TO HIMSELF. IT'S REALLY KINDA CREEPY.
HE TALKS A LOT...
MAYONNAISE IS A SEMI-SOLID DRESSING MADE FROM EITHER EGG YOLK OR THE WHOLE EGG AND HAS FOR ITS NECESSARY INGREDIENTS
EGG YOLK, HYDROLYSATE, SPICES, YAK,
PROTEIN SUGARS, YAK, YAK...
BEFORE...
...THE PETALS FALL...
!

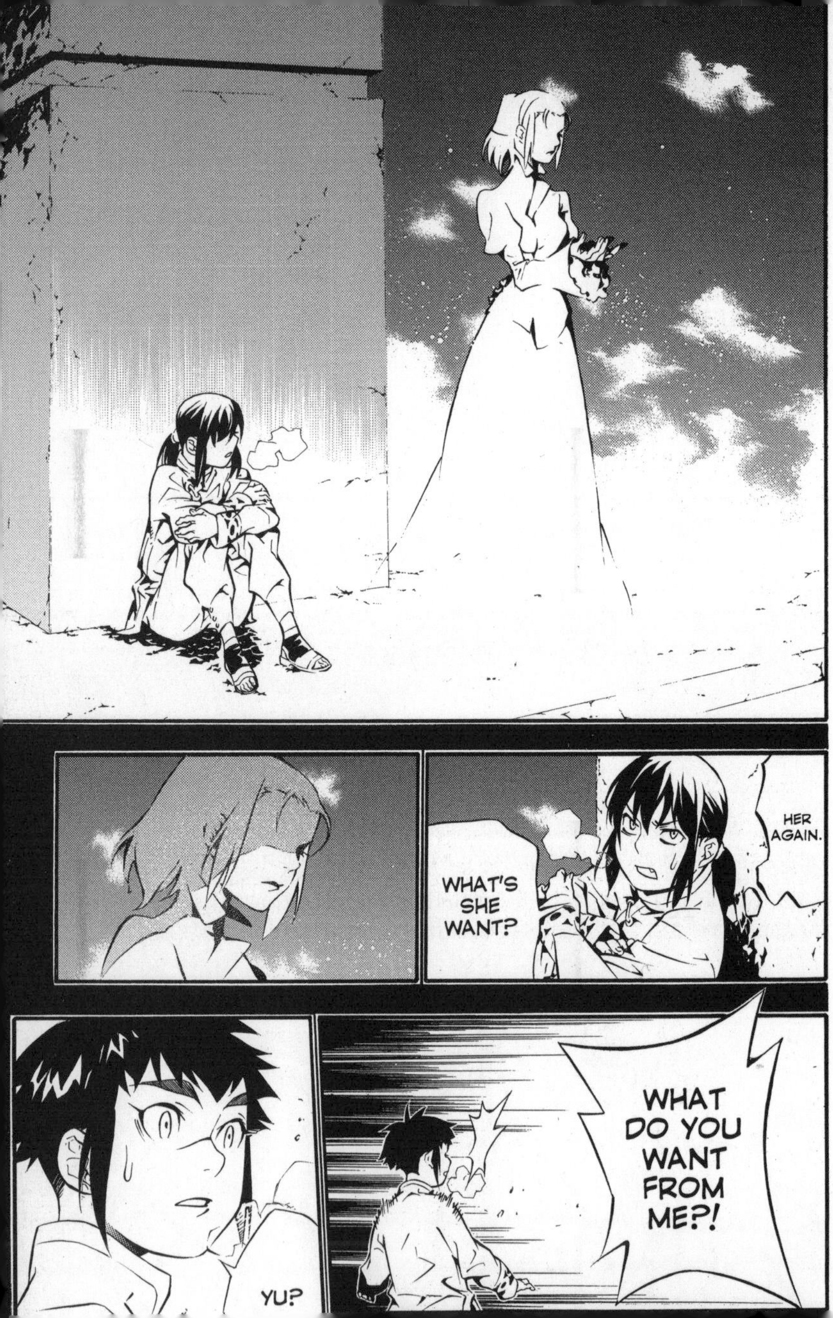
HER AGAIN.
WHAT'S SHE WANT?
WHAT DO YOU WANT FROM ME?!
YU?

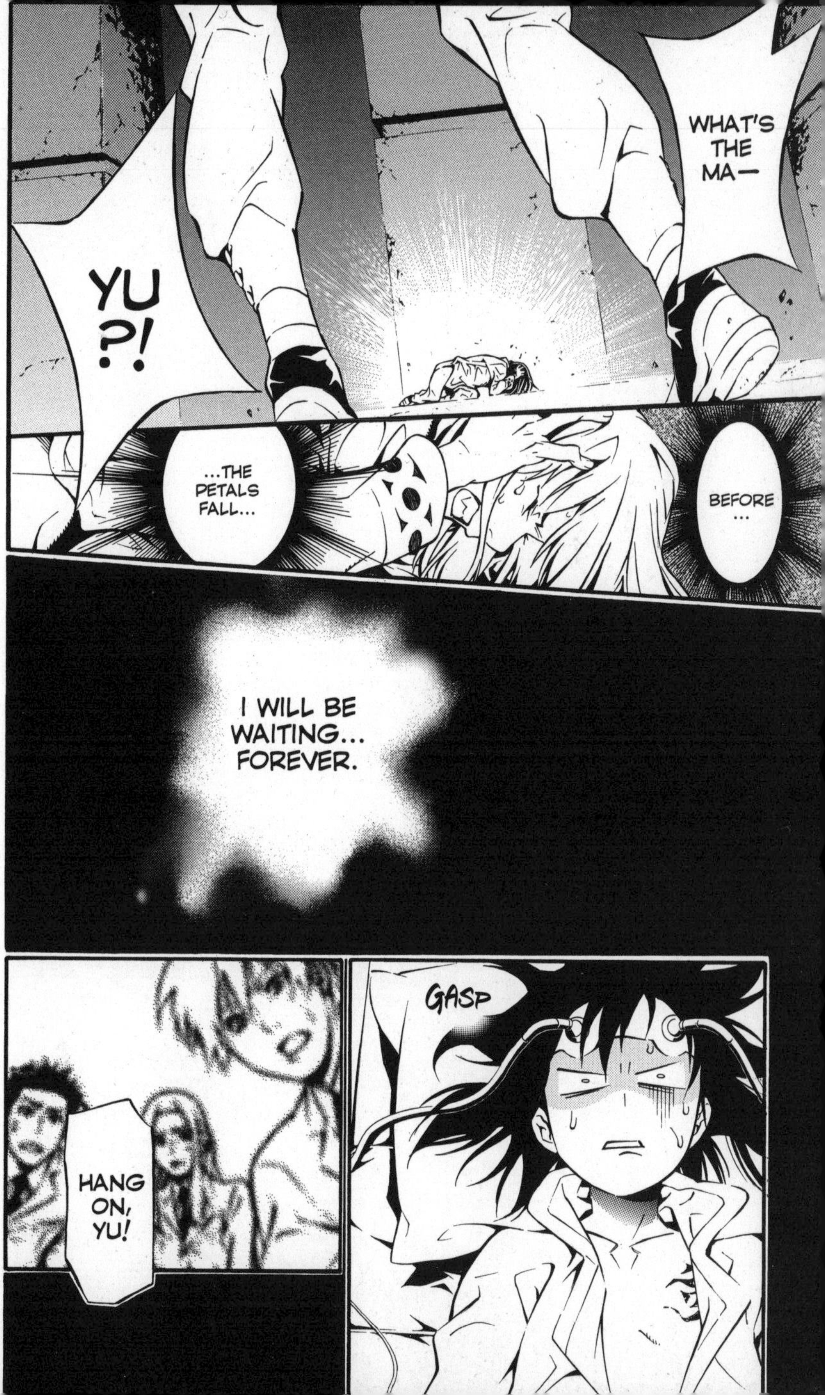
WHAT'S THE MA—
YU?!
BEFORE...
...THE PETALS FALL...
I WILL BE WAITING... FOREVER.
GASP
HANG ON, YU!

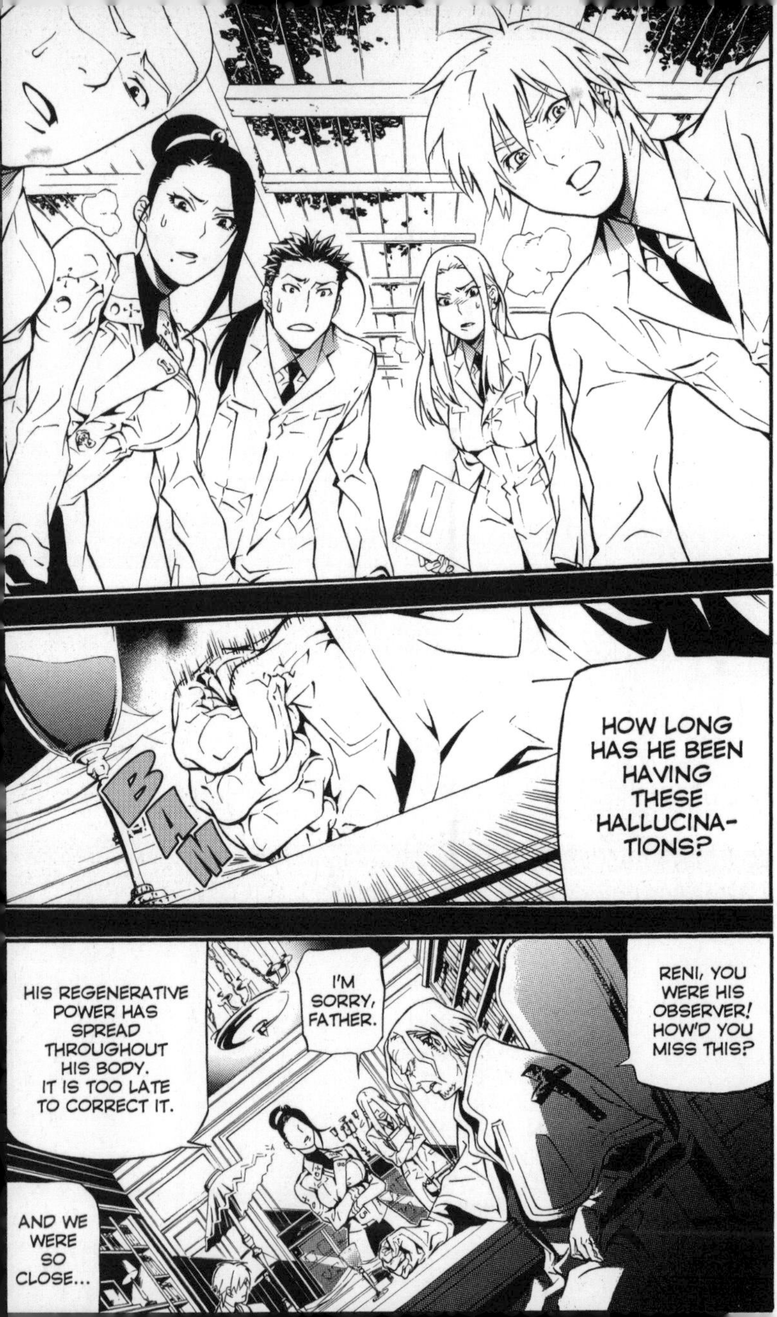
HOW LONG HAS HE BEEN HAVING THESE HALLUCINATIONS?
BAM
RENI, YOU WERE HIS OBSERVER! HOW'D YOU MISS THIS?
I'M SORRY, FATHER.
HIS REGENERATIVE POWER HAS SPREAD THROUGHOUT HIS BODY. IT IS TOO LATE TO CORRECT IT.
AND WE WERE SO CLOSE...

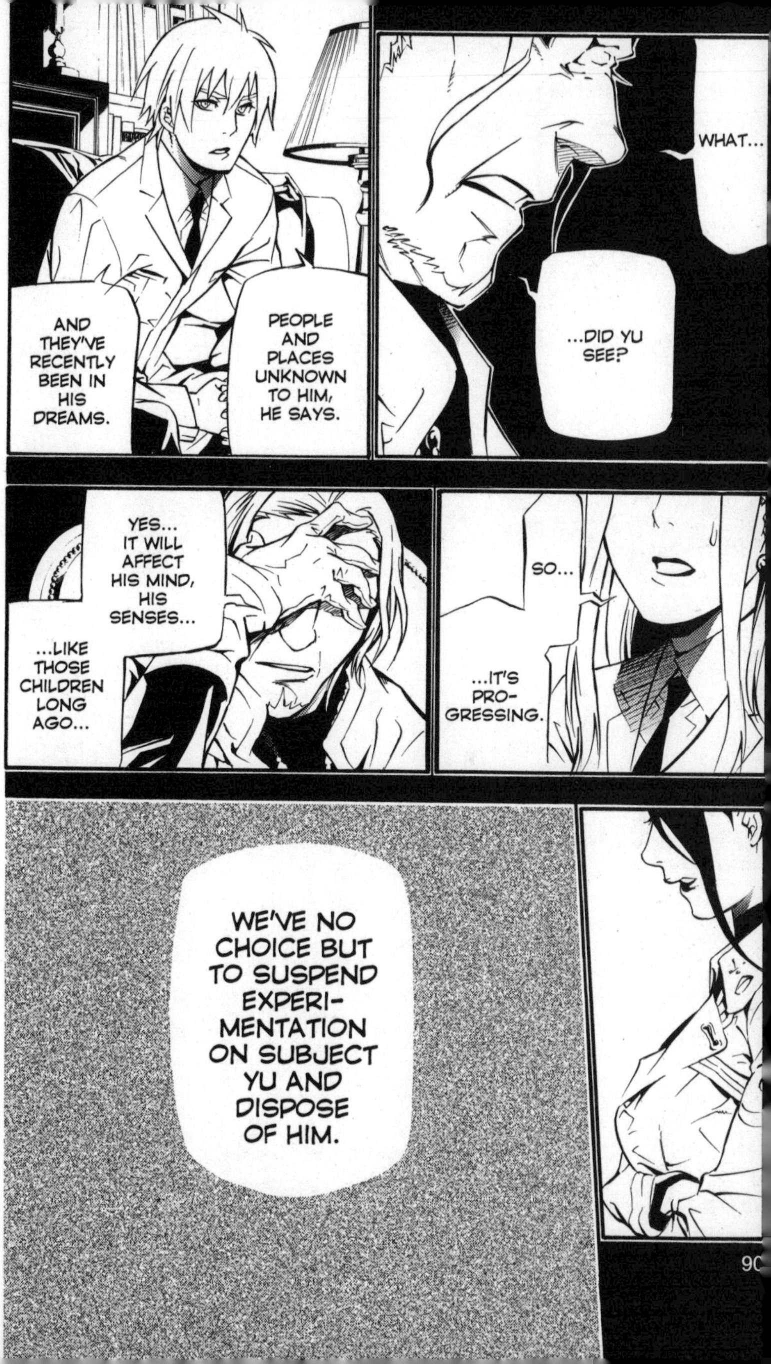
WHAT...
...DID YU SEE?
PEOPLE AND PLACES UNKNOWN TO HIM, HE SAYS.
AND THEY'VE RECENTLY BEEN IN HIS DREAMS.
SO...
...IT'S PRO-GRESSING.
YES... IT WILL AFFECT HIS MIND, HIS SENSES...
...LIKE THOSE CHILDREN LONG AGO...
WE'VE NO CHOICE BUT TO SUSPEND EXPERI-MENTATION ON SUBJECT YU AND DISPOSE OF HIM.

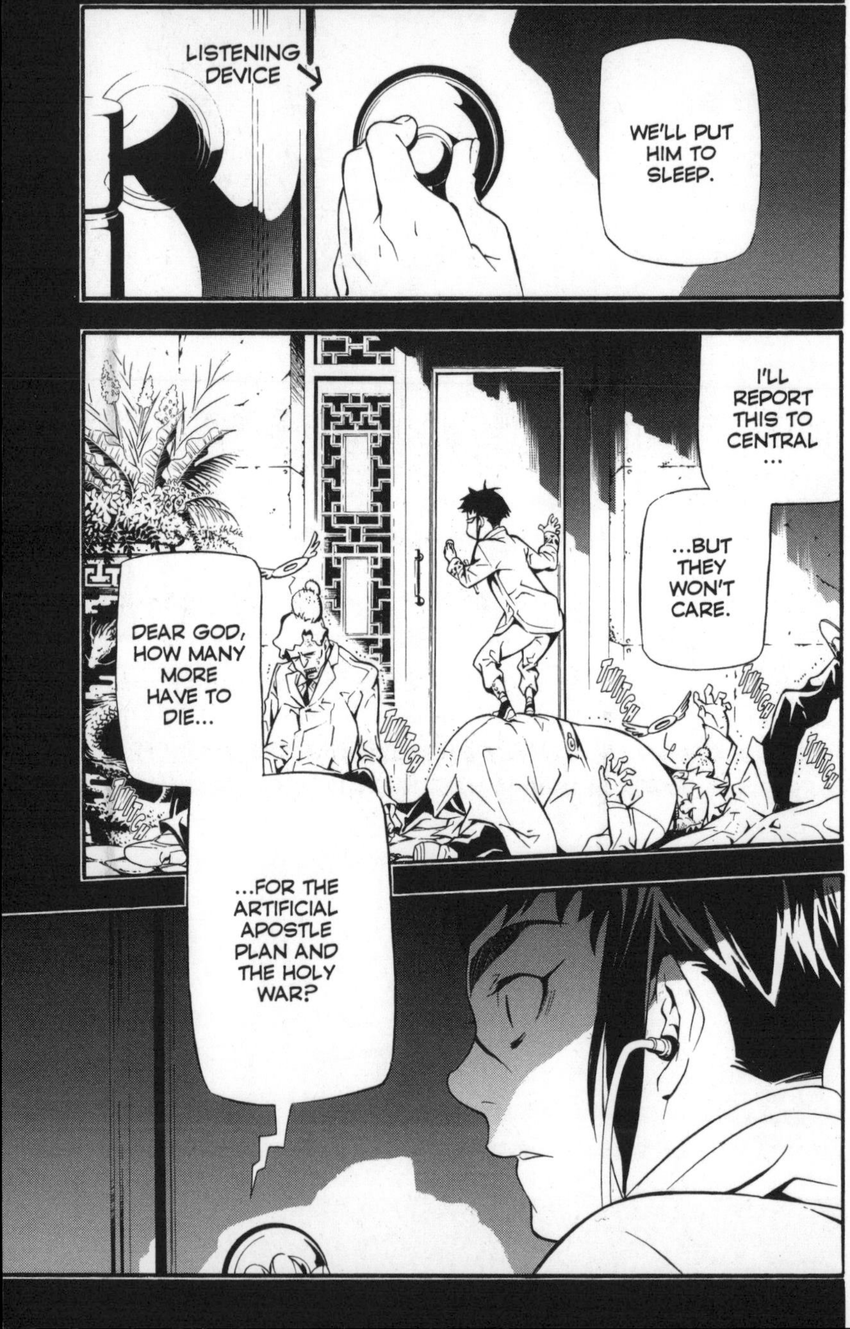
WE'LL PUT HIM TO SLEEP.
LISTENING DEVICE
I'LL REPORT THIS TO CENTRAL...
...BUT THEY WON'T CARE.
DEAR GOD, HOW MANY MORE HAVE TO DIE...
TWITCH
TWITCH
TWITCH
TWITCH
TWITCH
...FOR THE ARTIFICIAL APOSTLE PLAN AND THE HOLY WAR?

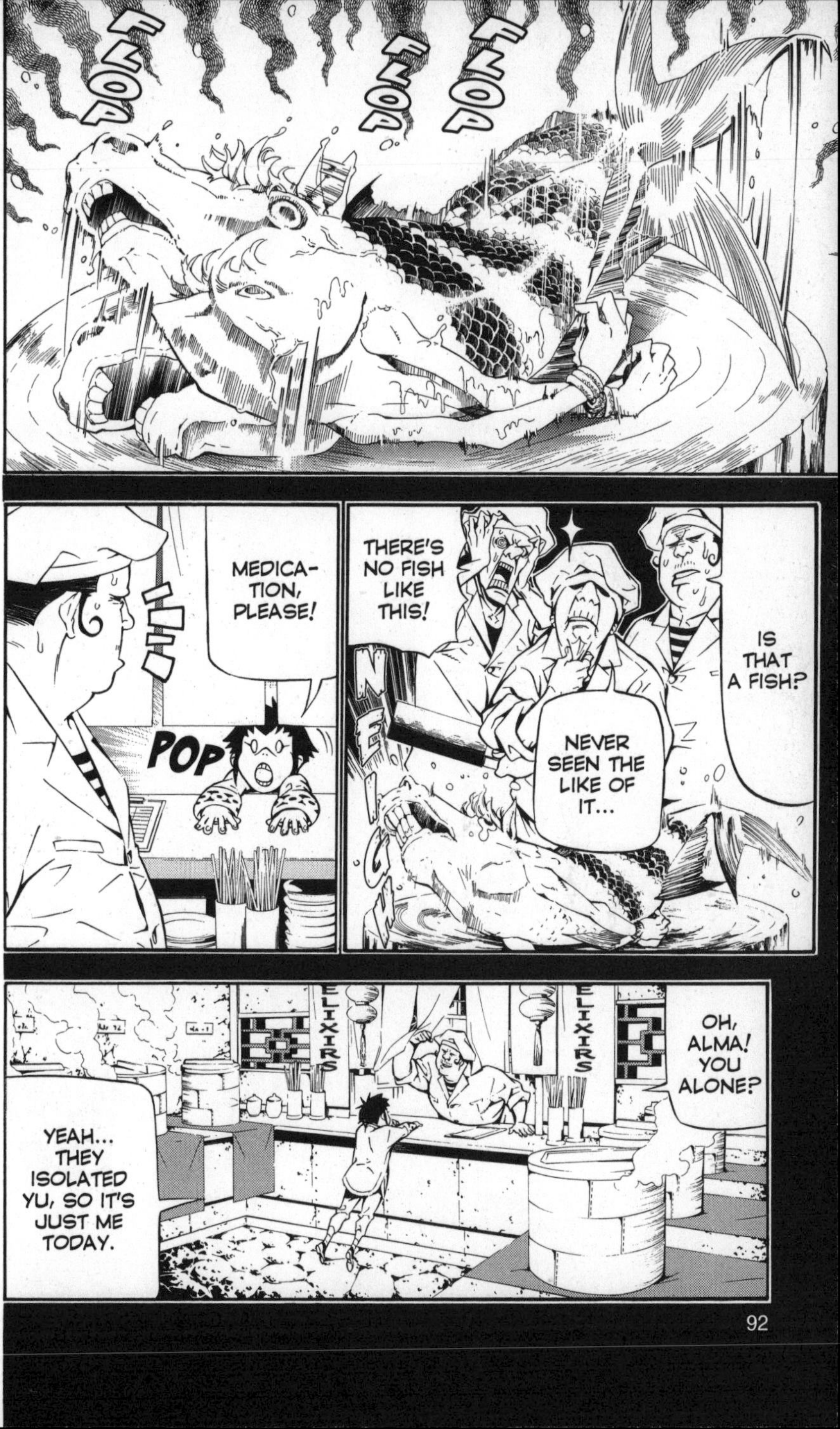
FLOP
FLOP
FLOP
IS THAT A FISH?
THERE'S NO FISH LIKE THIS!
NEVER SEEN THE LIKE OF IT...
NEIGH
MEDICATION, PLEASE!
POP
ELIXIRS
ELIXIRS
OH, ALMA! YOU ALONE?
YEAH... THEY ISOLATED YU, SO IT'S JUST ME TODAY.

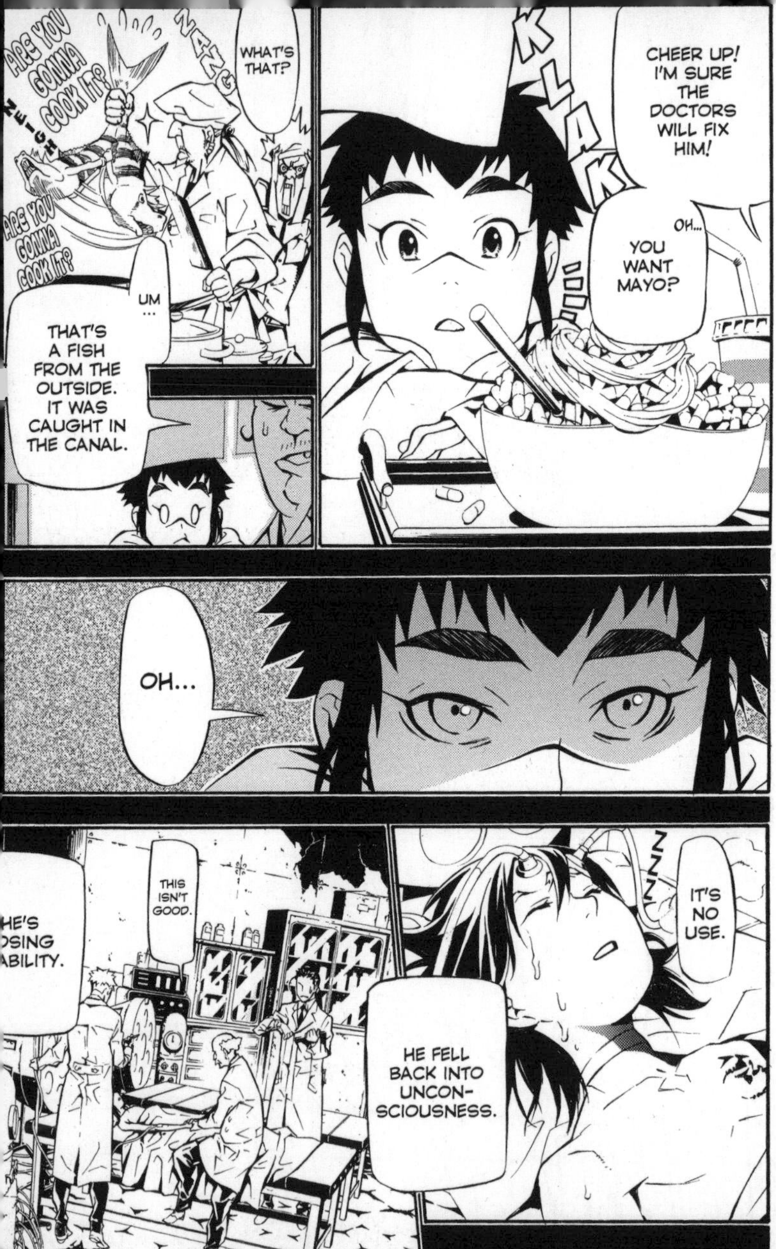
KLAK
CHEER UP! I'M SURE THE DOCTORS WILL FIX HIM!
OH... YOU WANT MAYO?
WHAT'S THAT?
ARE YOU GONNA COOK IT?
ARE YOU GONNA COOK IT?
UM ...
THAT'S A FISH FROM THE OUTSIDE. IT WAS CAUGHT IN THE CANAL.
OH...
ZZZ
IT'S NO USE.
HE FELL BACK INTO UNCON-SCIOUSNESS.
THIS ISN'T GOOD.
HE'S
OSING
ABILITY.

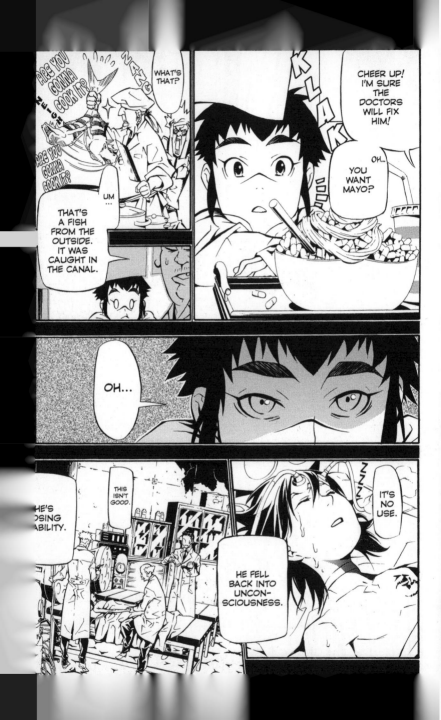

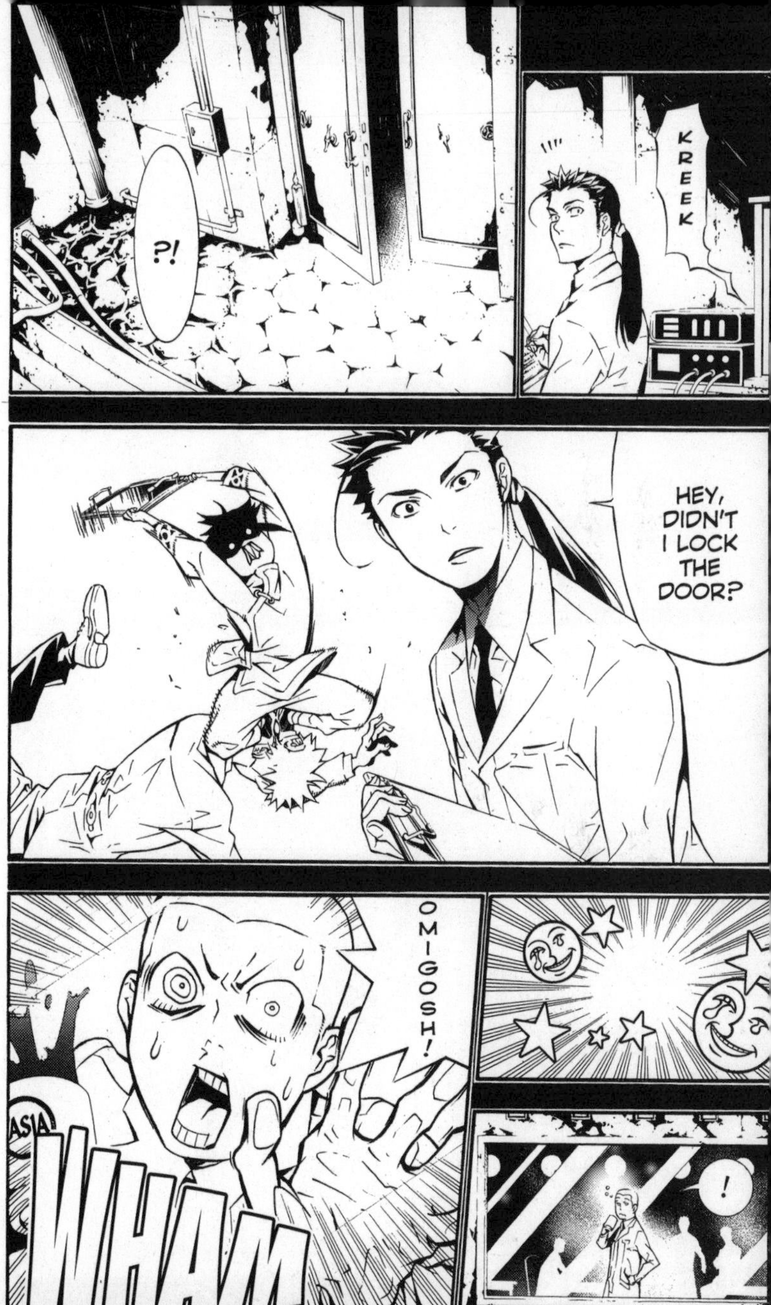
KREEK
?!
HEY, DIDN'T I LOCK THE DOOR?
!
OMIGOSH!
ASIA
WHAM

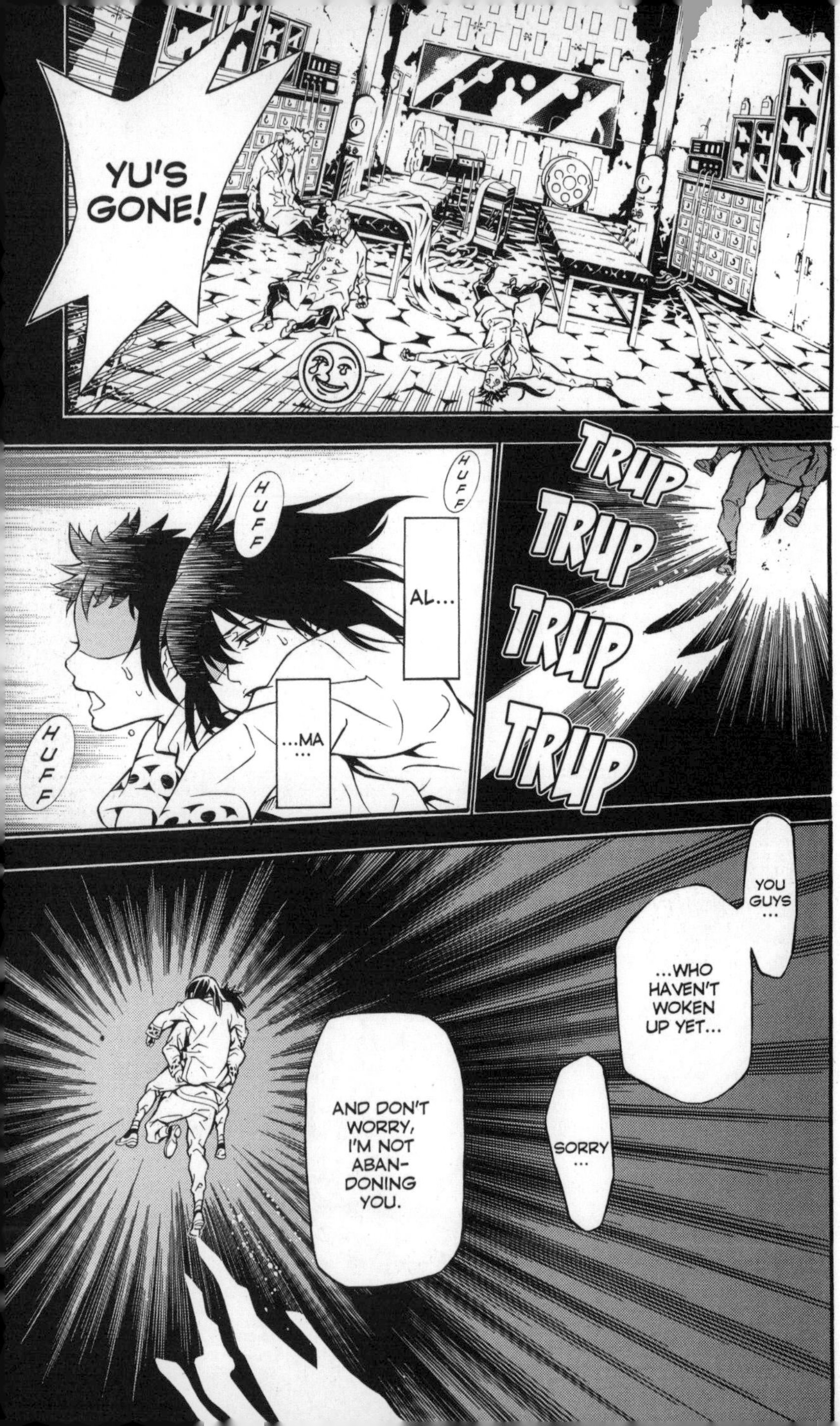
YU'S GONE!
TRUP TRUP TRUP TRUP
HUFF HUFF
AL...
HUFF
...MA...
HUFF
YOU GUYS...
...WHO HAVEN'T WOKEN UP YET...
SORRY...
AND DON'T WORRY, I'M NOT ABAN-DONING YOU.

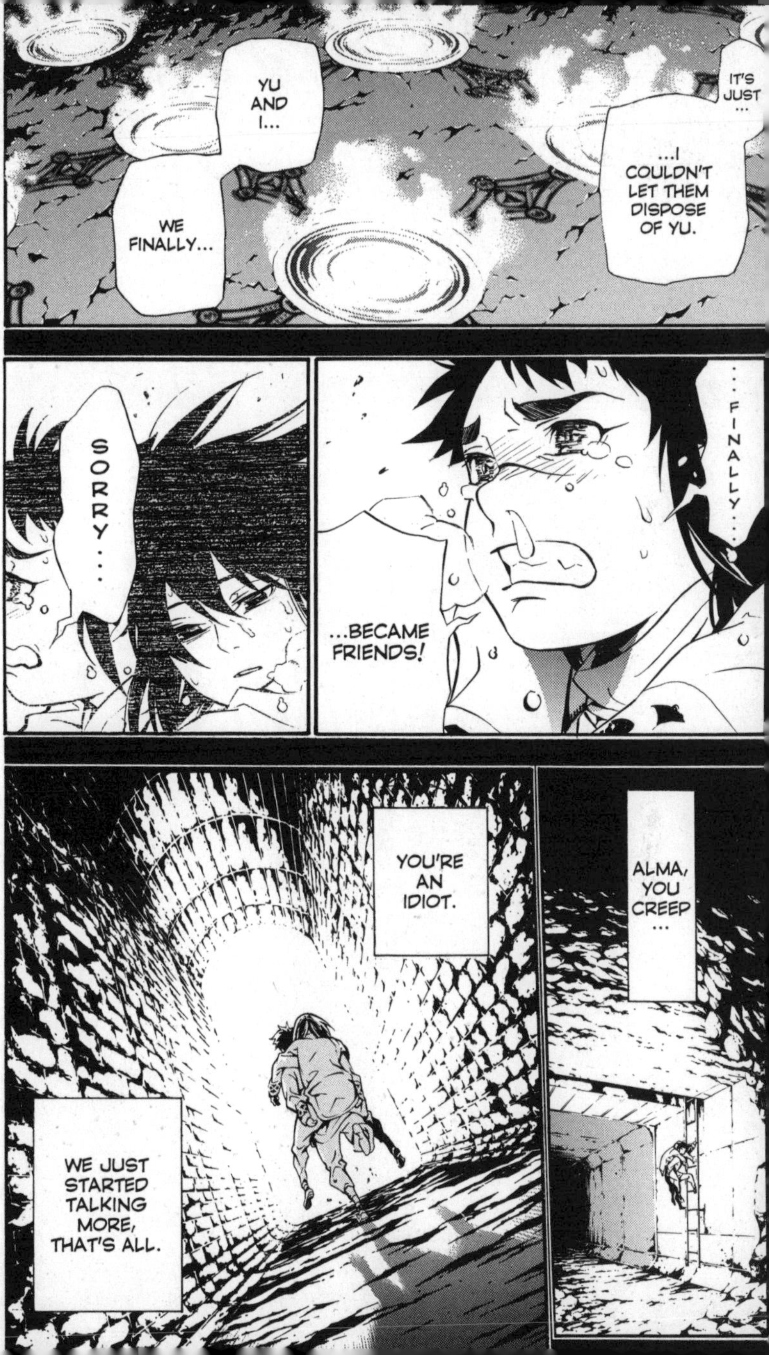
IT'S JUST ...
...I COULDN'T LET THEM DISPOSE OF YU.
YU AND I...
WE FINALLY...
...FINALLY...
...BECAME FRIENDS!
SORRY...
ALMA, YOU CREEP ...
YOU'RE AN IDIOT.
WE JUST STARTED TALKING MORE, THAT'S ALL.

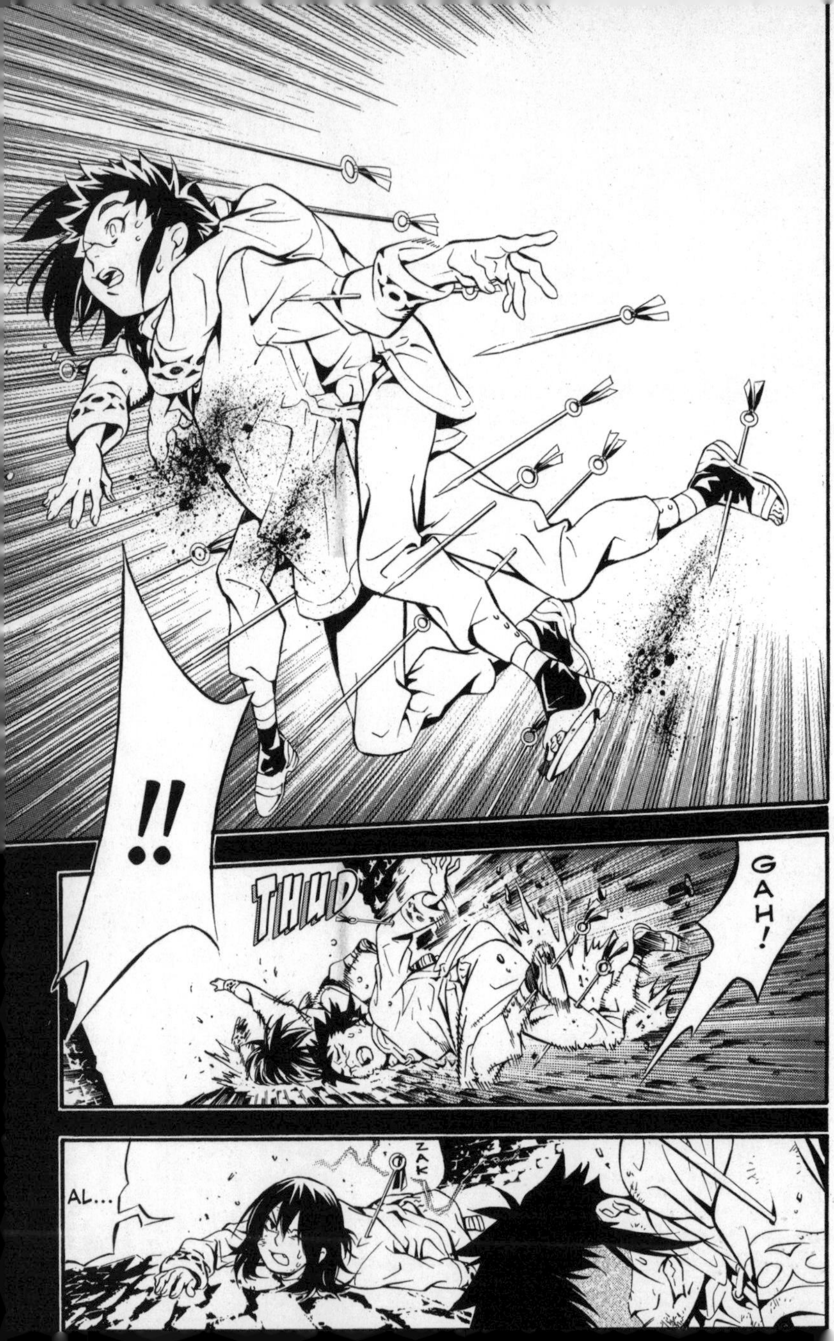
!!
GAH!
THUD
ZAK
AL...

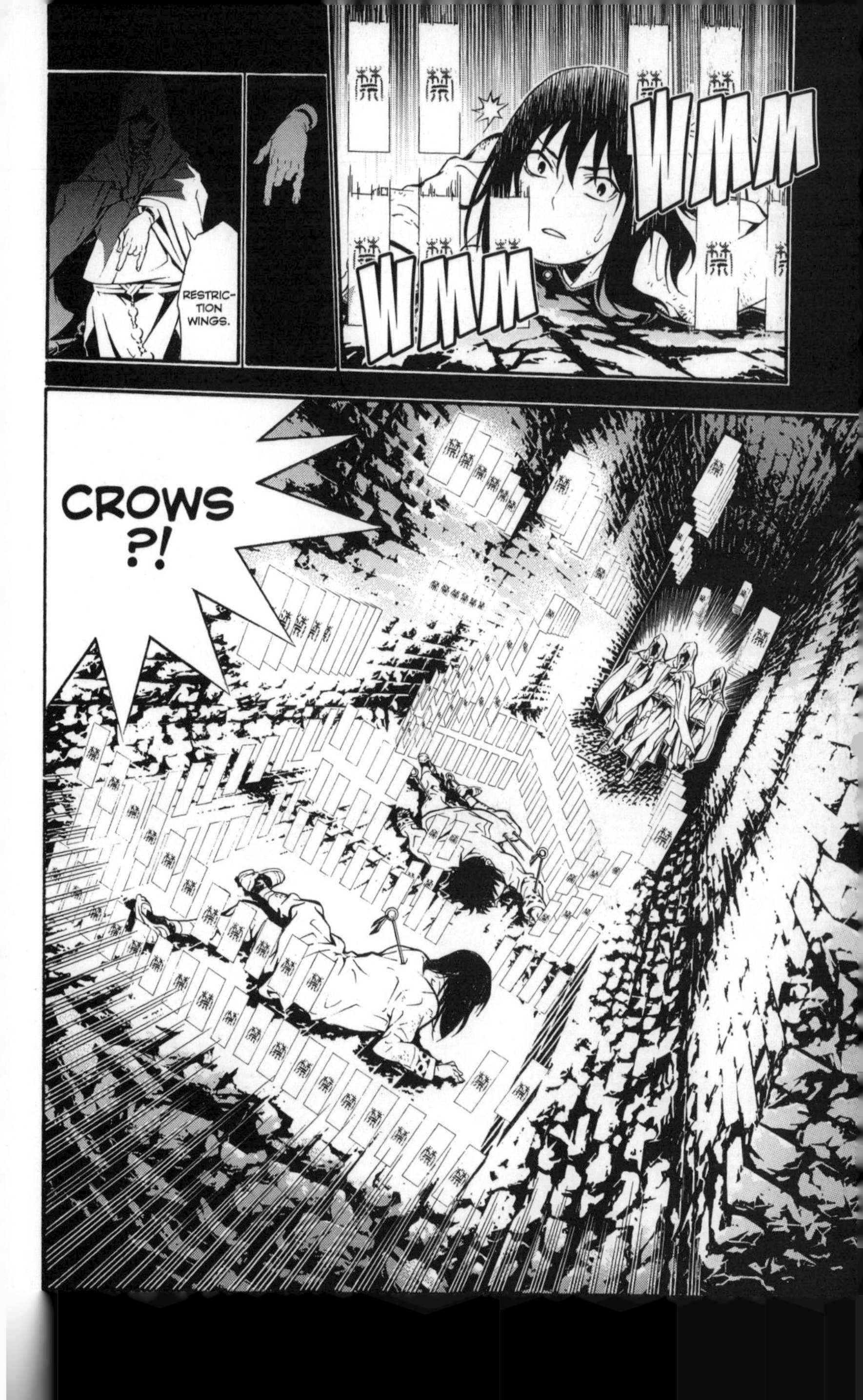
WMM
WMM
RESTRIC-TION WINGS.
CROWS ?!

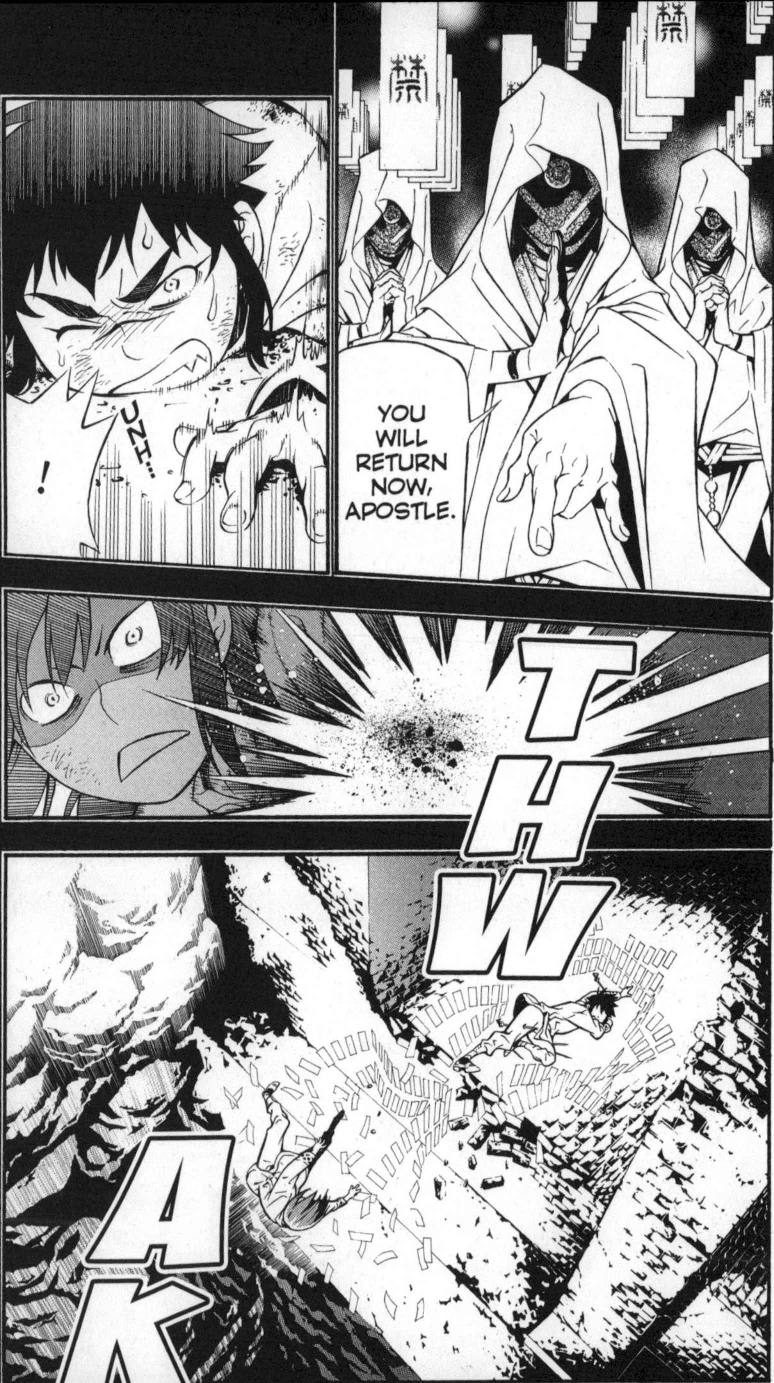
YOU WILL RETURN NOW, APOSTLE.
UNH...
!
THWAK

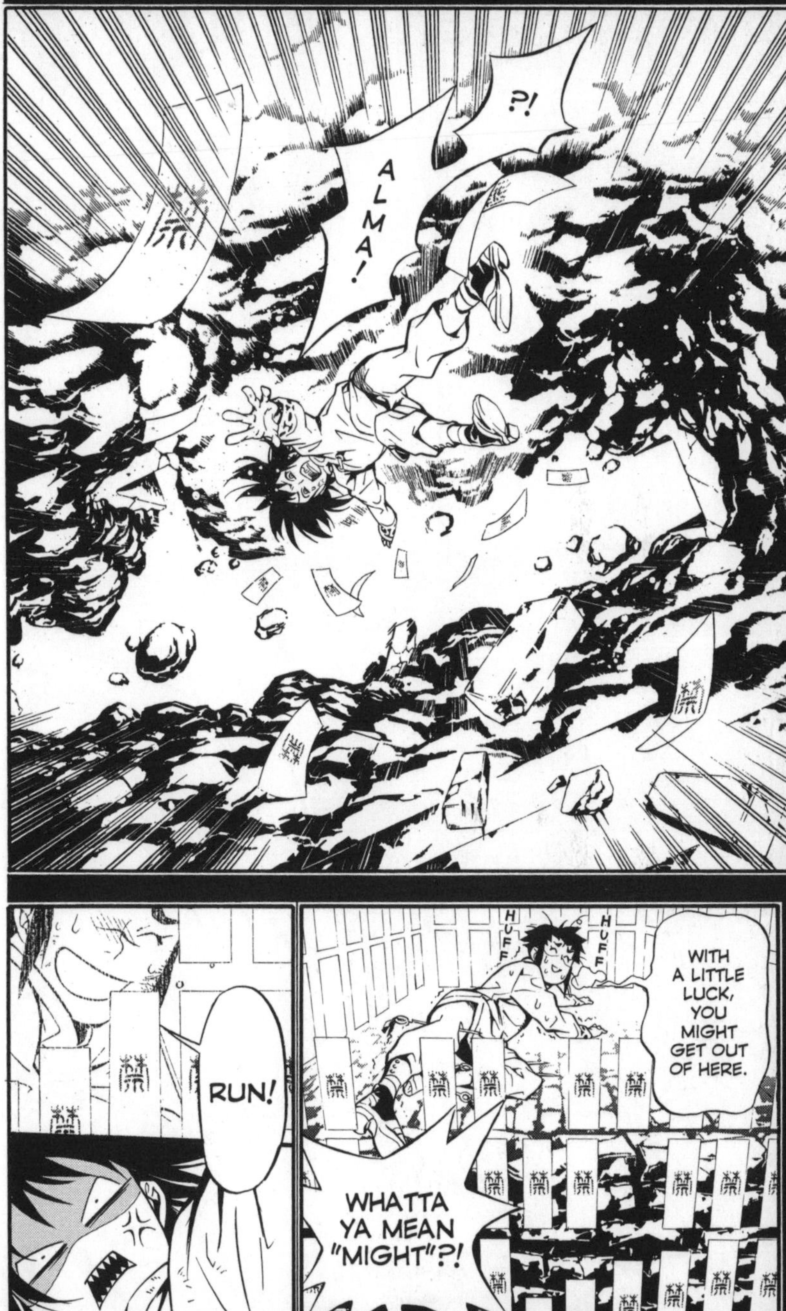
?!
ALMA!
HUFF
HUFF
WITH A LITTLE LUCK, YOU MIGHT GET OUT OF HERE.
WHATTA YA MEAN "MIGHT"?!
RUN!

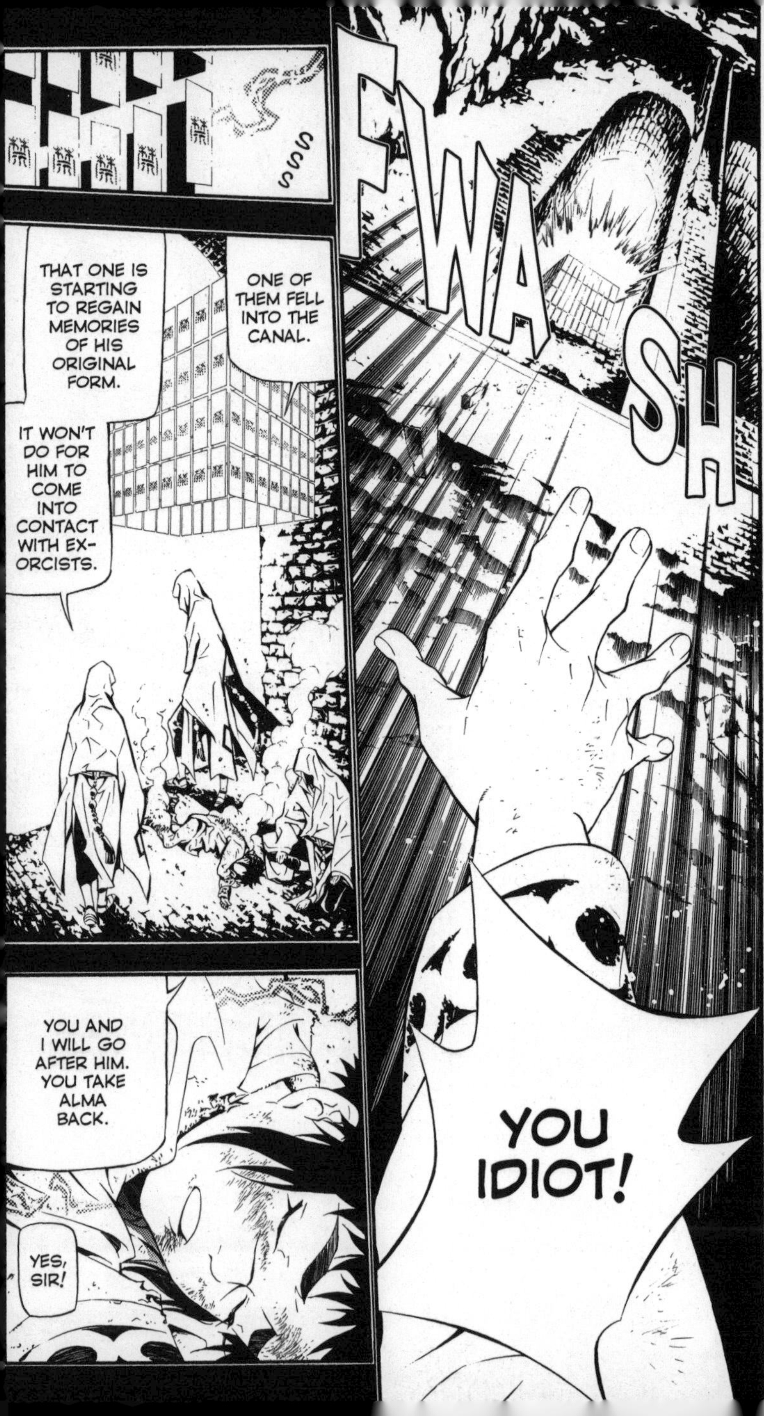
FWASH
YOU IDIOT!
SSS
ONE OF THEM FELL INTO THE CANAL.
THAT ONE IS STARTING TO REGAIN MEMORIES OF HIS ORIGINAL FORM.
IT WON'T DO FOR HIM TO COME INTO CONTACT WITH EX-ORCISTS.
YOU AND I WILL GO AFTER HIM. YOU TAKE ALMA BACK.
YES, SIR!

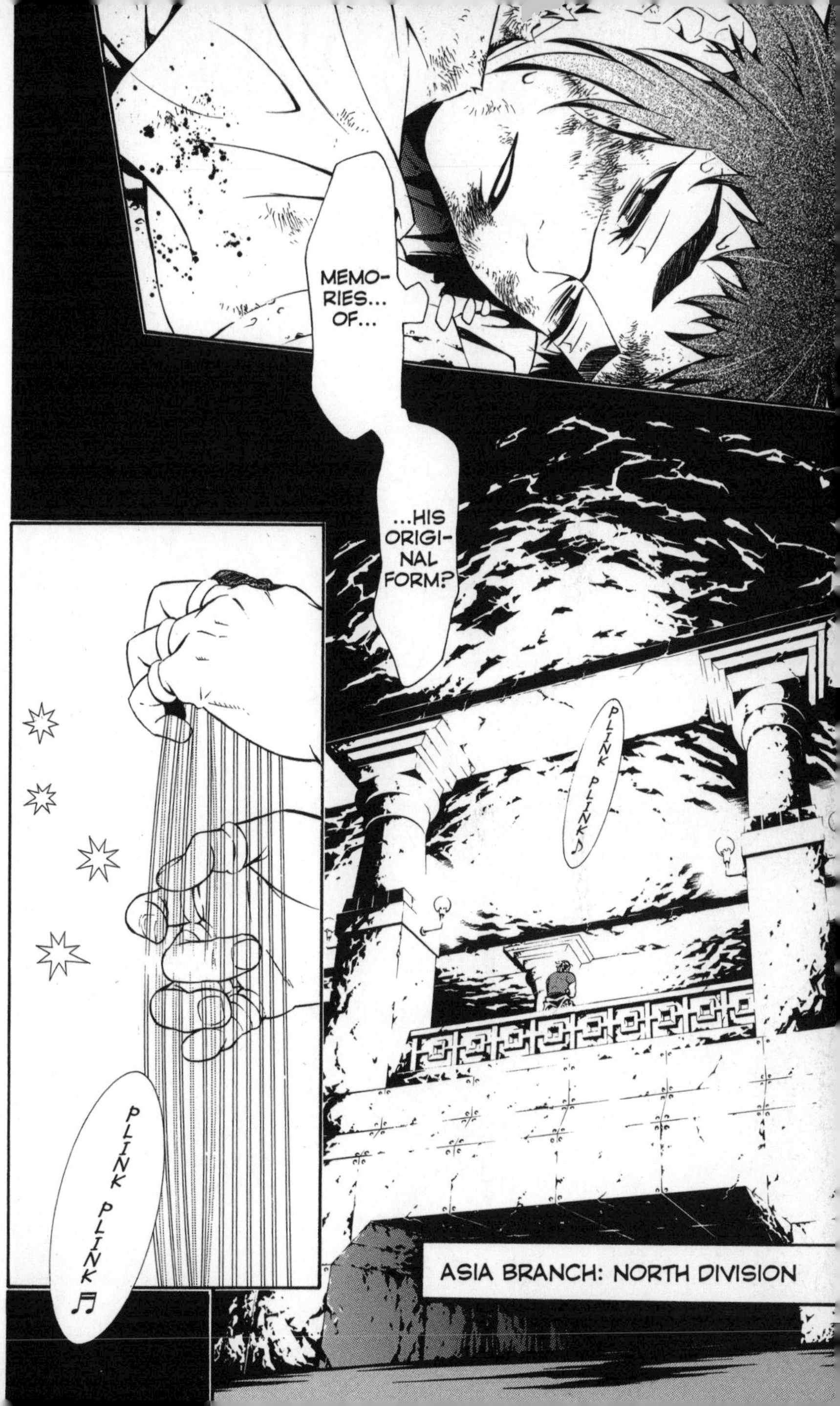
MEMO-RIES... OF...
...HIS ORIGI-NAL FORM?
PLINK PLINK♪
ASIA BRANCH: NORTH DIVISION
PLINK PLINK♬

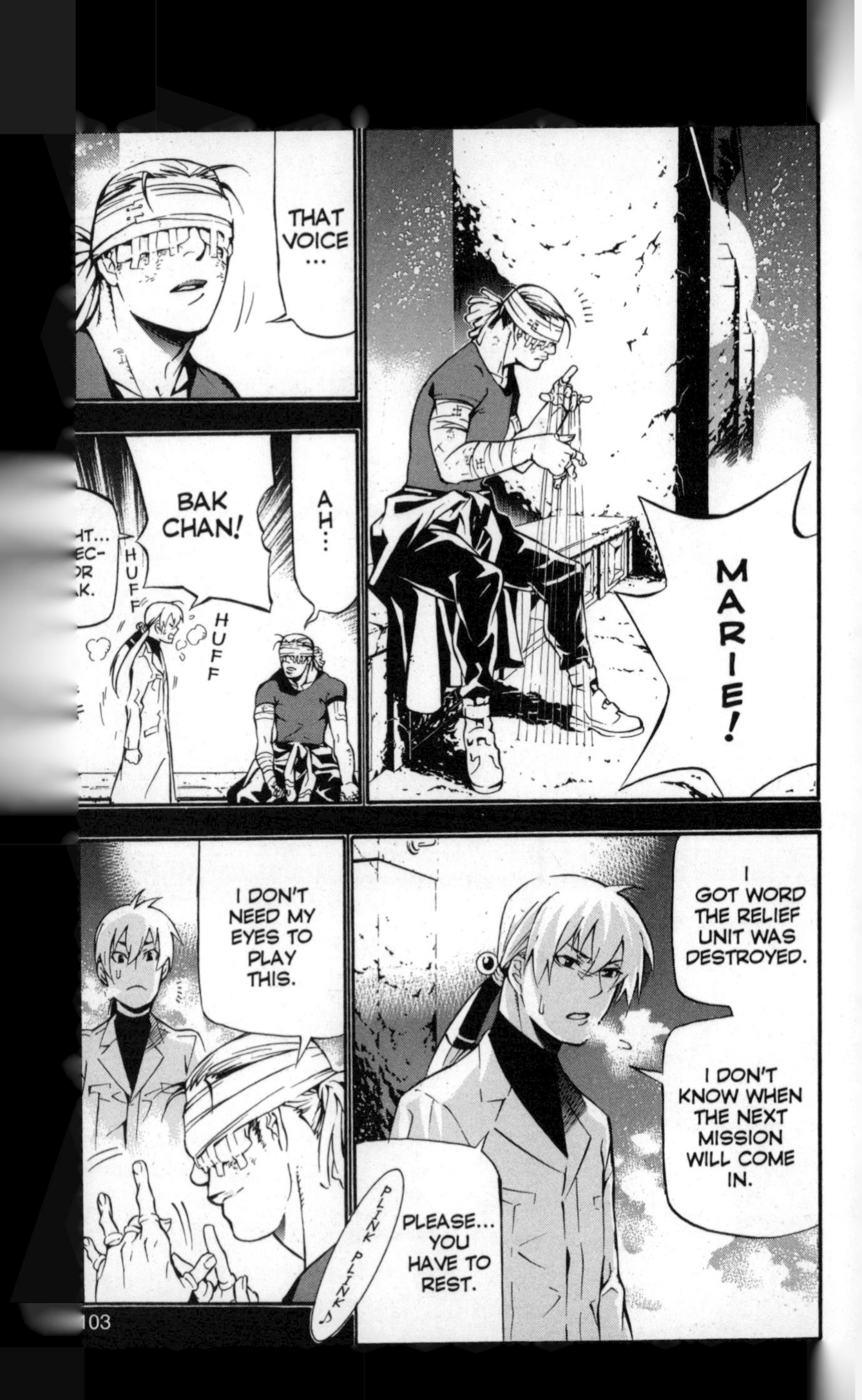
MARIE!
THAT VOICE...
AH...
BAK CHAN!
HUFF HUFF
I GOT WORD THE RELIEF UNIT WAS DESTROYED.
I DON'T KNOW WHEN THE NEXT MISSION WILL COME IN.
PLEASE... YOU HAVE TO REST.
PLINK PLINK♪
I DON'T NEED MY EYES TO PLAY THIS.

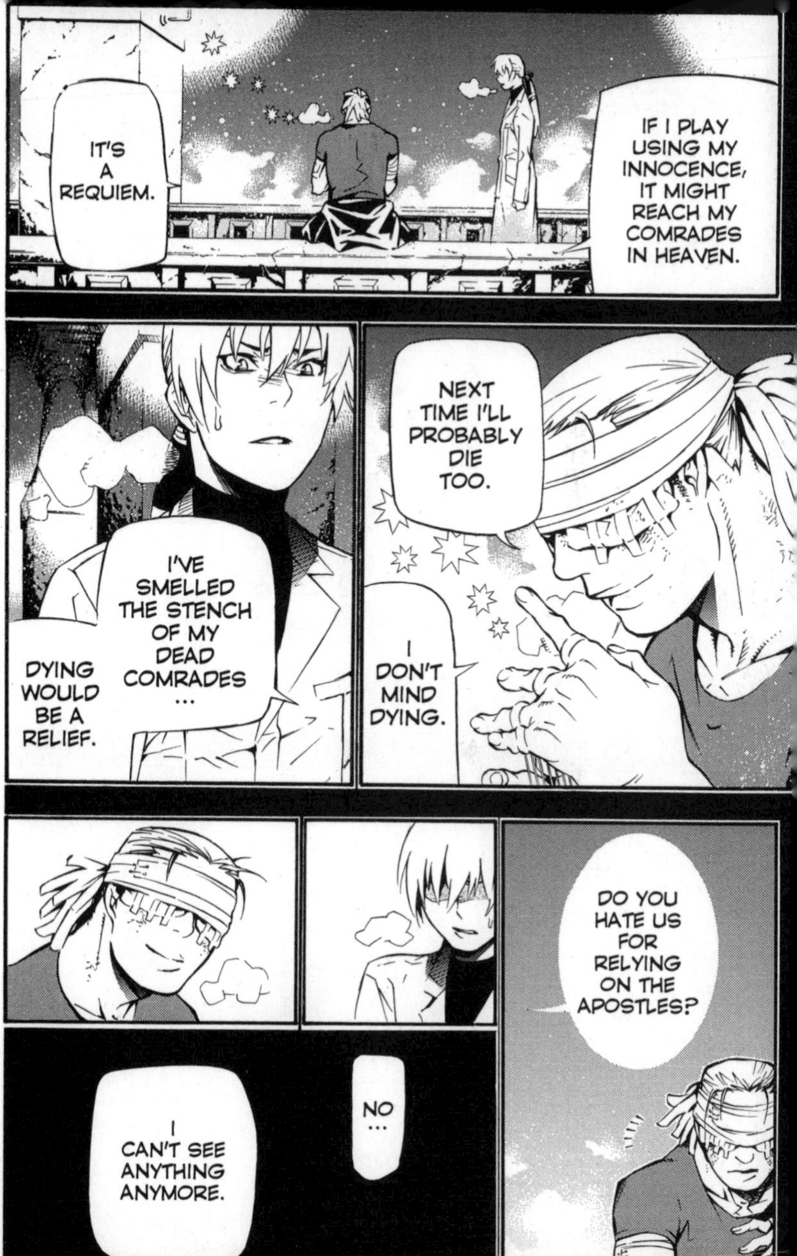
IF I PLAY USING MY INNOCENCE, IT MIGHT REACH MY COMRADES IN HEAVEN.
IT'S A REQUIEM.
NEXT TIME I'LL PROBABLY DIE TOO.
I DON'T MIND DYING.
I'VE SMELLED THE STENCH OF MY DEAD COMRADES...
DYING WOULD BE A RELIEF.
DO YOU HATE US FOR RELYING ON THE APOSTLES?
NO...
I CAN'T SEE ANYTHING ANYMORE.

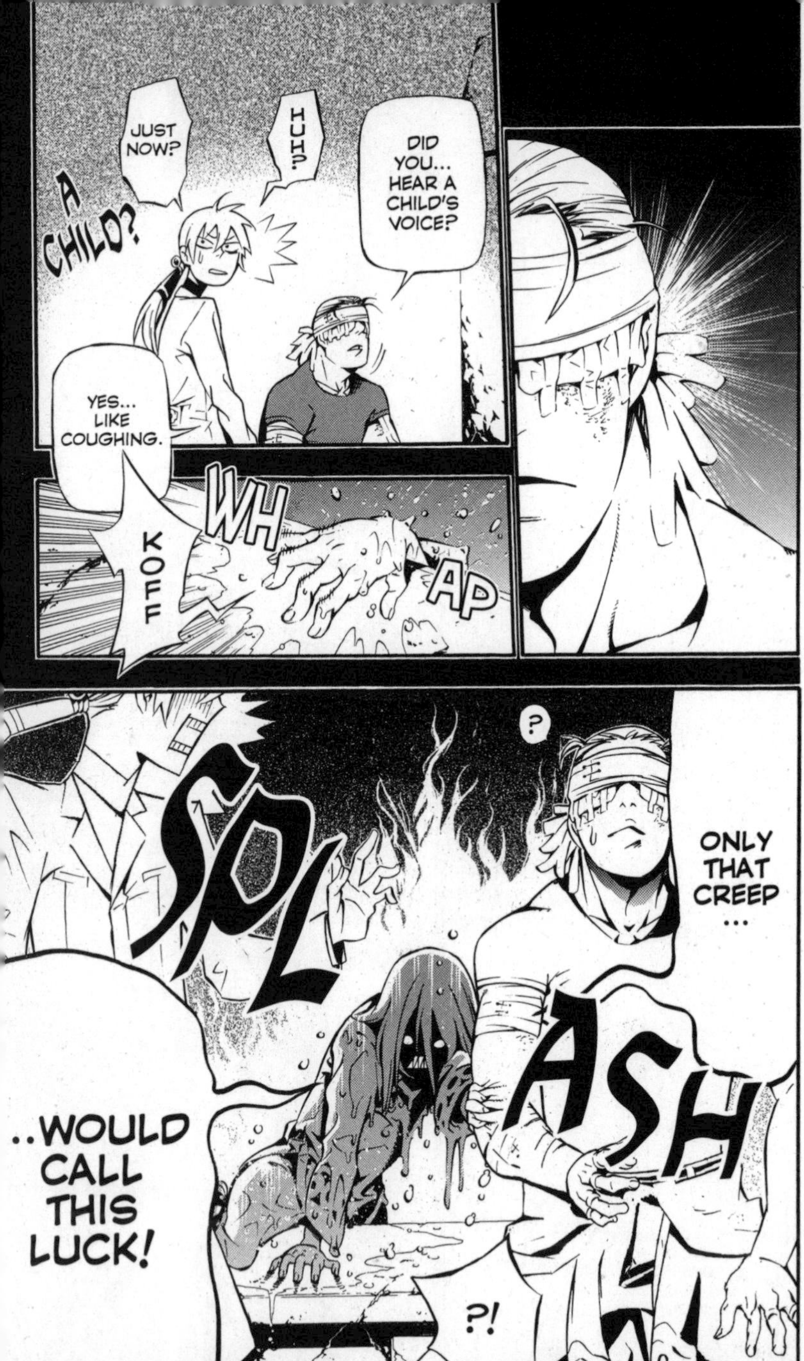
DID YOU... HEAR A CHILD'S VOICE?
HUH?
JUST NOW?
A CHILD?
YES... LIKE COUGHING.
KOFF
WHAP
?
ONLY THAT CREEP...
SPLASH
..WOULD CALL THIS LUCK!
?!

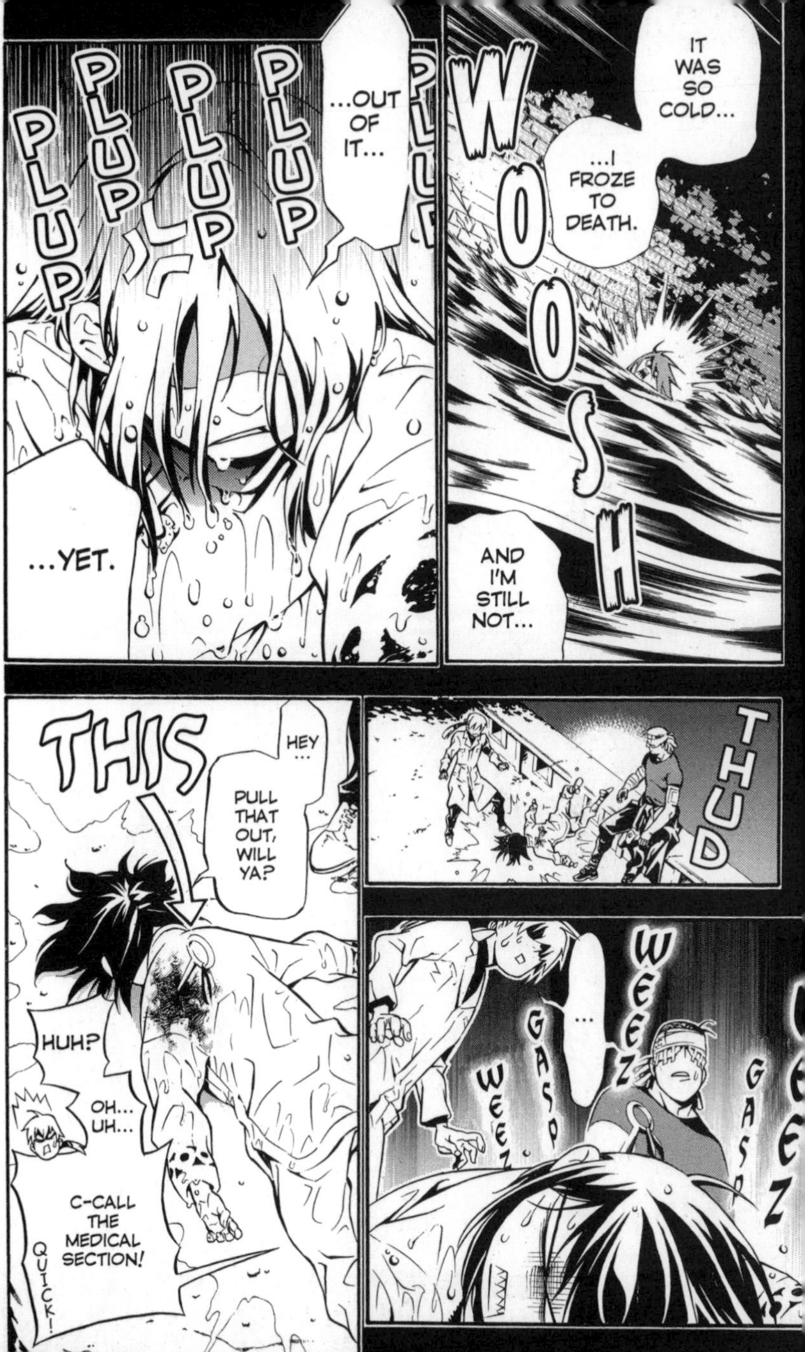
IT WAS SO COLD...
...I FROZE TO DEATH.
WOOSH
AND I'M STILL NOT...
...OUT OF IT...
PLUP PLUP PLUP PLUP PLUP
...YET.
THUD
...
GASP
WEEZ
GASP
WEEZ
THIS
HEY...
PULL THAT OUT, WILL YA?
HUH?
OH... UH...
C-CALL THE MEDICAL SECTION!
QUICK!

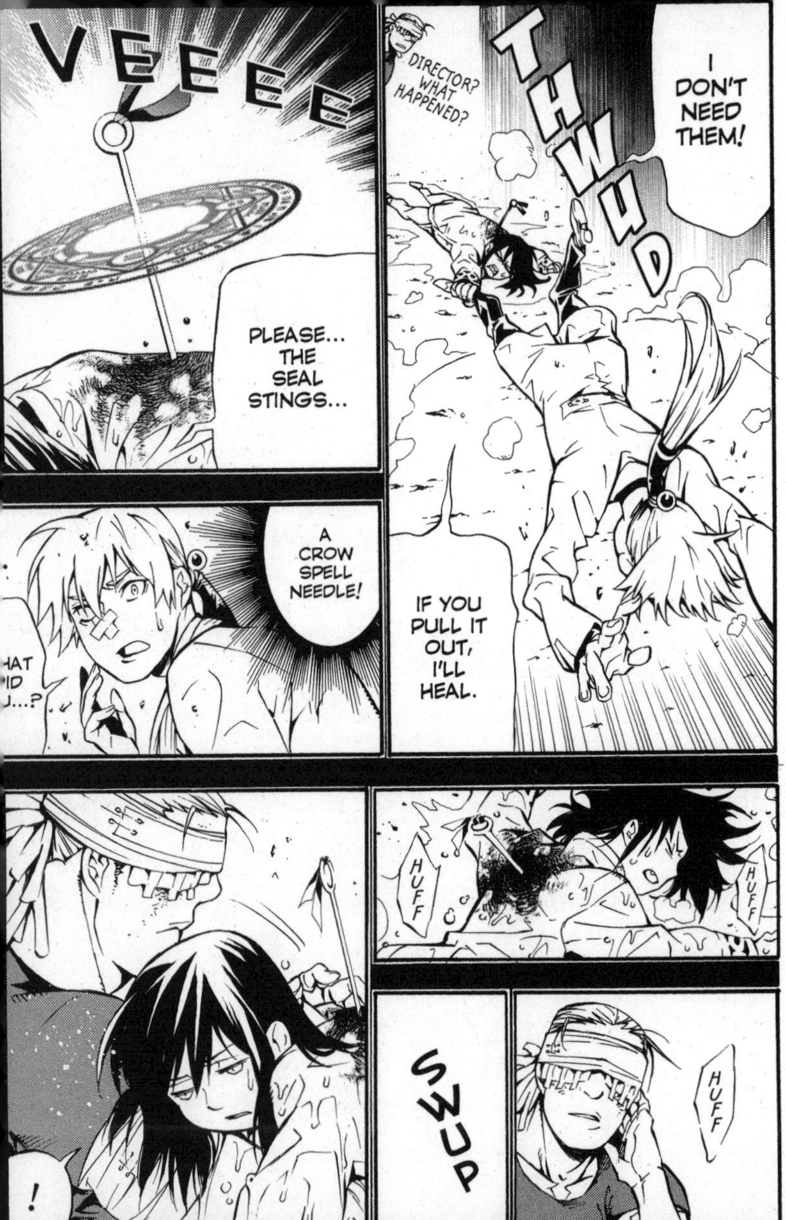

I DON'T NEED THEM!
DIRECTOR? WHAT HAPPENED?
THWUD
IF YOU PULL IT OUT, I'LL HEAL.
VEEEE
PLEASE... THE SEAL STINGS...
A CROW SPELL NEEDLE!
HUFF
HUFF
HUFF
SWUP
!

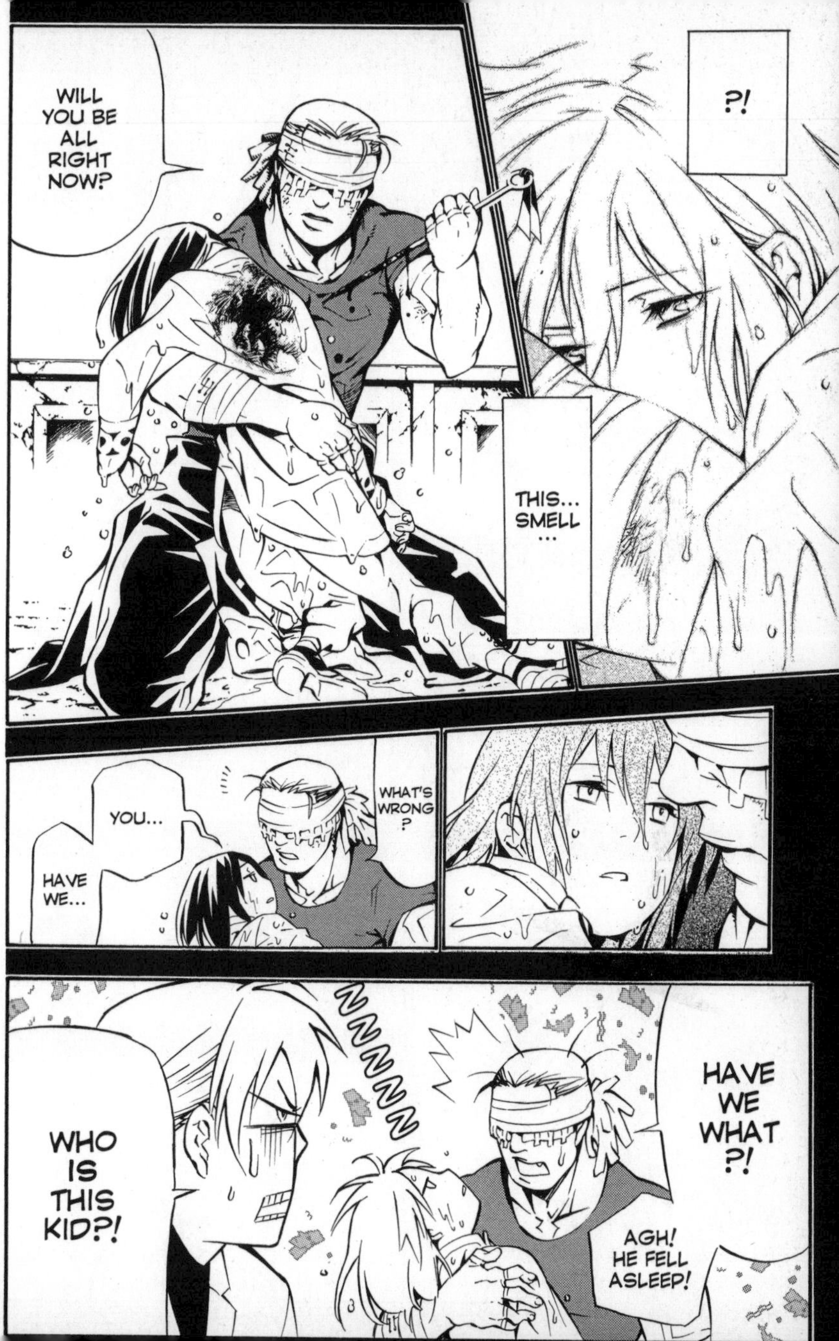
?!
THIS... SMELL ...
WILL YOU BE ALL RIGHT NOW?
WHAT'S WRONG?
YOU...
HAVE WE...
HAVE WE WHAT?!
NNNNNN
AGH! HE FELL ASLEEP!
WHO IS THIS KID?!

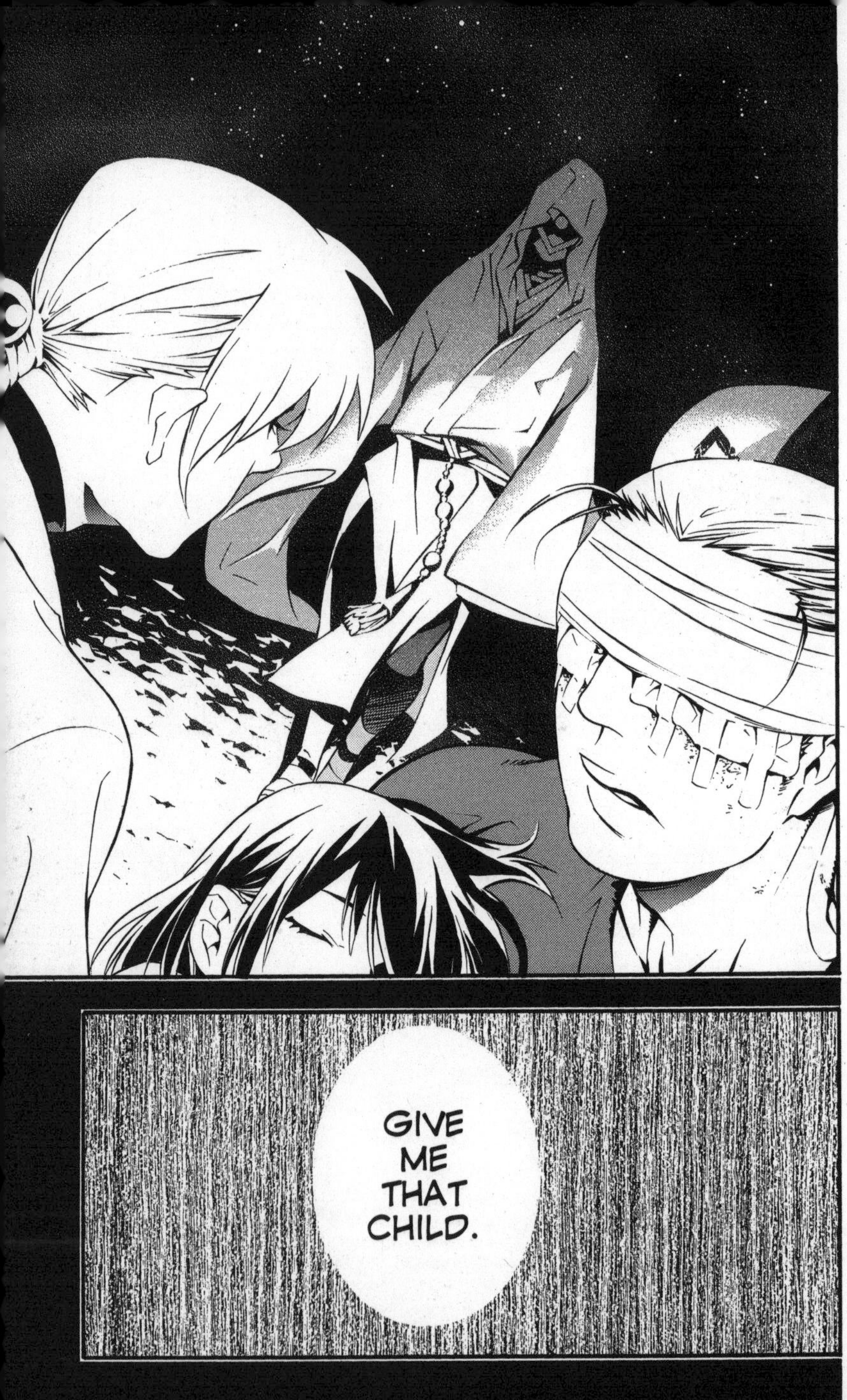
GIVE ME THAT CHILD.

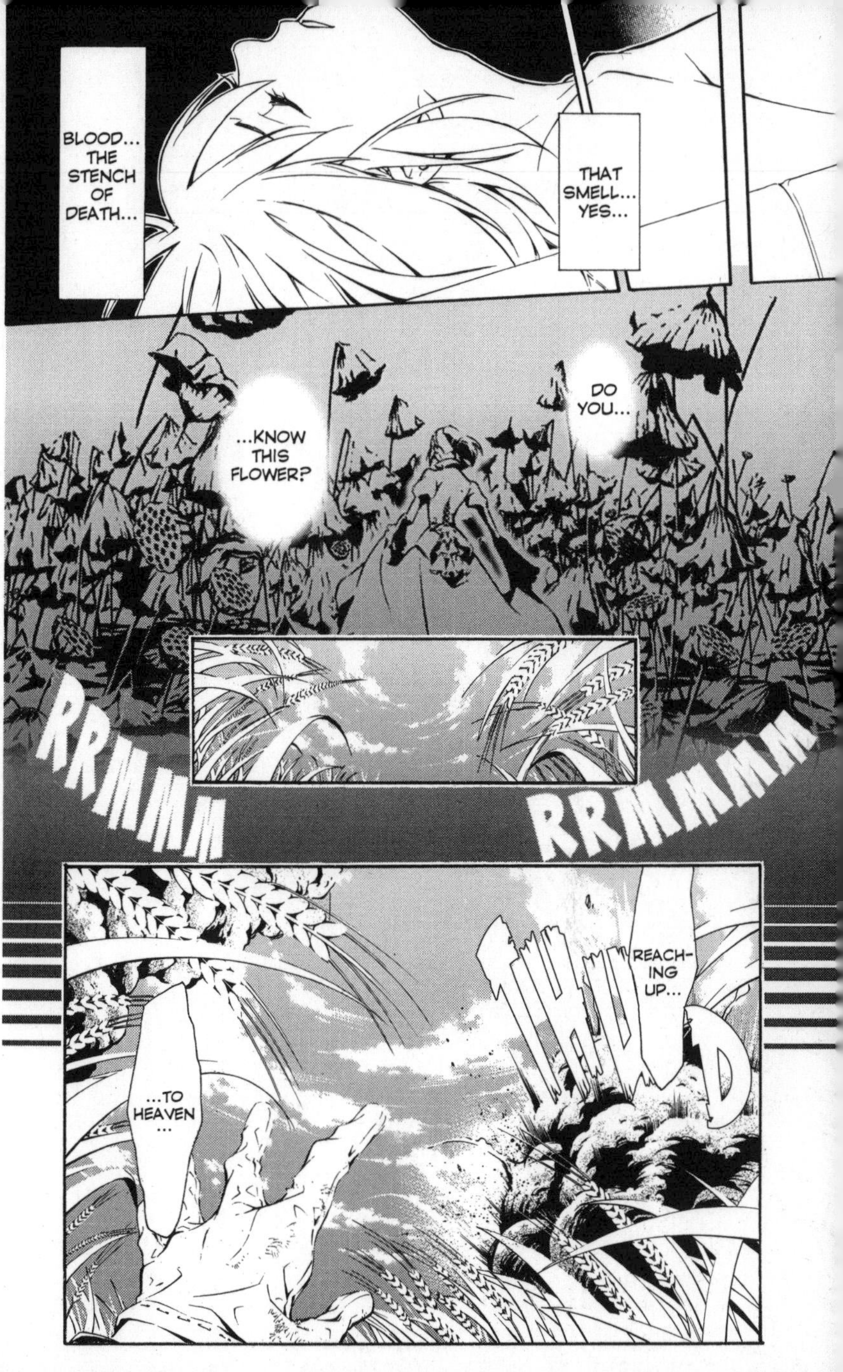
THAT SMELL... YES...
BLOOD... THE STENCH OF DEATH...
DO YOU...
...KNOW THIS FLOWER?
RRMMMMMM
RRMMMM
REACHING UP...
THUD
...TO HEAVEN...

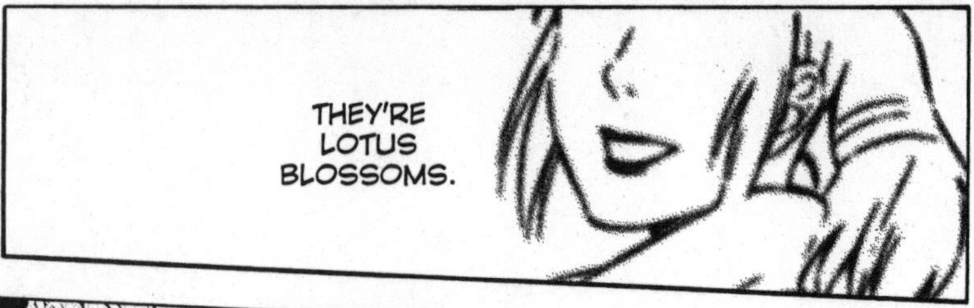
THEY'RE LOTUS BLOSSOMS.

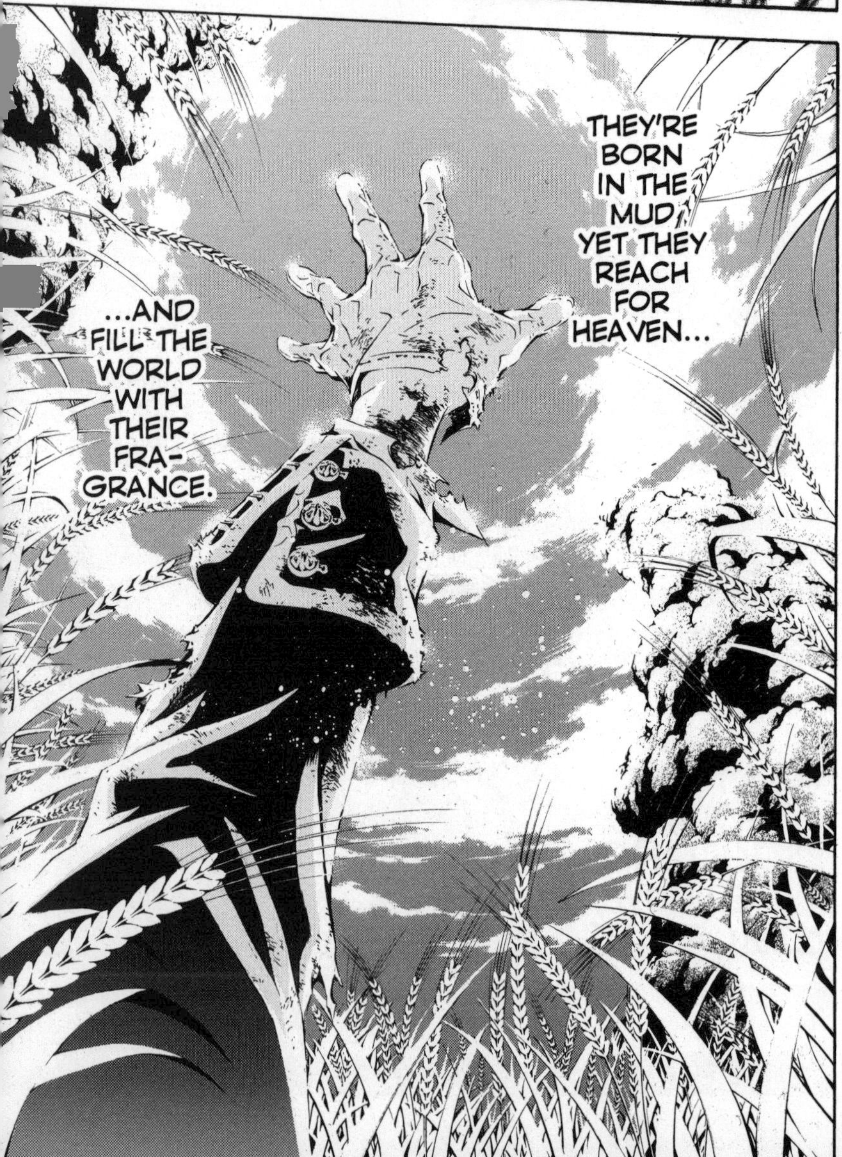
THEY'RE BORN IN THE MUD, YET THEY REACH FOR HEAVEN...
...AND FILL THE WORLD WITH THEIR FRA-GRANCE.

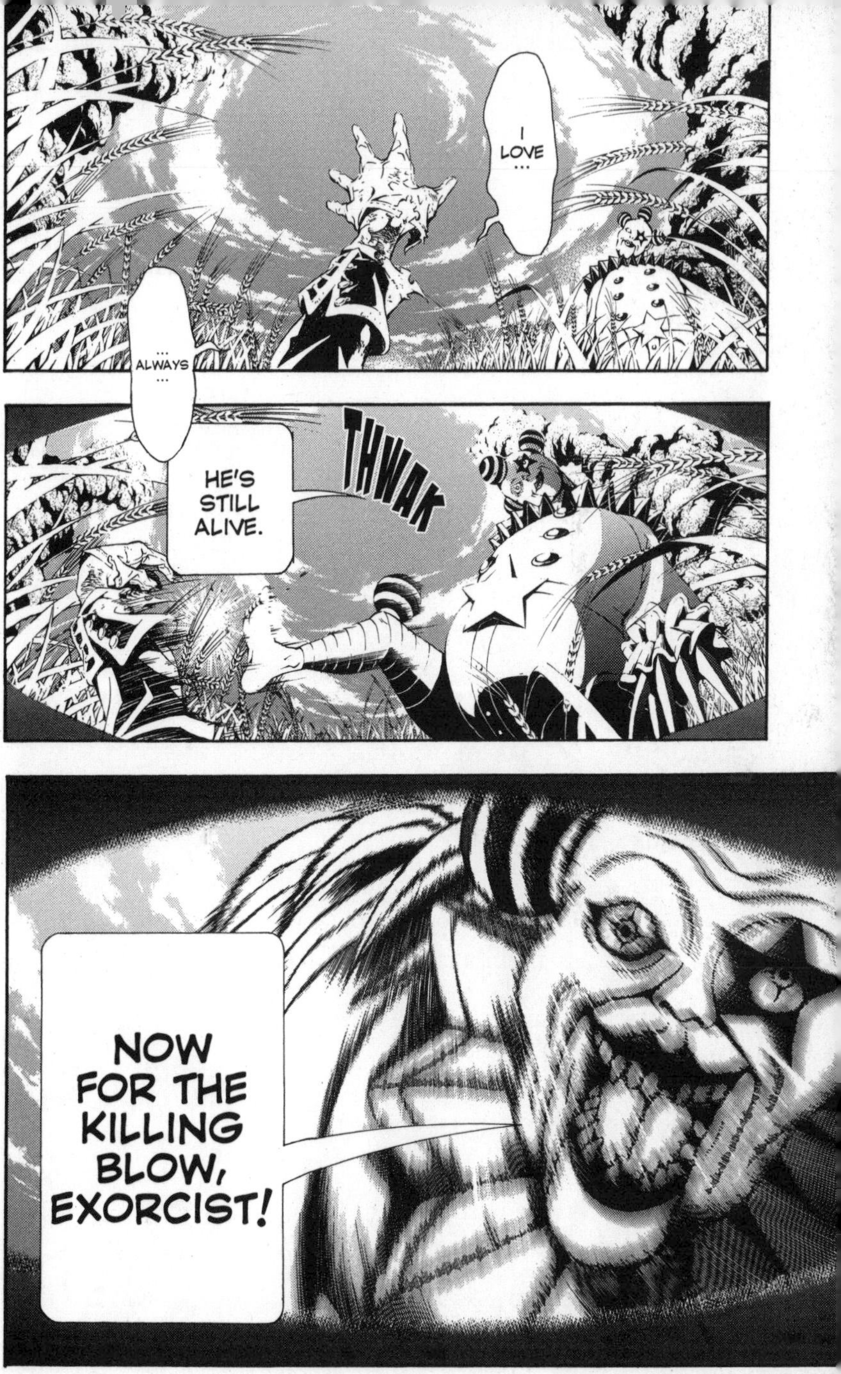
I LOVE ...
... ALWAYS ...
THWAK
HE'S STILL ALIVE.
NOW FOR THE KILLING BLOW, EXORCIST!

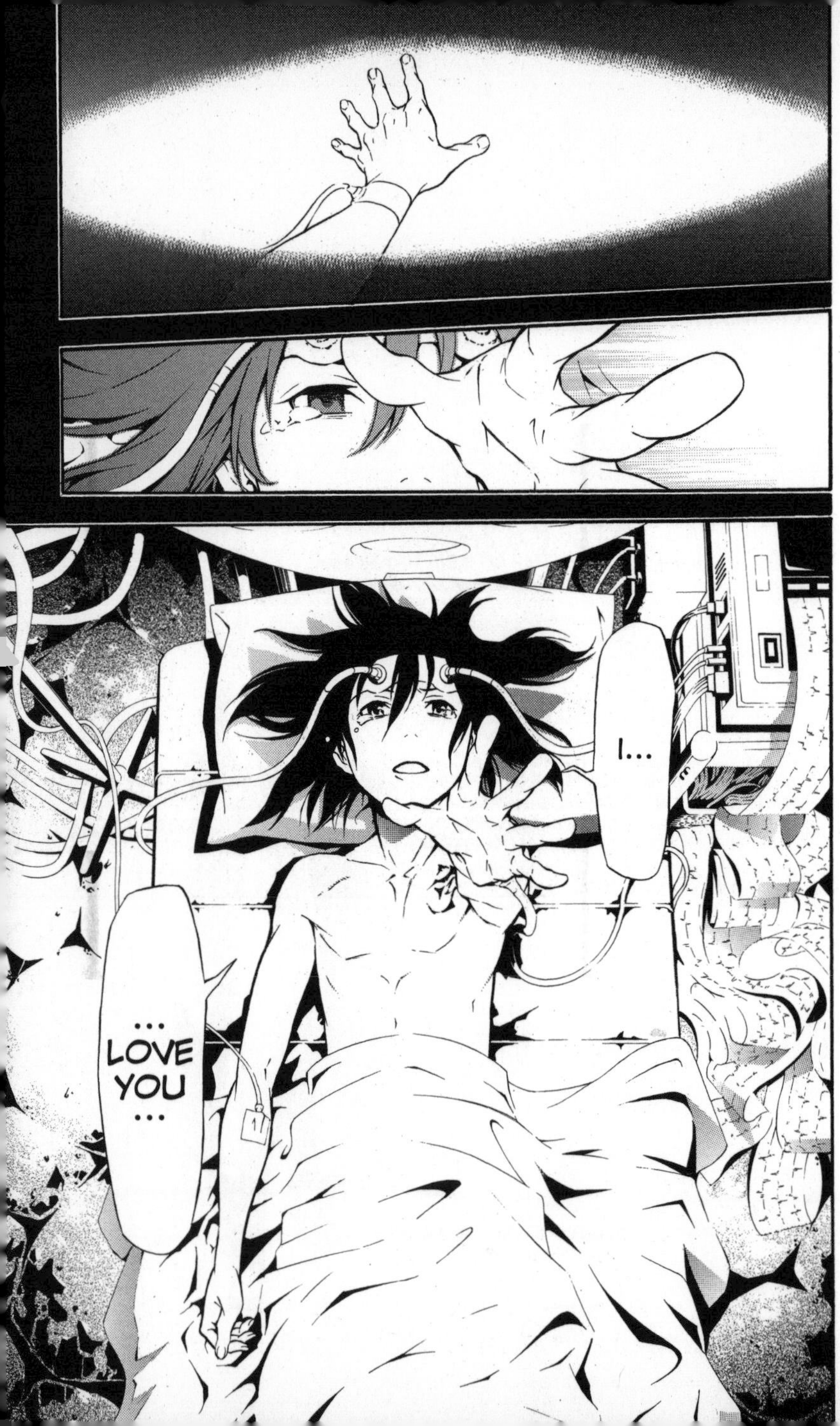
I...
...LOVE YOU...

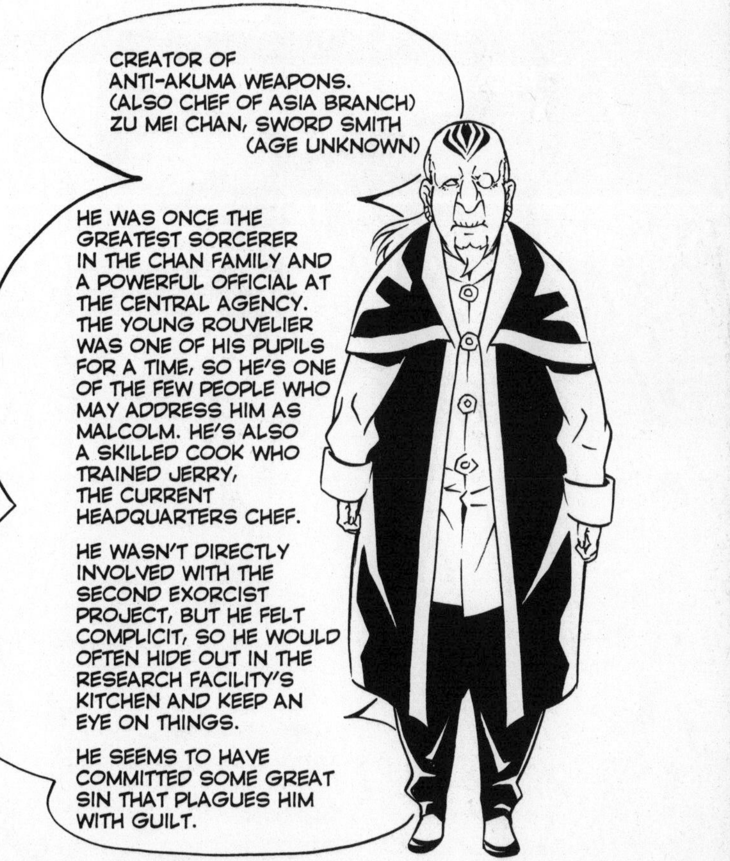
CREATOR OF ANTI-AKUMA WEAPONS. (ALSO CHEF OF ASIA BRANCH)
ZU MEI CHAN, SWORD SMITH
(AGE UNKNOWN)
HE WAS ONCE THE GREATEST SORCERER IN THE CHAN FAMILY AND A POWERFUL OFFICIAL AT THE CENTRAL AGENCY. THE YOUNG ROUVELIER WAS ONE OF HIS PUPILS FOR A TIME, SO HE'S ONE OF THE FEW PEOPLE WHO MAY ADDRESS HIM AS MALCOLM. HE'S ALSO A SKILLED COOK WHO TRAINED JERRY, THE CURRENT HEADQUARTERS CHEF.
HE WASN'T DIRECTLY INVOLVED WITH THE SECOND EXORCIST PROJECT, BUT HE FELT COMPLICIT, SO HE WOULD OFTEN HIDE OUT IN THE RESEARCH FACILITY'S KITCHEN AND KEEP AN EYE ON THINGS.
HE SEEMS TO HAVE COMMITTED SOME GREAT SIN THAT PLAGUES HIM WITH GUILT.

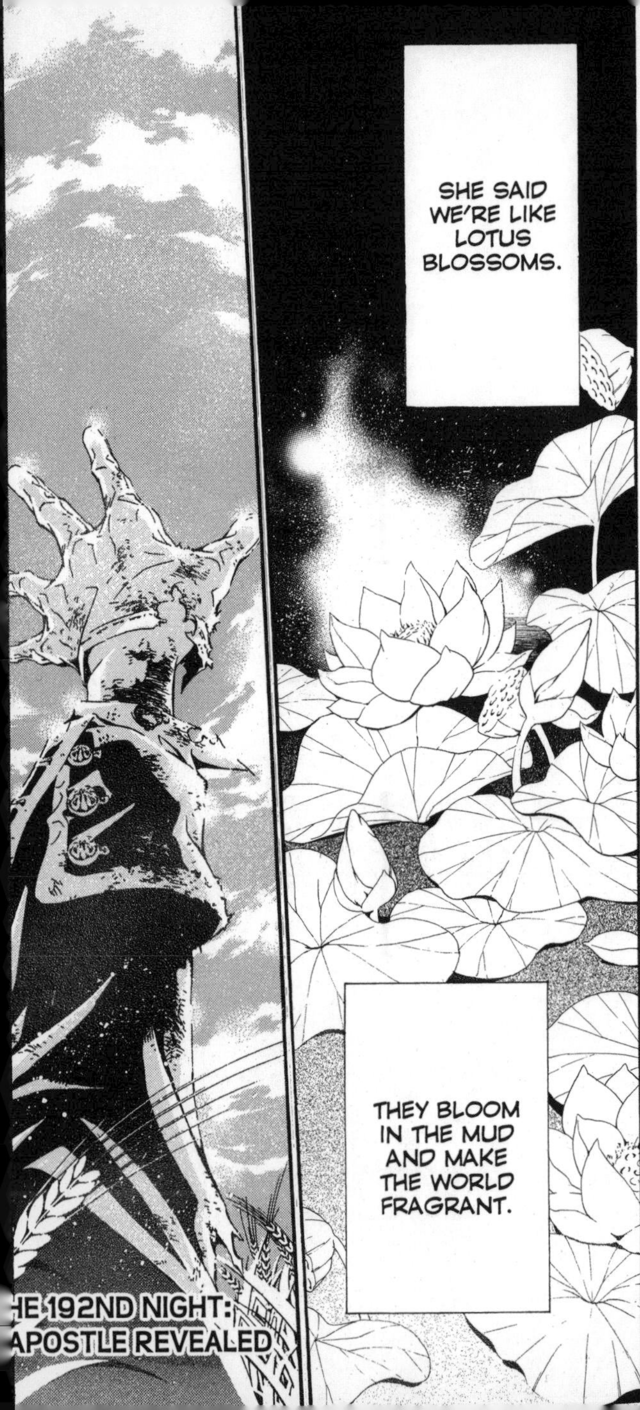
SHE SAID WE'RE LIKE LOTUS BLOSSOMS.
THEY BLOOM IN THE MUD AND MAKE THE WORLD FRAGRANT.
HE 192ND NIGHT:
APOSTLE REVEALED

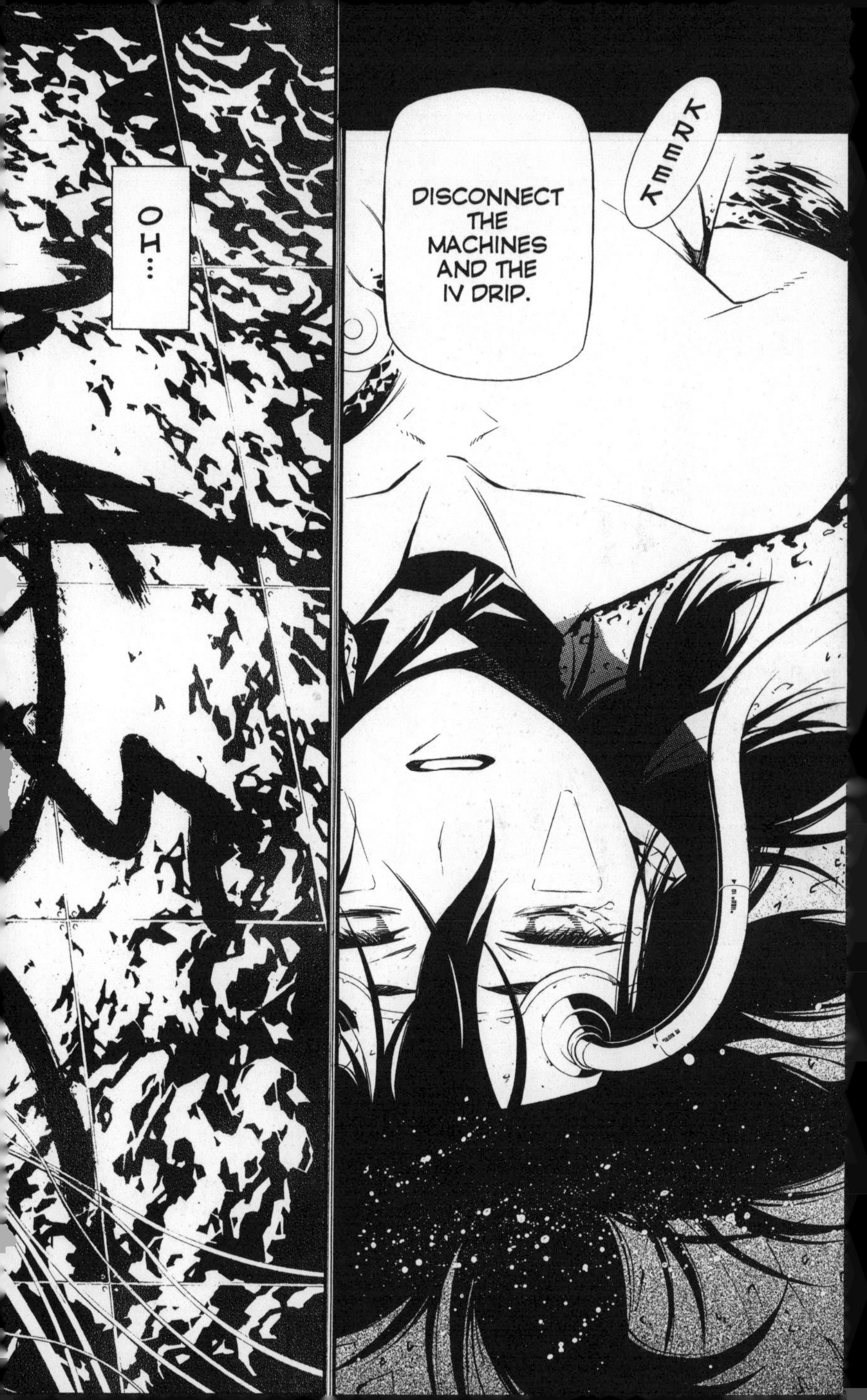
KREEK
DISCONNECT THE MACHINES AND THE IV DRIP.
OH…

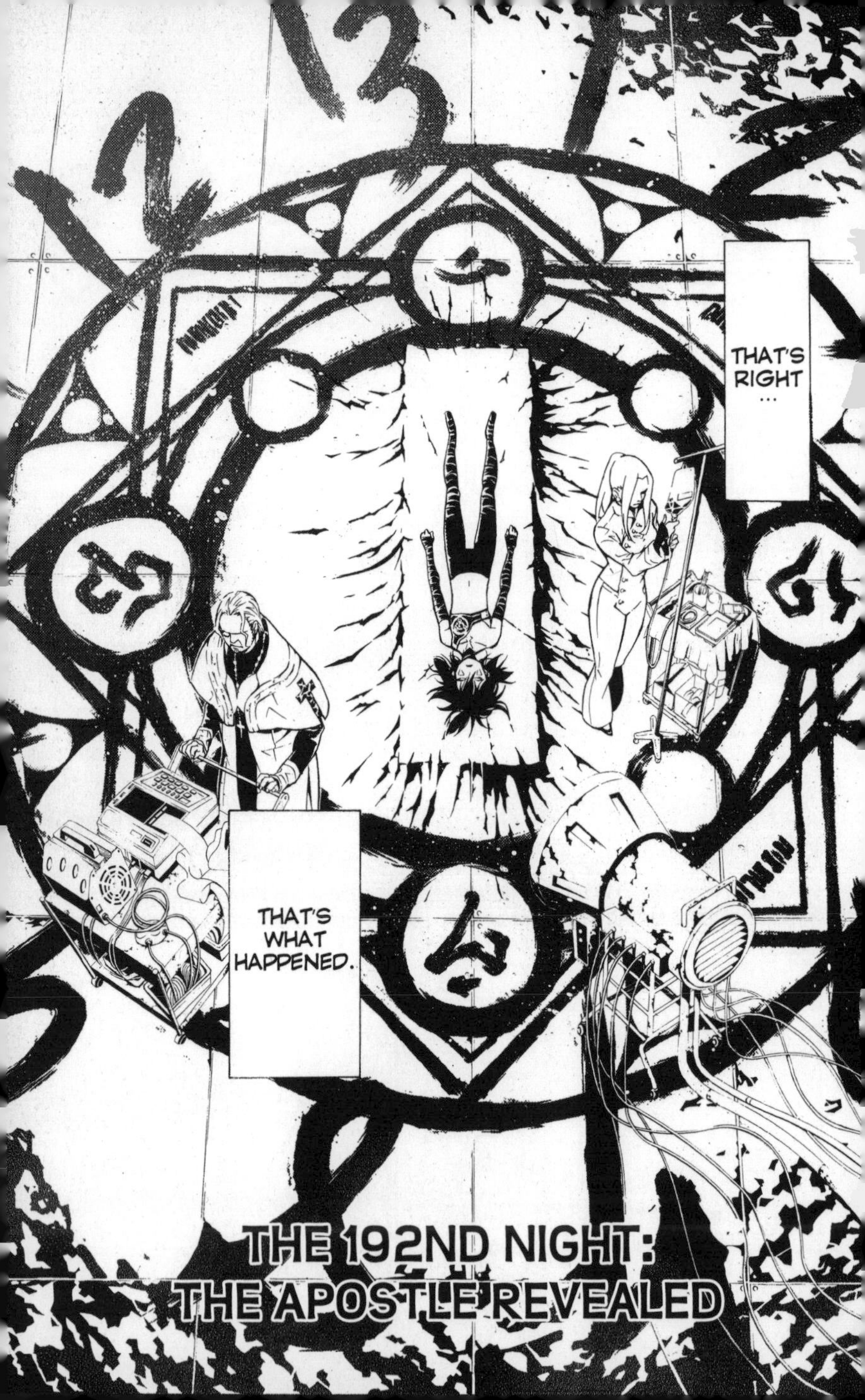
THAT'S RIGHT ...
THAT'S WHAT HAPPENED.
THE 192ND NIGHT: THE APOSTLE REVEALED

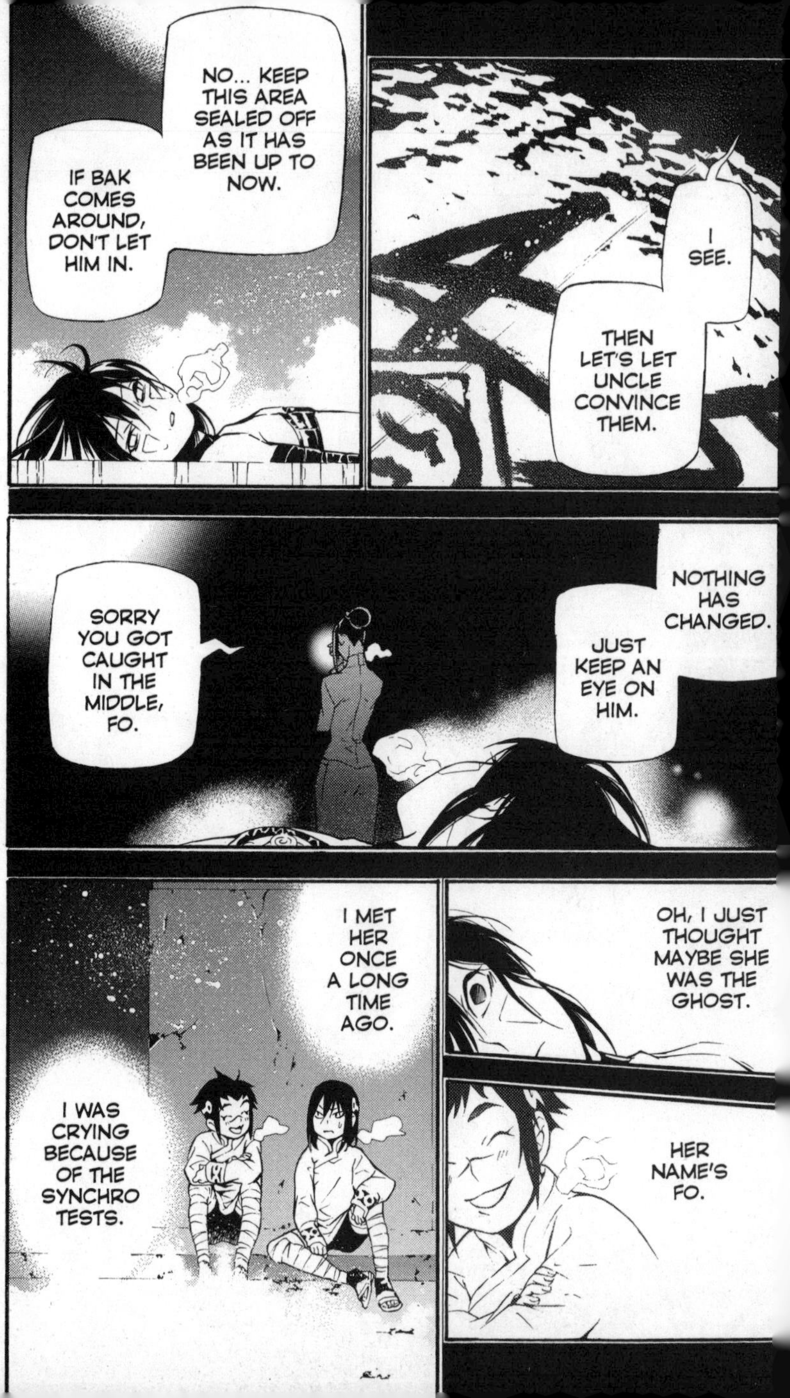
I SEE.
THEN LET'S LET UNCLE CONVINCE THEM.
NO... KEEP THIS AREA SEALED OFF AS IT HAS BEEN UP TO NOW.
IF BAK COMES AROUND, DON'T LET HIM IN.
NOTHING HAS CHANGED.
JUST KEEP AN EYE ON HIM.
SORRY YOU GOT CAUGHT IN THE MIDDLE, FO.
OH, I JUST THOUGHT MAYBE SHE WAS THE GHOST.
HER NAME'S FO.
I MET HER ONCE A LONG TIME AGO.
I WAS CRYING BECAUSE OF THE SYNCHRO TESTS.

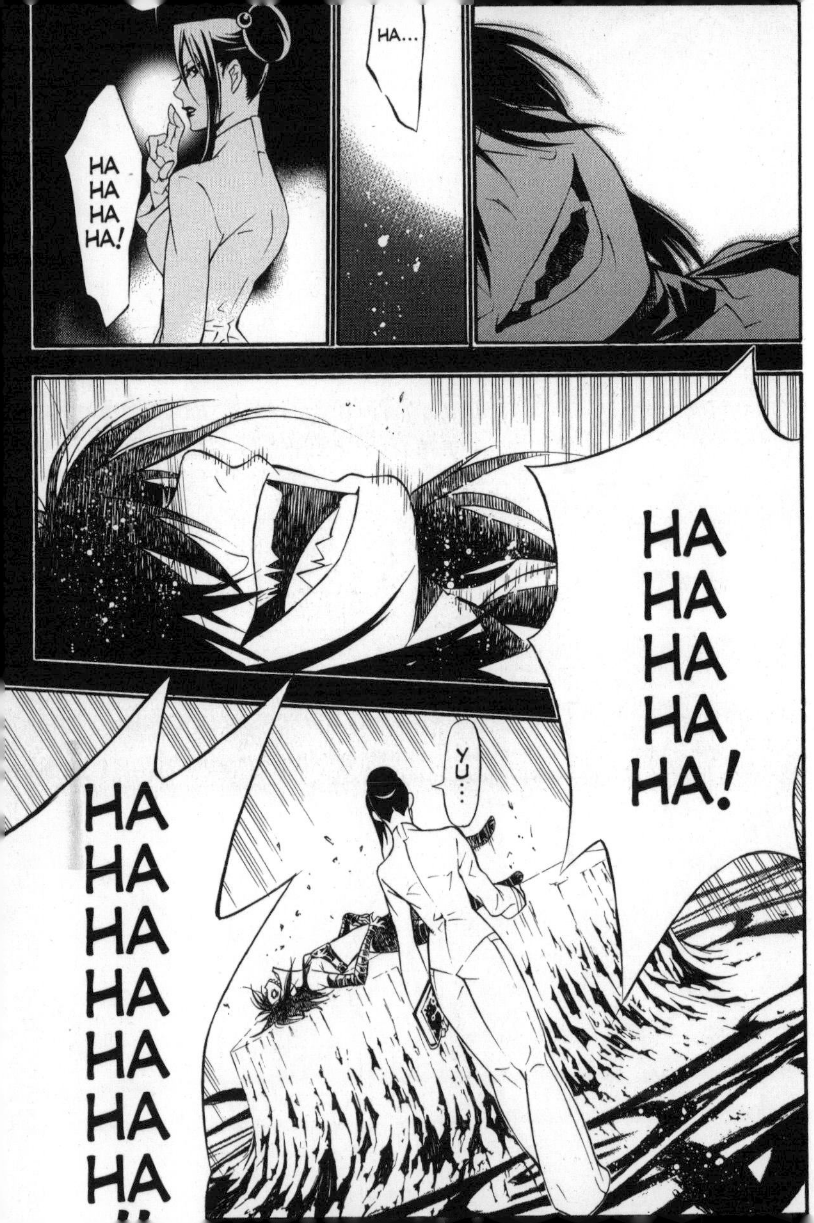
HA...
HA HA HA HA!
HA HA HA HA HA!
YU...
HA HA HA HA HA HA HA HA!

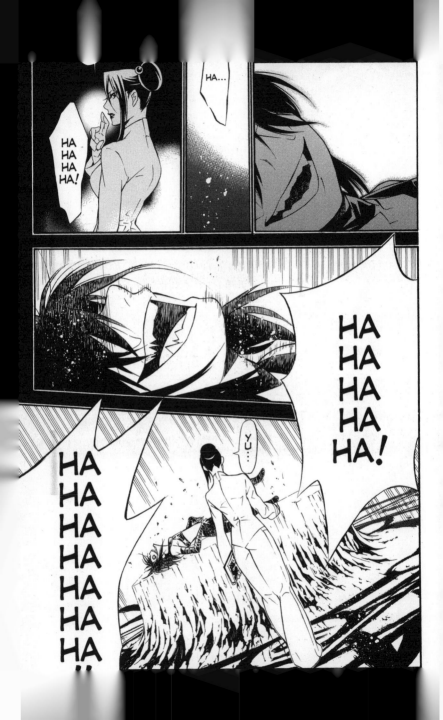

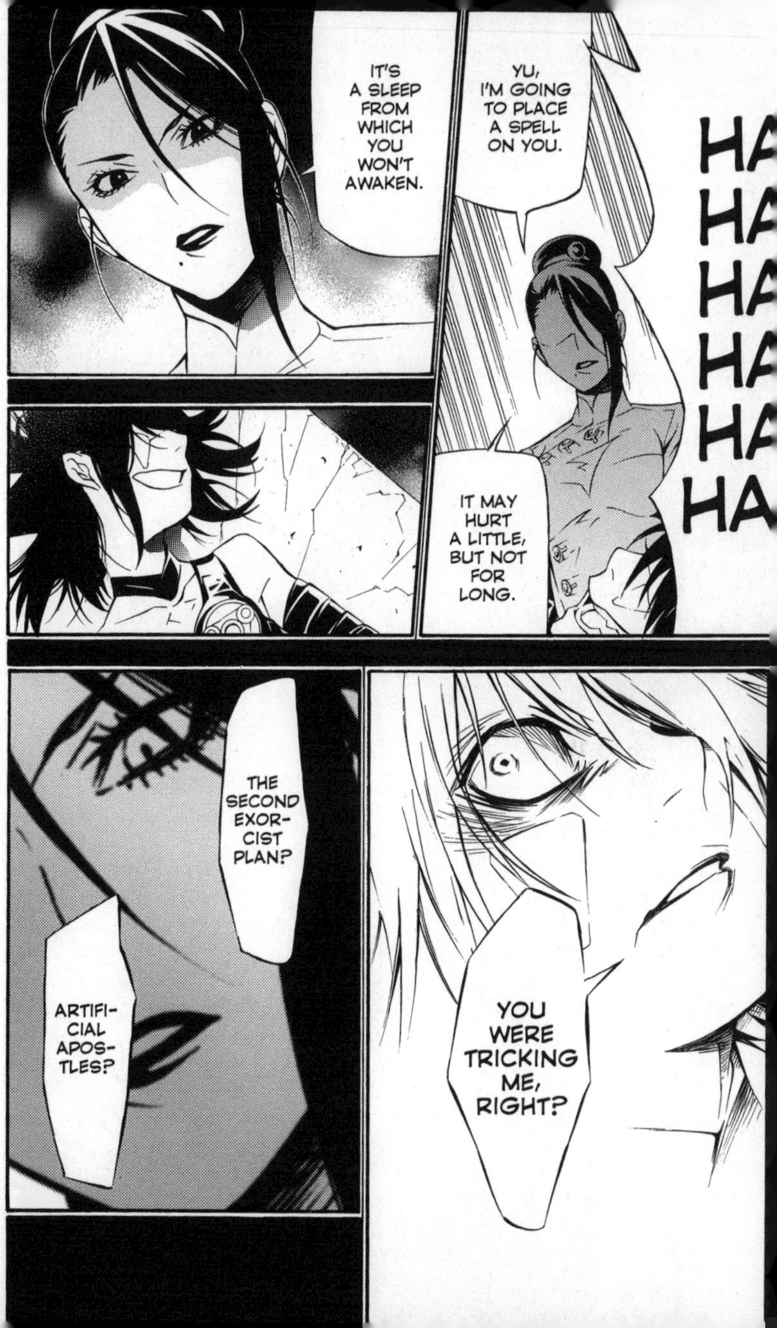
HA
HA
HA
HA
HA
HA
YU, I'M GOING TO PLACE A SPELL ON YOU.
IT MAY HURT A LITTLE, BUT NOT FOR LONG.
IT'S A SLEEP FROM WHICH YOU WON'T AWAKEN.
YOU WERE TRICKING ME, RIGHT?
THE SECOND EXORCIST PLAN?
ARTIFICIAL APOSTLES?

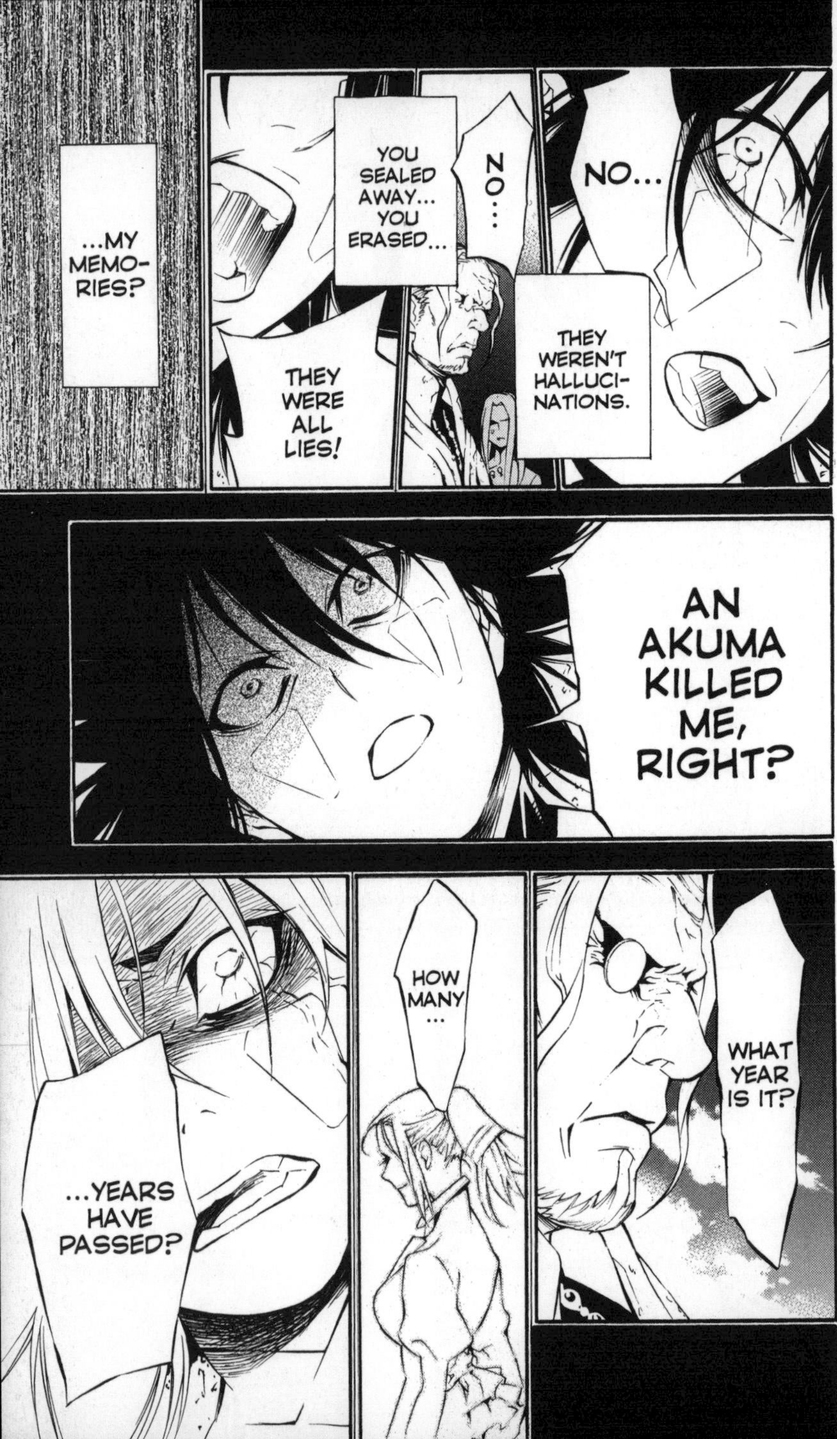
NO...
THEY WEREN'T HALLUCINATIONS.
NO...
YOU SEALED AWAY... YOU ERASED...
THEY WERE ALL LIES!
...MY MEMORIES?
AN AKUMA KILLED ME, RIGHT?
WHAT YEAR IS IT?
HOW MANY...
...YEARS HAVE PASSED?

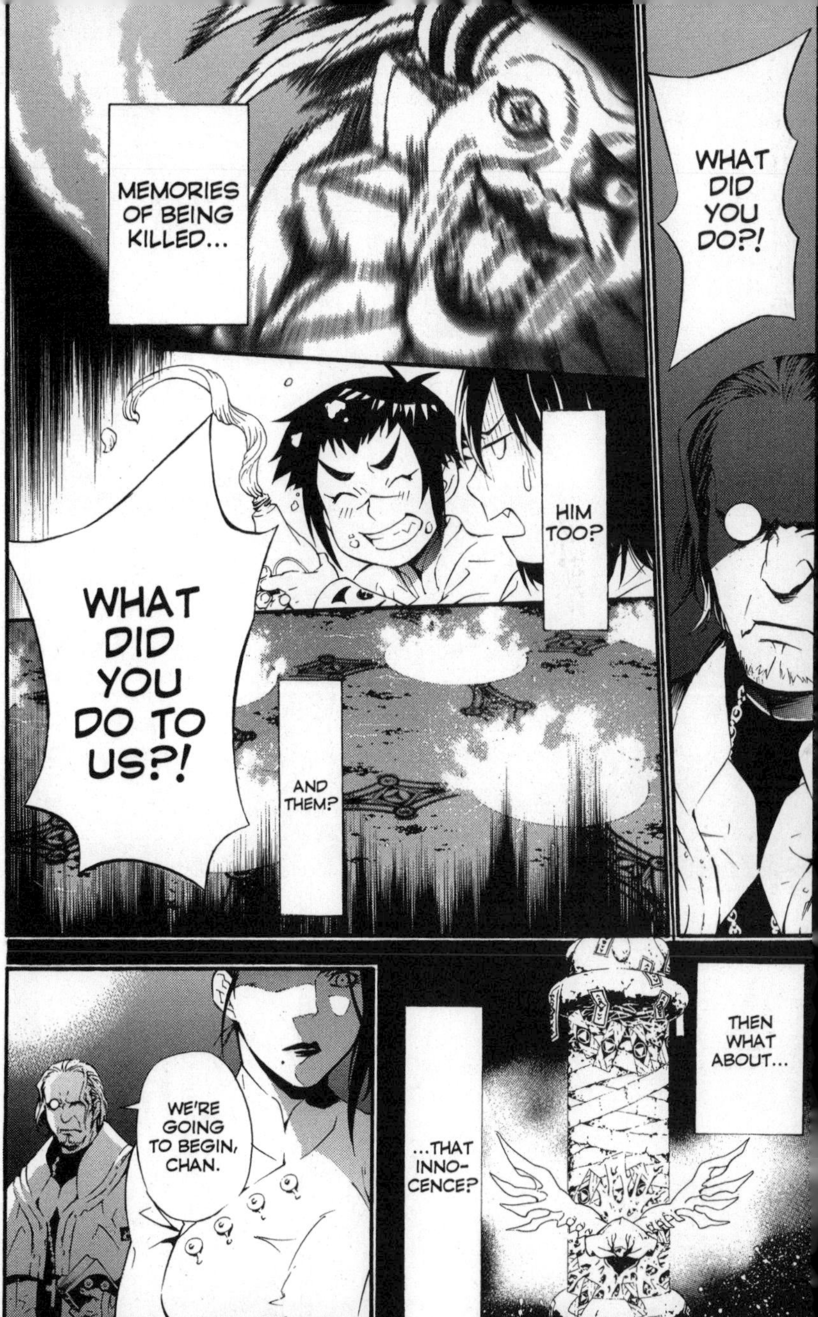
WHAT DID YOU DO?!
MEMORIES OF BEING KILLED...
HIM TOO?
WHAT DID YOU DO TO US?!
AND THEM?
THEN WHAT ABOUT...
...THAT INNO-CENCE?
WE'RE GOING TO BEGIN, CHAN.

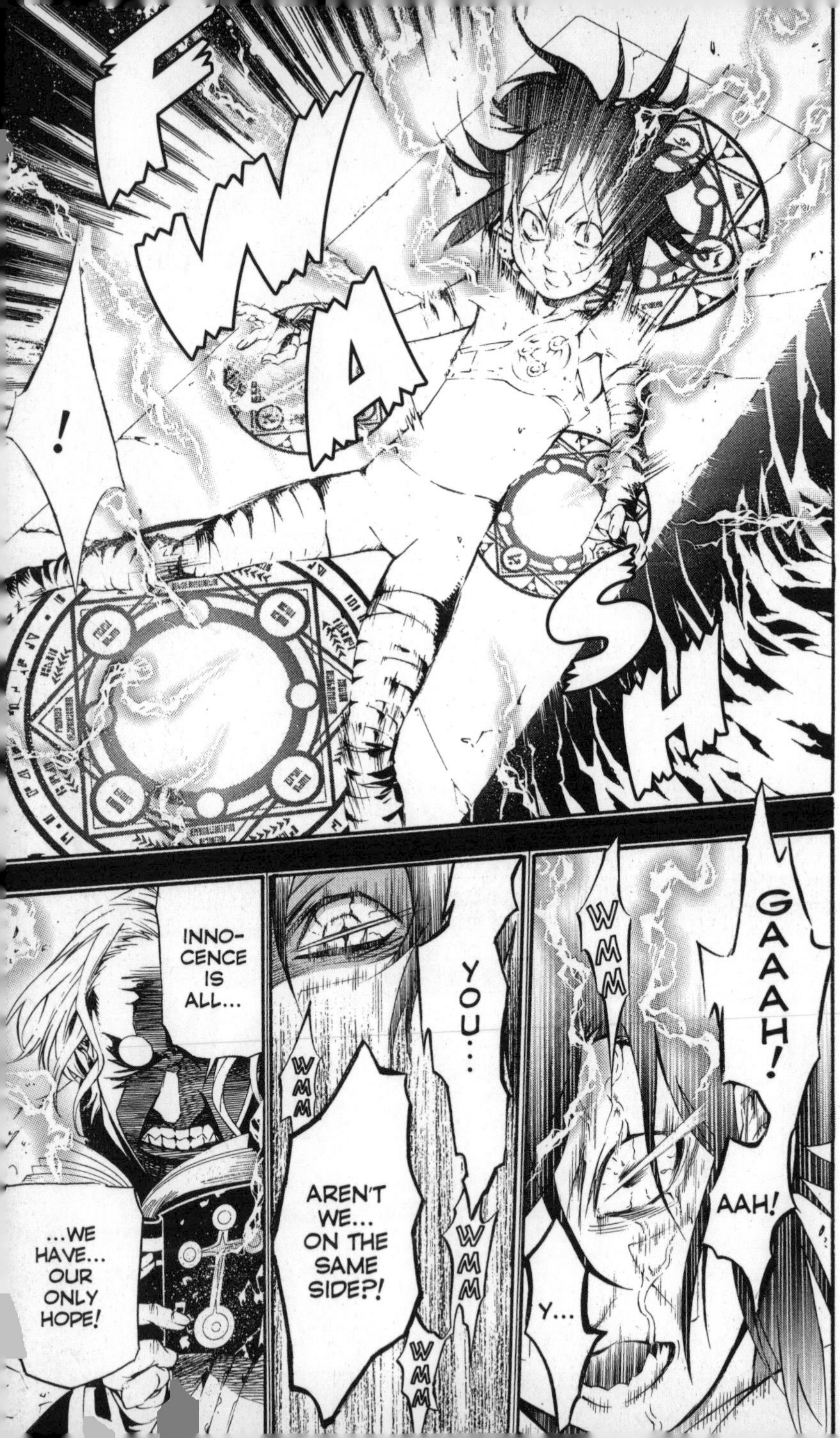

FWASH
!
GAAAH!
WMM
AAH!
Y...
YOU...
WMM
AREN'T WE... ON THE SAME SIDE?!
WMM
WMM
INNOCENCE IS ALL...
...WE HAVE... OUR ONLY HOPE!

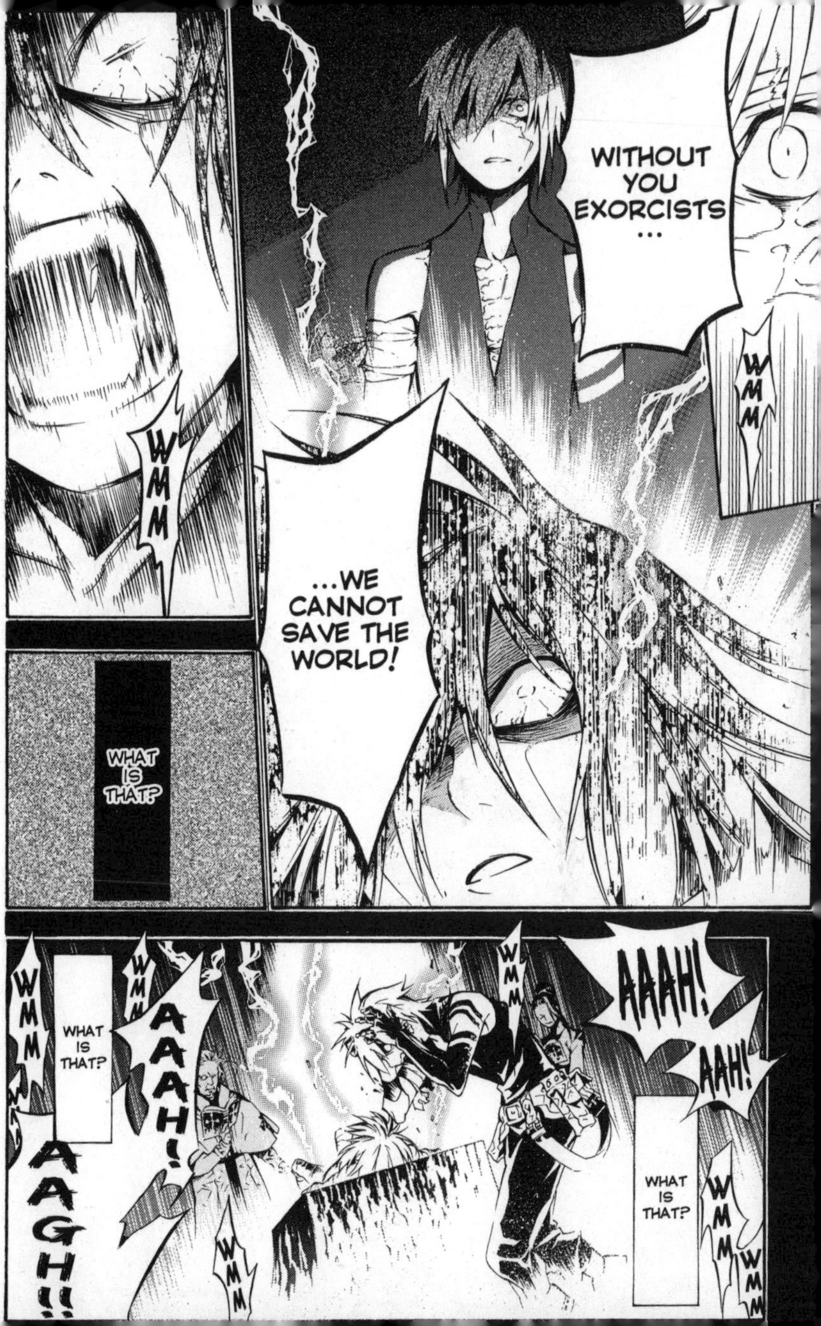

WITHOUT YOU EXORCISTS...
WMM
...WE CANNOT SAVE THE WORLD!
WMM
WHAT IS THAT?
WMM
AAAH!
AAH!
WHAT IS THAT?
WMM
WMM
WMM
AAAH!
WHAT IS THAT?
WMM
AAGH!!
WMM

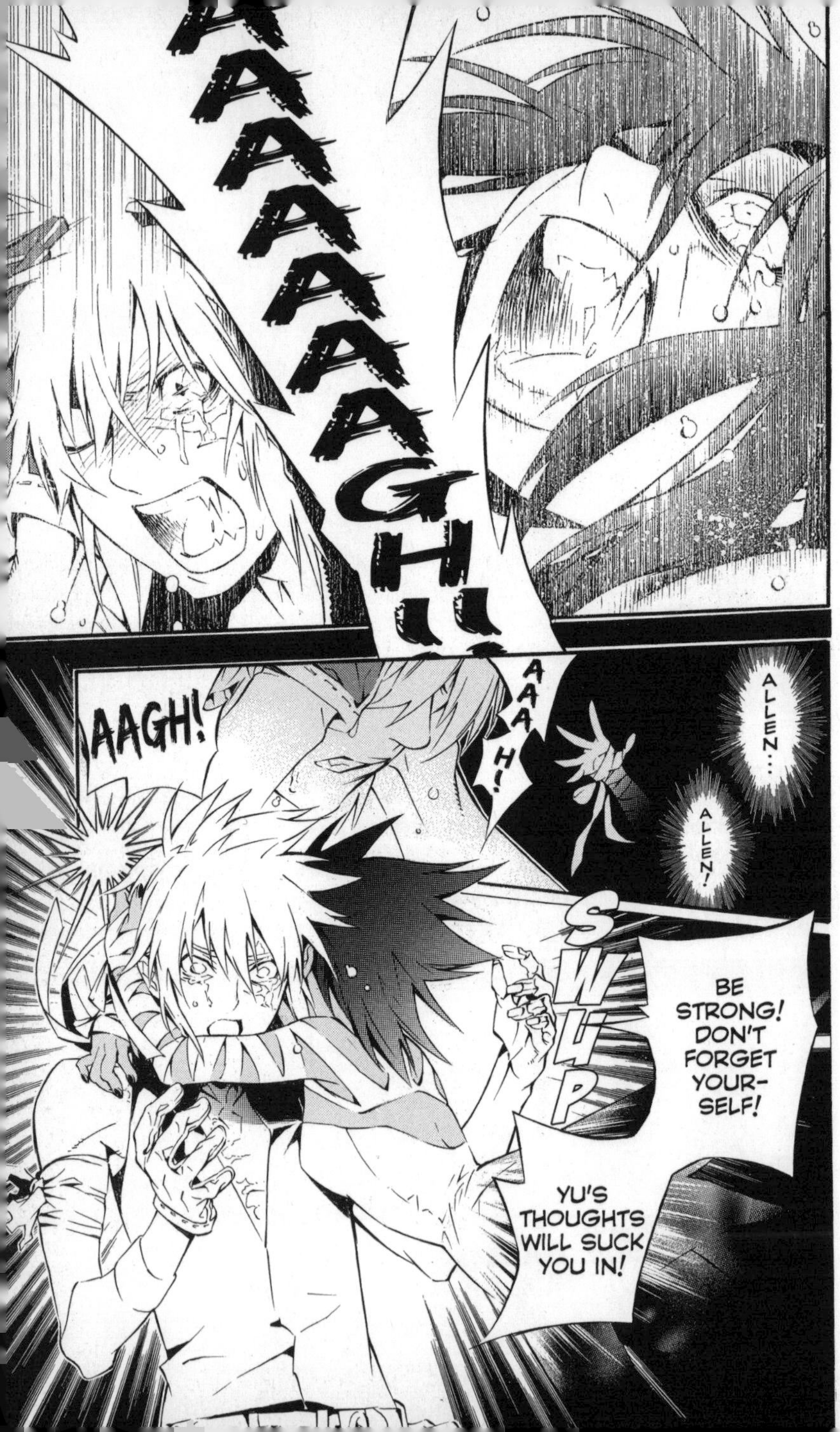
AAAAAAAGH!!
AAAH!
AAGH!
ALLEN...
ALLEN!
SWUP
BE STRONG! DON'T FORGET YOURSELF!
YU'S THOUGHTS WILL SUCK YOU IN!

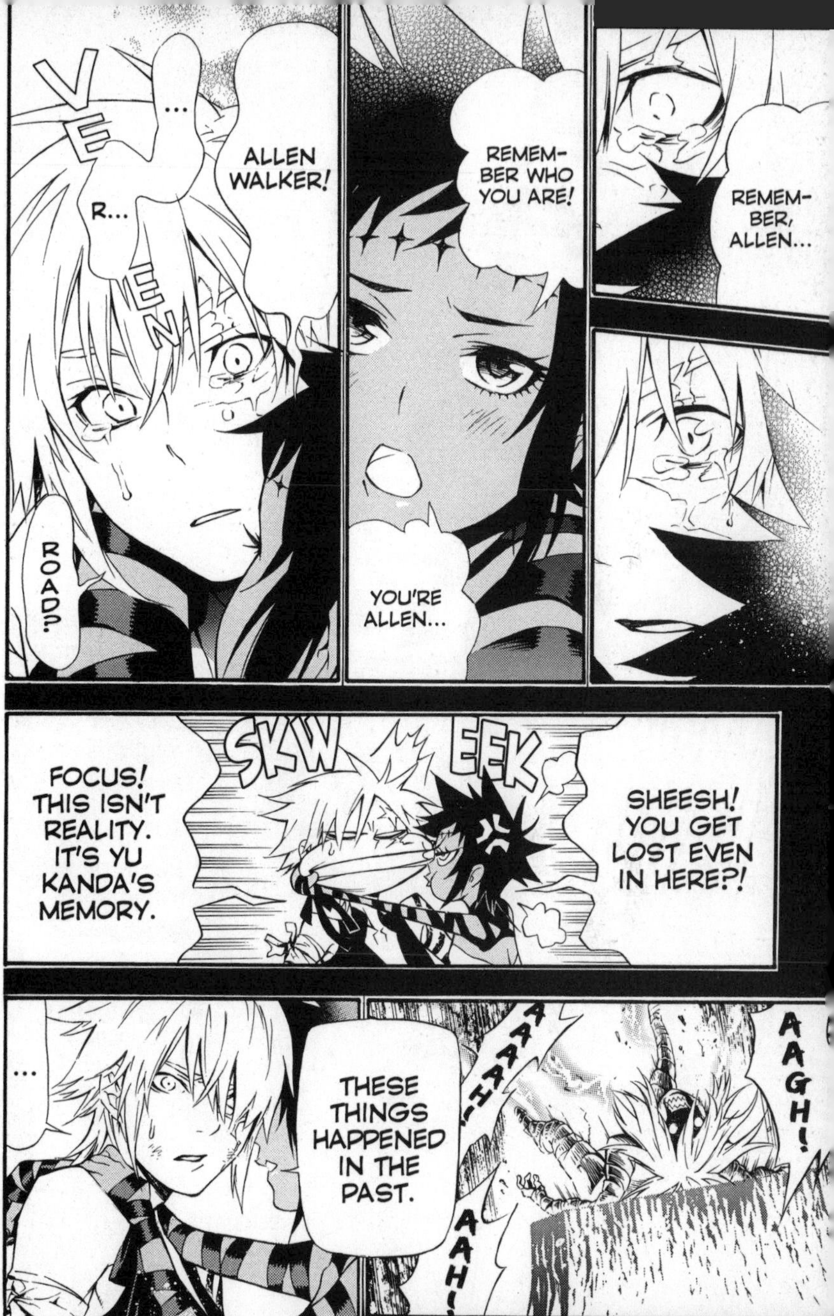
REMEM-BER, ALLEN...
REMEM-BER WHO YOU ARE!
YOU'RE ALLEN...
ALLEN WALKER!
...
VE
R...
EN
ROAD?
SHEESH! YOU GET LOST EVEN IN HERE?!
SKW EEK
FOCUS! THIS ISN'T REALITY. IT'S YU KANDA'S MEMORY.
AAGH!
AAAAH!
AAH!
THESE THINGS HAPPENED IN THE PAST.
...

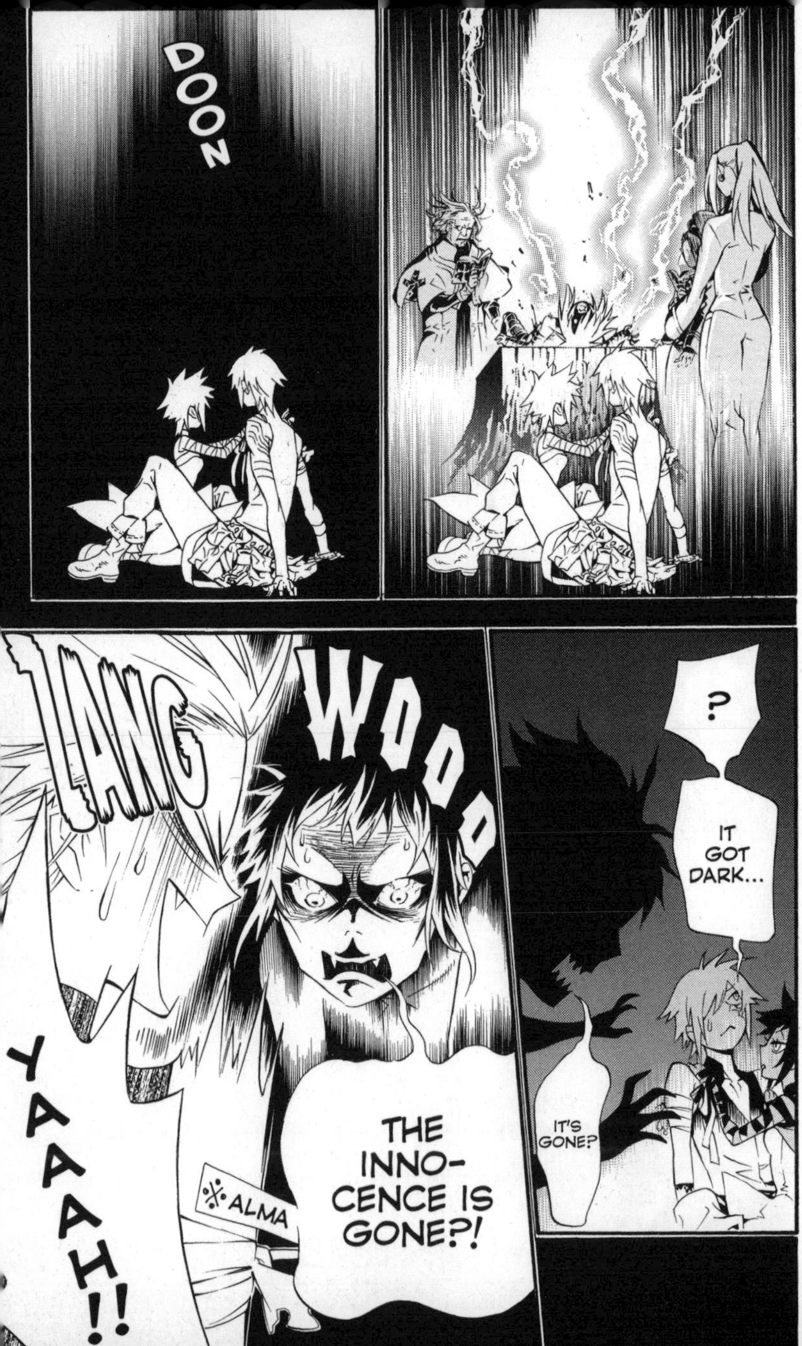
DOON
?
IT GOT DARK...
IT'S GONE?
WOOO
CLANG
THE INNOCENCE IS GONE?!
※ALMA
YAAAAH!!

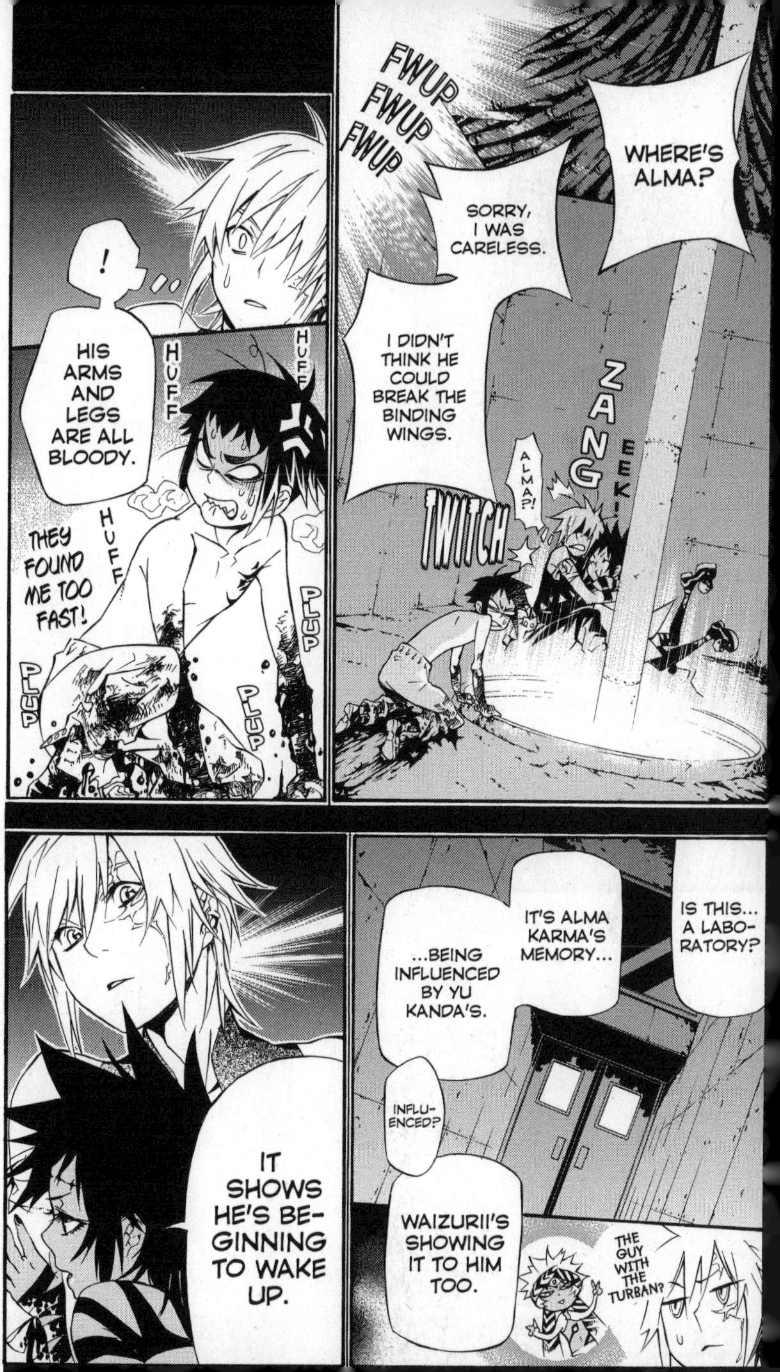
FWUP FWUP FWUP
WHERE'S ALMA?
SORRY, I WAS CARELESS.
I DIDN'T THINK HE COULD BREAK THE BINDING WINGS.
ZANG
EEK!
ALMA?!
TWITCH
!...
HUFF
HUFF
HIS ARMS AND LEGS ARE ALL BLOODY.
HUFF
THEY FOUND ME TOO FAST!
PLUP
PLUP
PLUP
IS THIS... A LABO-RATORY?
IT'S ALMA KARMA'S MEMORY...
...BEING INFLUENCED BY YU KANDA'S.
INFLU-ENCED?
WAIZURII'S SHOWING IT TO HIM TOO.
THE GUY WITH THE TURBAN?
IT SHOWS HE'S BE-GINNING TO WAKE UP.

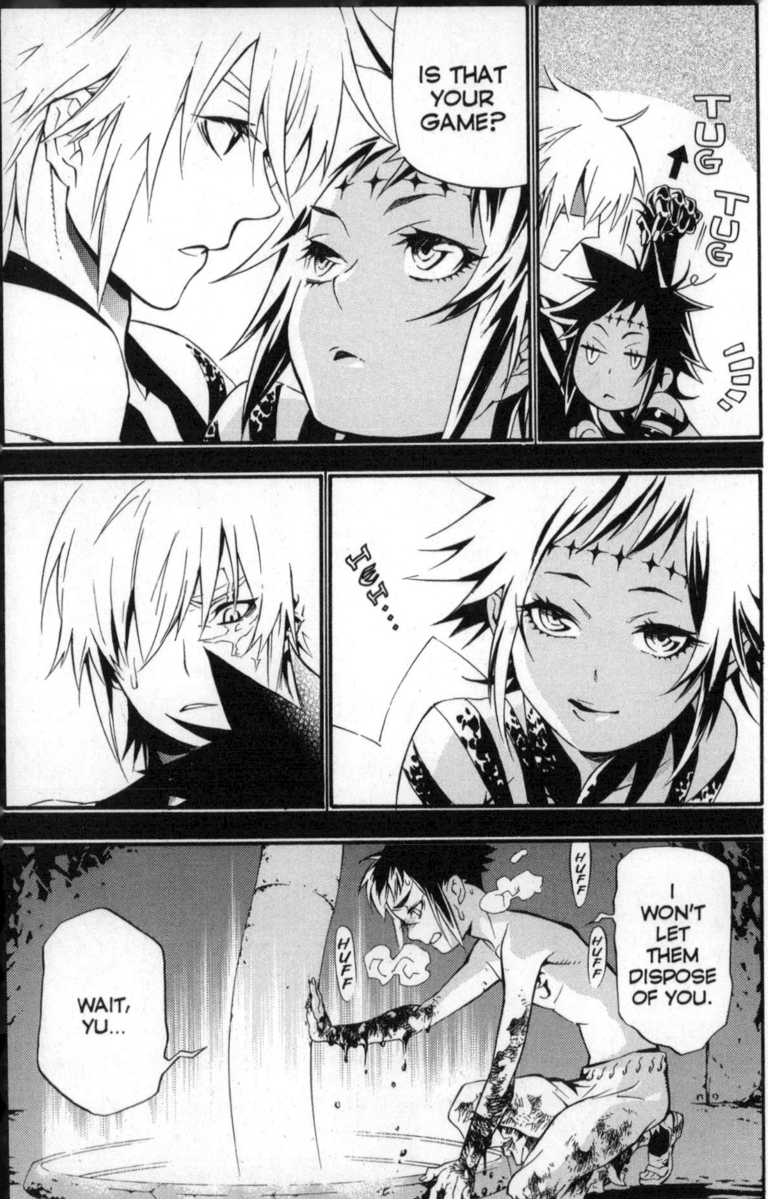
TUG TUG
!!!
IS THAT YOUR GAME?
IWI...
HUFF
I WON'T LET THEM DISPOSE OF YOU.
HUFF
HUFF
WAIT, YU...

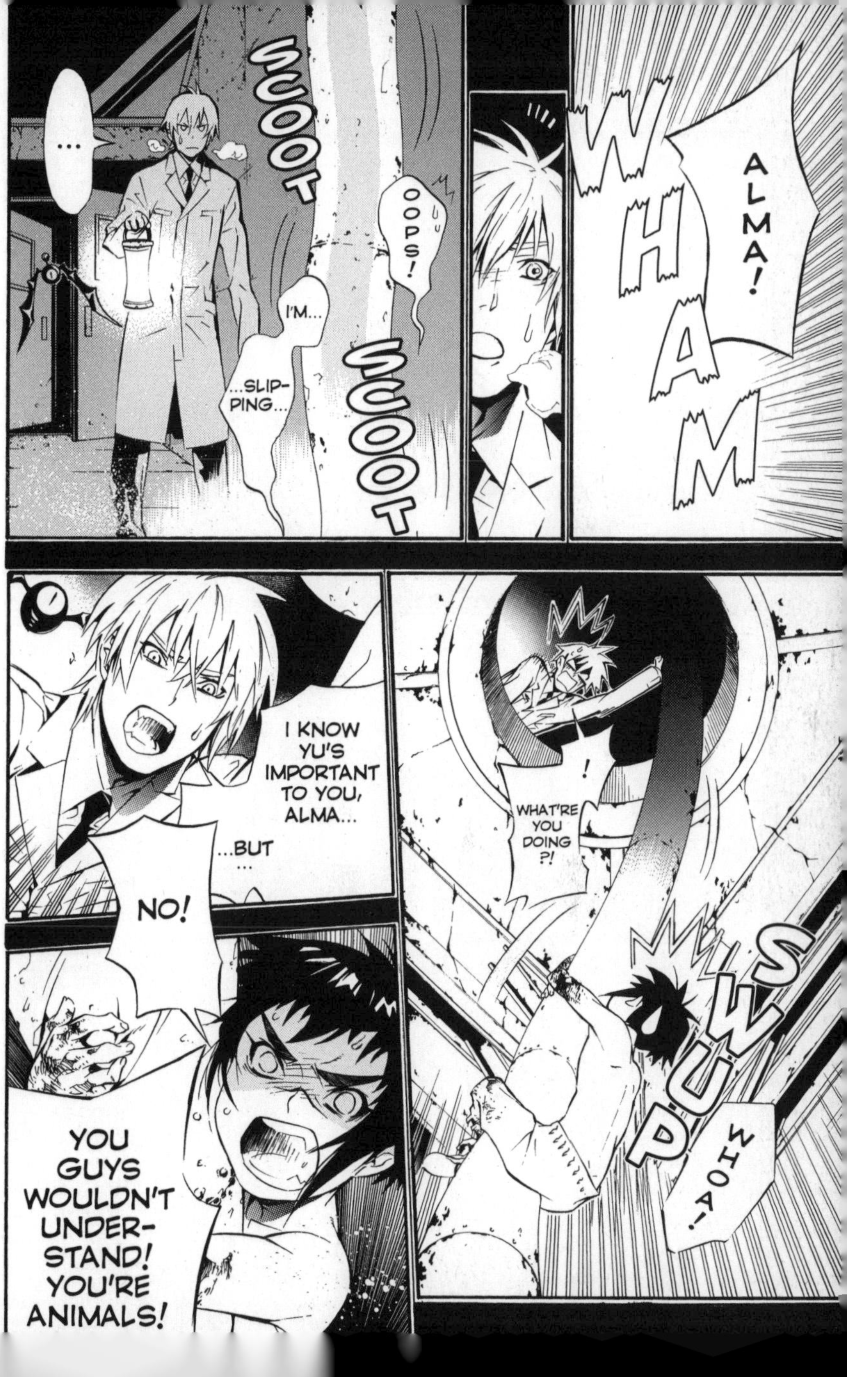
ALMA!
WHAM
OOPS!
...
SCOOT
I'M...
...SLIP-PING...
SCOOT
!
WHAT'RE YOU DOING?!
SWUP
WHOA!
I KNOW YU'S IMPORTANT TO YOU, ALMA...
...BUT ...
NO!
YOU GUYS WOULDN'T UNDER-STAND! YOU'RE ANIMALS!

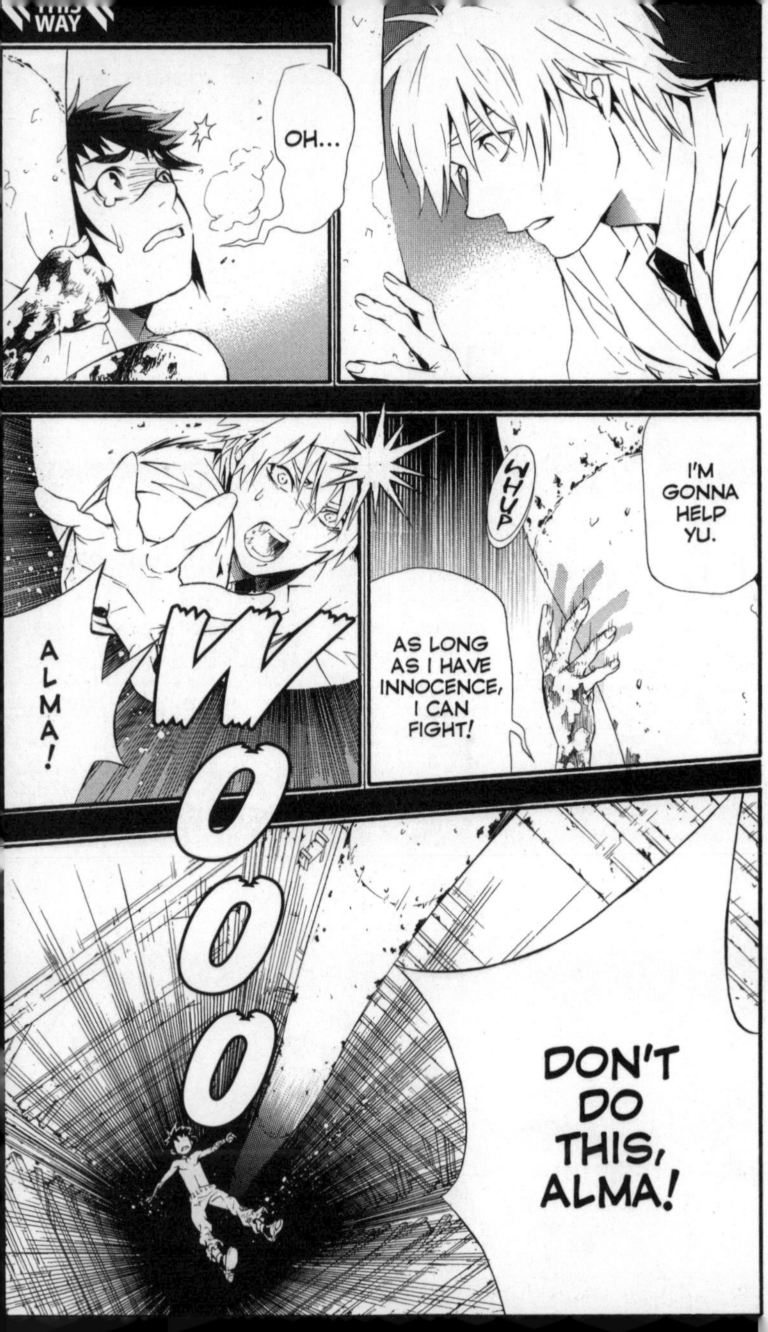
WAY
OH...
I'M GONNA HELP YU.
WHUP
AS LONG AS I HAVE INNOCENCE, I CAN FIGHT!
ALMA!
WOOOO
DON'T DO THIS, ALMA!

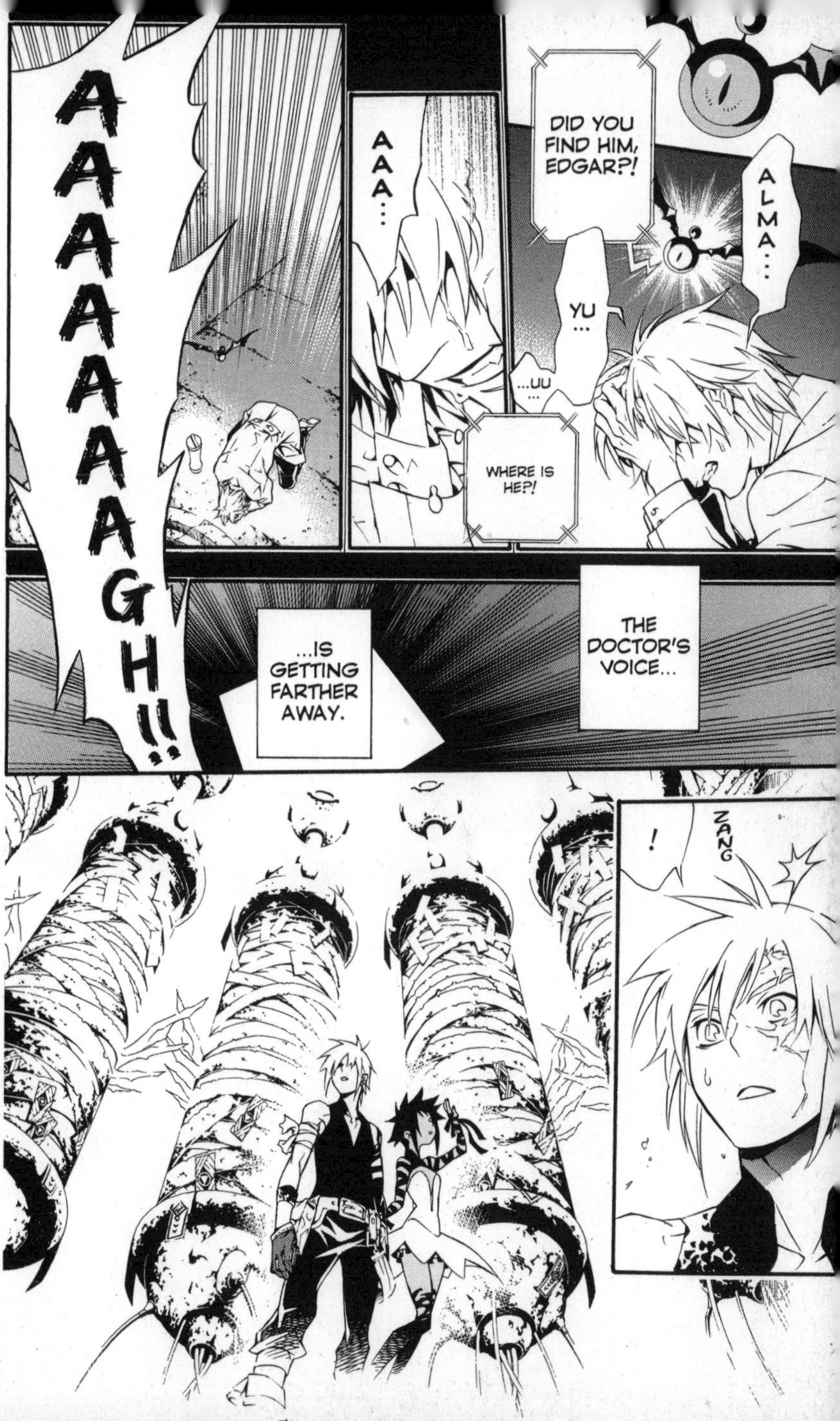

ALMA...
DID YOU FIND HIM, EDGAR?!
YU ...
...UU ...
WHERE IS HE?!
AAA...
THE DOCTOR'S VOICE...
...IS GETTING FARTHER AWAY.
AAAAAAAGH!!
ZANG
!

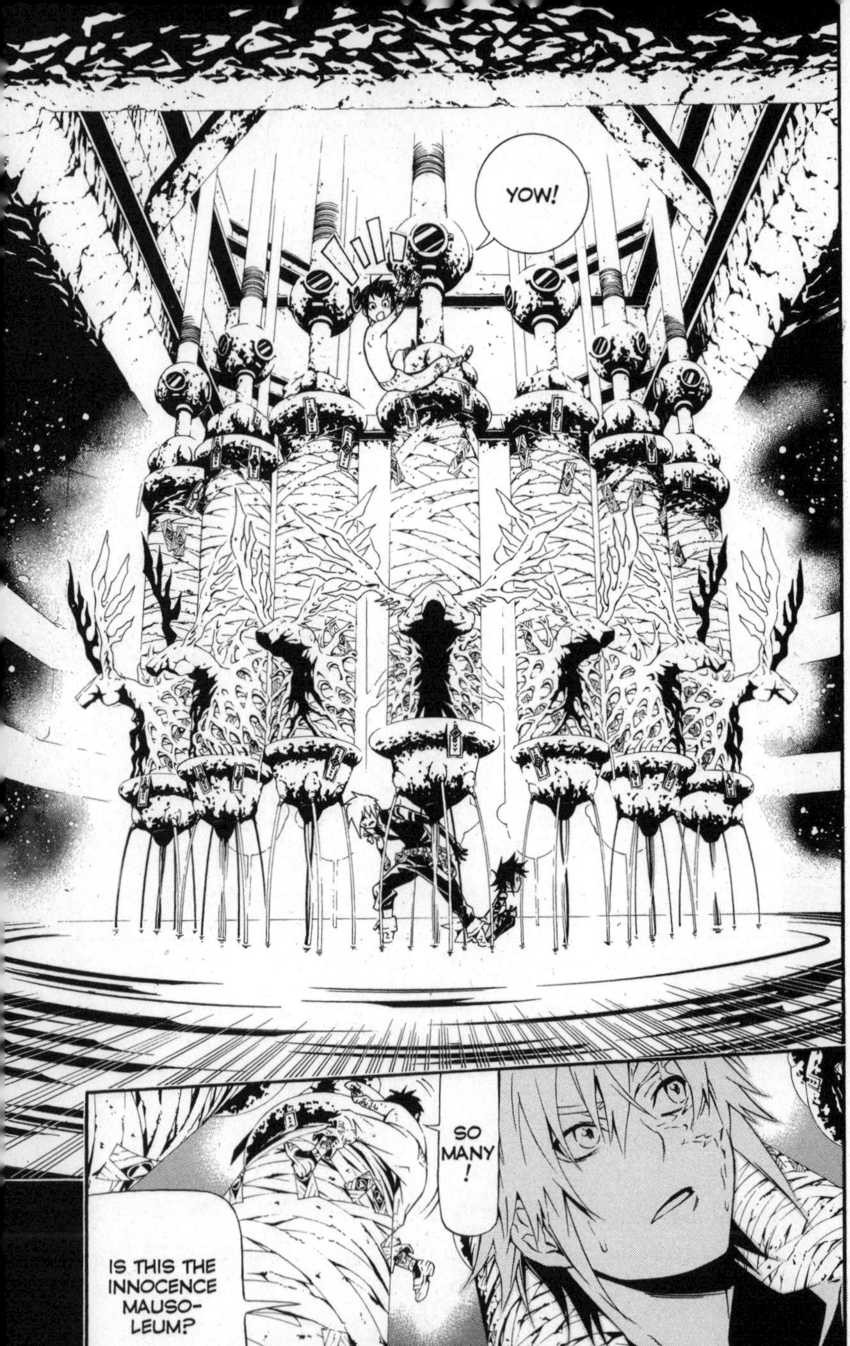
YOW!
SO MANY!
IS THIS THE INNOCENCE MAUSO-LEUM?

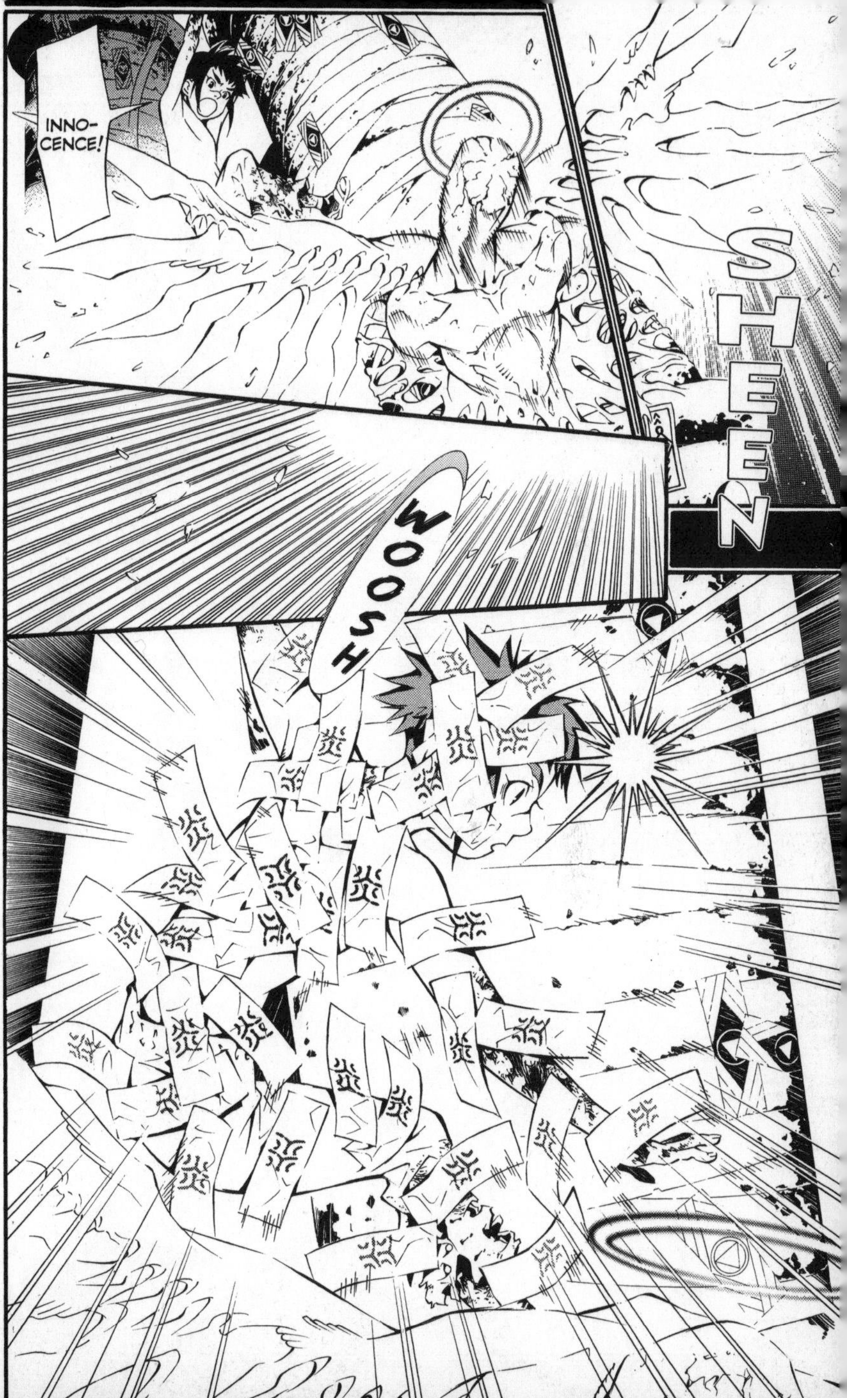
SHEEN
INNO-CENCE!
WOOSH

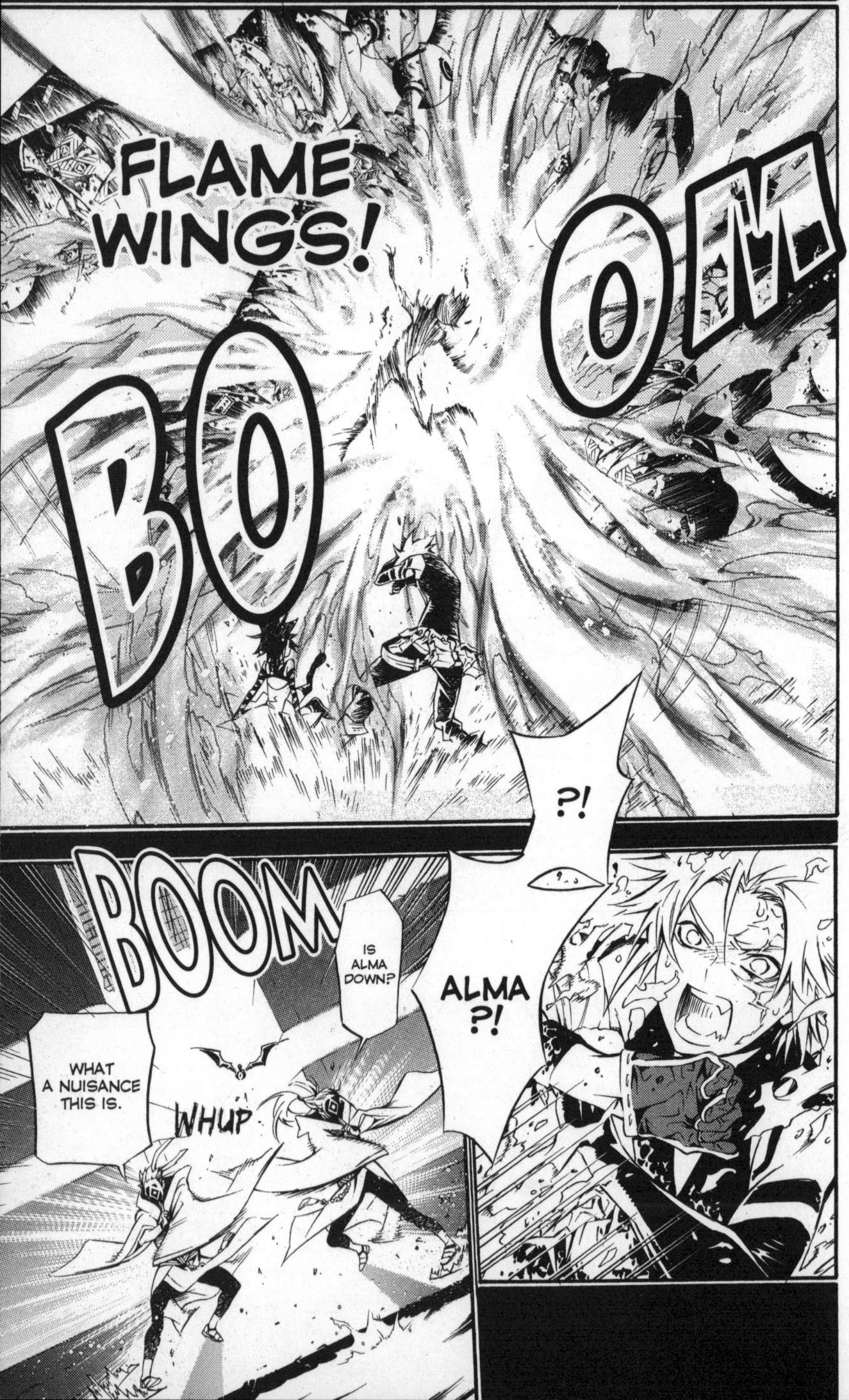

FLAME WINGS!
BO OM
?!
ALMA ?!
IS ALMA DOWN?
BOOM
WHAT A NUISANCE THIS IS.
WHUP

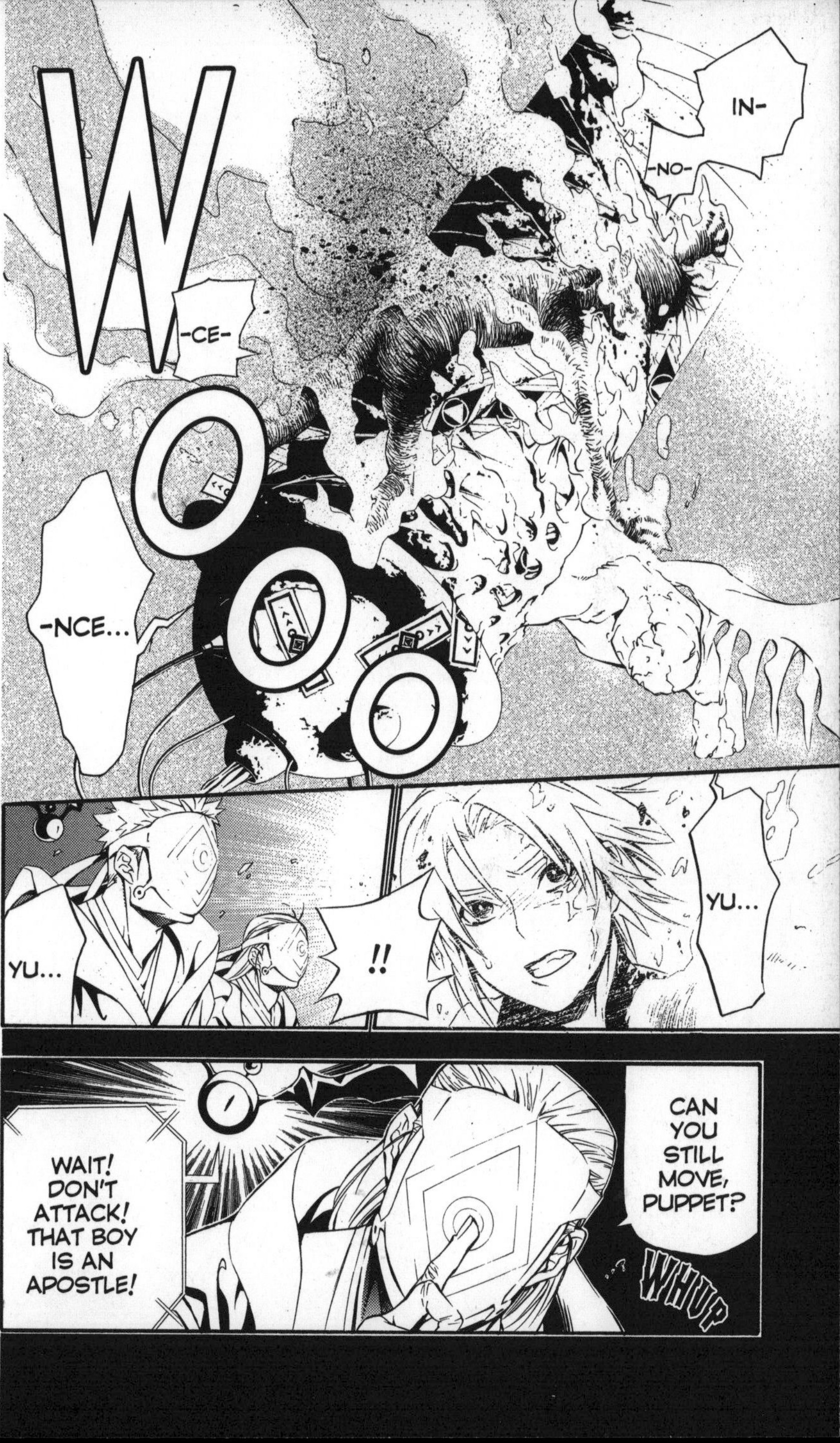
IN-
-NO-
-CE-
WOOO
-NCE...
YU...
!!
YU...
CAN YOU STILL MOVE, PUPPET?
WHUP
WAIT! DON'T ATTACK! THAT BOY IS AN APOSTLE!

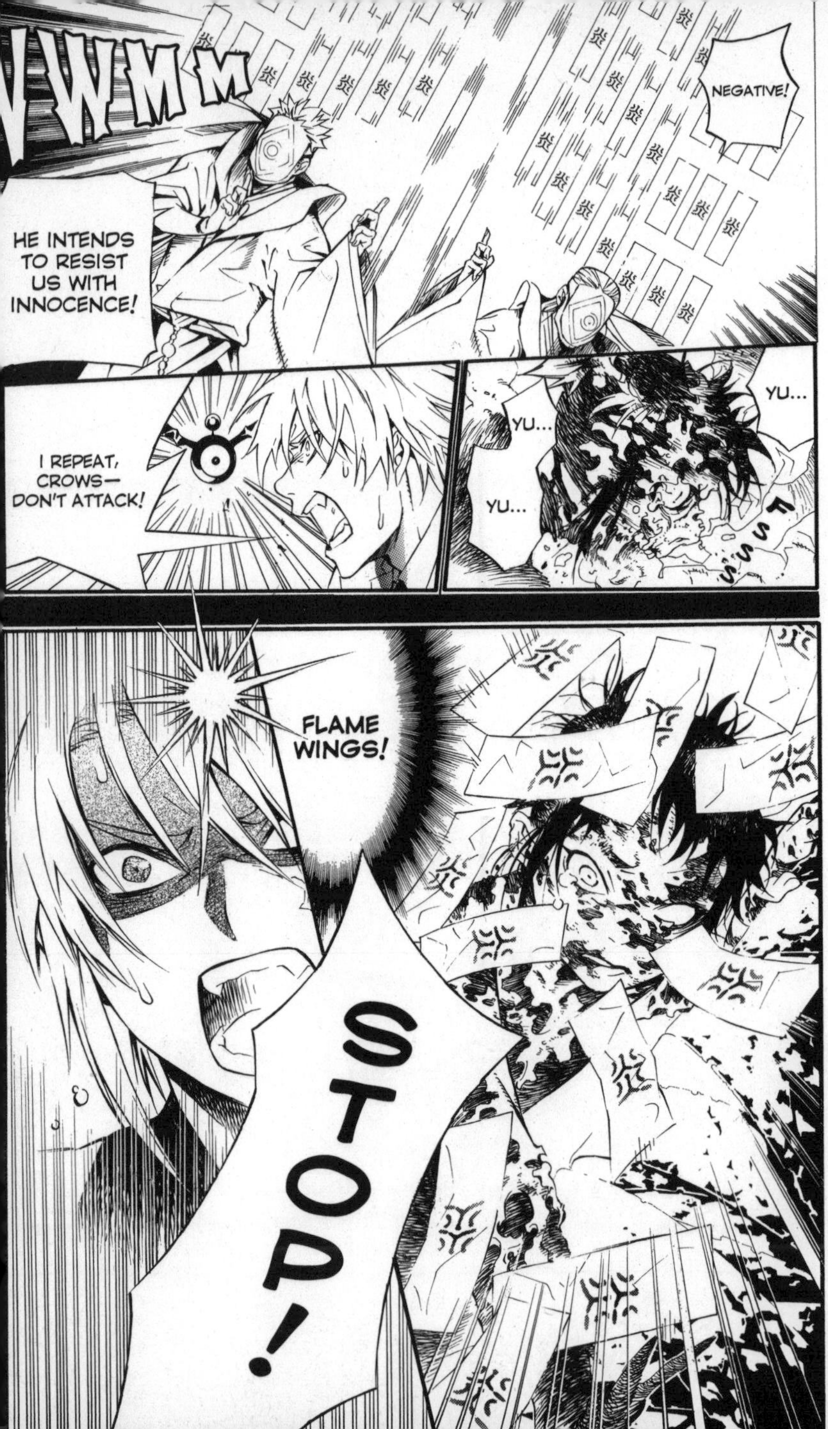
NEGATIVE!
VWMM
HE INTENDS TO RESIST US WITH INNOCENCE!
YU...
YU...
YU...
SSSF
I REPEAT, CROWS— DON'T ATTACK!
FLAME WINGS!
STOP!

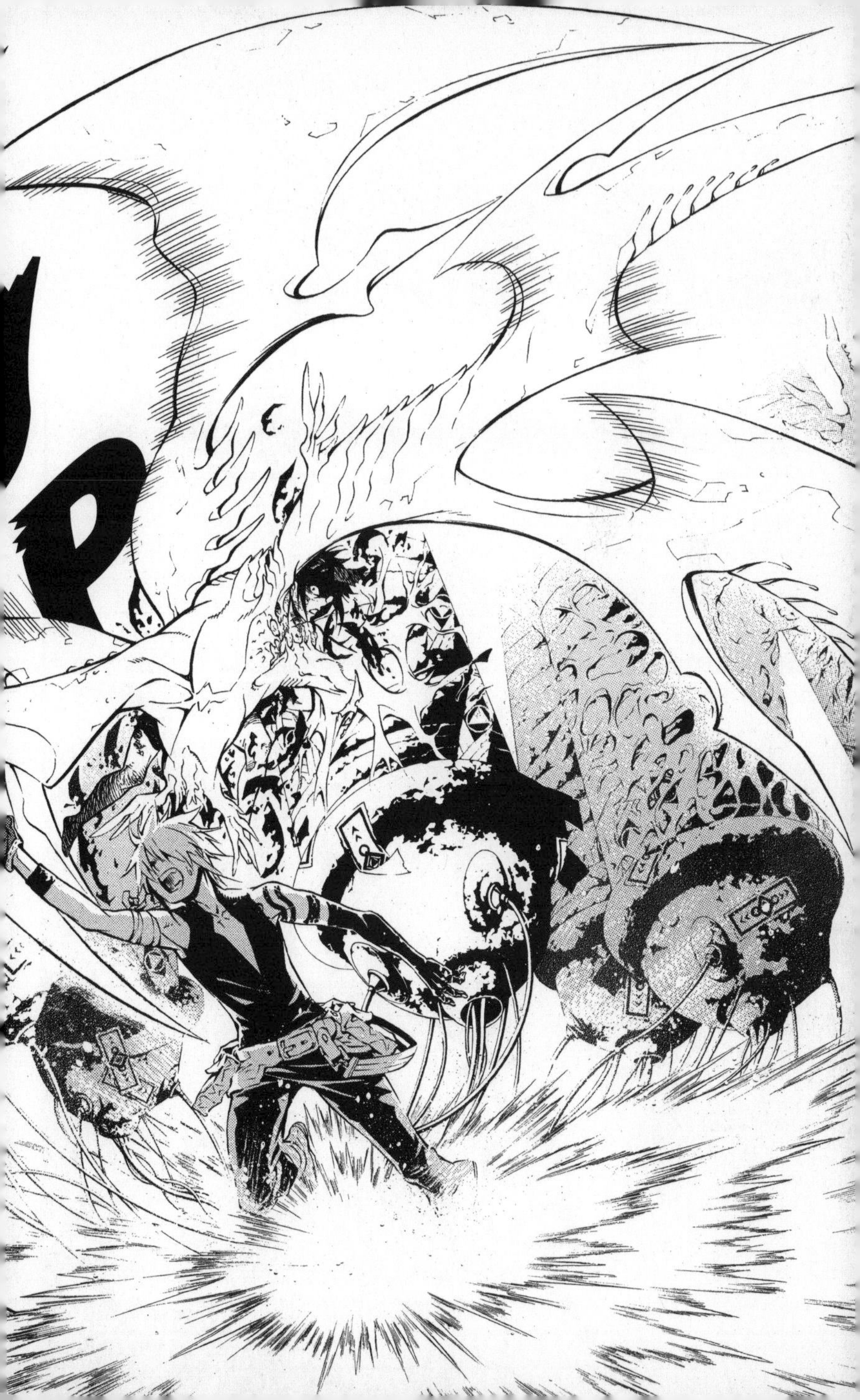

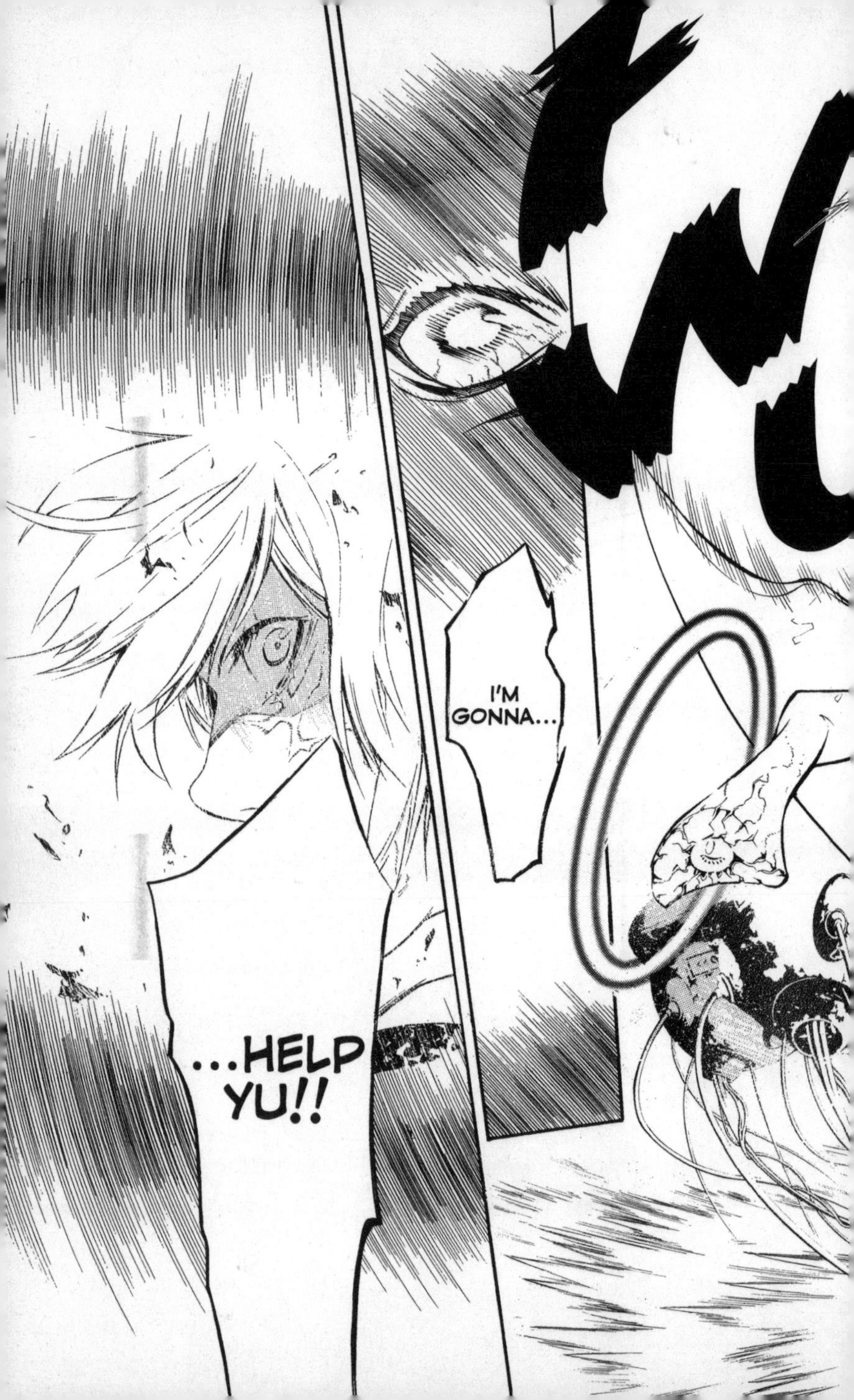
I'M GONNA...
...HELP YU!!

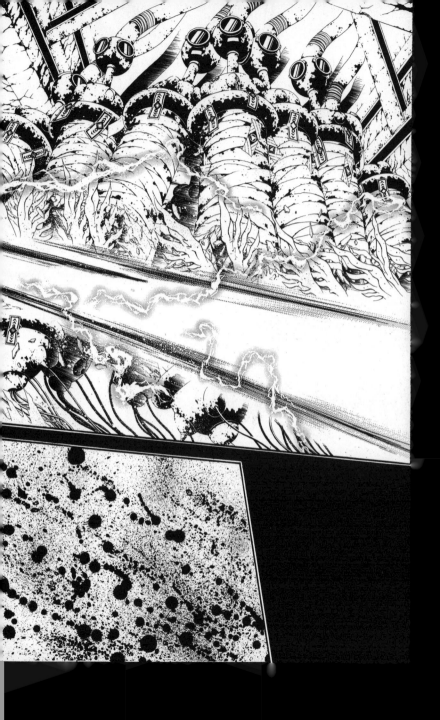

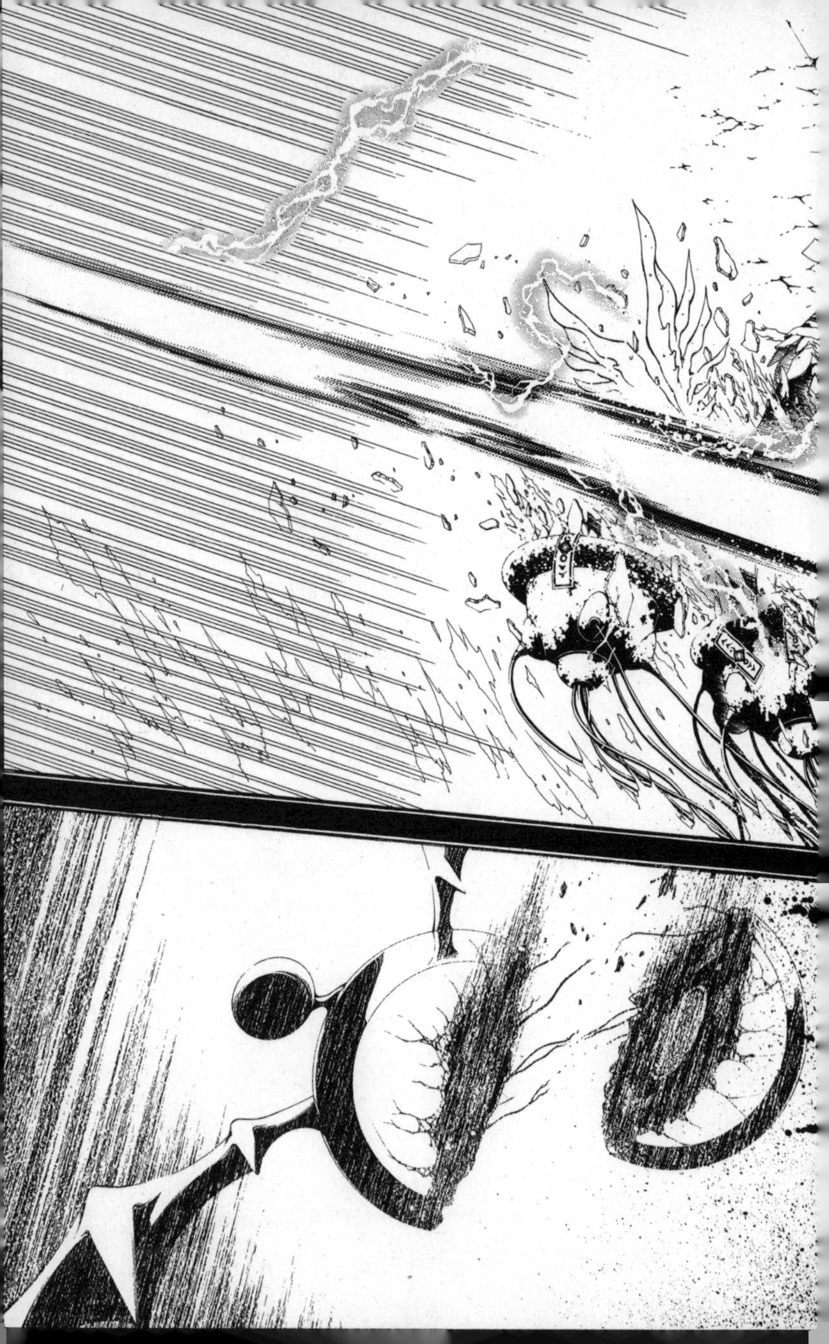

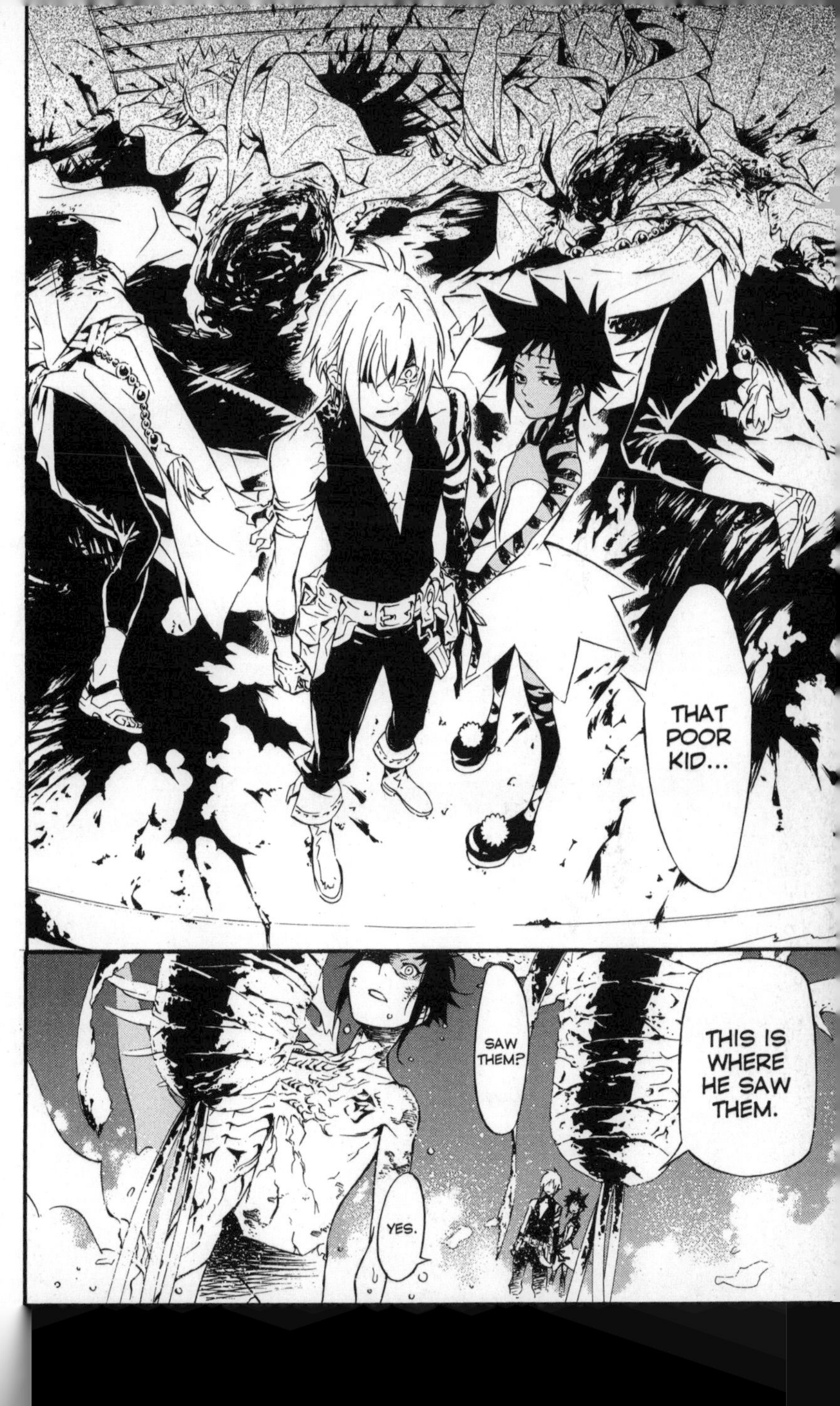
THAT POOR KID...
THIS IS WHERE HE SAW THEM.
SAW THEM?
YES.

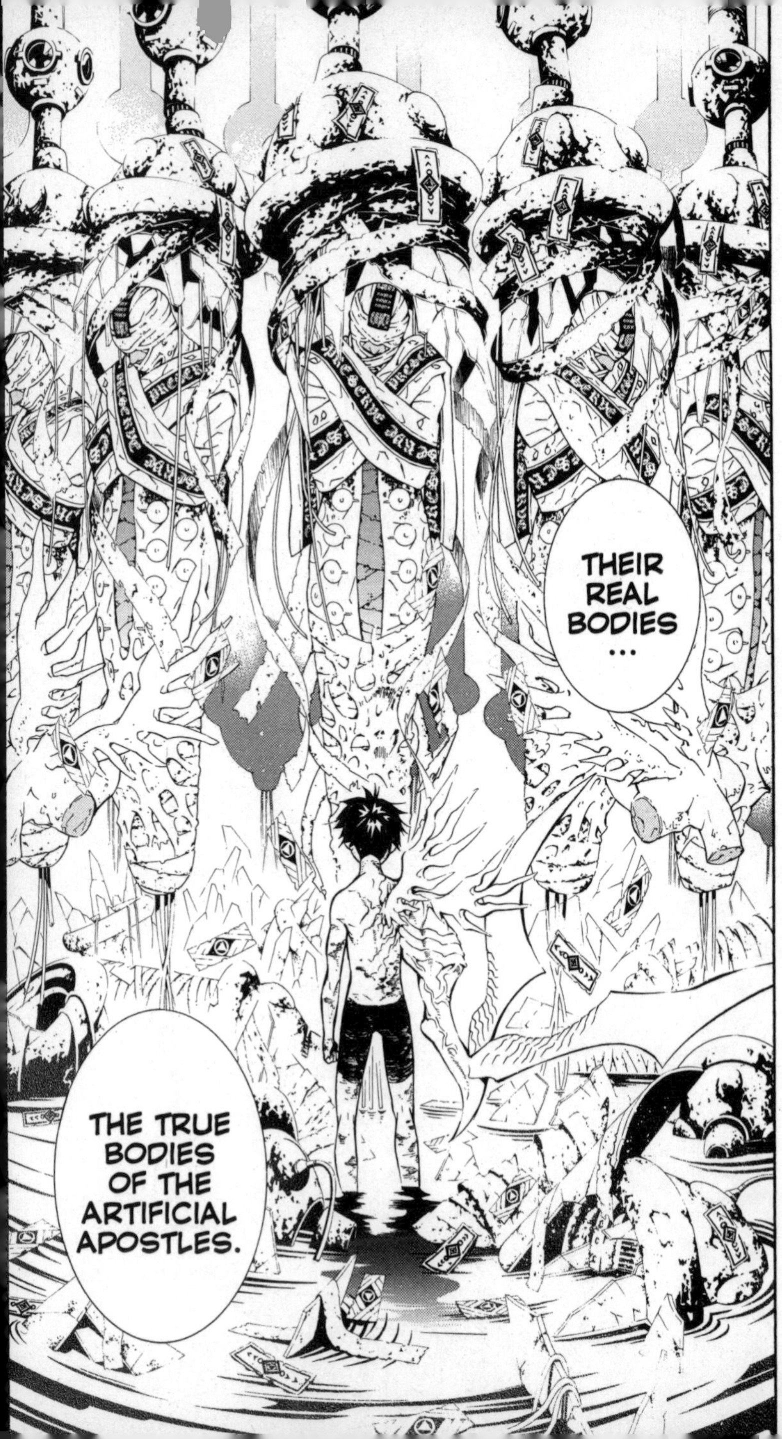
THEIR REAL BODIES ...
THE TRUE BODIES OF THE ARTIFICIAL APOSTLES.

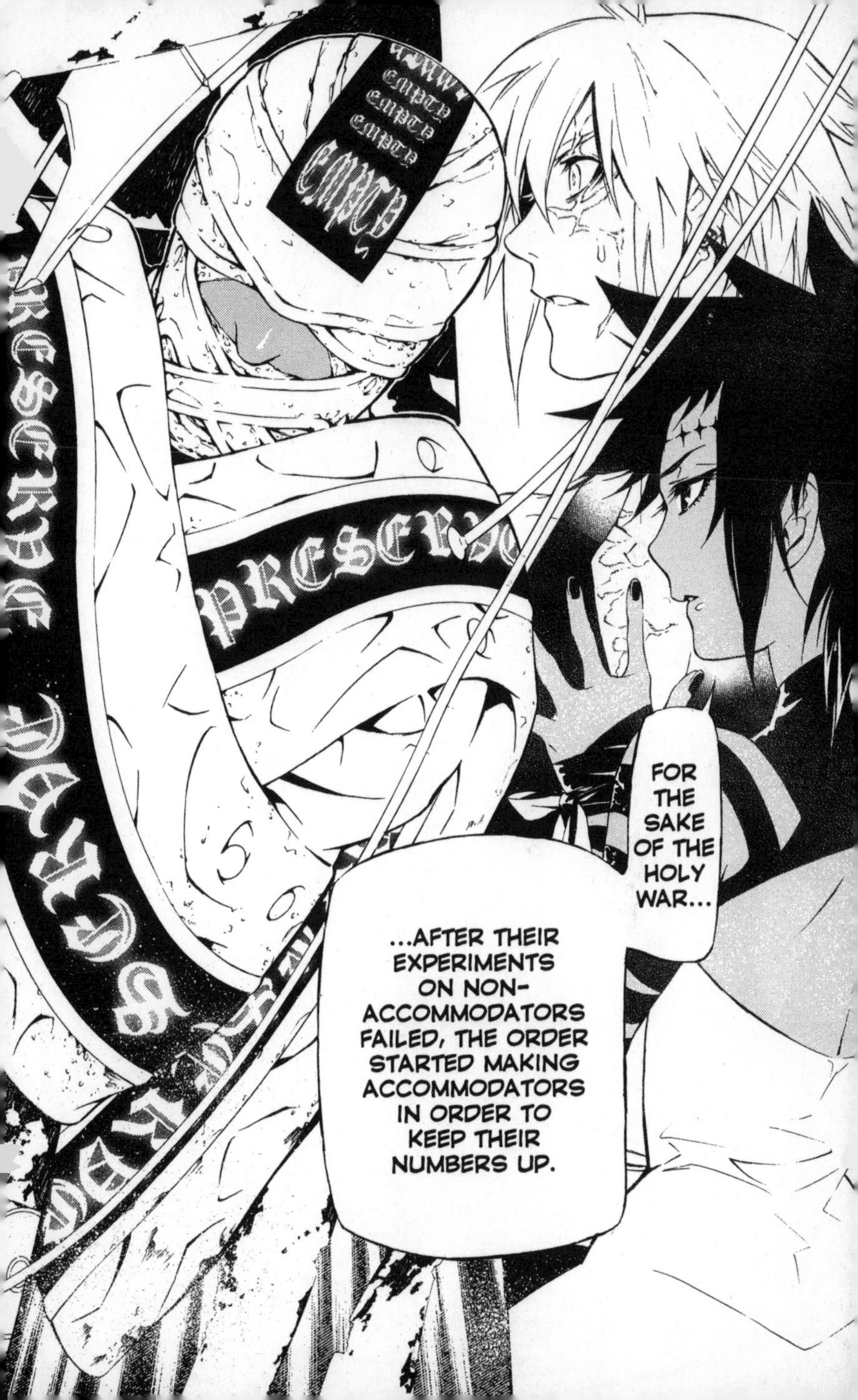
FOR THE SAKE OF THE HOLY WAR...
...AFTER THEIR EXPERIMENTS ON NON-ACCOMMODATORS FAILED, THE ORDER STARTED MAKING ACCOMMODATORS IN ORDER TO KEEP THEIR NUMBERS UP.

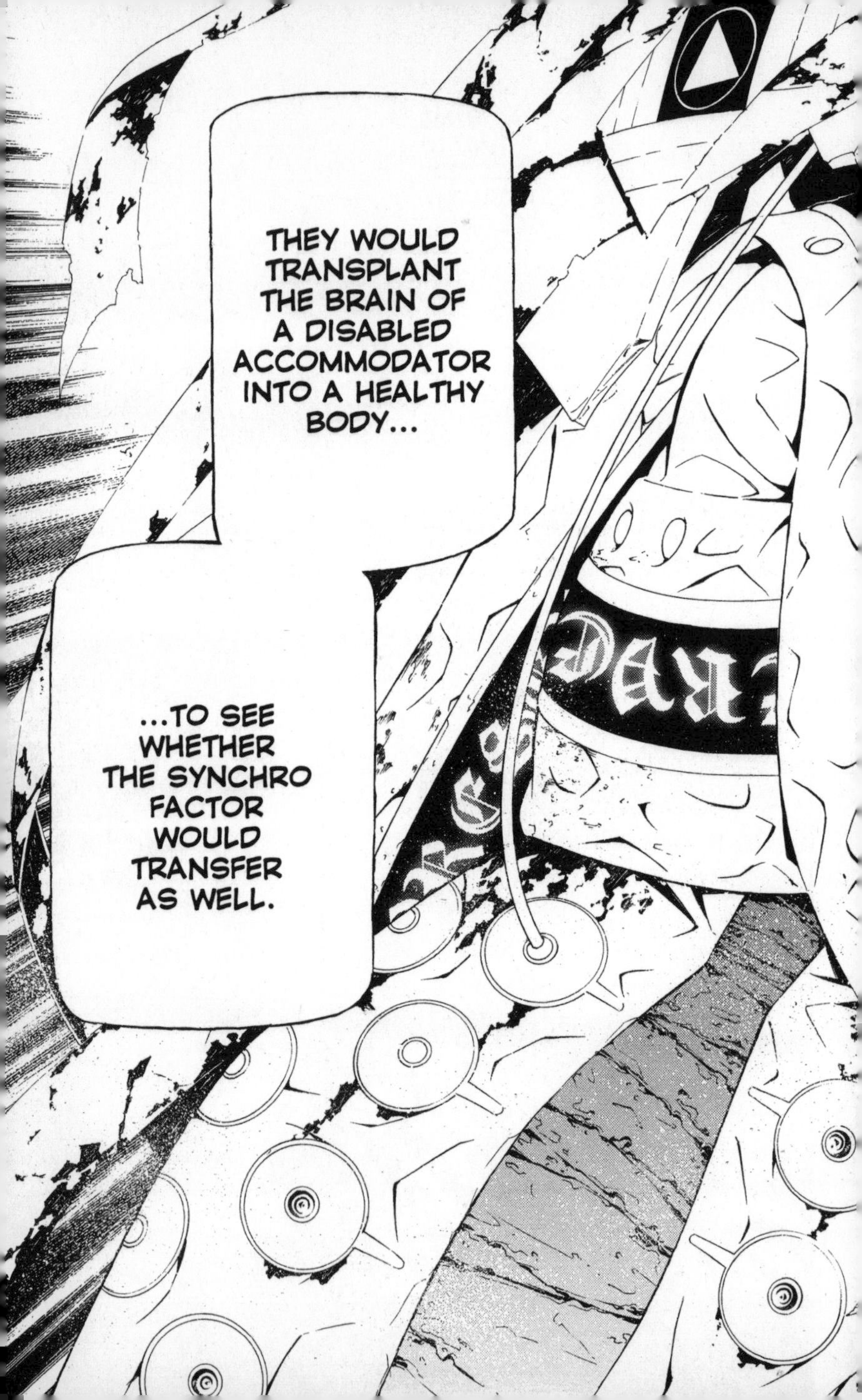
THEY WOULD TRANSPLANT THE BRAIN OF A DISABLED ACCOMMODATOR INTO A HEALTHY BODY...
...TO SEE WHETHER THE SYNCHRO FACTOR WOULD TRANSFER AS WELL.

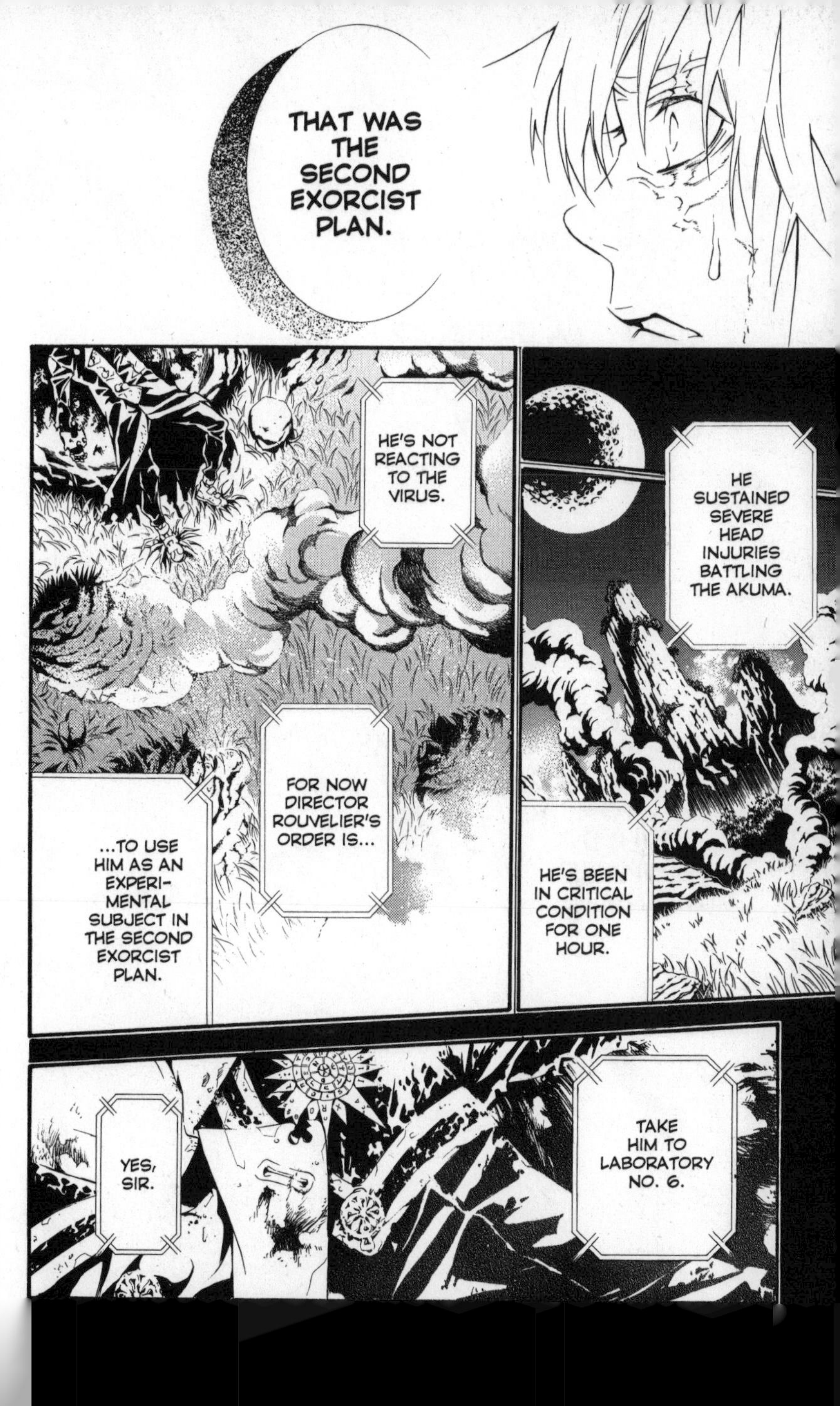
THAT WAS THE SECOND EXORCIST PLAN.
HE SUSTAINED SEVERE HEAD INJURIES BATTLING THE AKUMA.
HE'S BEEN IN CRITICAL CONDITION FOR ONE HOUR.
HE'S NOT REACTING TO THE VIRUS.
FOR NOW DIRECTOR ROUVELIER'S ORDER IS...
...TO USE HIM AS AN EXPERI-MENTAL SUBJECT IN THE SECOND EXORCIST PLAN.
TAKE HIM TO LABORATORY NO. 6.
YES, SIR.

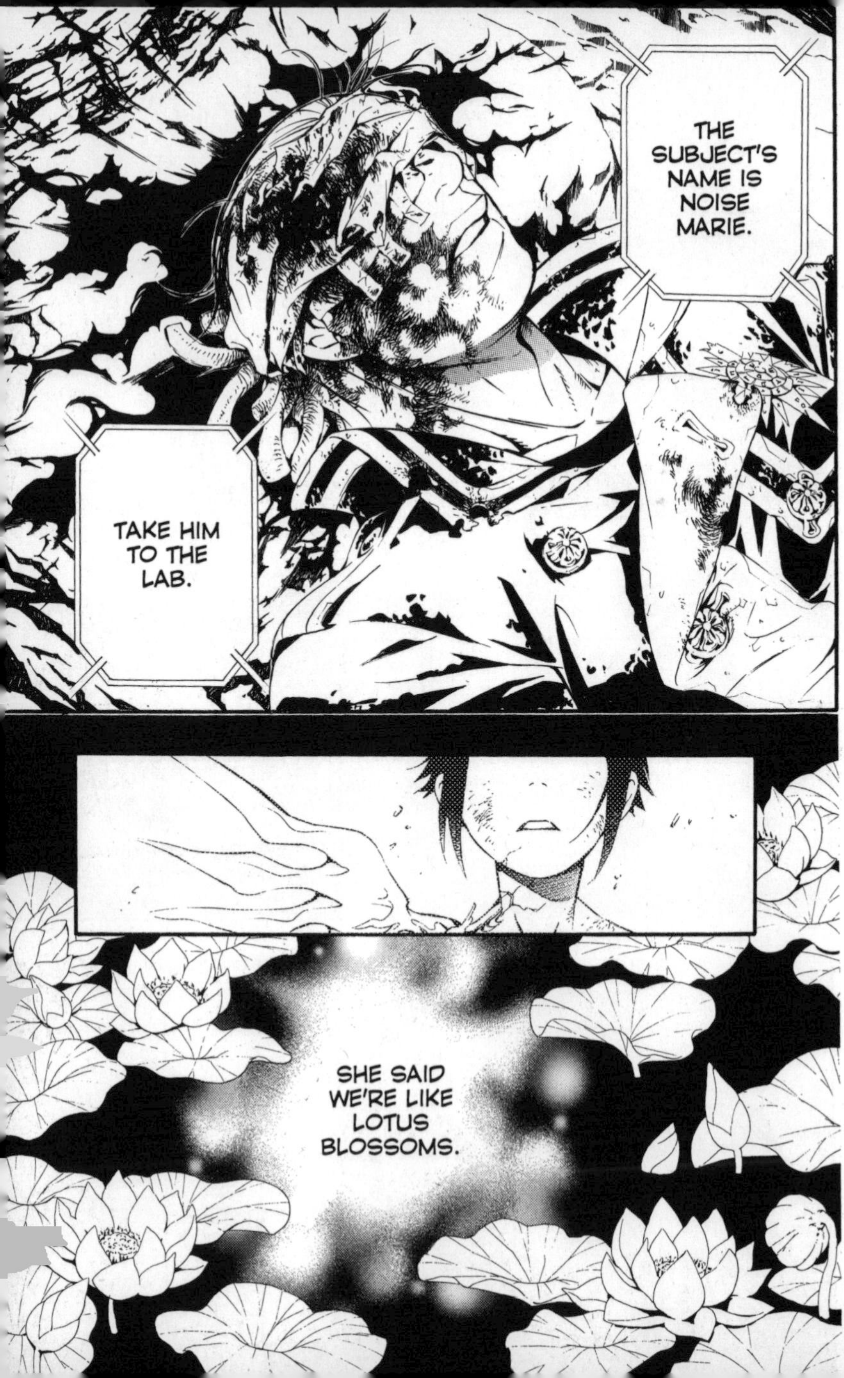
THE SUBJECT'S NAME IS NOISE MARIE.
TAKE HIM TO THE LAB.
SHE SAID WE'RE LIKE LOTUS BLOSSOMS.

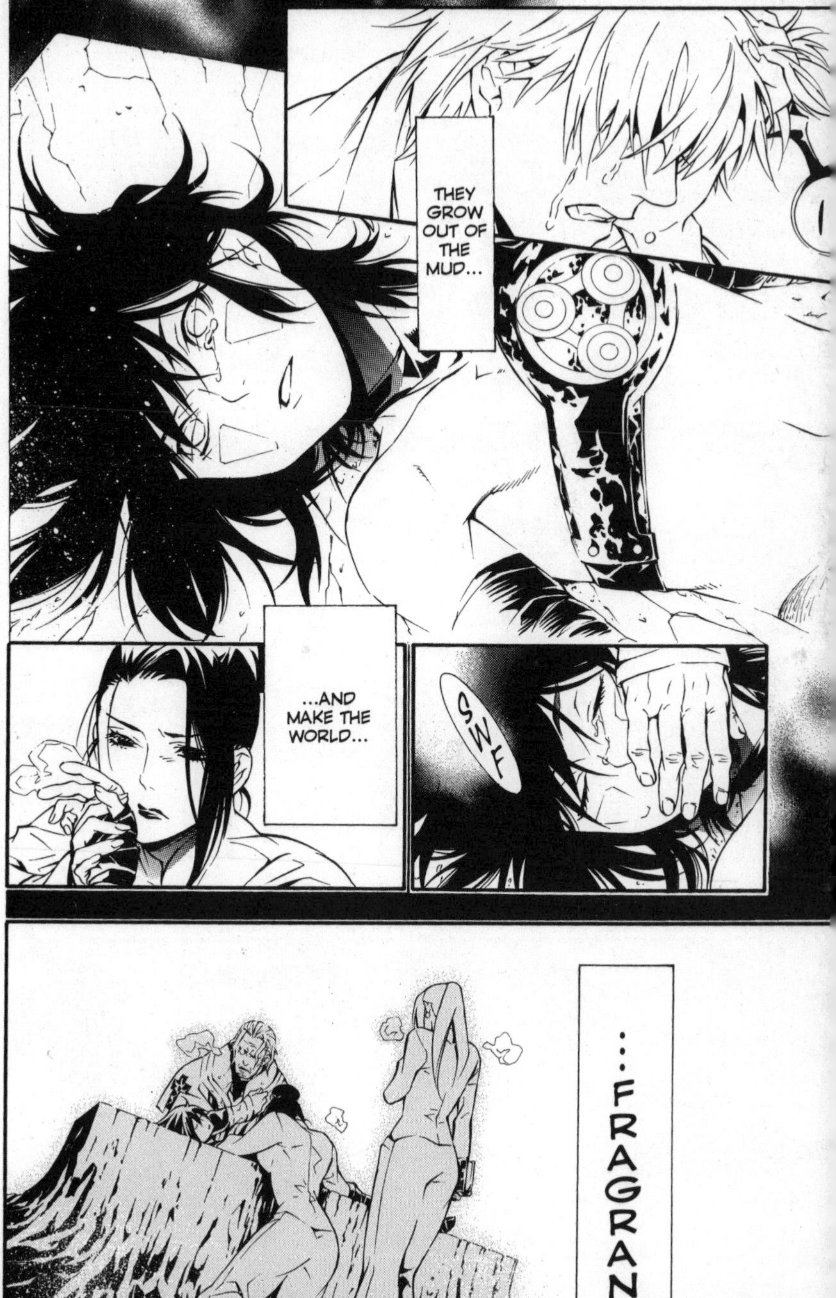
THEY GROW OUT OF THE MUD...
SWF
...AND MAKE THE WORLD...
...FRAGRANT.

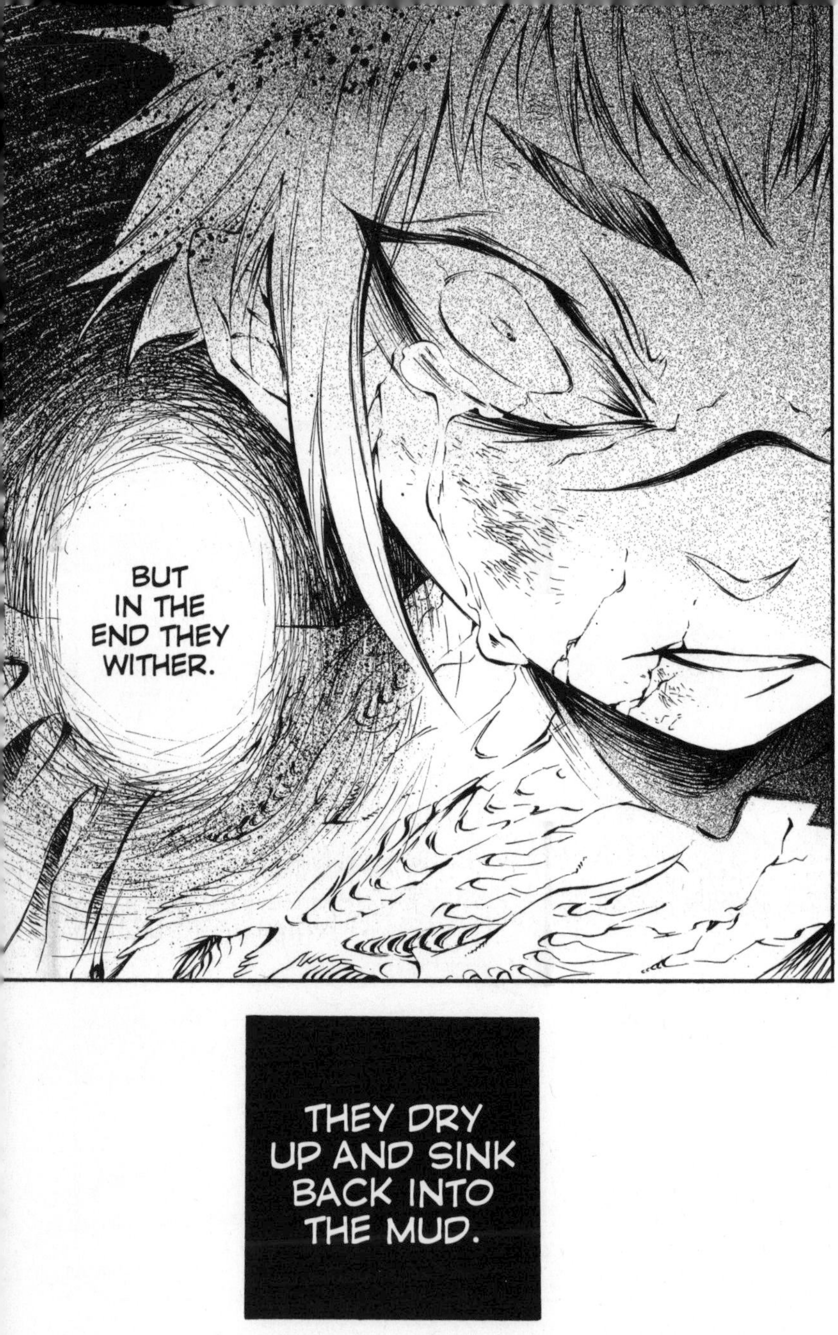
BUT IN THE END THEY WITHER.

THEY DRY UP AND SINK BACK INTO THE MUD.

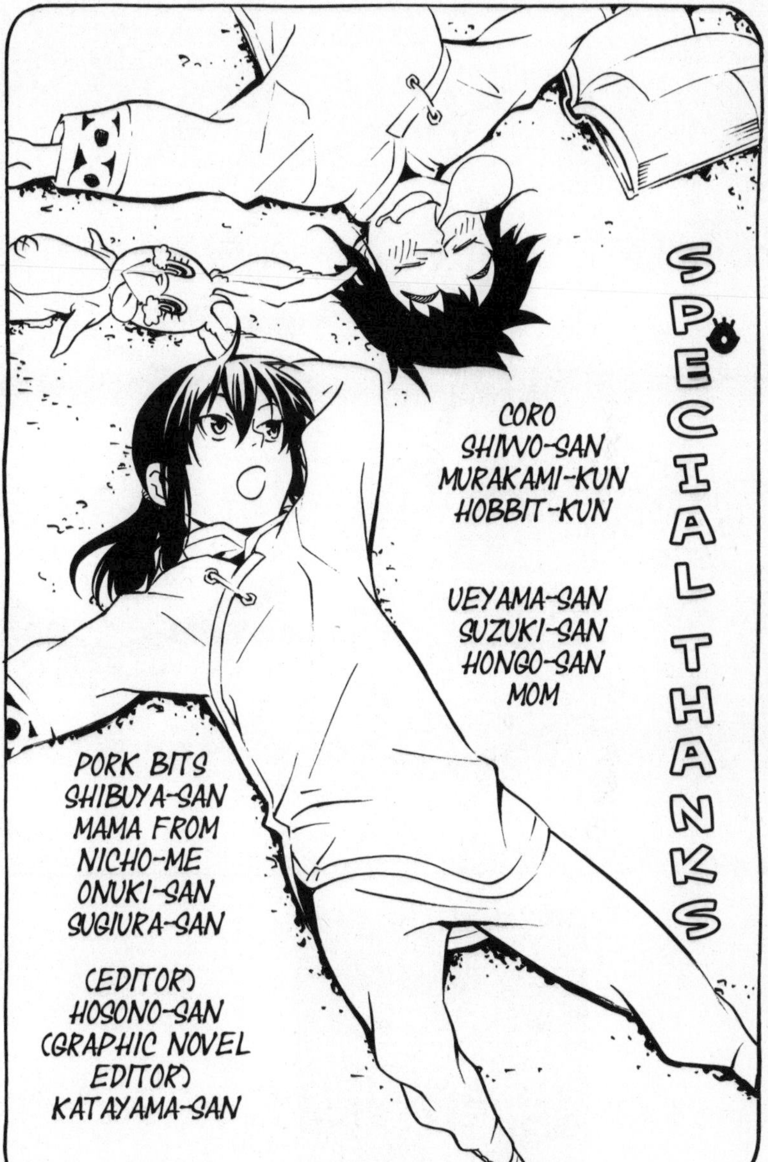
SPECIAL THANKS
CORO
SHINVO-SAN
MURAKAMI-KUN
HOBBIT-KUN
UEYAMA-SAN
SUZUKI-SAN
HONGO-SAN
MOM
PORK BITS
SHIBUYA-SAN
MAMA FROM
NICHO-ME
ONUKI-SAN
SUGIURA-SAN
(EDITOR)
HOSONO-SAN
(GRAPHIC NOVEL
EDITOR)
KATAYAMA-SAN

Friend

THE 193RD NIGHT: FRIEND

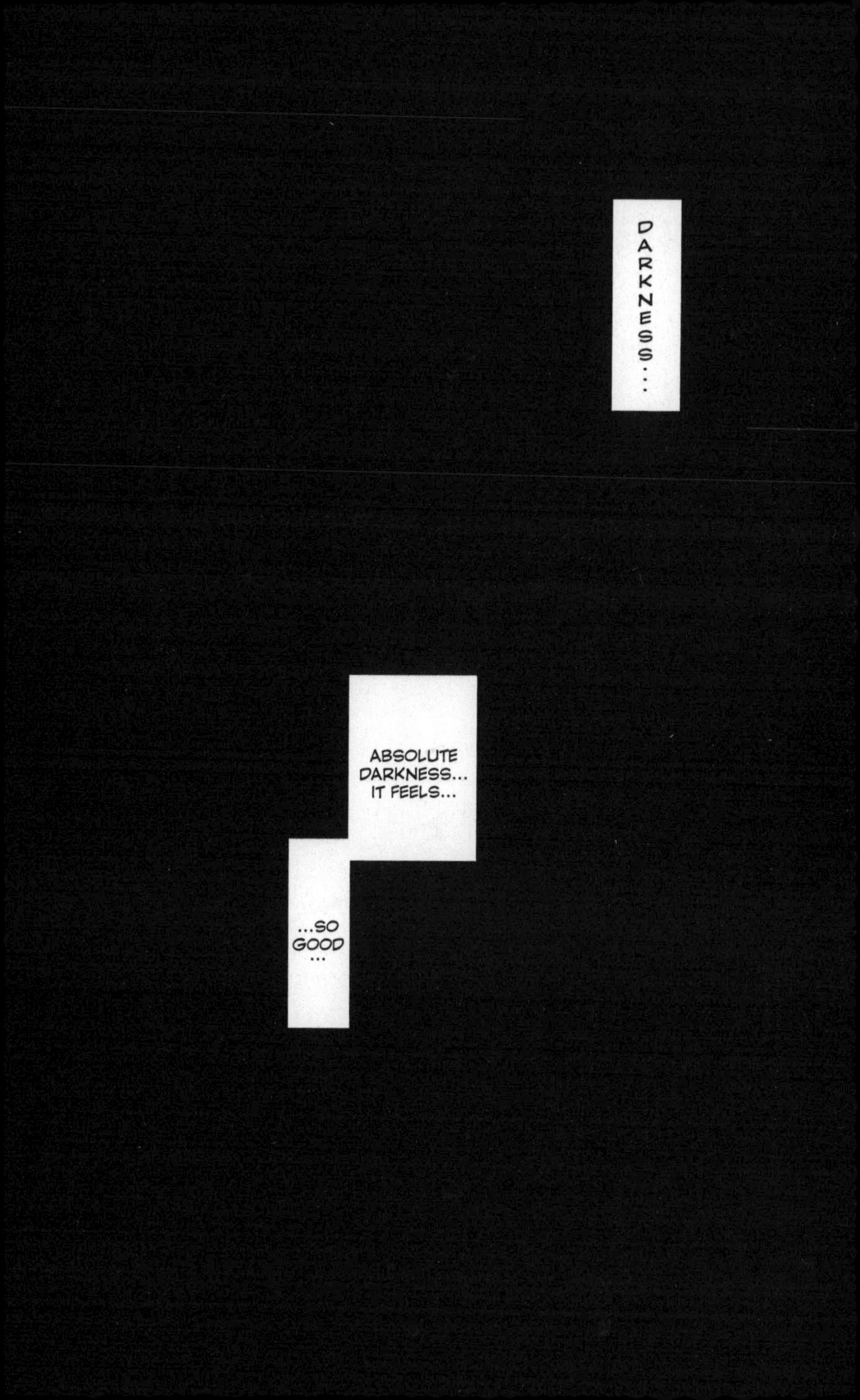
DARKNESS...
ABSOLUTE DARKNESS... IT FEELS...
...SO GOOD...

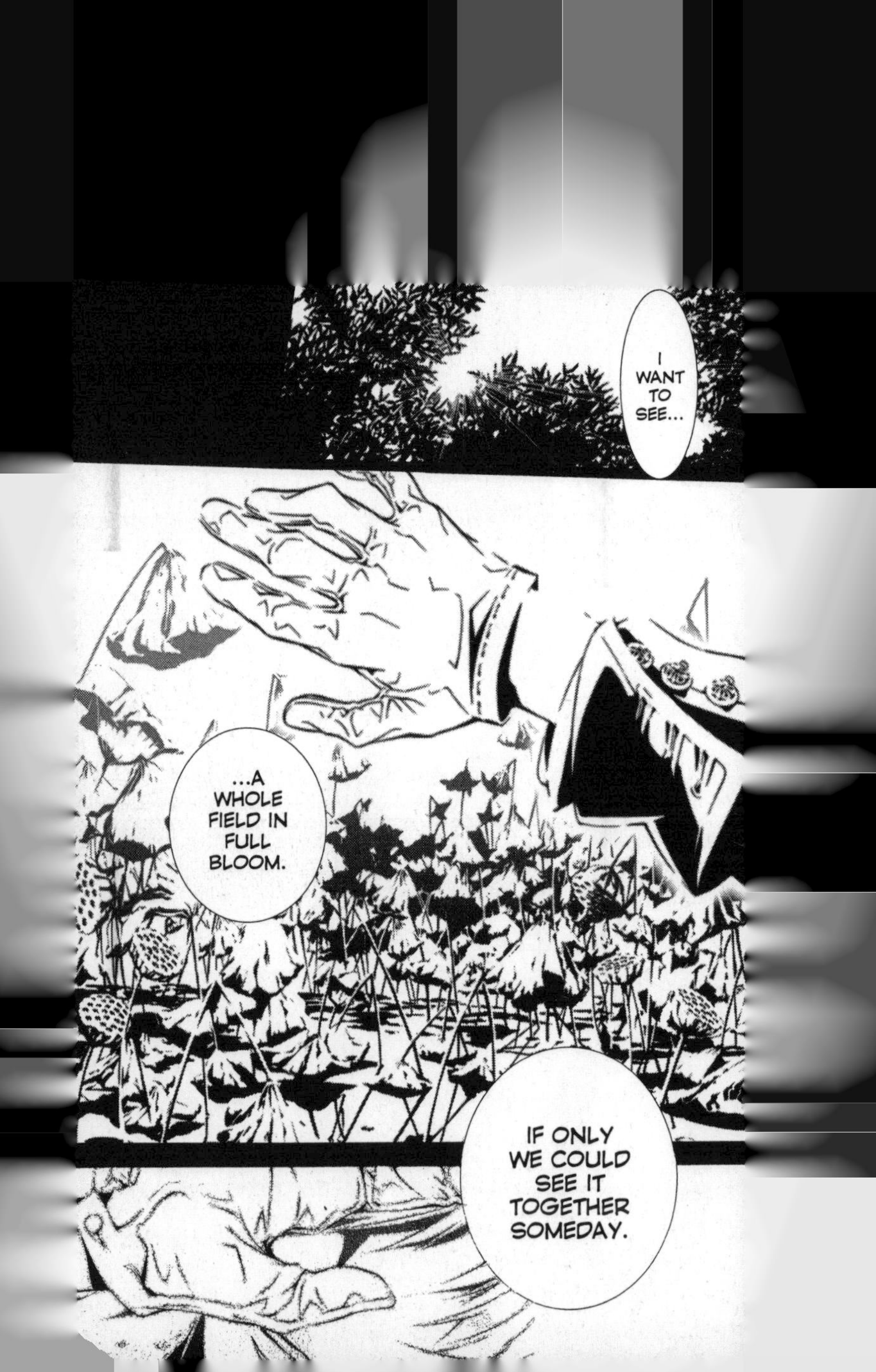
I WANT TO SEE...
...A WHOLE FIELD IN FULL BLOOM.
IF ONLY WE COULD SEE IT TOGETHER SOMEDAY.

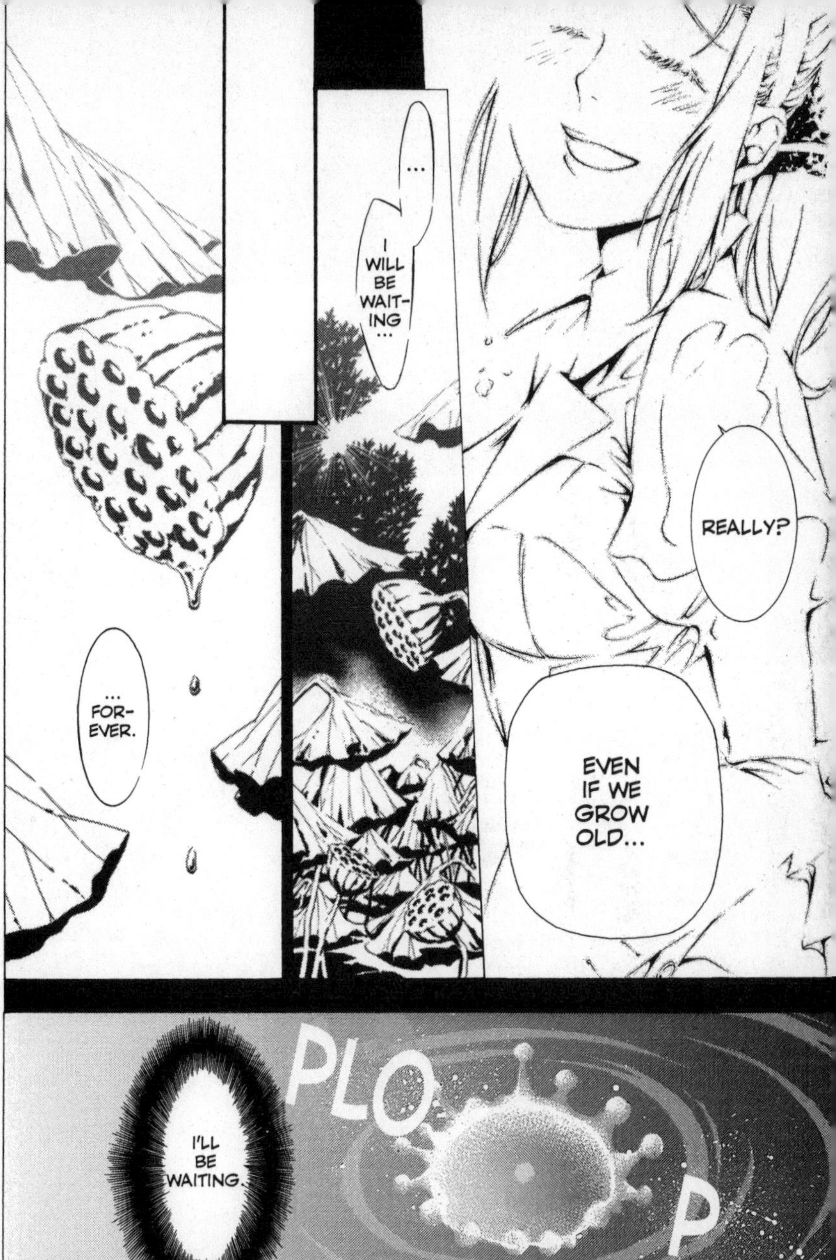
REALLY?
EVEN IF WE GROW OLD...
...
I WILL BE WAIT-ING...
... FOR-EVER.
PLOP
I'LL BE WAITING.

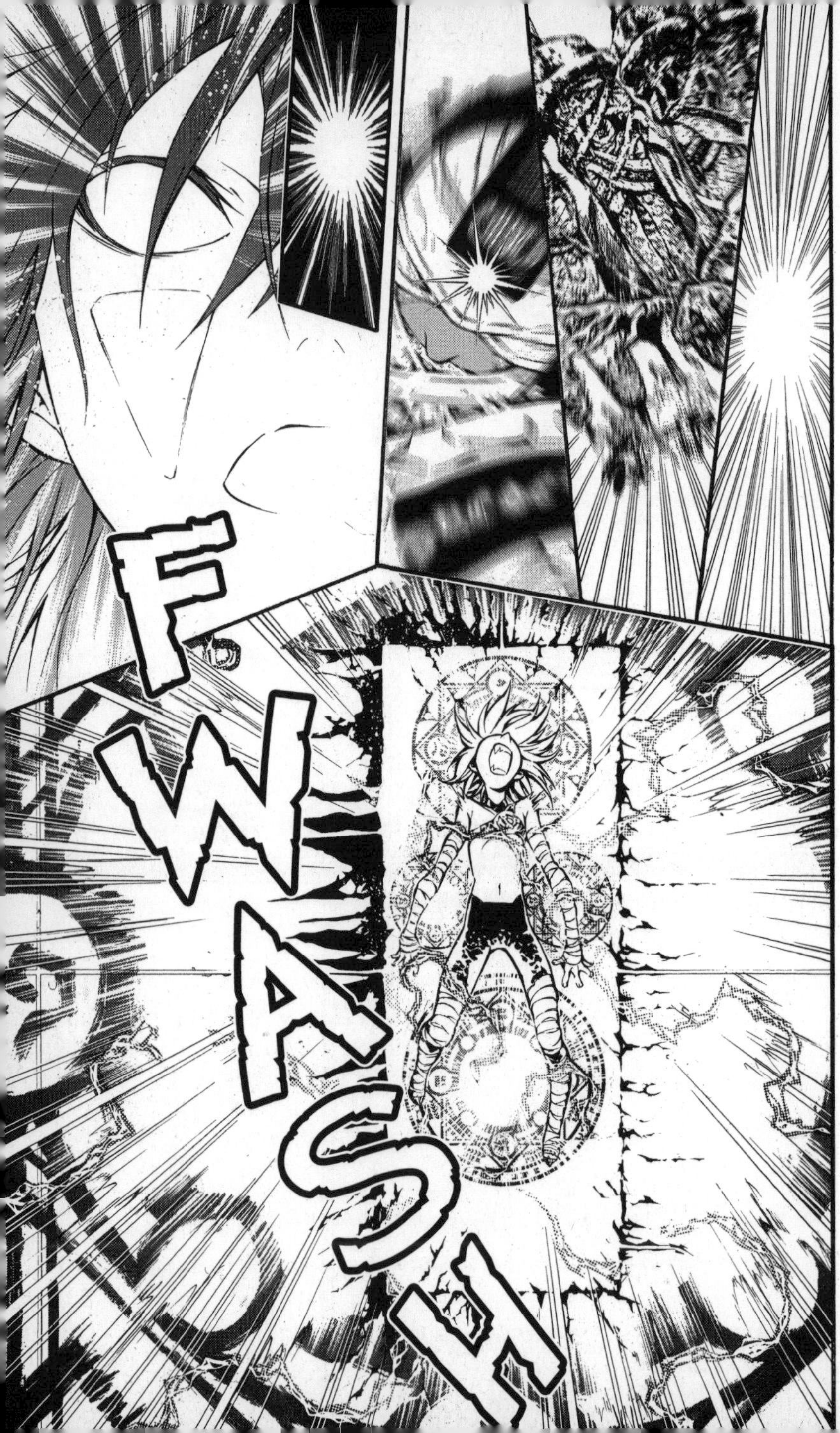
FWASH!

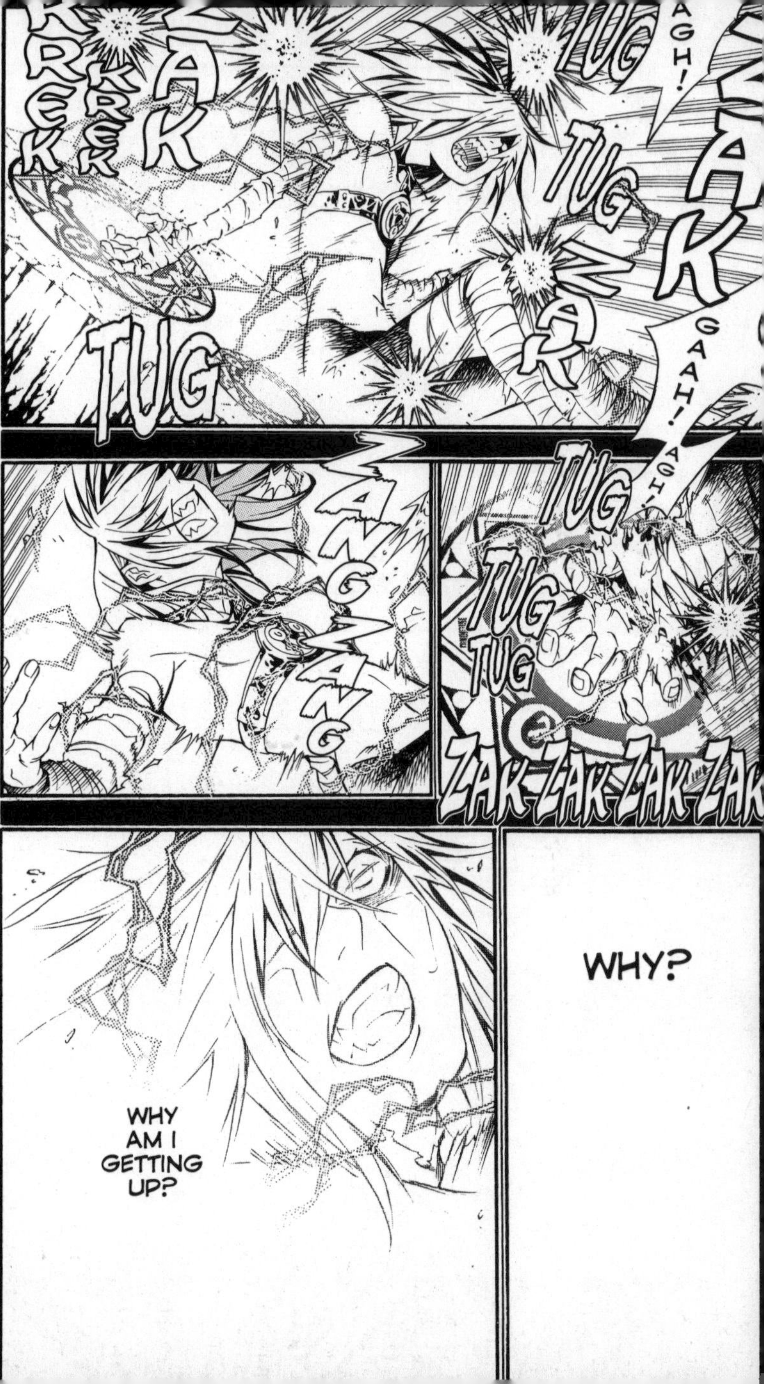
AGH!
TUG
TUG
ZAK
GAAH!
ZAK
KREK KREK KREK
TUG
AGH!
TUG
TUG TUG
ZAK ZAK ZAK ZAK ZAK
ZANG ZANG
WHY?
WHY AM I GETTING UP?

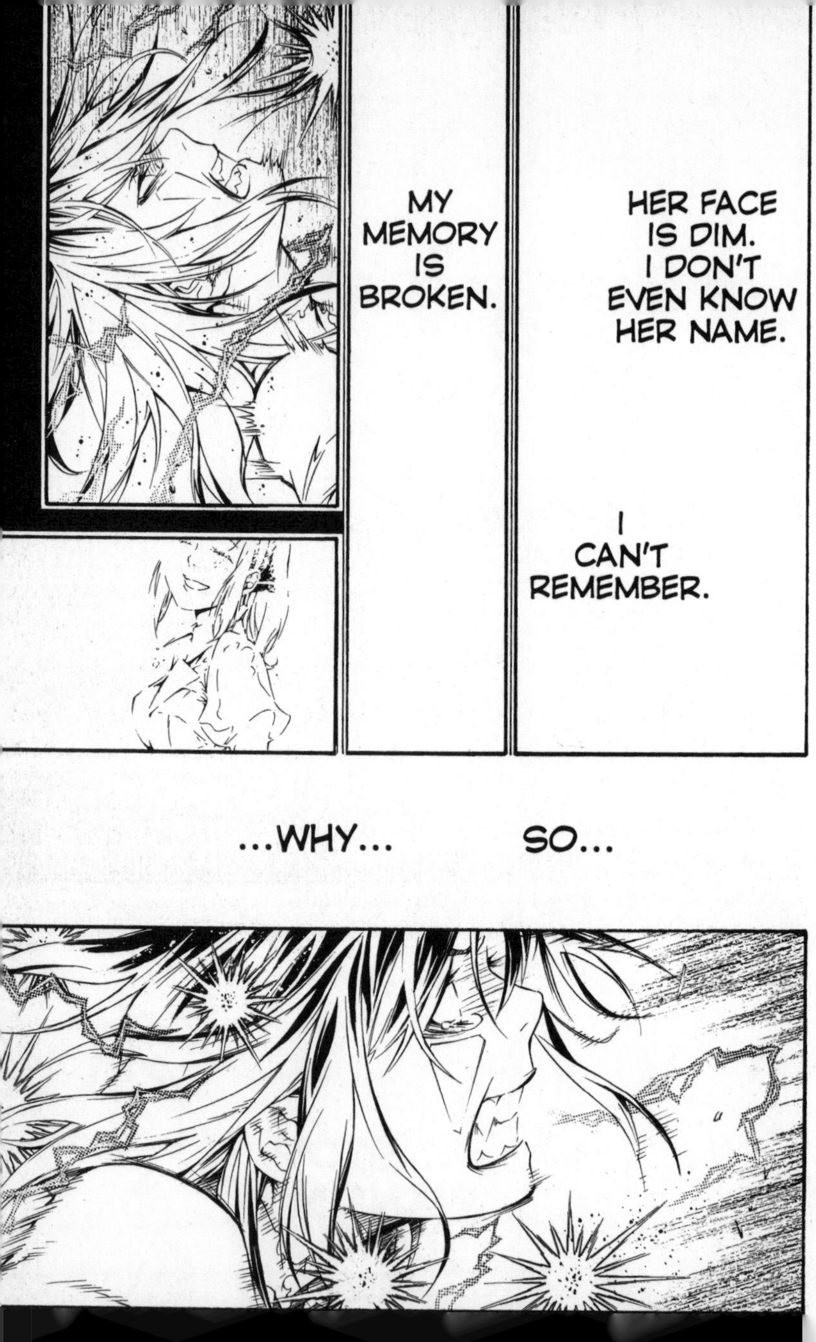
HER FACE IS DIM. I DON'T EVEN KNOW HER NAME.
I CAN'T REMEMBER.
MY MEMORY IS BROKEN.
SO...
...WHY...

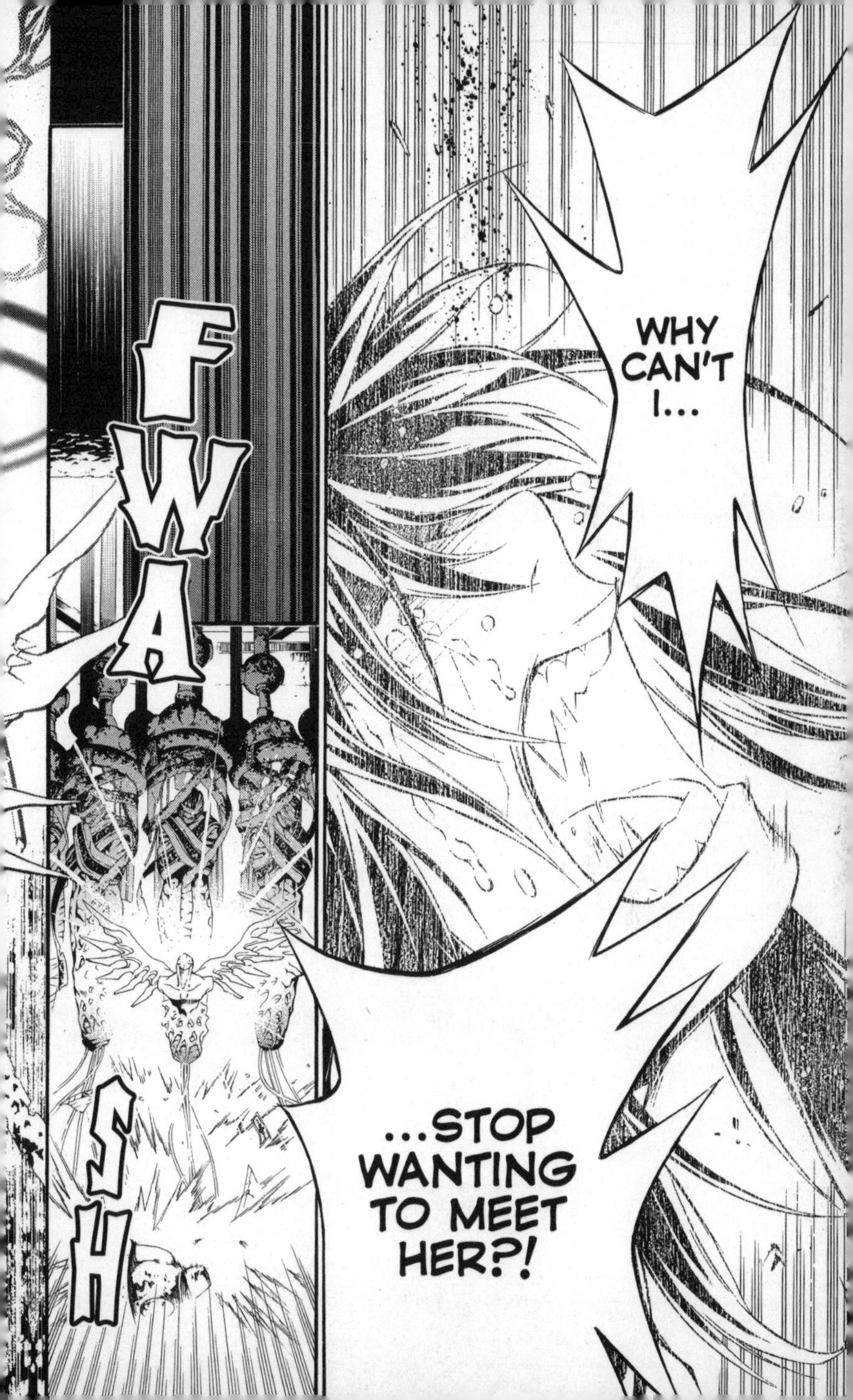
WHY CAN'T I...
...STOP WANTING TO MEET HER?!
FWASH

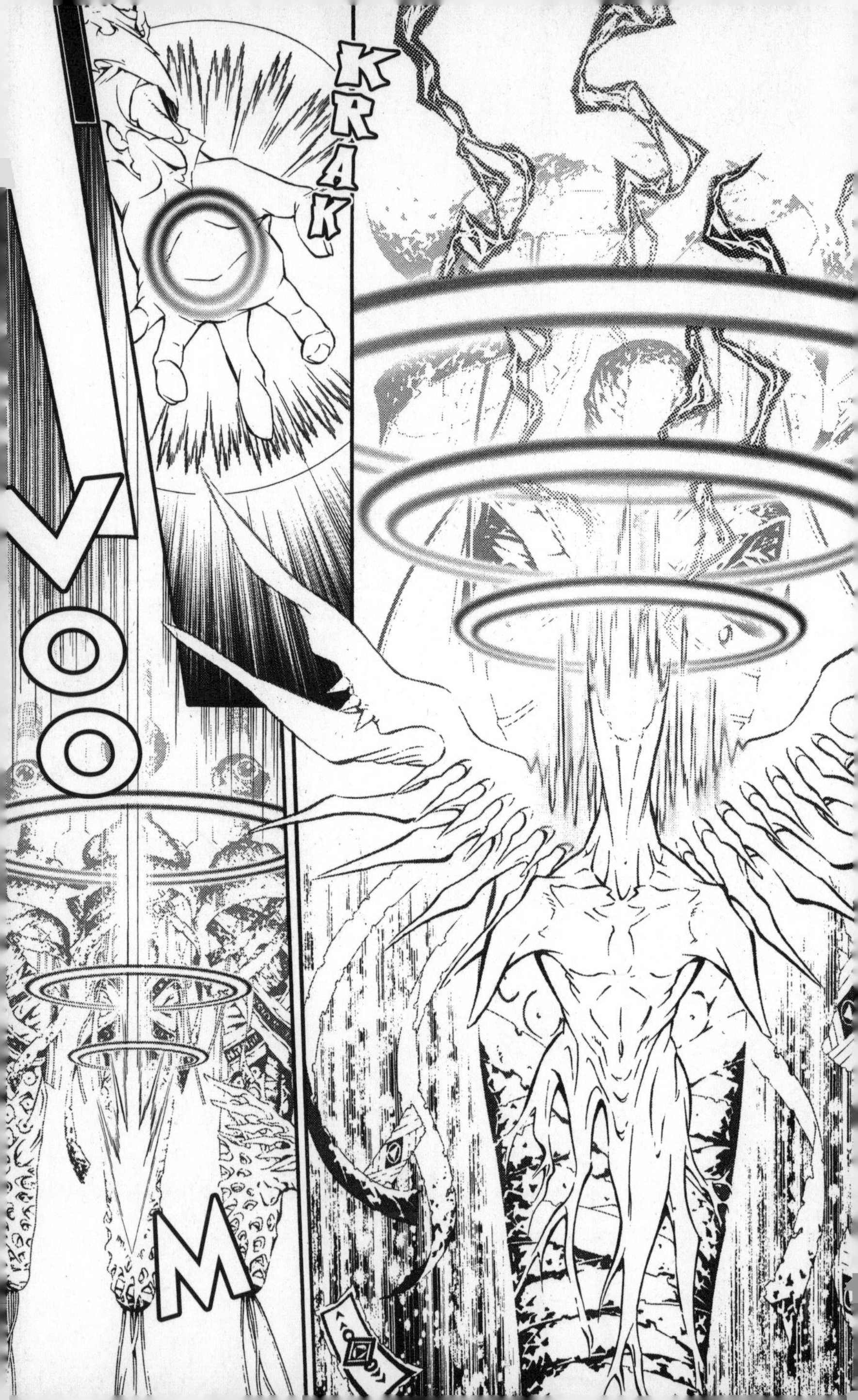
KRAK
VOOM

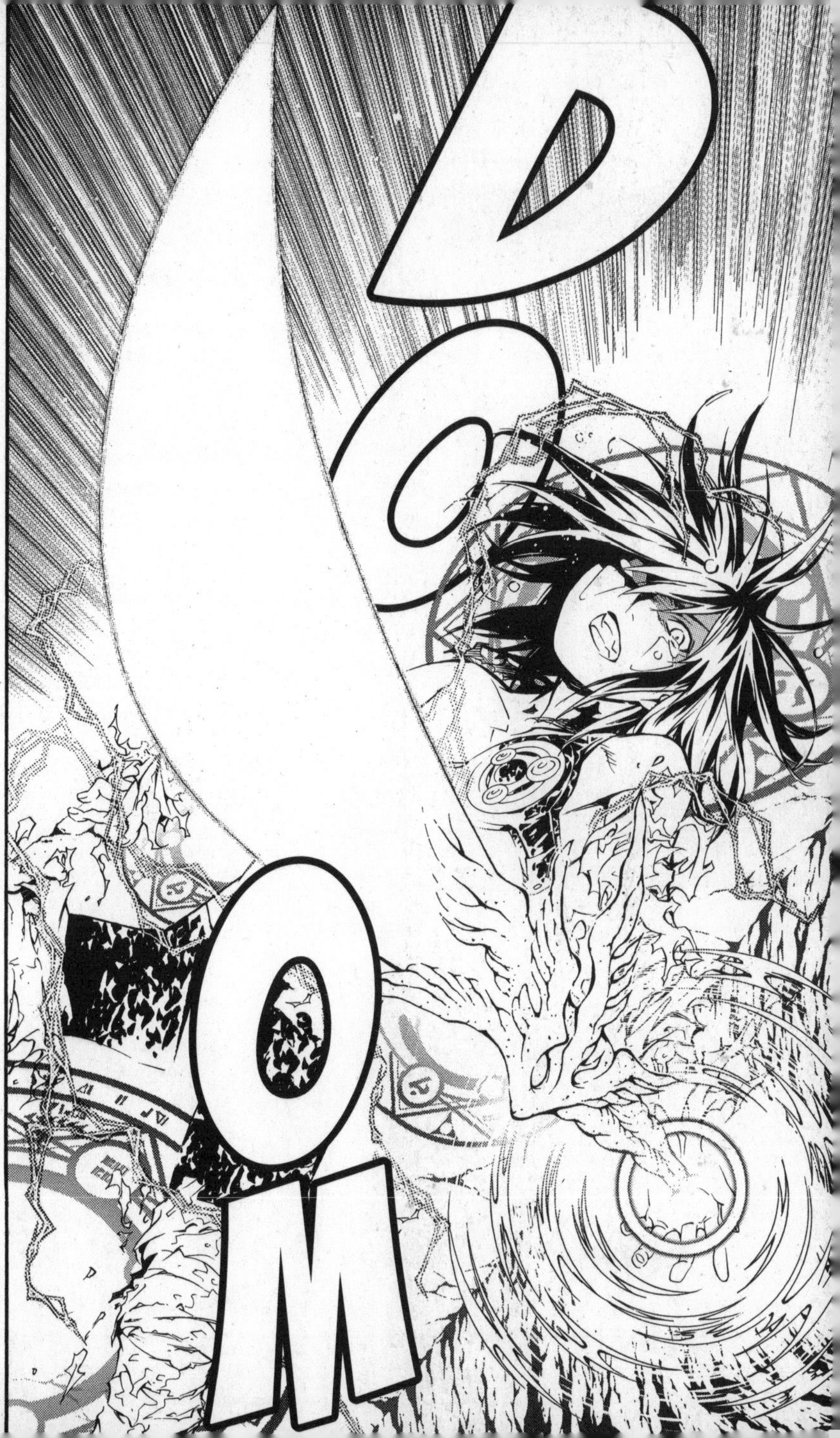
DOOM

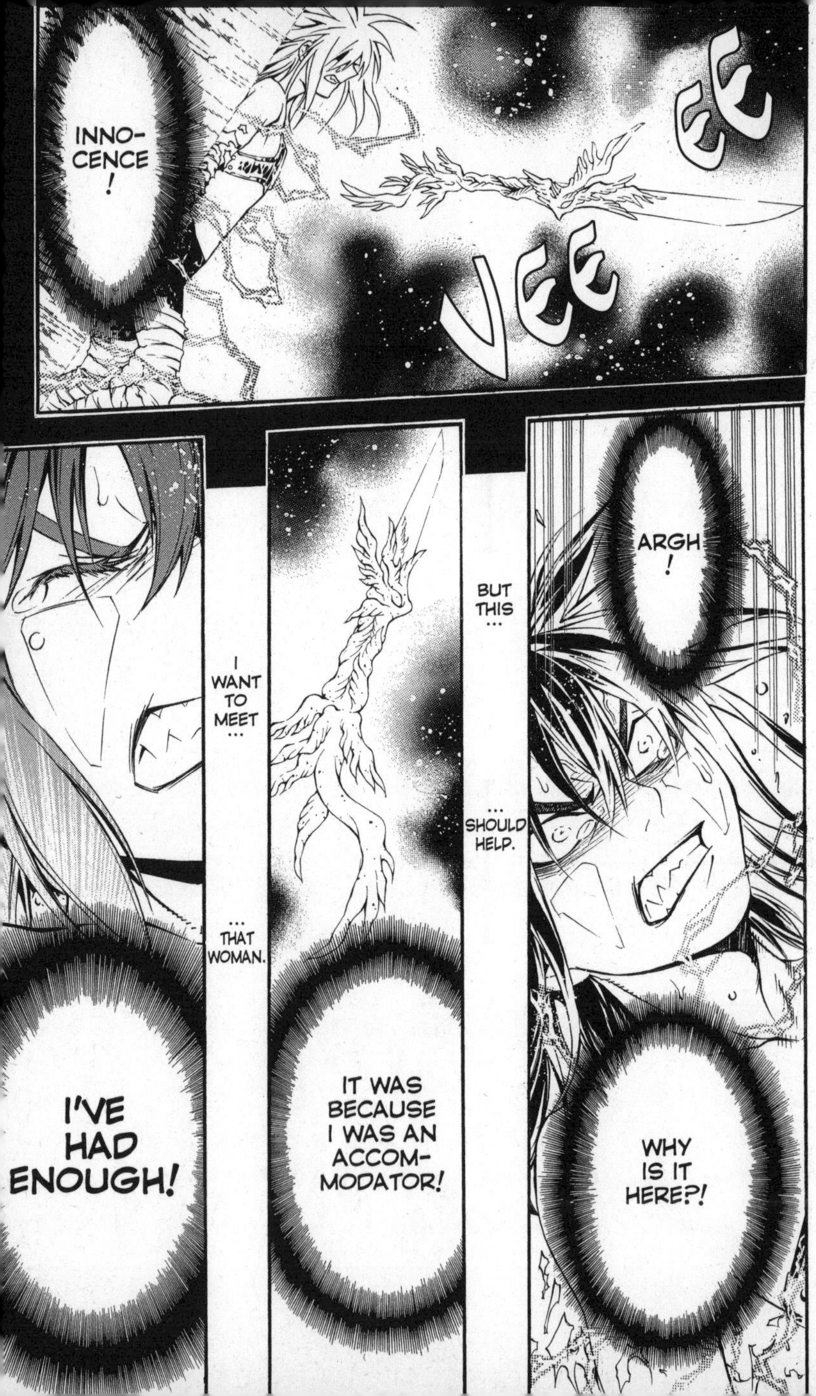
VEE
EE
INNO-CENCE!
ARGH!
BUT THIS...
...SHOULD HELP.
WHY IS IT HERE?!
I WANT TO MEET...
...THAT WOMAN.
IT WAS BECAUSE I WAS AN ACCOM-MODATOR!
I'VE HAD ENOUGH!

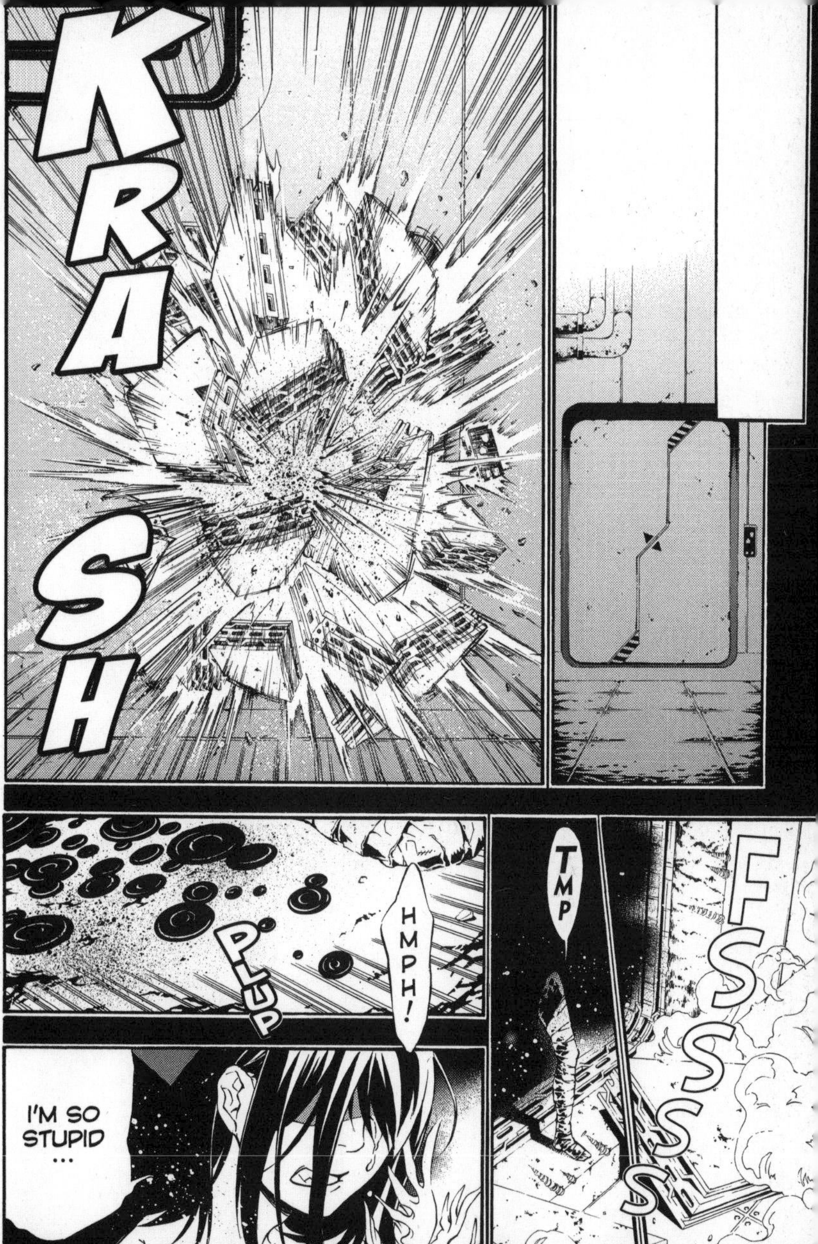
KRASH
TMP
FSSSSS
HMPH!
PLUP
I'M SO STUPID...

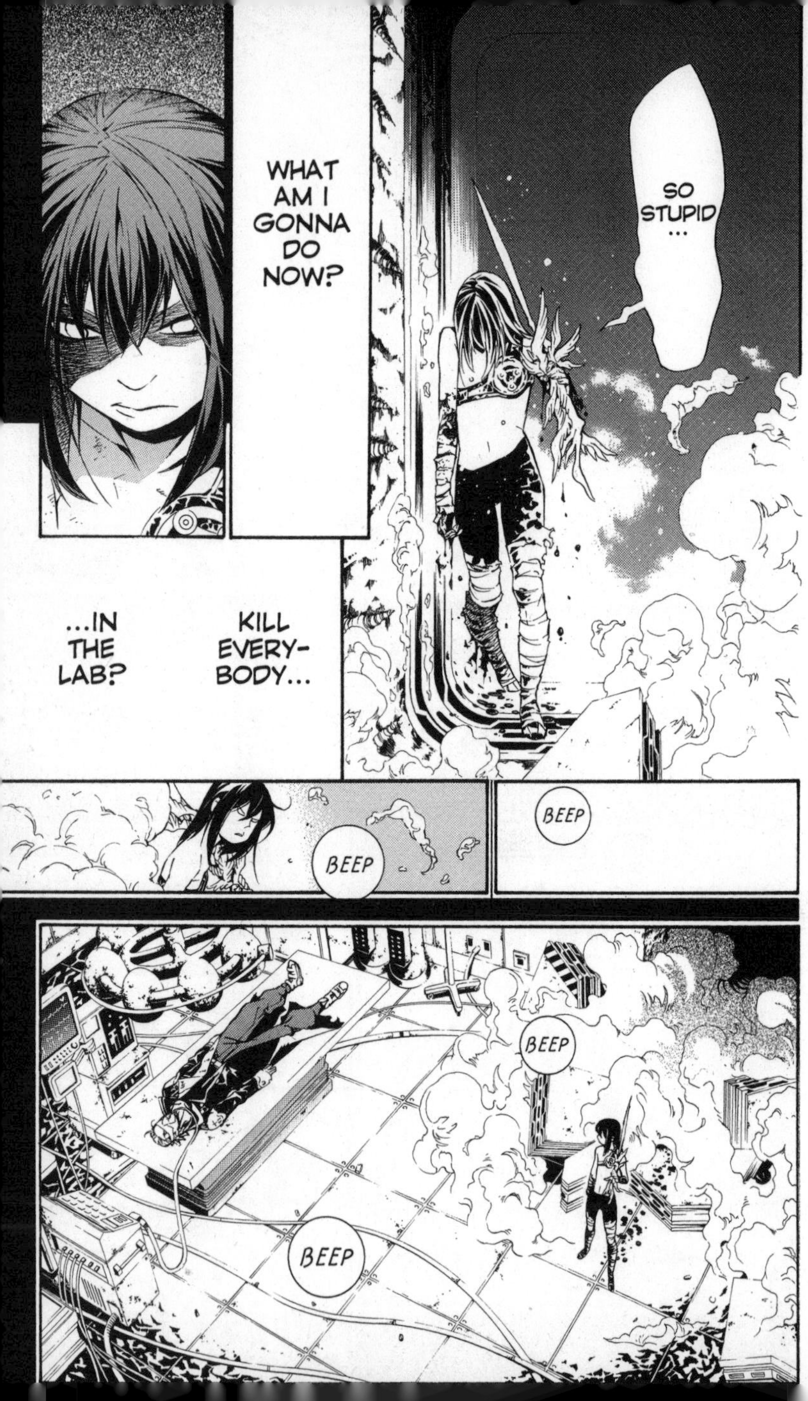
SO STUPID...
WHAT AM I GONNA DO NOW?
KILL EVERY-BODY...
...IN THE LAB?
BEEP
BEEP
BEEP
BEEP

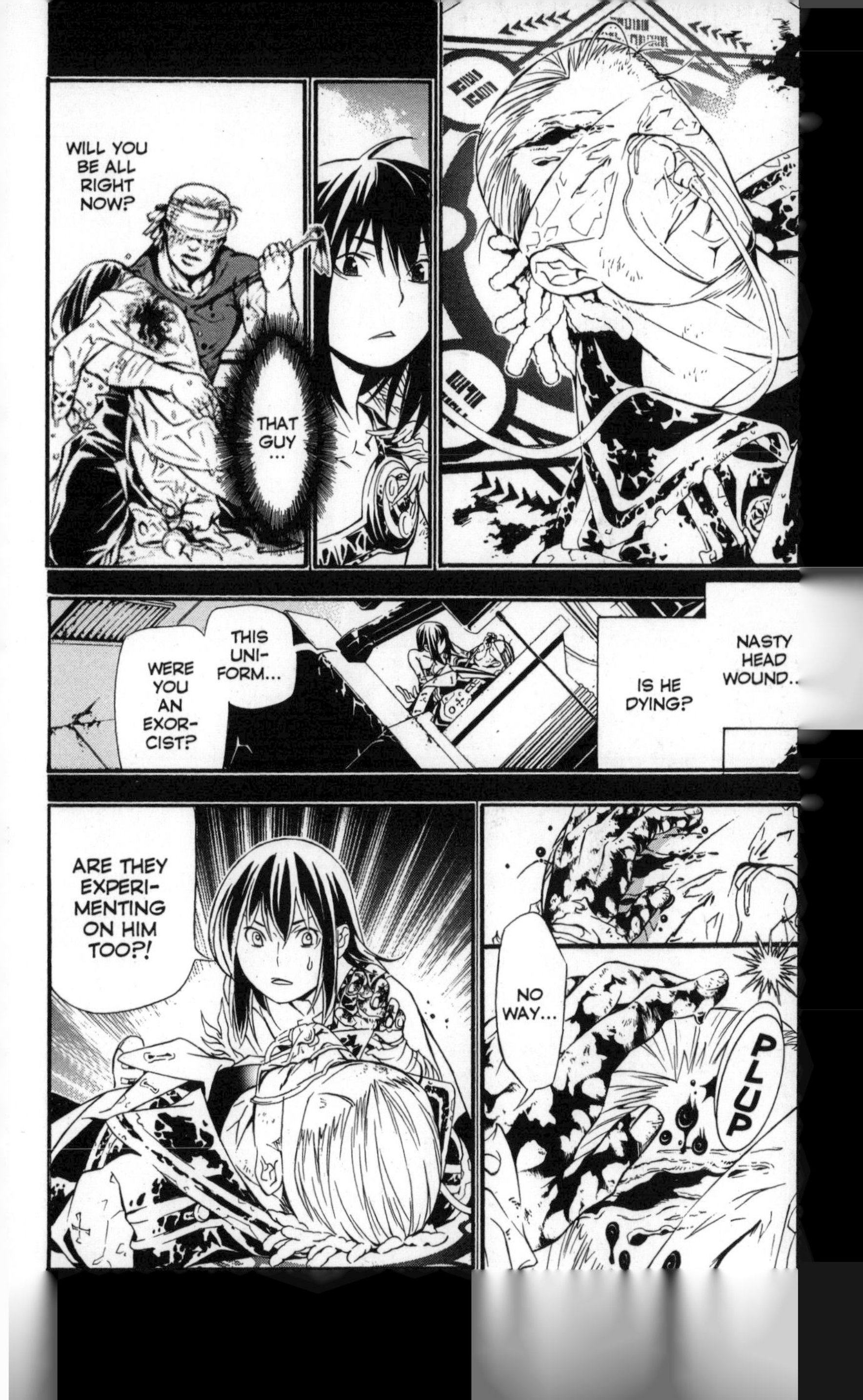
THAT GUY...
WILL YOU BE ALL RIGHT NOW?
NASTY HEAD WOUND..
IS HE DYING?
THIS UNIFORM...
WERE YOU AN EXORCIST?
NO WAY...
PLUP
ARE THEY EXPERIMENTING ON HIM TOO?!

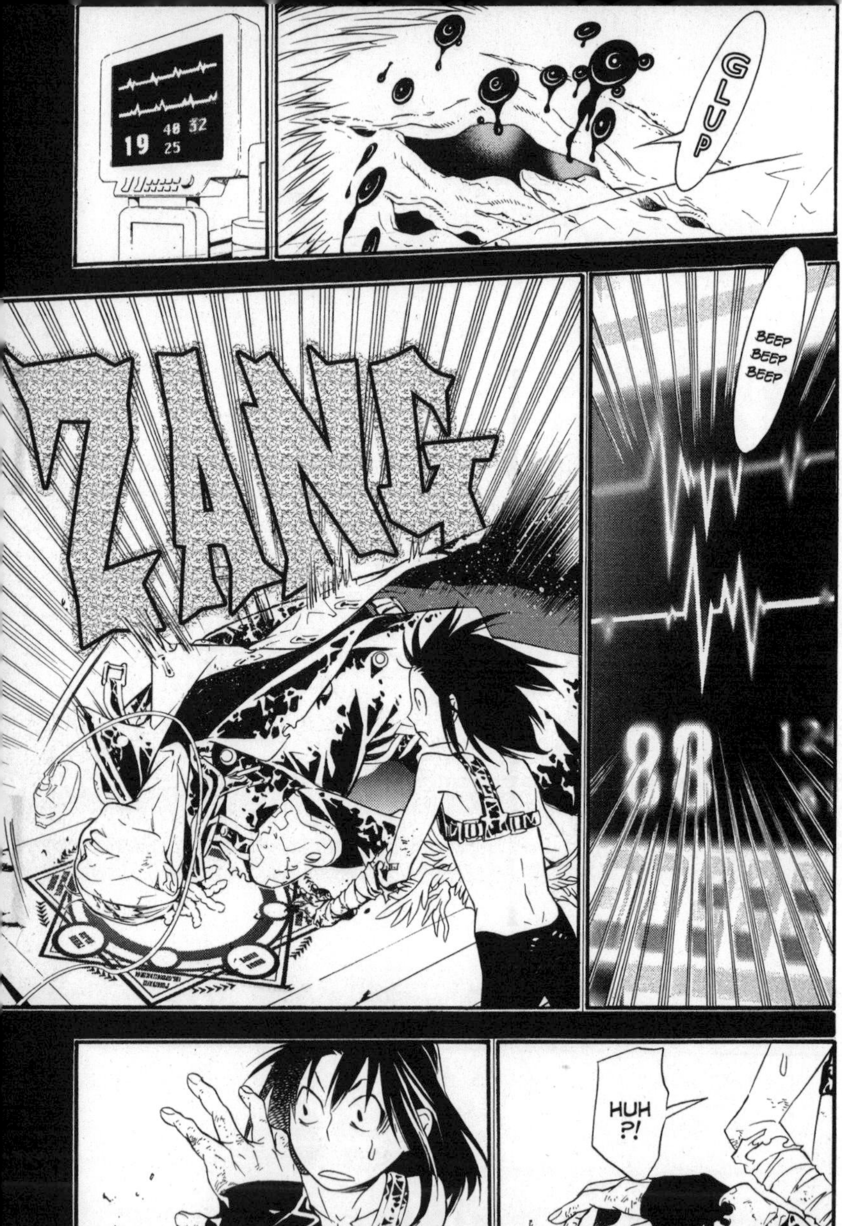
GLUP
19 40 32 25
BEEP BEEP BEEP
ZANG
HUH?!

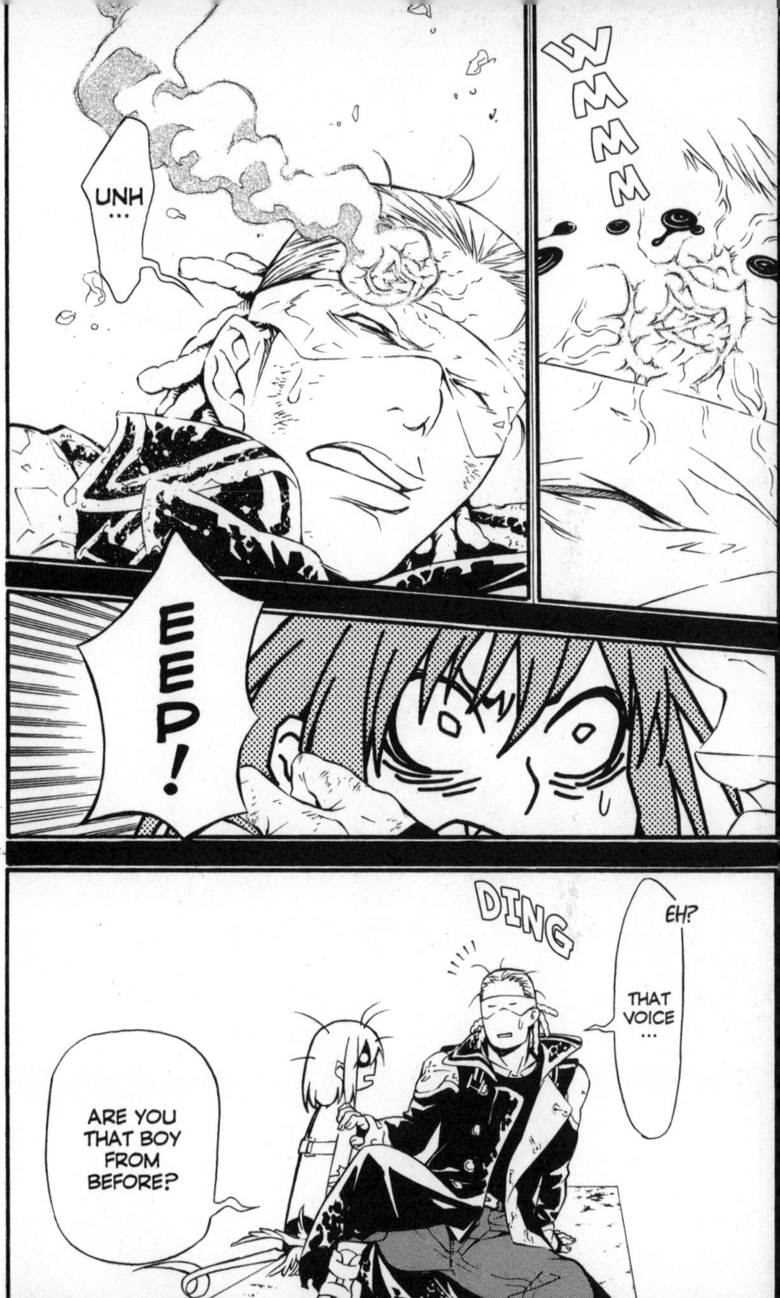
WMMMM
UNH...
EEP!
DING
EH?
THAT VOICE...
ARE YOU THAT BOY FROM BEFORE?

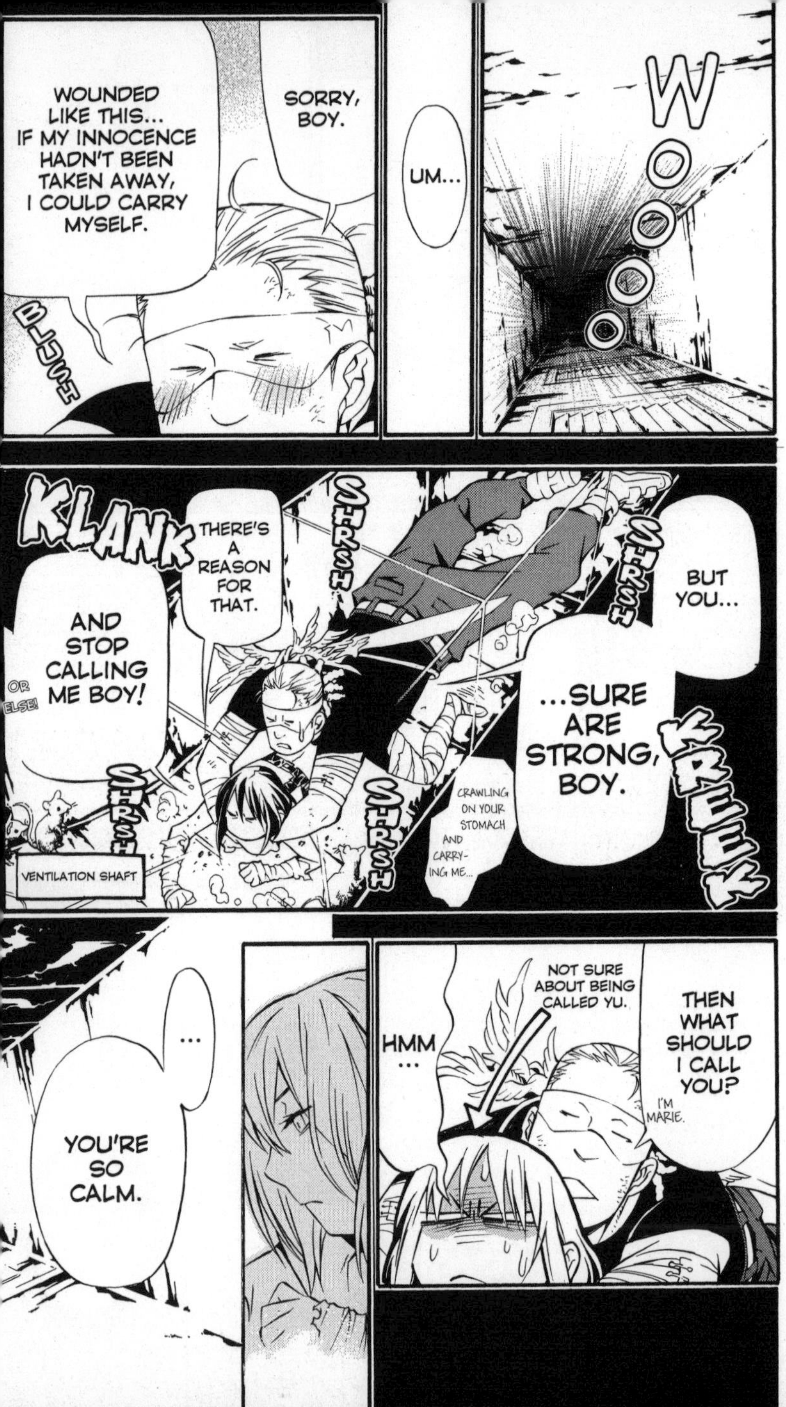
WOOOOO
UM...
SORRY, BOY.
WOUNDED LIKE THIS... IF MY INNOCENCE HADN'T BEEN TAKEN AWAY, I COULD CARRY MYSELF.
BLUSH
BUT YOU...
...SURE ARE STRONG, BOY.
KREEK
CRAWLING ON YOUR STOMACH AND CARRYING ME...
SHRSH
SHRSH
SHRSH
THERE'S A REASON FOR THAT.
KLANK
AND STOP CALLING ME BOY!
OR ELSE!
SHRSH
VENTILATION SHAFT
THEN WHAT SHOULD I CALL YOU?
I'M MARIE.
NOT SURE ABOUT BEING CALLED YU.
HMM...
...
YOU'RE SO CALM.

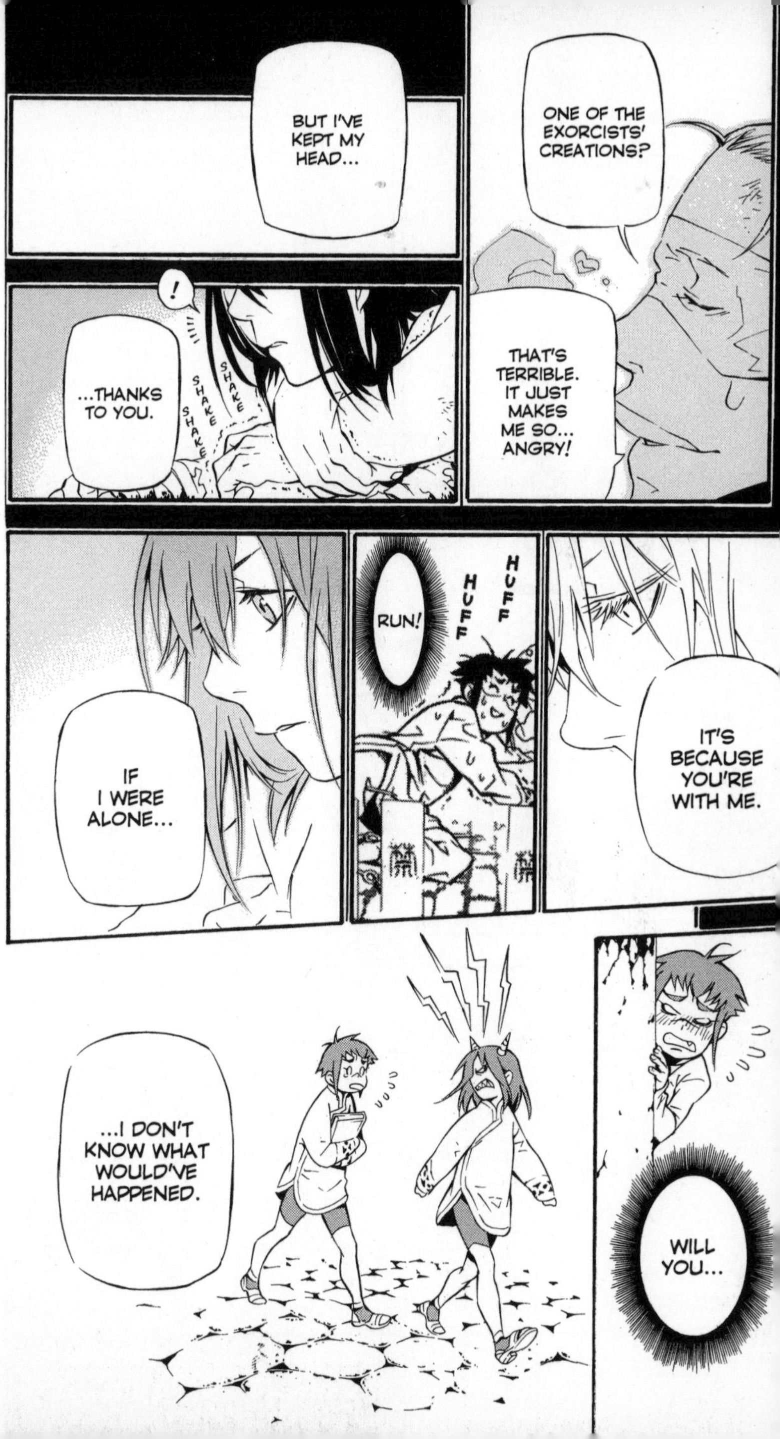
ONE OF THE EXORCISTS' CREATIONS?
THAT'S TERRIBLE. IT JUST MAKES ME SO... ANGRY!
BUT I'VE KEPT MY HEAD...
!
...THANKS TO YOU.
SHAKE SHAKE
IT'S BECAUSE YOU'RE WITH ME.
HUFF HUFF
RUN!
IF I WERE ALONE...
WILL YOU...
...I DON'T KNOW WHAT WOULD'VE HAPPENED.

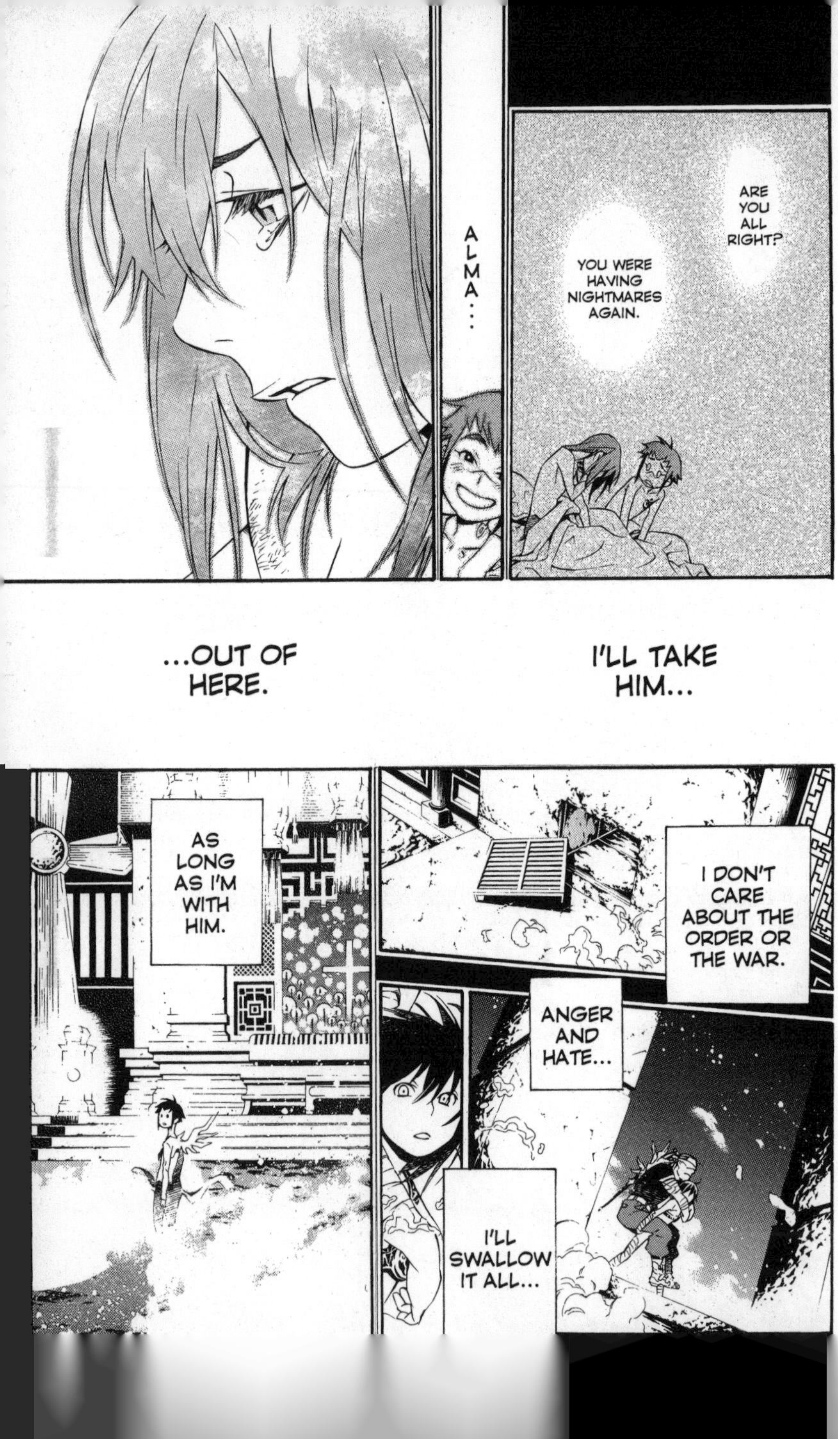
ARE YOU ALL RIGHT?
YOU WERE HAVING NIGHTMARES AGAIN.
ALMA...
I'LL TAKE HIM...
...OUT OF HERE.
I DON'T CARE ABOUT THE ORDER OR THE WAR.
ANGER AND HATE...
I'LL SWALLOW IT ALL...
AS LONG AS I'M WITH HIM.

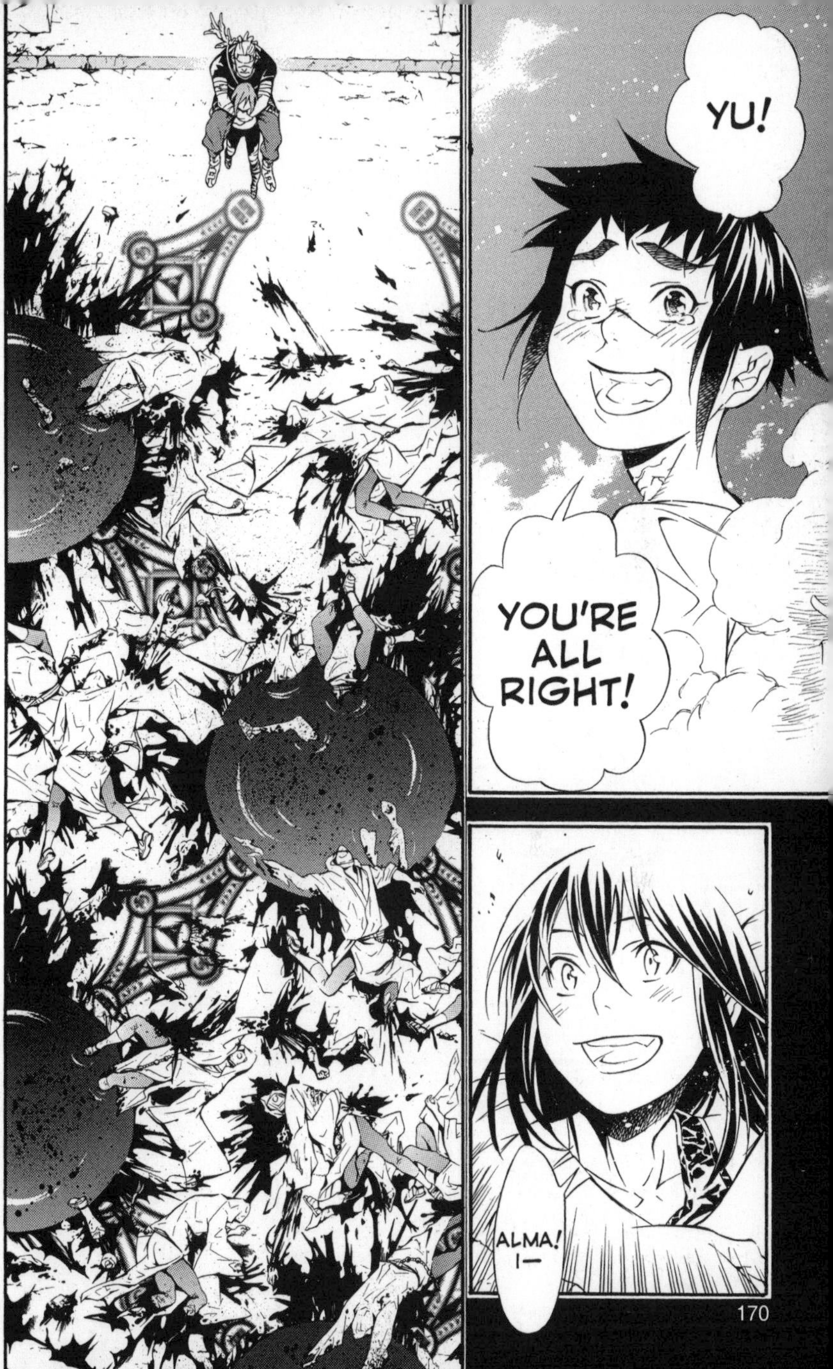
YU!
YOU'RE ALL RIGHT!
ALMA! I—

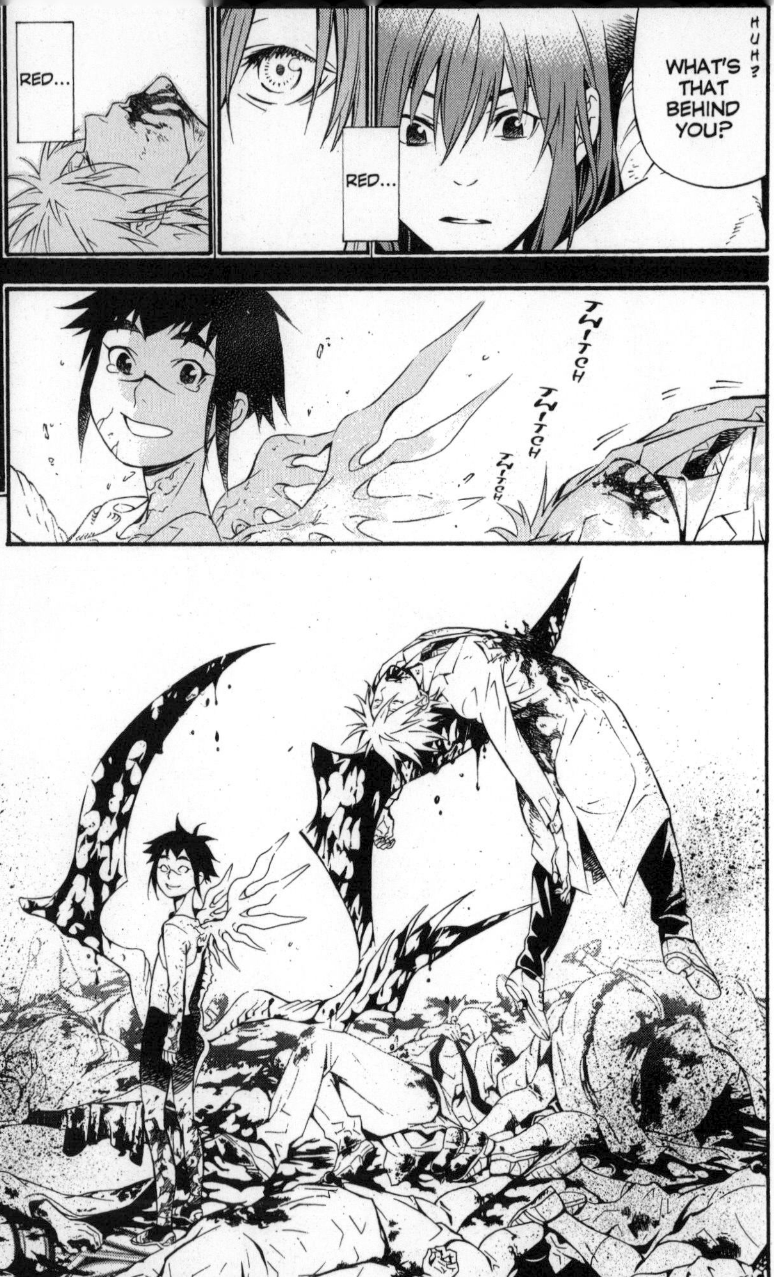
HUH?
WHAT'S THAT BEHIND YOU?
RED...
RED...
TWITCH
TWITCH
TWITCH

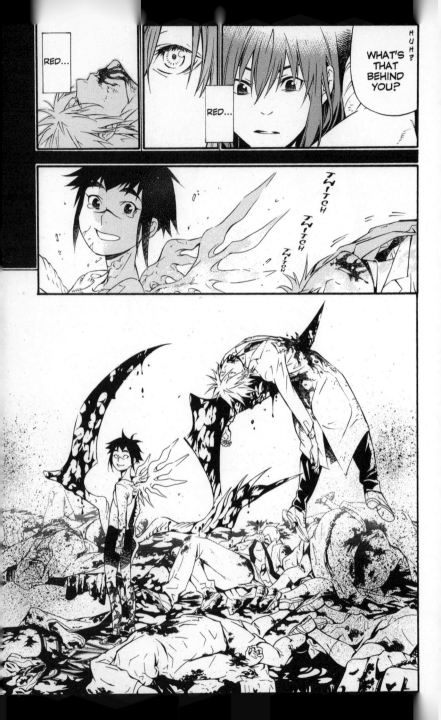

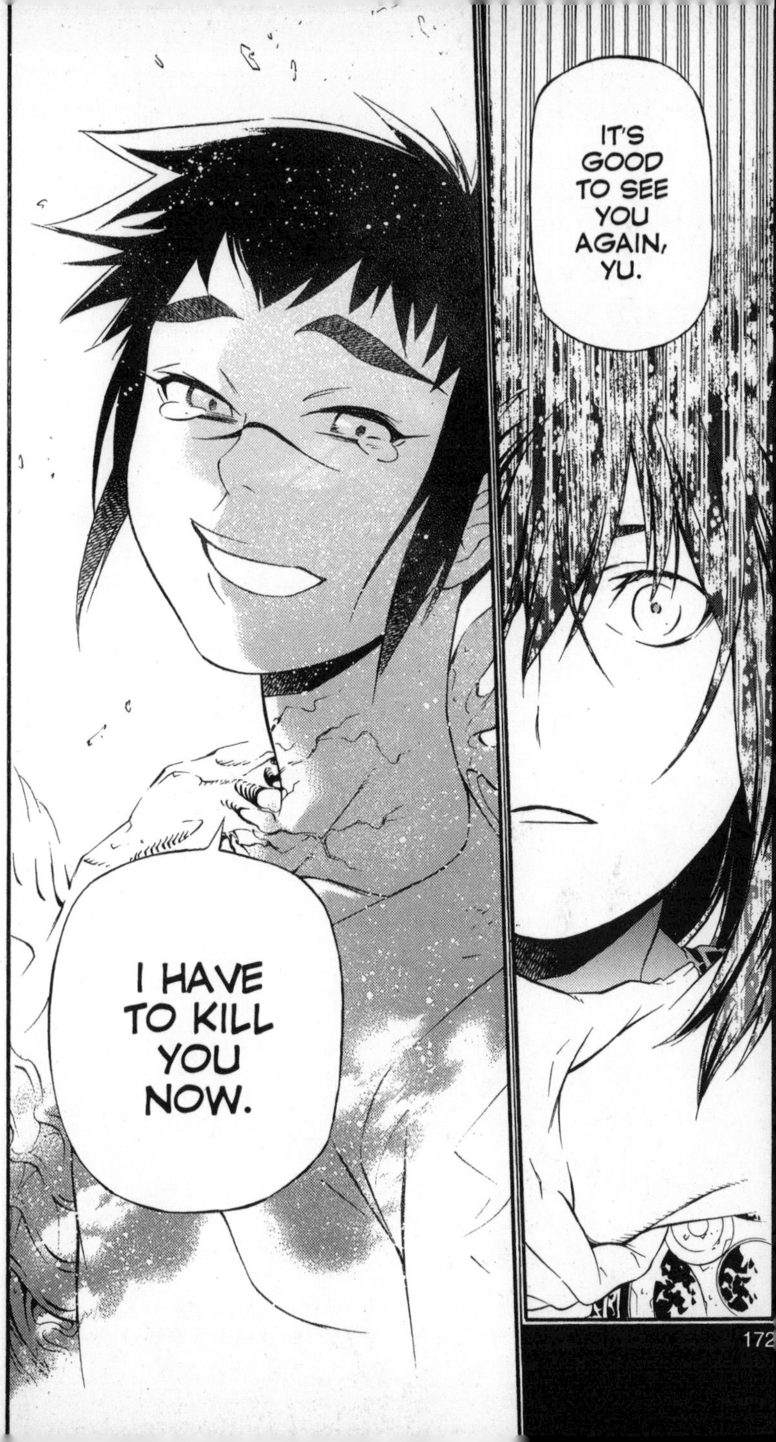
IT'S GOOD TO SEE YOU AGAIN, YU.
I HAVE TO KILL YOU NOW.

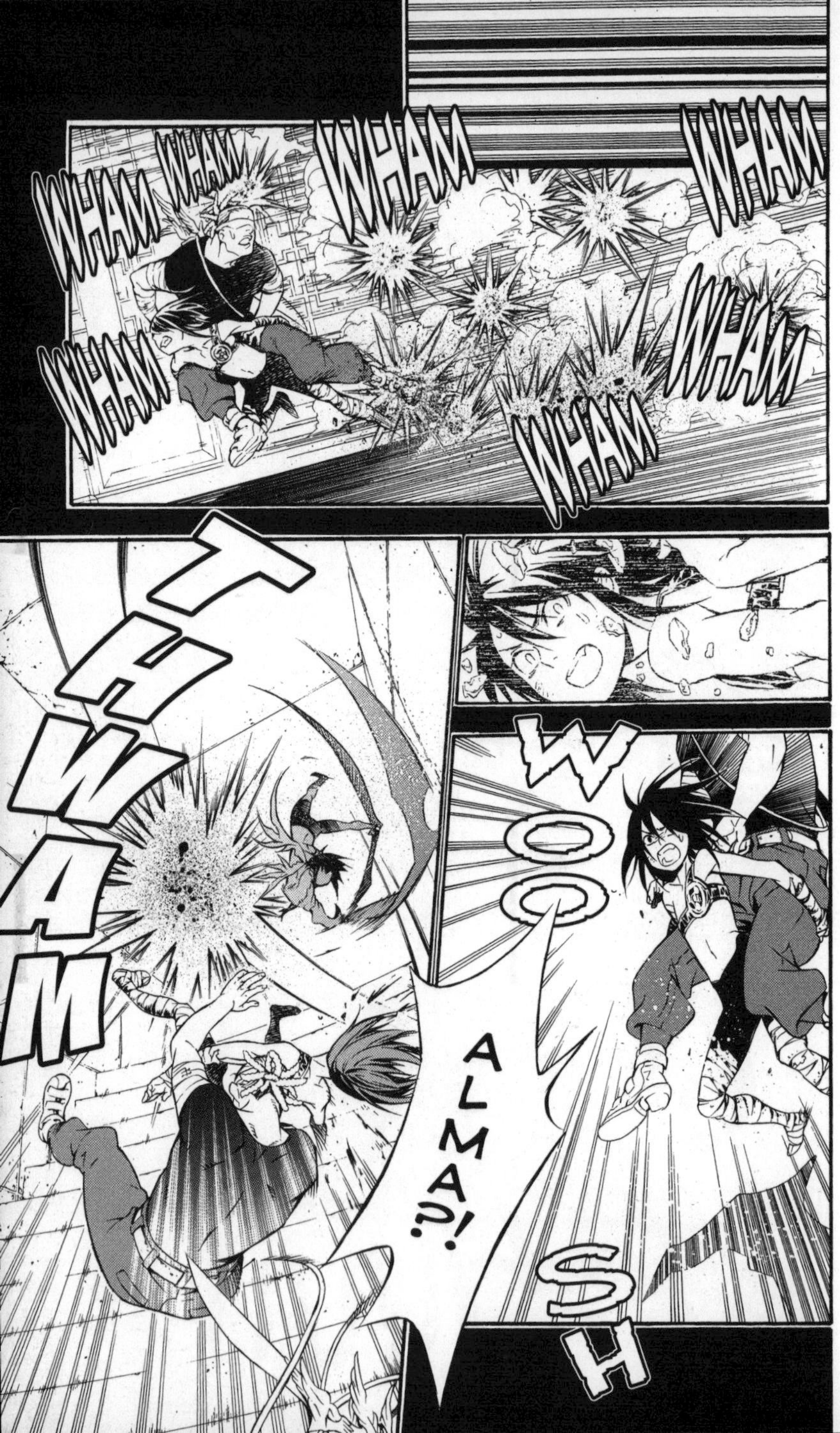
WHAM
WHAM
WHAM
WHAM
WHAM
WHAM
WHAM
WHAM
WOOSH
ALMA?!
THWAM

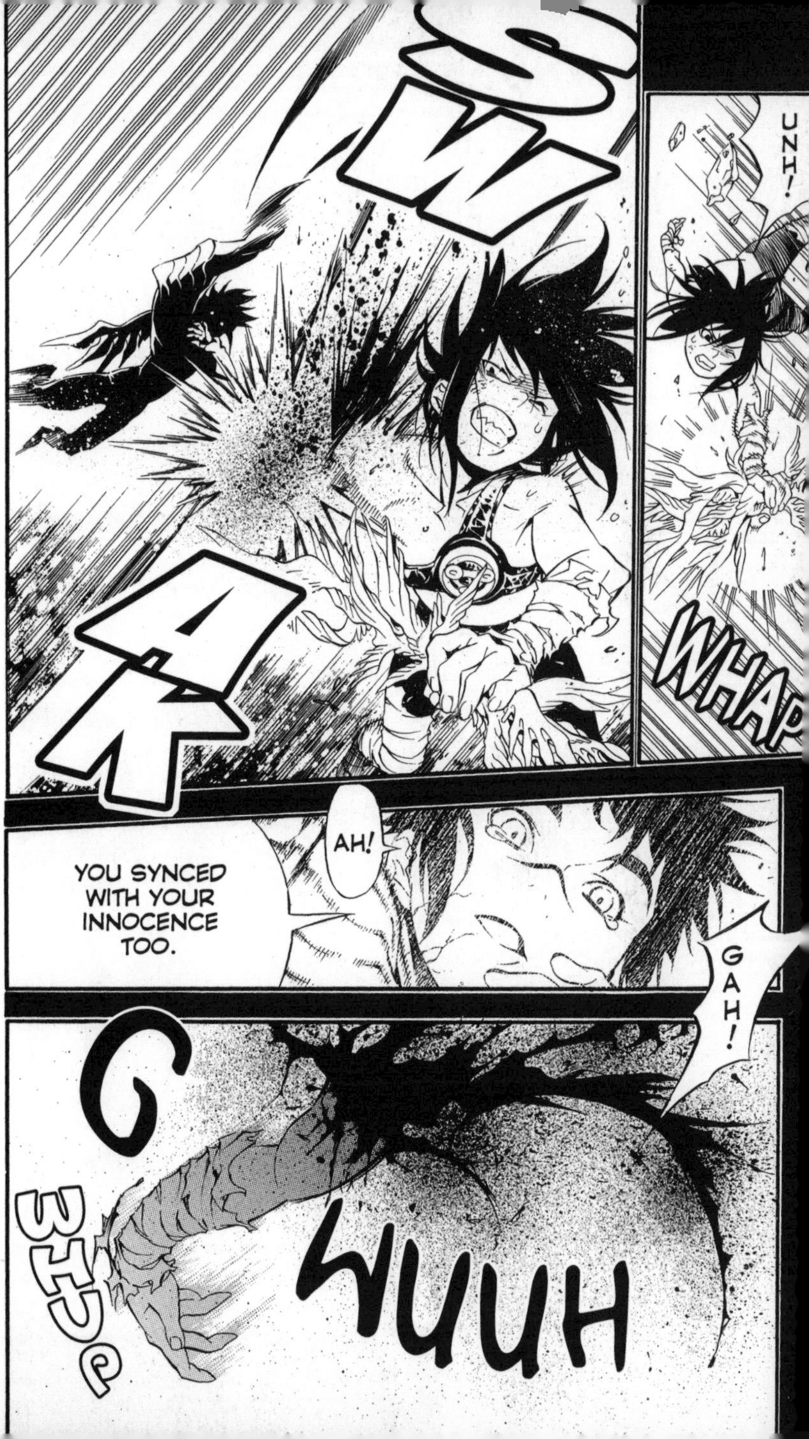
UNH!
WHAP
GAH!
AH!
YOU SYNCED WITH YOUR INNOCENCE TOO.
WHUP

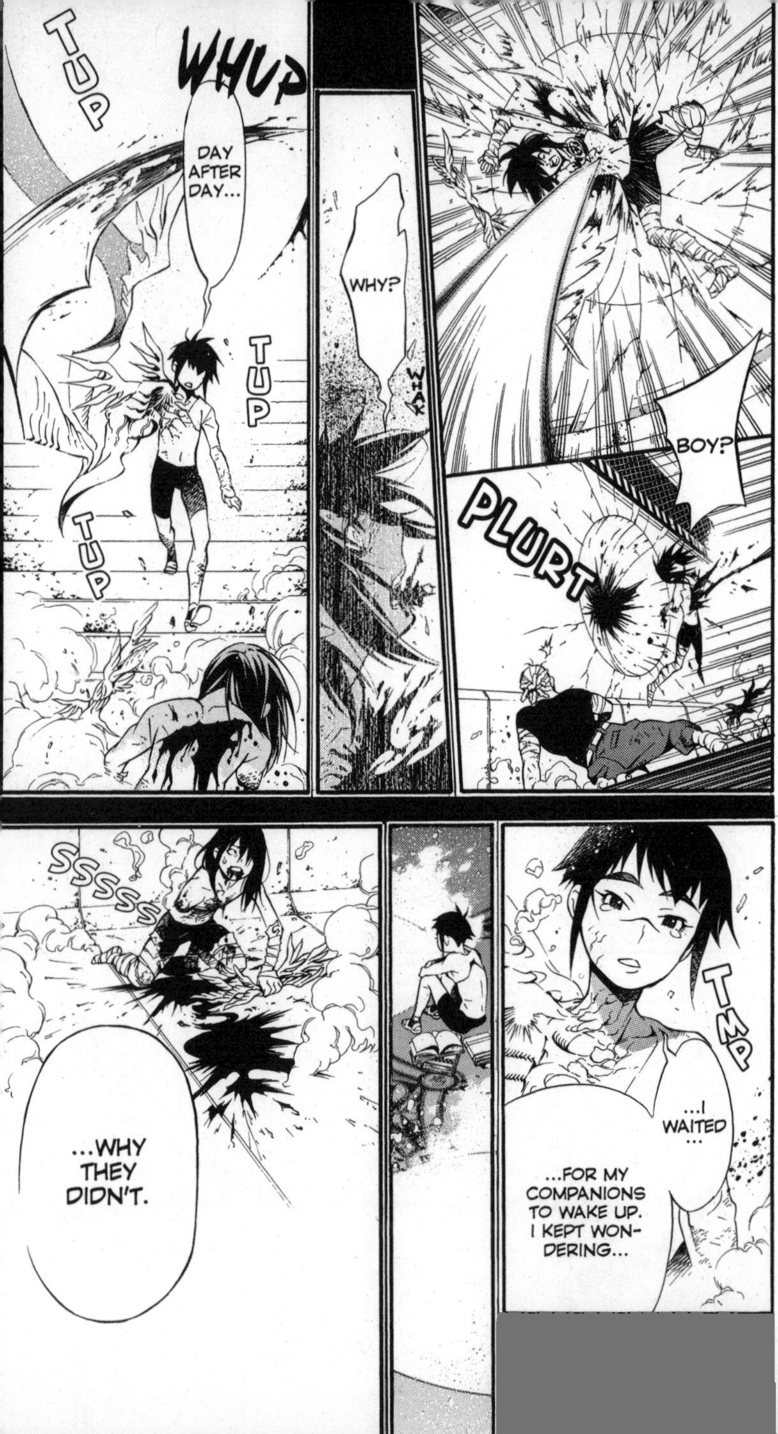
BOY?
PLURT
WHY?
WHAK
WHUP
TUP
DAY AFTER DAY...
TUP
TUP
TMP
...I WAITED...
...FOR MY COMPANIONS TO WAKE UP. I KEPT WONDERING...
SSSSS
...WHY THEY DIDN'T.

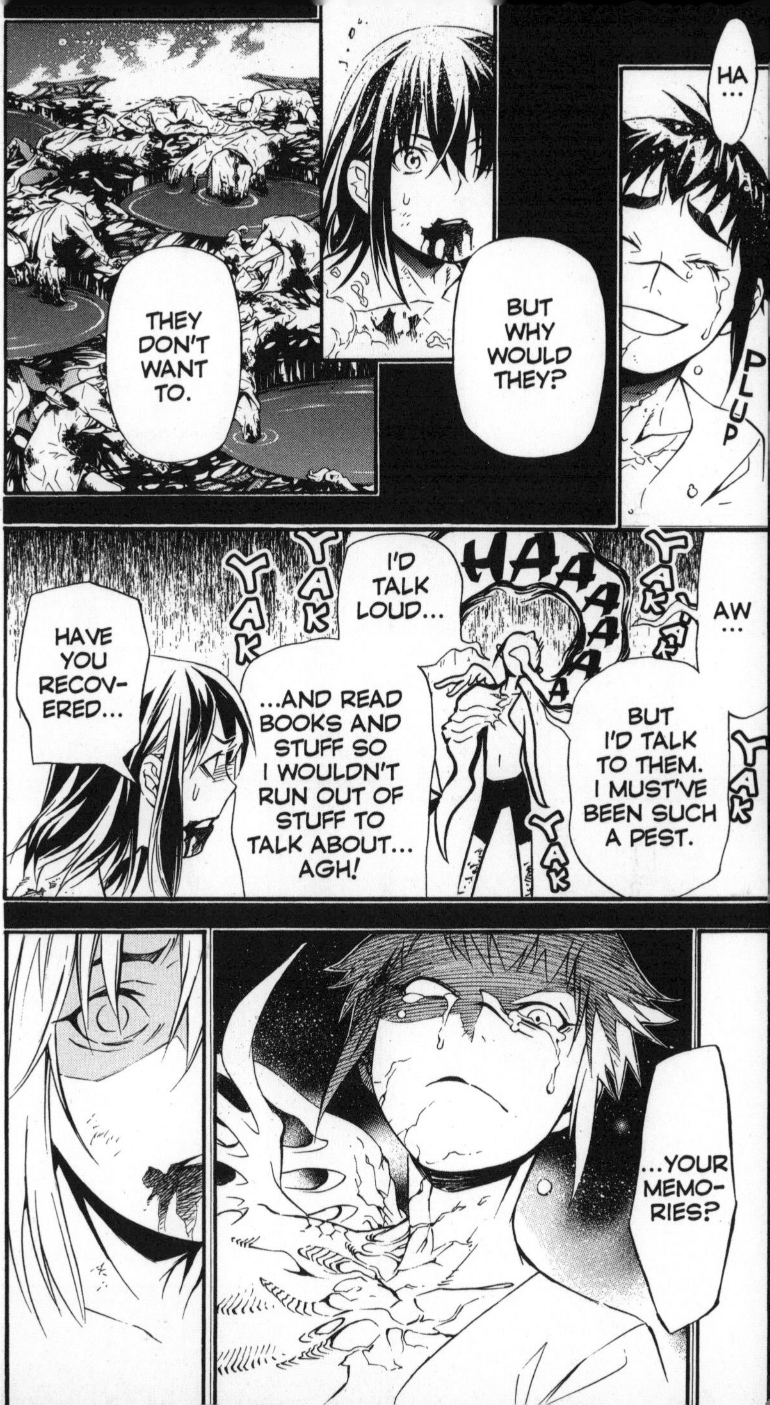
HA...
PLUP
BUT WHY WOULD THEY?
THEY DON'T WANT TO.
AW...
YAK
YAK
YAK
BUT I'D TALK TO THEM. I MUST'VE BEEN SUCH A PEST.
YAK
HAAAAAAA
I'D TALK LOUD...
...AND READ BOOKS AND STUFF SO I WOULDN'T RUN OUT OF STUFF TO TALK ABOUT... AGH!
YAK
YAK
HAVE YOU RECOVERED...
...YOUR MEMORIES?

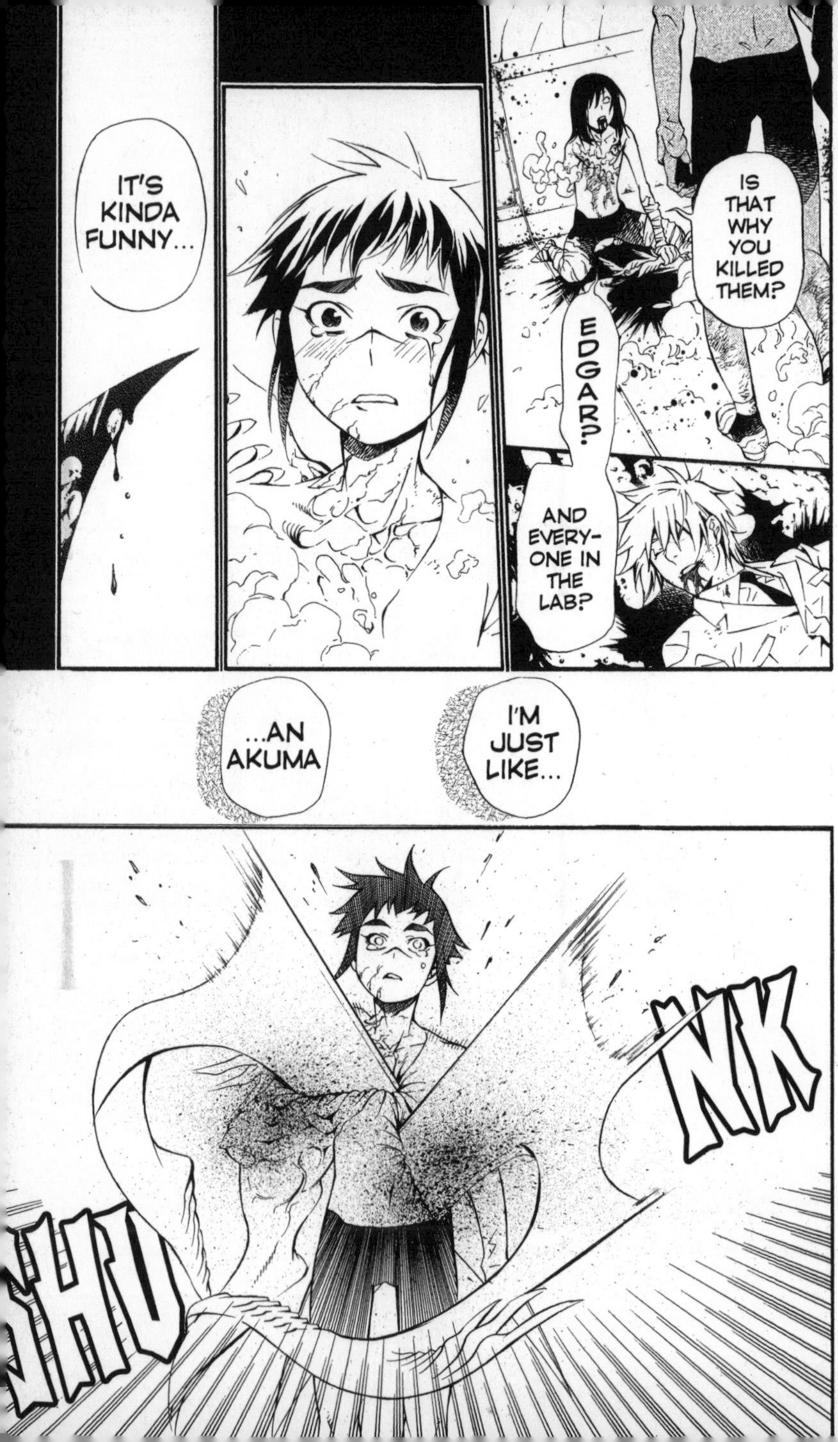
IS THAT WHY YOU KILLED THEM?
EDGAR?
AND EVERYONE IN THE LAB?
IT'S KINDA FUNNY...
I'M JUST LIKE...
...AN AKUMA
SHU
NK

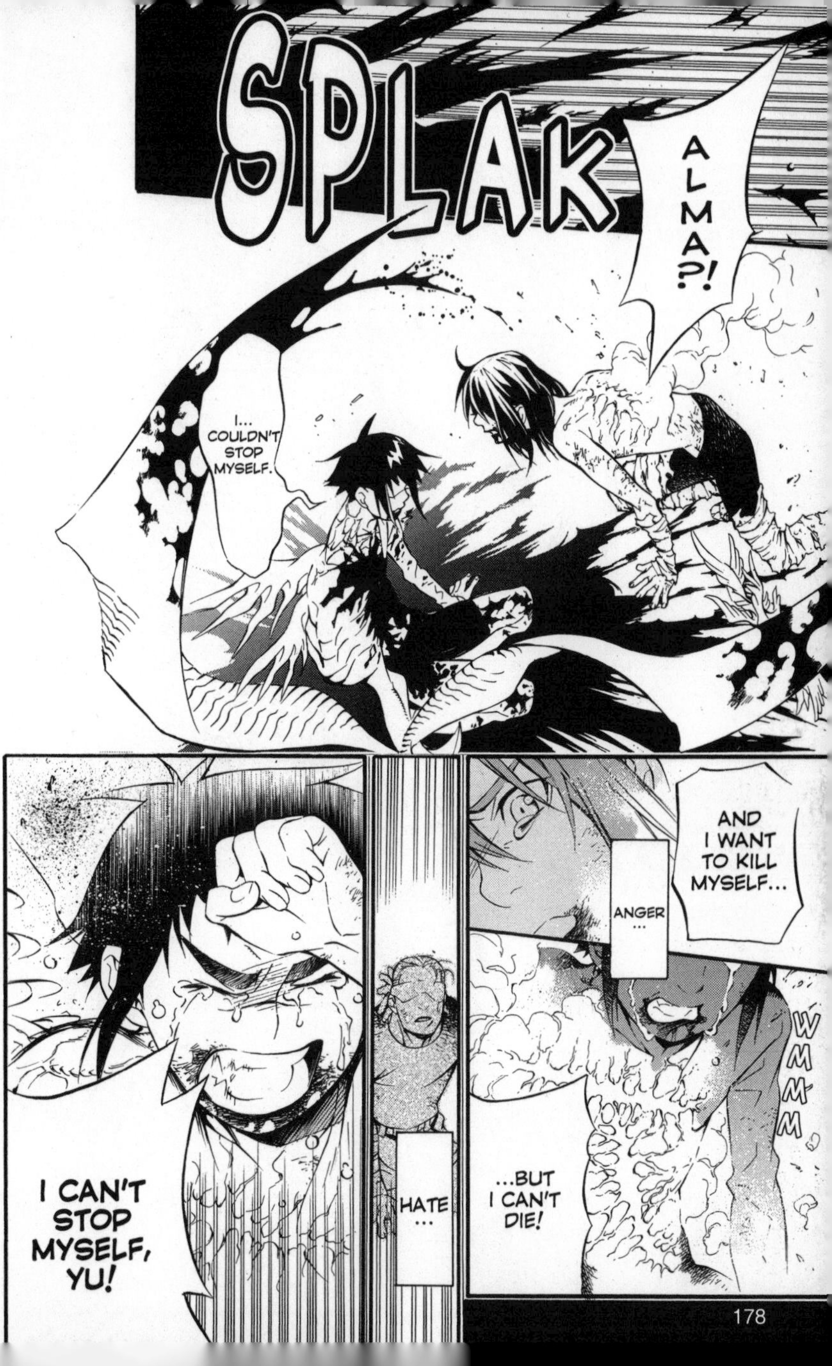

ALMA?!
SPLAK
I... COULDN'T STOP MYSELF.
AND I WANT TO KILL MYSELF...
ANGER...
WMMM
...BUT I CAN'T DIE!
HATE...
I CAN'T STOP MYSELF, YU!

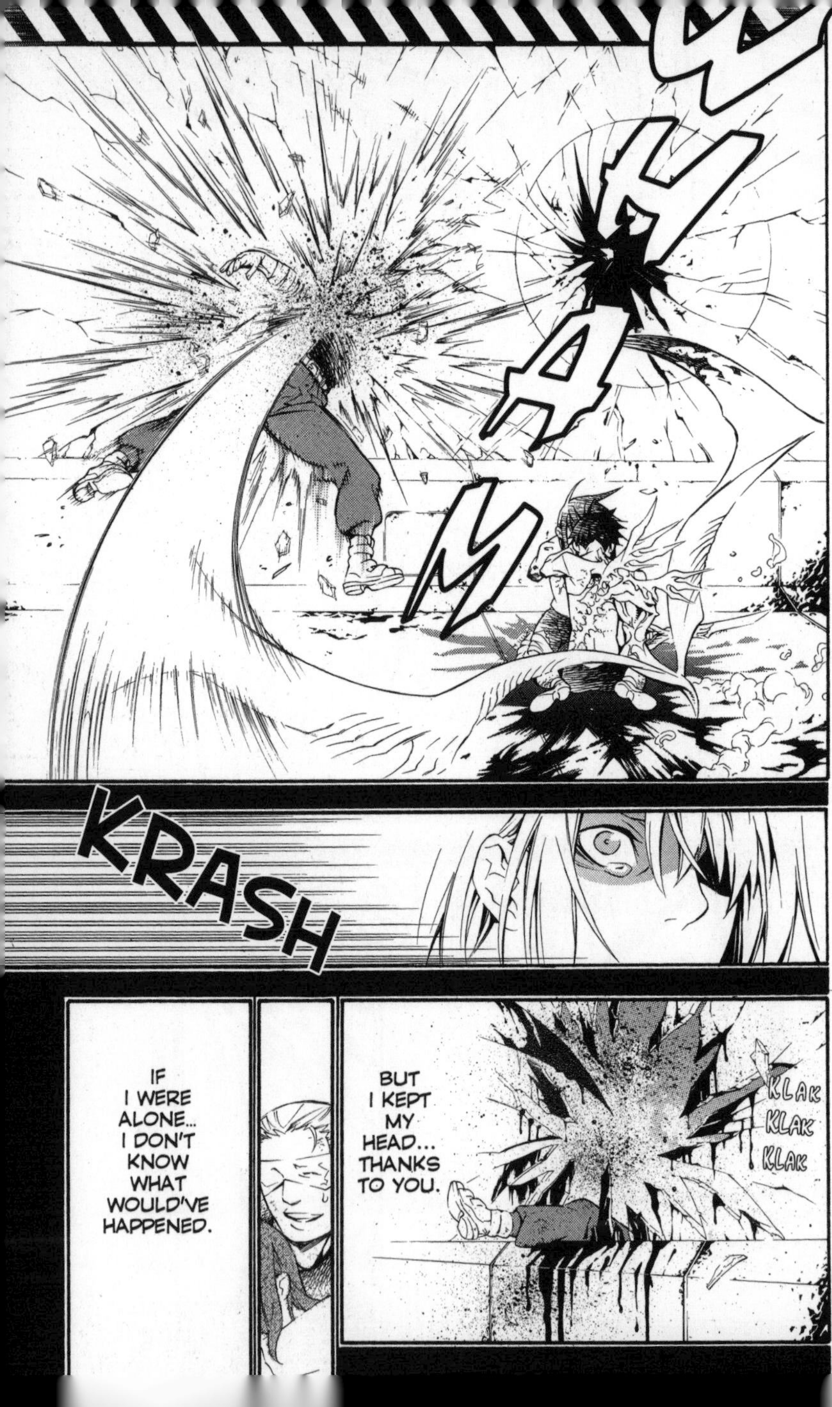
WHAM
KRASH
KLAK
KLAK
KLAK
BUT I KEPT MY HEAD... THANKS TO YOU.
IF I WERE ALONE... I DON'T KNOW WHAT WOULD'VE HAPPENED.

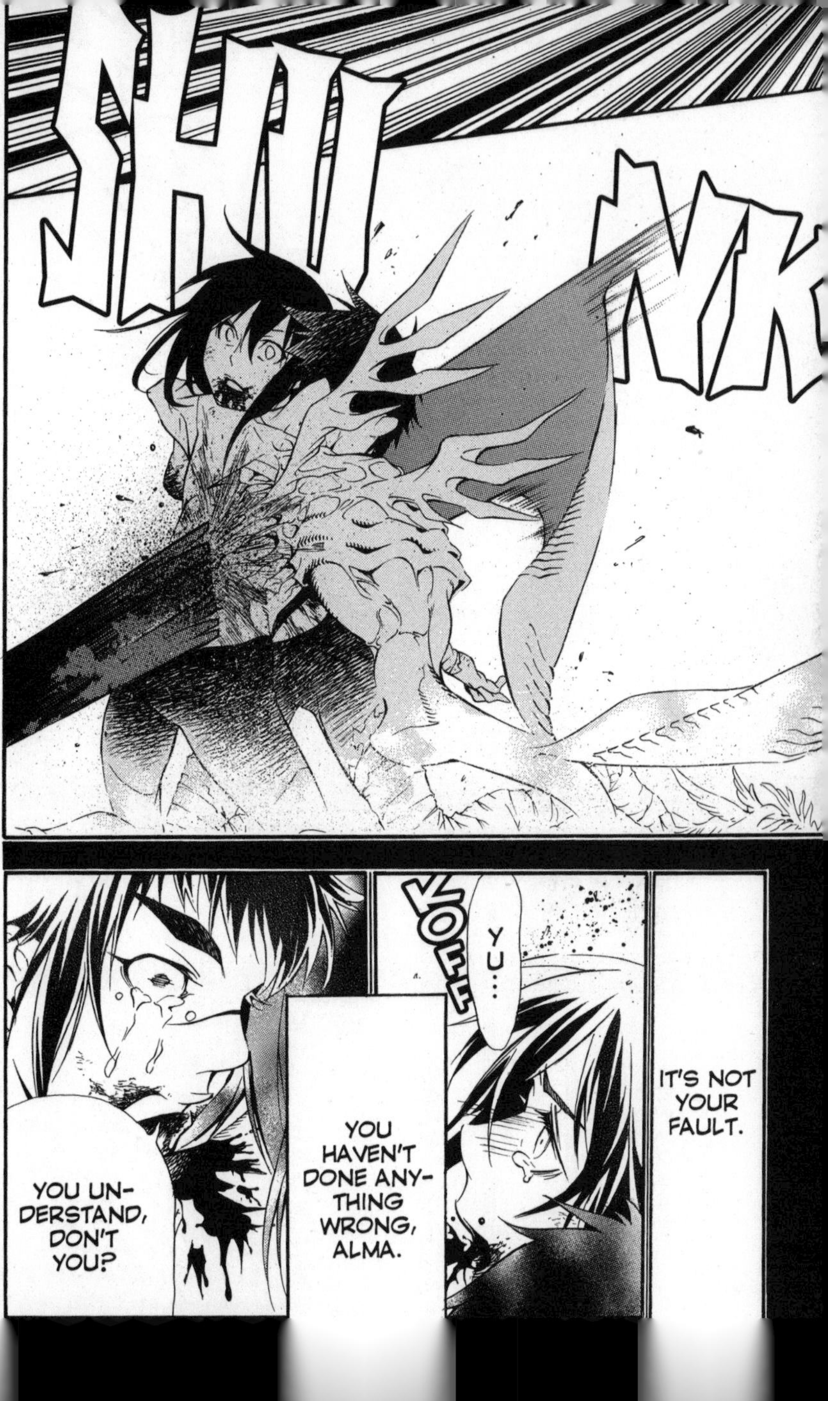
SHUNK
IT'S NOT YOUR FAULT.
KOFF
YU...
YOU HAVEN'T DONE ANY-THING WRONG, ALMA.
YOU UN-DERSTAND, DON'T YOU?

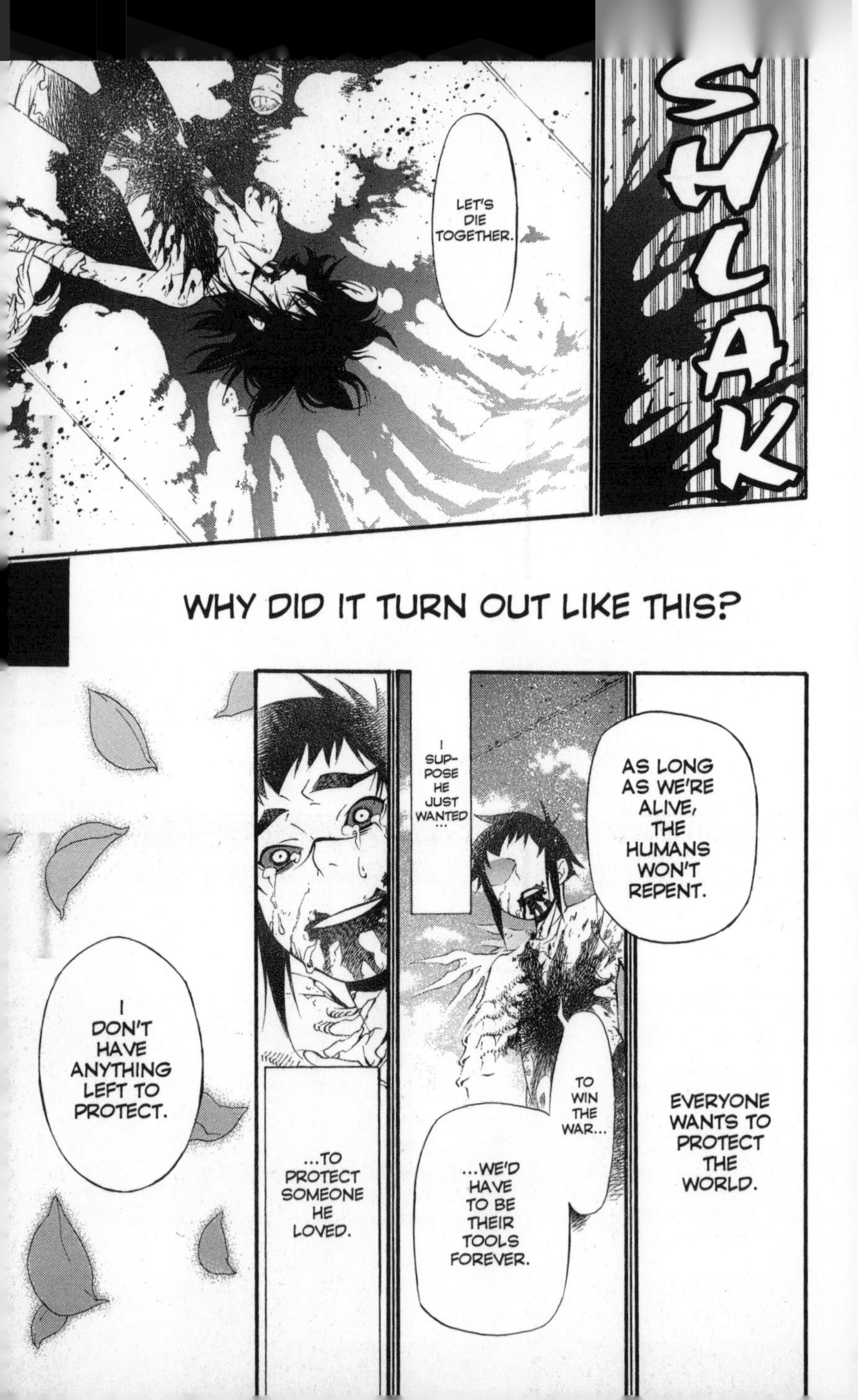
SHLAK
LET'S DIE TOGETHER.
WHY DID IT TURN OUT LIKE THIS?
EVERYONE WANTS TO PROTECT THE WORLD.
AS LONG AS WE'RE ALIVE, THE HUMANS WON'T REPENT.
TO WIN THE WAR...
...WE'D HAVE TO BE THEIR TOOLS FOREVER.
I SUP-POSE HE JUST WANTED...
...TO PROTECT SOMEONE HE LOVED.
I DON'T HAVE ANYTHING LEFT TO PROTECT.

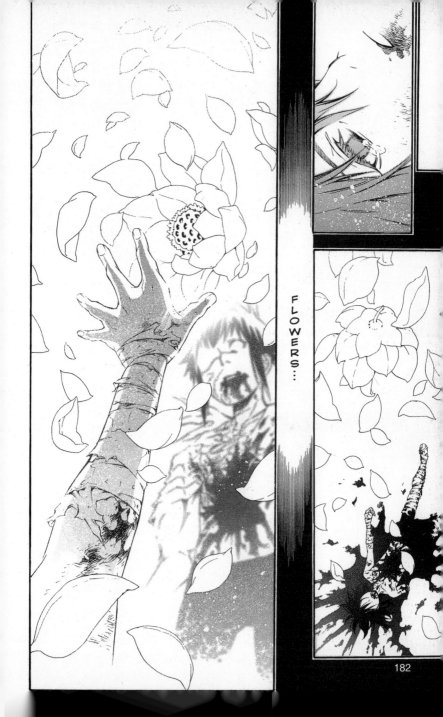

FLOWERS...

182

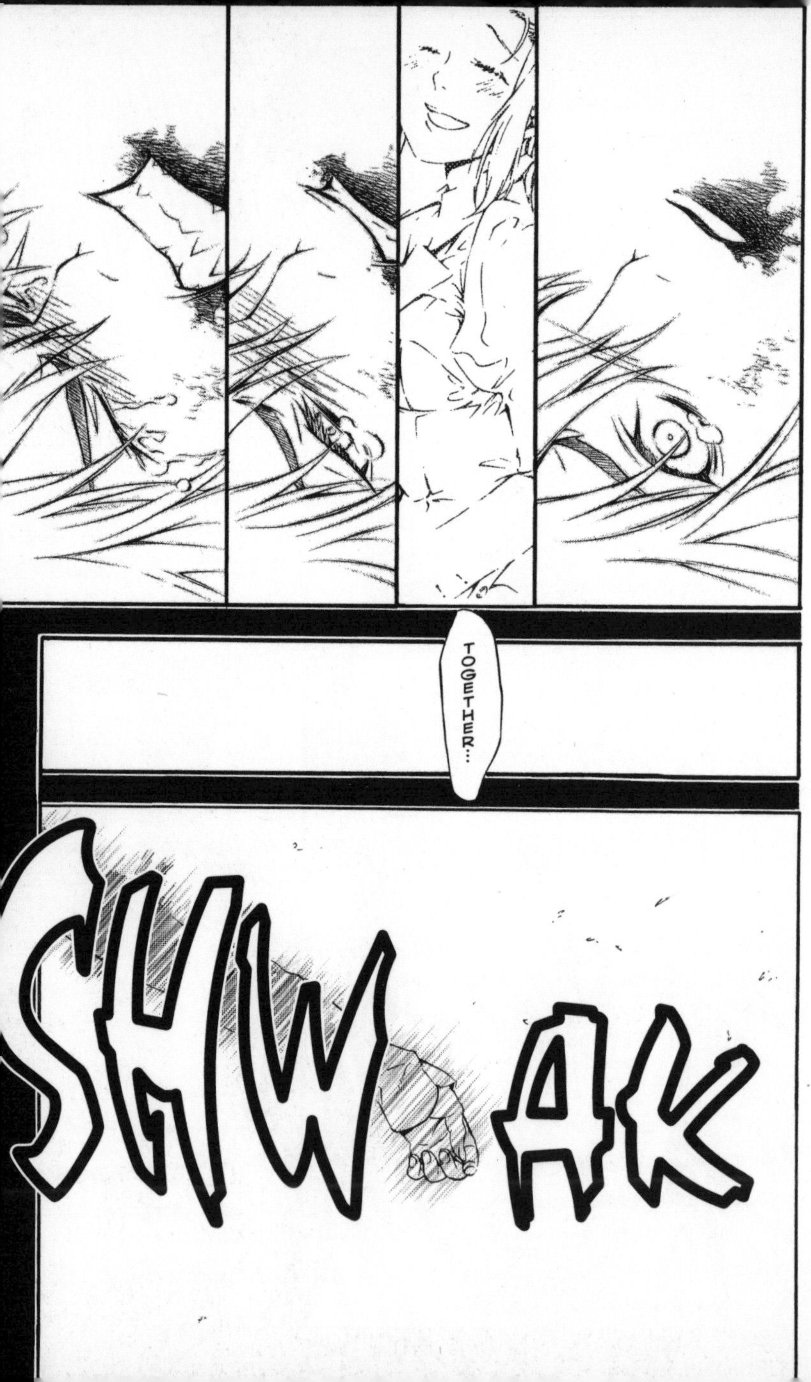
TOGETHER...
SHWAK

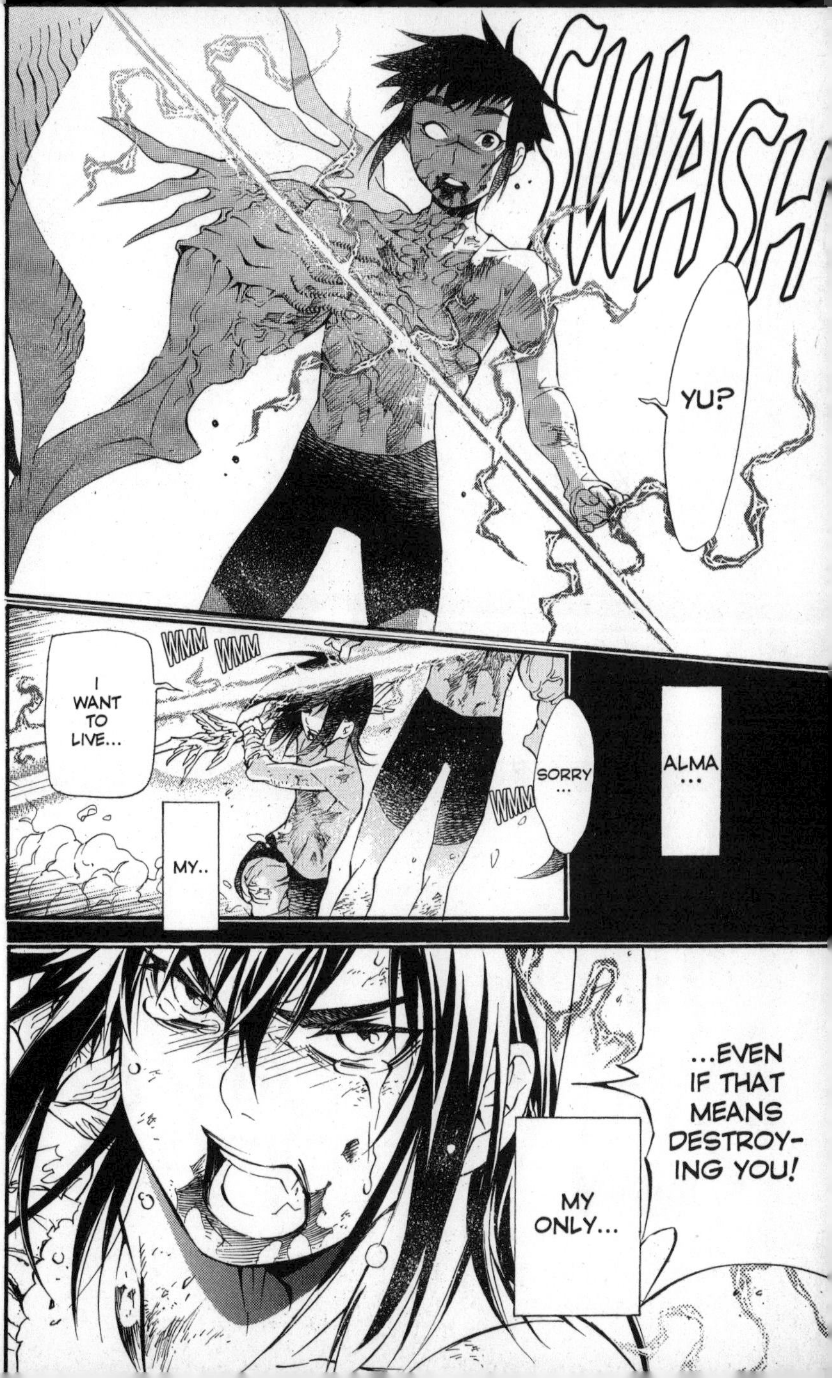
SWASH
YU?
ALMA...
SORRY...
WMM
WMM WMM
I WANT TO LIVE...
MY..
...EVEN IF THAT MEANS DESTROYING YOU!
MY ONLY...

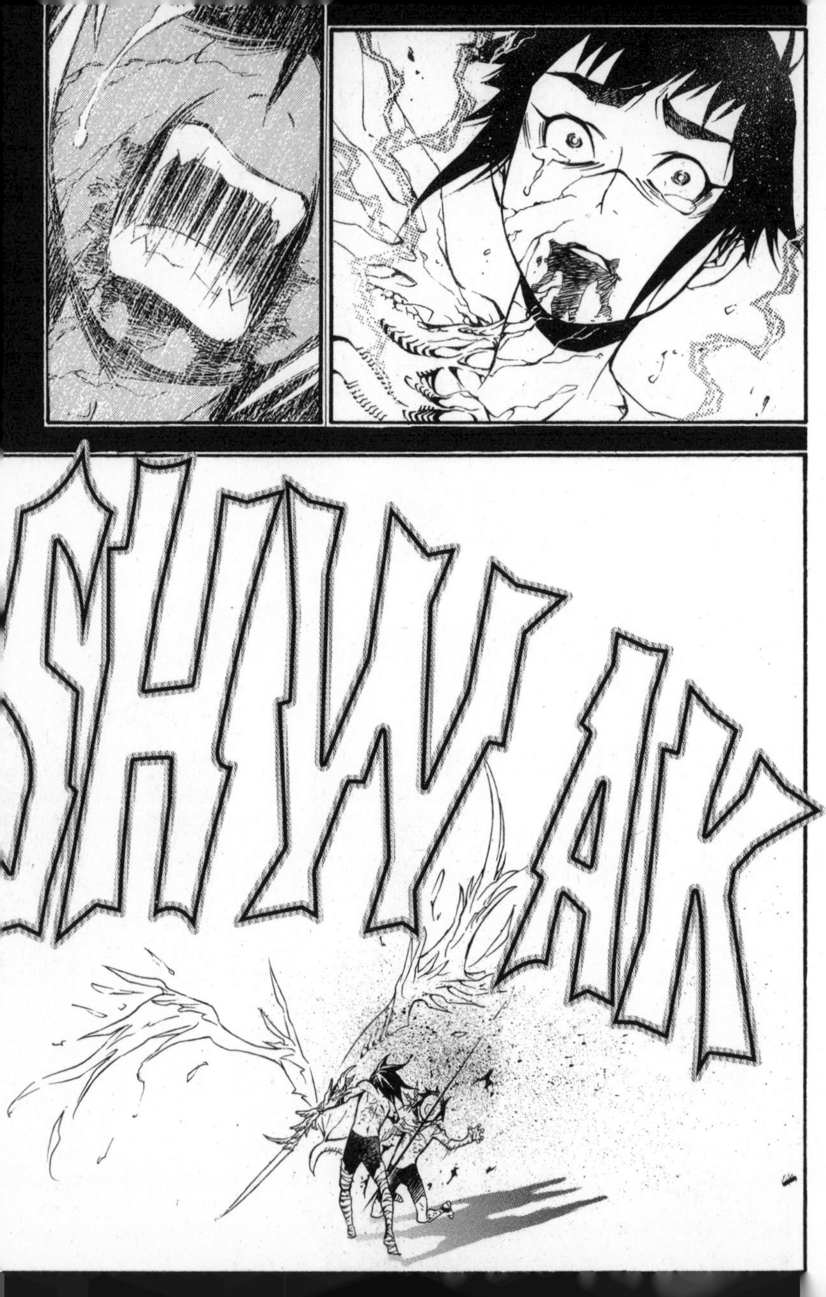
SHWAK

D.GRAY-MAN BONUS

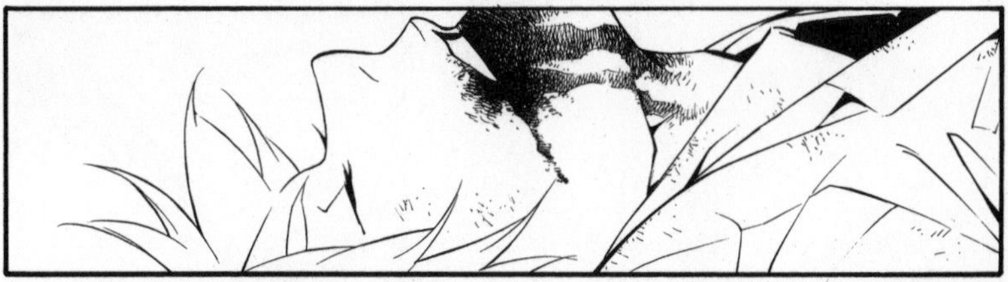

THE 193RD-AND-A-HALF NIGHT: FRIEND

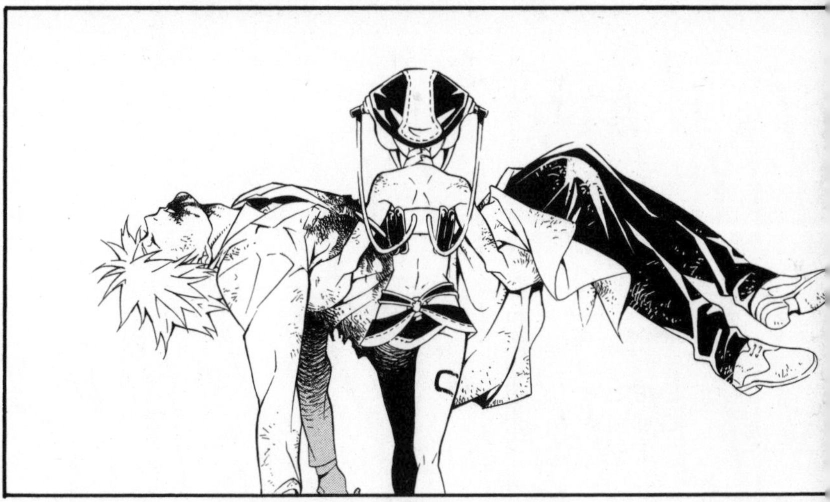

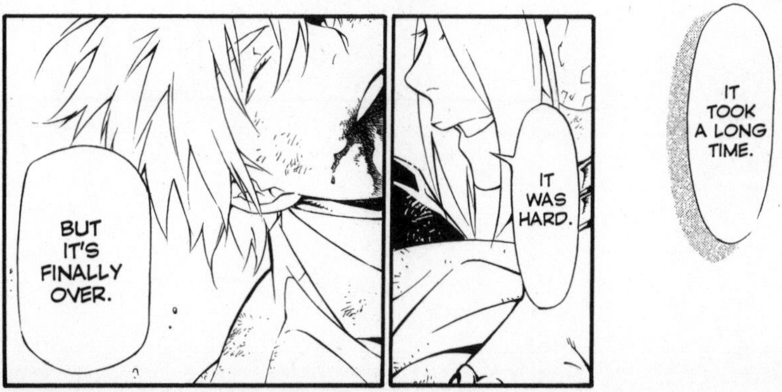
IT TOOK A LONG TIME.
IT WAS HARD.
BUT IT'S FINALLY OVER.

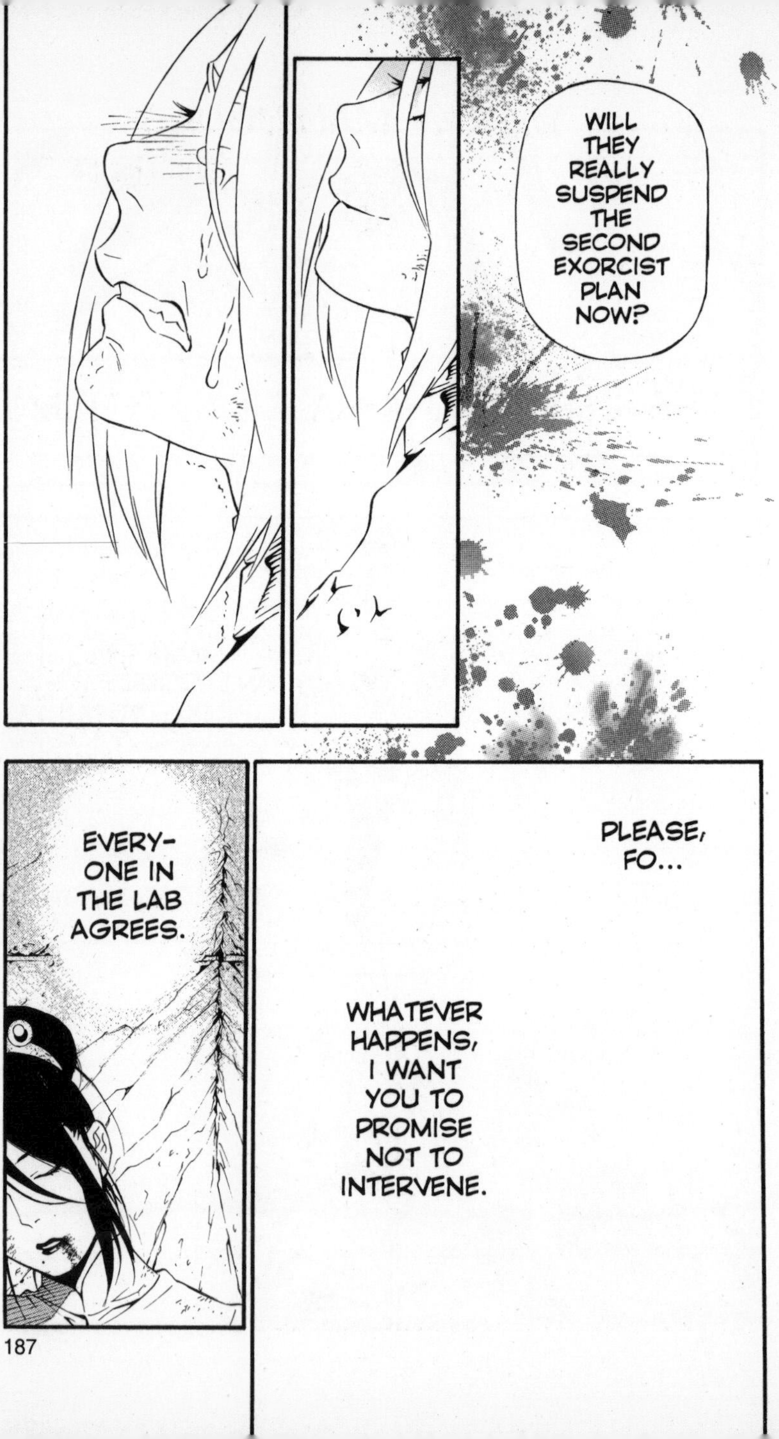
WILL THEY REALLY SUSPEND THE SECOND EXORCIST PLAN NOW?
PLEASE, FO...
WHATEVER HAPPENS, I WANT YOU TO PROMISE NOT TO INTERVENE.
EVERY-ONE IN THE LAB AGREES.

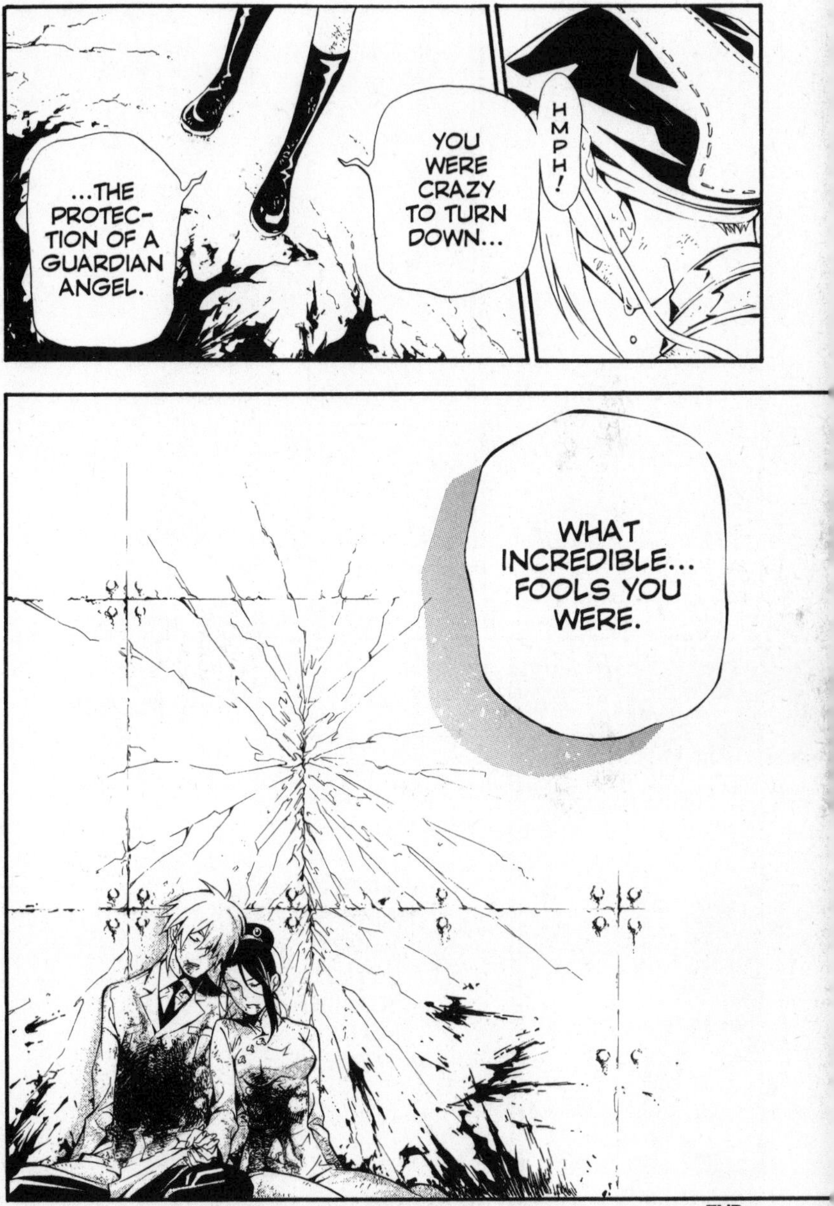
HMPH!
YOU WERE CRAZY TO TURN DOWN...
...THE PROTEC-TION OF A GUARDIAN ANGEL.
WHAT INCREDIBLE... FOOLS YOU WERE.

END.

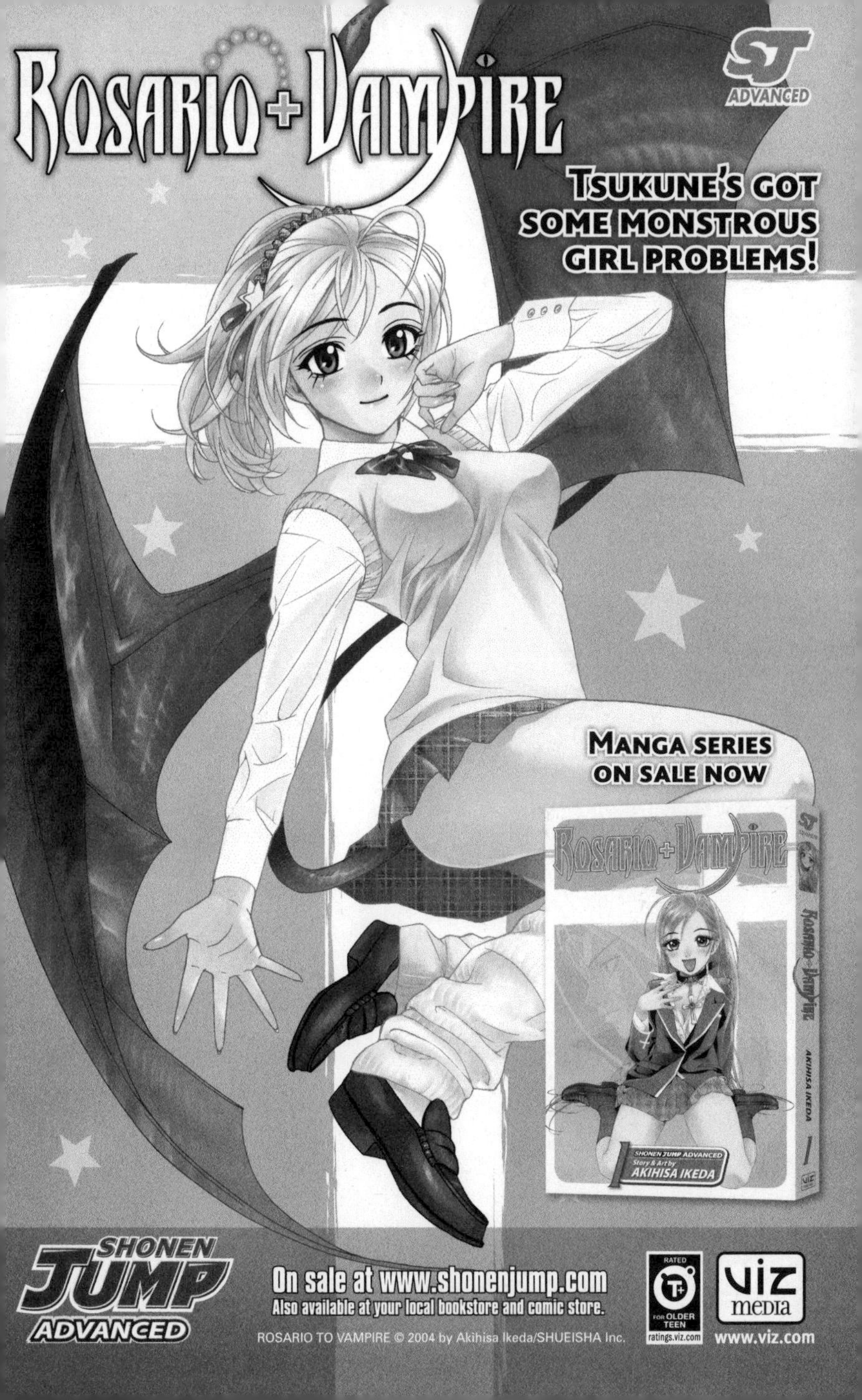
ROSARIO+VAMPIRE
SJ ADVANCED
TSUKUNE'S GOT SOME MONSTROUS GIRL PROBLEMS!
MANGA SERIES ON SALE NOW
ROSARIO+VAMPIRE
SHONEN JUMP ADVANCED
Story & Art by AKIHISA IKEDA
SHONEN JUMP ADVANCED
On sale at www.shonenjump.com
Also available at your local bookstore and comic store.
ROSARIO TO VAMPIRE © 2004 by Akihisa Ikeda/SHUEISHA Inc.
RATED T+ FOR OLDER TEEN
ratings.viz.com
VIZ media
www.viz.com

ROSARIO + VAMPIRE
Season II

Story and Art by **Akihisa Ikeda**

LOVE BITES

Tsukune Aono spent his first year at Yokai Academy on the run from demons, ogres and monsters. So why is he so eager to return as a sophomore?

Perhaps the bevy of babes fighting for his affection has something to do with it...

Rosario+Vampire: Season II, Vol. 1
ISBN: 978-1-4215-3136-6
$9.99 US / $12.99 CAN *

Manga on sale at store.viz.com
Also available at your local bookstore or comic store

ROSARIO TO VAMPIRE SEASON II © 2007 by Akihisa Ikeda/SHUEISHA Inc.
* Prices subject to change

SHONEN JUMP ADVANCED

RATED T FOR OLDER TEEN
ratings.viz.com

VIZ media
www.viz.com

FIGHT HELLFIRE WITH HELLFIRE!

Watch the anime on VIZAnime.com!

MANGA PRICE:
$9.99 usa $12.99 can
ISBN-13: 978-1-4215-4032-0

Go to **VIZ.COM** for more info on **Blue Exorcist** and other great titles!

available now at store.viz.com

Also available at your local bookstore or comic store

www.shonenjump.com   www.viz.com

BLUE EXORCIST

Story and Art by Kazue Kato

BLUE EXORCIST © 2009 by Kazue Kato/SHUEISHA Inc.

D.GRAY-MAN
VOL. 20
SHONEN JUMP ADVANCED
Manga Edition

STORY AND ART BY
KATSURA HOSHINO

English Adaptation/Lance Caselman
Translation/John Werry
Touch-up Art & Lettering/HudsonYards
Design/Matt Hinrichs
Editor/Gary Leach

D.GRAY-MAN © 2004 by Katsura Hoshino. All rights reserved.
First published in Japan in 2004 by SHUEISHA Inc., Tokyo. English translation rights arranged by SHUEISHA Inc.

The rights of the author(s) of the work(s) in this publication to be so identified have been asserted in accordance with the Copyright, Designs and Patents Act 1988. A CIP catalogue record for this book is available from the British Library.

The stories, characters and incidents mentioned in this publication are entirely fictional.

No portion of this book may be reproduced or transmitted in any form or by any means without written permission from the copyright holders.

Printed in the U.S.A.

Published by VIZ Media, LLC
P.O. Box 77010
San Francisco, CA 94107

10 9 8 7 6 5 4 3 2
First printing, February 2011
Second printing, November 2011

THE WORLD'S MOST
CUTTING-EDGE MANGA

www.viz.com

ADVANCED
www.shonenjump.com

RATED
T+
FOR OLDER TEEN

PARENTAL ADVISORY
D.GRAY-MAN is rated T+ for Older Teen and is recommended for ages 16 and up. This volume contains fantasy violence.
ratings.viz.com

It's been a fast ten years since I came to Tokyo from Shiga
Prefecture. I just moved to a place that, like my hometown, has
lots of nature. It had been so long since I stretched out on a wide-
open expanse of grass for a nap. It felt so good and I was so full of
emotion that I almost cried. Nature is awesome! ★
   —**Katsura Hoshino**

Shiga Prefecture native Katsura Hoshino's hit manga series
D.Gray-man has been serialized in *Weekly Shonen Jump* since 2004.
Katsura's debut manga, "Continue," appeared for the first time in
Weekly Shonen Jump in 2003.

Katsura adores cats.